RENAISSANCE IN ITALY

By the Same Author.

RENAISSANCE IN ITALY. In Seven Volumes.
  Vol. I. THE AGE OF THE DESPOTS.
  ,, II. THE REVIVAL OF LEARNING.
  ,, III. THE FINE ARTS.
  ,, IV. ITALIAN LITERATURE, PART I.
  ,,   V. ITALIAN LITERATURE, PART II.
  ,, VI. THE CATHOLIC REACTION, PART I.
  ,, VII. THE CATHOLIC REACTION, PART II.

SKETCHES AND STUDIES IN ITALY AND GREECE. In Three Volumes.

ESSAYS: SPECULATIVE AND SUGGESTIVE. With an Introduction by HORATIO F. BROWN.

SHAKESPERE'S PREDECESSORS IN THE ENGLISH DRAMA.

NEW AND OLD. A Volume of Verse.

MANY MOODS. A Volume of Verse.

THE SONNETS OF MICHAEL ANGELO BUONARROTI. The Italian Text is printed on the pages opposite the Translation.

JOHN ADDINGTON SYMONDS. A Biography. By HORATIO F. BROWN. With Portrait.

LETTERS OF JOHN ADDINGTON SYMONDS. Chiefly to Professor Henry Sidgwick and Mr. Horatio F. Brown. Edited by HORATIO F. BROWN.

OUT OF THE PAST. By MARGARET SYMONDS (Mrs. W. W. Vaughan). With an Account of Janet Catherine Symonds by Mrs. WALTER LEAF. Illustrated.

[*All rights reserved*]

Engraved by G. Cook, from a Photograph.

London Published by Smith, Elder & Co. 15. Waterloo Place.

RENAISSANCE IN ITALY

THE CATHOLIC REACTION

BY

JOHN ADDINGTON SYMONDS

AUTHOR OF
'STUDIES OF THE GREEK POETS' 'SKETCHES IN ITALY AND GREECE'
ETC.

> 'Deh! per Dio, donna,
> Se romper si potria quelle grandi ale!
> . . . . .
> Tu piangi e taci; e questo meglio parmi'
> SAVONAROLA: *De Ruina Ecclesiae*

IN TWO PARTS—PART I.

LONDON
JOHN MURRAY, ALBEMARLE STREET, W.

FIRST EDITION (Smith, Elder & Co.) .	October	1886
SECOND EDITION	June	1898
Reprinted	March	1900
Reprinted	November	1906
Reprinted	January	1910
Reprinted	January	1914
Reprinted (John Murray) .	October	1920
Reprinted	November	1926

Printed in Great Britain at THE BALLANTYNE PRESS
SPOTTISWOODE, BALLANTYNE & CO. LTD.
Colchester, London & Eton

PREFACE[1]

AT the end of the second volume of my 'Renaissance in Italy' I indulged the hope that I might live to describe the phase of culture which closed that brilliant epoch. It was in truth demanded that a work pretending to display the manifold activity of the Italian genius during the fifteenth century and the first quarter of the sixteenth, should also deal with the causes which interrupted its further development upon the same lines.

This study, forming a logically necessitated supplement to the five former volumes of 'Renaissance in Italy,' I have been permitted to complete. The results are now offered to the public in these two parts.

So far as it was possible, I have conducted my treatment of the Catholic Revival on a method analogous to that adopted for the Renaissance. I found it, however, needful to enter more minutely into details

[1] To the original edition of this and the succeeding volume.

regarding facts and institutions connected with the main theme of national culture.

The Catholic Revival was by its nature reactionary. In order to explain its influences, I have been compelled to analyse the position of Spain in the Italian peninsula, the conduct of the Tridentine Council, the specific organisation of the Holy Office and the Company of Jesus, and the state of society upon which those forces were brought to bear.

In the list of books which follows these prefatory remarks, I have indicated the most important of the sources used by me. Special references will be made in their proper places to works of a subordinate value for the purposes of my inquiry.

DAVOS PLATZ: *July* 1886

*WORKS COMMONLY REFERRED TO IN THIS AND THE
SUCCEEDING VOLUME OF THIS BOOK*

SISMONDI.—Histoire des Républiques Italiennes du Moyen-Age.
RANKE.—History of the Popes. 3 vols. English edition: Bohn.
CREIGHTON.—History of the Papacy during the Reformation. 2 vols. Macmillan.
BOTTA.—Storia d' Italia. Continuata da quella del Guicciardini sino al 1789.
FERRARI.—Rivoluzioni d' Italia. 3 vols.
QUINET.—Les Révolutions d'Italie.
GALLUZZI.—Storia del Granducato di Toscana.
PALLAVICINI.—Storia del Concilio Tridentino.
SARPI.—Storia del Concilio. Vols. 1 and 2 of Sarpi's Opere.
DENNISTOUN's Dukes of Urbino. 3 vols.
ALBERI.—Relazioni degli Ambasciatori Veneti.
MUTINELLI.—Storia Arcana ed Aneddotica d' Italia. Raccontata dai Veneti Ambasciatori. 4 vols. Venice. 1858.
MUTINELLI.—Annali Urbani di Venezia.
LITTA.—Famiglie Celebri Italiane.
PHILIPPSON.—La Contre-Révolution Religieuse au XVIme Siècle. Bruxelles. 1884.
DEJOB.—De l'Influence du Concile de Trente. Paris. 1884.
GIORDANI.—Della Venuta e Dimora in Bologna del Sommo Pontefice Clemente VII. per la Coronazione di Carlo V., Imperatore. Bologna. 1832.
BALBI.—Sommario della Storia d' Italia.
CANTÙ.—Gli Eretici d' Italia. 3 vols. Torino. 1866.
LLORENTE.—Histoire Critique de l'Inquisition d'Espagne. 4 vols. Paris. 1818.

LAVALLÉE.—Histoire des Inquisitions Religieuses. 2 vols. Paris. 1808.
McCRIE.—History of the Reformation in Italy. Edinburgh. 1827.
TIRABOSCHI.—Storia della Letteratura Italiana.
DE SANCTIS.—Storia della Letteratura Italiana. 2 vols.
SETTEMBRINI.—Storia della Letteratura Italiana. 8 vols.
CANTÙ.—Storia della Letteratura Italiana.
Decreta, &c., Societatis Jesu. Avignon. 1827.
CANTÙ.—Storia della Diocesi di Como. 2 vols.
DANDOLO.—La Signora di Monza e le Streghe del Tirolo. Milano. 1855.
BONGHI.—Storia di Lucrezia Buonvisi. Lucca. 1864.
Archivio Storico Italiano.
Bandi Lucchesi.—Bologna: Romagnoli. 1868.
BERTOLOTTI.—Francesco Cenci e la sua Famiglia. Firenze. 1877.
GNOLI.—Vittoria Accoramboni. Firenze: Le Monnier. 1870.
DAELLI.—Lorenzino de' Medici. Milano. 1862.
DE STENDHAL.—Chroniques et Nouvelles. Paris. 1855.
GIORDANO BRUNO.—Opere Italiane (Wagner). 2 vols. Leipzig. 1830.
JORDANUS BRUNUS.—Opera Latina. 2 vols. Neapoli. 1879.
BRUNO.—Scripta Latina (Gförer). Stuttgart. 1836.
BERTI.—Vita di Giordano Bruno. Firenze, Torino, Milano. 1868.
BRUNNHOFER.—Giordano Bruno's Weltanschauung und Verhängniss. Leipzig. 1882.
PAOLO SARPI.—Opere. 6 vols. Helmstat. 1765.
FRA FULGENZIO MICANZI.—Vita del Sarpi.
BIANCHI GIOVINI.—Biografia di Fra Paolo Sarpi. 2 vols. Bruxelles. 1836.
Lettere di Fra Paolo Sarpi. 2 vols. Firenze. 1863.
CAMPBELL.—Life of Fra Paolo Sarpi. London: Molini and Green. 1869.
DEJOB.—Marc-Antoine Muret. Paris: Thorin. 1881.
CHRISTIE.—Etienne Dolet. London: Macmillan. 1880.
RENOUARD.—Imprimerie des Aldes.
TORQUATO TASSO.—Opere. Ed. Rosini. 33 vols. Pisa. 1822 and on.
TASSO.—Le Lettere. Ed. Guasti. 5 vols. Firenze. 1855.
CECCHI.—T. Tasso, e la Vita Italiana. Firenze. 1877.
CECCHI.—T. Tasso. Il Pensiero e le Belle Lettere, &c. Firenze. 1877.
D' OVIDIO.—Saggi Critici. Napoli. 1878.

WORKS COMMONLY REFERRED TO

MANSO.—Vita di T. Tasso, in Rosini's edition, vol. 33.
ROSINI.—Saggio sugli Amori di T. Tasso, in edition cited above, vol. 33.
GUARINI.—Il Pastor Fido. Ed. Casella. Firenze: Barbèra. 1866.
MARINO.—Adone, &c. Napoli. 1861.
CHIABRERA.—Ed. Polidori. Firenze: Barbèra. 1865.
TASSONI.—La Secchia Rapita. Ed. Carducci. Firenze: Barbèra. 1861.
Il Parnaso Italiano.
BAINI.—Vita di G. P. L. Palestrina.
Felsina Pittrice.—2 vols. Bologna. 1841.
LANZI.—History of Painting in Italy. English Edition. London: Bohn. Vol. 3.

CONTENTS

OF

THE FIRST PART

CHAPTER I

THE SPANISH HEGEMONY

Italy in the Renaissance—The Five Great Powers—The Kingdom of Naples—The Papacy—The Duchy of Milan—Venice—The Florentine Republic—Wars of Invasion closed by the Sack of Rome in 1527—Concordat between Clement VII. and Charles V.—Treaty of Barcelona and Paix des Dames—Charles lands at Genoa—His Journey to Bologna—Entrance into Bologna and Reception by Clement—Mustering of Italian Princes—Francesco Sforza replaced in the Duchy of Milan—Venetian Embassy—Italian League signed on Christmas Eve 1529—Florence alone excluded—The Siege of Florence pressed by the Prince of Orange—Charles's Coronation as King of Italy and Holy Roman Emperor—The Significance of this Ceremony at Bologna—Ceremony in S. Petronio—Settlement of the Duchy of Ferrara—Men of Letters and Arts at Bologna—The Emperor's Use of the Spanish Habit—Charles and Clement leave Bologna in March 1530—Review of the Settlement of Italy effected by Emperor and Pope—Extinction of Republics—Subsequent Absorption of Ferrara and Urbino into the Papal States—Savoy becomes an Italian Power—Period between Charles's Coronation and the Peace of Cateau Cambrésis in 1559—Economical and Social Condition of the Italians under Spanish Hegemony—The

Nation still exists in Separate Communities—Intellectual Conditions—Predominance of Spain and Rome—Both Cosmopolitan Powers—Levelling down of the Component Portions of the Nation in a Common Servitude—The Evils of Spanish Rule 1

CHAPTER II

THE PAPACY AND THE TRIDENTINE COUNCIL

The Counter-Reformation—Its Intellectual and Moral Character—Causes of the Gradual Extinction of Renaissance Energy—Transition from the Renaissance to the Catholic Revival—New Religious Spirit in Italy—Attitude of Italians toward German Reformation—Oratory of Divine Love—Gasparo Contarini and the Moderate Reformers—New Religious Orders—Paul III.—His early History and Education—Political Attitude between France and Spain—Creation of the Duchy of Parma—Imminence of a General Council—Review of previous Councils—Paul's Uneasiness—Opens a Council at Trent in 1542—Protestants virtually excluded, and Catholic Dogmas confirmed in the first Sessions—Death of Paul in 1549—Julius III.—Paul IV.—Character and Ruling Passions of G. P. Caraffa—His Futile Opposition to Spain—Tyranny of his Nephews—Their Downfall—Paul devotes himself to Church Reform and the Inquisition—Pius IV.—His Minister Morone—Diplomatic Temper of this Pope—His Management of the Council—Assistance rendered by his Nephew Carlo Borromeo—Alarming State of Northern Europe—The Council reopened at Trent in 1562—Subsequent History of the Council—It closes with a complete Papal Triumph in 1563—Place of Pius IV. in History—Pius V.—The Inquisitor Pope—Population of Rome—Social Corruption—Sale of Offices and Justice—Tridentine Reforms depress Wealth—Ascetic Purity of Manners becomes fashionable—Piety—The Catholic Reaction generates the Counter-Reformation—Battle of Lepanto—Gregory XIII.—His Relatives—Policy of enriching the Church at Expense of the Barons—Brigandage in States of the Church—Sixtus V.—His Stern Justice—Rigid Economy—Great Public Works—Taxation—The City of Rome assumes its present Form—Nepotism in the Counter-Reformation Period—Various Estimates of the Wealth accumulated by Papal Nephews—Rise of Princely Roman Families . . . 49

CHAPTER III

THE INQUISITION AND THE INDEX

Different Spirit in the Holy Office and the Company of Jesus—Both needed by the Counter-Reformation—Heresy in the Early Church—First Origins of the Inquisition in 1203—S. Dominic—The Holy Office becomes a Dominican Institution—Recognised by the Empire—Its early Organisation—The Spanish Inquisition—Founded in 1484—How it differed from the earlier Apostolical Inquisition—Jews, Moors, New Christians—Organisation and History of the Holy Office in Spain—Torquemada and his Successors—The Spanish Inquisition never introduced into Italy—How the Roman Inquisition organised by Caraffa differed from it—*Autos da fe* in Rome—Proscription of suspected Lutherans—The Calabrian Waldenses—Protestants at Locarno and Venice—Digression on the Venetian Holy Office—Persecution of Free Thought in Literature—Growth of the Index Librorum Prohibitorum—Sanction given to it by the Council of Trent—The Roman Congregation of the Index—Final Form of the Censorship of Books under Clement VIII.—Analysis of its Regulations—Proscription of Heretical Books—Correction of Texts—Purgation and Castration—Inquisitorial and Episcopal Licences—Working of the System of this Censorship in Italy—Its Long Delays—Hostility to Sound Learning—Ignorance of the Censors—Interference with Scholars in their Work—Terrorism of Booksellers—Vatican Scheme for the Restoration of Christian Erudition—Frustrated by the Tyranny of the Index—Dishonesty of the Vatican Scholars—Biblical Studies rendered nugatory by the Tridentine Decree on the Vulgate—Decline of Learning in Universities—Miserable Servitude of Professors—Greek dies out—Muretus and Manutius in Rome—The Index and its Treatment of Political Works—Machiavelli—*Ratio Status*—Encouragement of Literature on Papal Absolutism—Sarpi's Attitude—Comparative Indifference of Rome to Books of Obscene or Immoral Tendency—Bandello and Boccaccio—Papal Attempts to control Intercourse of Italians with Heretics . . 124

CHAPTER IV

THE COMPANY OF JESUS

PAGE

Vast Importance of the Jesuits in the Counter-Reformation—Ignatius Loyola—His Youth—Retreat at Manresa—Journey to Jerusalem—Studies in Spain and Paris—First Formation of his Order at Sainte Barbe—Sojourn at Venice—Settlement at Rome—Papal Recognition of the Order—Its Military Character—Absolutism of the General—Devotion to the Roman Church—Choice of Members—Practical and Positive Aims of the Founder—Exclusion of the Ascetic, Acceptance of the Worldly Spirit—Review of the Order's Rapid Extension over Europe—Loyola's Dealings with his Chief Lieutenants—Propaganda—The Virtue of Obedience—The 'Exercitia Spiritualia'—Materialistic Imagination—Intensity and Superficiality of Religious Training—The Status of the Novice—Temporal Coadjutors—Scholastics—Professed of the Three Vows—Professed of the Four Vows—The General—Control exercised over him by his Assistants—His Relation to the General Congregation—Espionage a part of the Jesuit System—Advantageous Position of a Contented Jesuit—The Vow of Poverty—Houses of the Professed and Colleges—The Constitutions and Declarations—Problem of the 'Monita Secreta'—Reciprocal Relations of Rome and the Company—Characteristics of Jesuit Education—Direction of Consciences—Moral Laxity—Sarpi's Critique—Casuistry—Interference in Affairs of State—Instigation to Regicide and Political Conspiracy—Theories of Church Supremacy—Insurgence of the European Nations against the Company 179

CHAPTER V

SOCIAL AND DOMESTIC MORALS: PART I

How did the Catholic Revival affect Italian Society?—Difficulty of Answering this Question—Frequency of Private Crimes of Violence—Homicides and Bandits—Savage Criminal Justice—Paid Assassins—Toleration of Outlaws—Honourable Murder—Example of the Lucchese Army—State of the Convents—The History of Virginia de Leyva—Lucrezia Buonvisi—The True Tale of the Cenci—The Brothers of the House of Massimo—Vittoria Accoramboni—The Duchess of Palliano—Wife-Murders—The Family of Medici 234

CHAPTER VI

SOCIAL AND DOMESTIC MORALS: PART II

Tales illustrative of Bravi and Banditti—Cecco Bibboni—Ambrogio Tremazzi—Lodovico dall' Armi—Brigandage—Piracy—Plagues—The Plagues of Milan, Venice, Piedmont—Persecution of the Untori—Moral State of the Proletariate—Witchcraft—Its Italian Features—History of Giacomo Centini . . . 301

CHAPTER VII

TORQUATO TASSO

Tasso's Relation to his Age—Balbi on that Period—The Life of Bernardo Tasso—Torquato's Boyhood—Sorrento, Naples, Rome, Urbino—His First Glimpse of the Court—Student Life at Padua and Bologna—The 'Rinaldo'—Dialogues on Epic Poetry—Enters the service of Cardinal d' Este—The Court of Ferrara—Alfonso II. and the Princesses—Problem of Tasso's Love—Goes to France with Cardinal d'Este—Enters the service of Duke Alfonso—The 'Aminta'—Tasso at Urbino—Return to Ferrara—Revision of the 'Gerusalemme'—Jealousies at Court—Tasso's Sense of His own Importance—Plans a Change from Ferrara to Florence—First Symptoms of Mental Disorder—Persecutions of the Ferrarese Courtiers—Tasso confined as a Semi-Madman—Goes with Duke Alfonso to Belriguardo—Flies in Disguise from Ferrara to Sorrento—Returns to Court-life at Ferrara—Problem of his Madness—Flies again—Mantua, Venice, Urbino, Turin—Returns once more to Ferrara—Alfonso's Third Marriage—Tasso's Discontent—Imprisoned for Seven Years in the Madhouse of S. Anna—Character of Tasso—Character of Duke Alfonso—Nature of the Poet's Malady—His Course of Life in Prison—Released at the Intercession of Vincenzo Gonzaga—Goes to Mantua—The 'Torrismondo'—An Odyssey of Nine Years—Death at Sant' Onofrio in Rome—Costantini's Sonnet . . 334

PORTRAIT OF JOHN ADDINGTON SYMONDS . . . . *Frontispiece*

RENAISSANCE IN ITALY

CHAPTER I

THE SPANISH HEGEMONY

Italy in the Renaissance—The Five Great Powers—The Kingdom of Naples—The Papacy—The Duchy of Milan—Venice—The Florentine Republic—Wars of Invasion closed by the Sack of Rome in 1527—Concordat between Clement VII. and Charles V.—Treaty of Barcelona and Paix des Dames—Charles lands at Genoa—His Journey to Bologna—Entrance into Bologna and Reception by Clement—Mustering of Italian Princes—Francesco Sforza replaced in the Duchy of Milan—Venetian Embassy—Italian League signed on Christmas Eve 1529—Florence alone excluded—The Siege of Florence pressed by the Prince of Orange—Charles's Coronation as King of Italy and Holy Roman Emperor—The Significance of this Ceremony at Bologna—Ceremony in S. Petronio—Settlement of the Duchy of Ferrara—Men of Letters and Arts at Bologna—The Emperor's Use of the Spanish Habit—Charles and Clement leave Bologna in March 1530—Review of the Settlement of Italy effected by Emperor and Pope—Extinction of Republics—Subsequent Absorption of Ferrara and Urbino into the Papal States—Savoy becomes an Italian Power—Period between Charles's Coronation and the Peace of Cateau Cambresis in 1559—Economical and Social Condition of the Italians under Spanish Hegemony—The Nation still exists in Separate Communities—Intellectual Conditions—Predominance of Spain and Rome—Both Cosmopolitan Powers—Levelling down of the Component Fortions of the Nation in a Common Servitude—The Evils of Spanish Rule.

IN the first volume of this work on 'Renaissance in Italy' I attempted to set forth the political and social phases through which the Italians passed before their principal States fell into the hands of despots, and to explain the conditions of mutual jealousy and military feebleness which exposed those States to the assaults of foreign armies at the close of the fifteenth century.

In the year 1494, when Charles VIII. of France, at Lodovico Sforza's invitation, crossed the Alps to make good his claim on Naples, the peninsula was independent. Internal peace had prevailed for a period of nearly fifty years. An equilibrium had been established between the five great native Powers, which secured the advantages of confederation and diplomatic interaction.

While using the word confederation I do not of course imply that anything similar to the federal union of Switzerland or of North America existed in Italy. The contrary is proved by patent facts. On a miniature scale, Italy then displayed political conditions analogous to those which now prevail in Europe. The parcels of the nation adopted different forms of self-government, sought divers foreign alliances, and owed no allegiance to any central legislative or administrative body. I therefore speak of the Italian confederation only in the same sense as Europe may now be called a confederation of kindred races.

In the year 1530, when Charles V. (of Austria and Spain) was crowned Emperor at Bologna, this national independence had been irretrievably lost by the Italians. This confederation of evenly balanced Powers was now exchanged for servitude beneath a foreign monarchy, and for subjection to a cosmopolitan elective priesthood.

The history of social, intellectual, and moral conditions in Italy during the seventy years of the sixteenth century which followed Charles's coronation at Bologna, forms the subject of this work; but before entering upon these topics it will be well to devote one chapter to considering with due brevity the partition of Italy into five States in 1494, the dislocation of this order by the wars between Spain and France for supremacy, the position in which the same States found themselves respectively at the termination of those wars in 1527, and the new settlement of the peninsula effected by Charles V. in 1529-30.

The five members of the Italian federation in 1494 were the Kingdom of Naples, the Papacy, the Duchy of Milan, and the Republics of Venice and Florence. Round them, in various relations of amity or hostility, were grouped these minor Powers: the Republics of Genoa, Lucca, Siena; the Duchy of Ferrara, including Modena and Reggio; the Marquisates of Mantua and Montferrat; and the Duchy of Urbino. For our immediate purpose it is not worth taking separate account of the Republic of Pisa, which was practically though not thoroughly enslaved by Florence; or of the Despots in the cities of Romagna, the March, Umbria, and the Patrimony of S. Peter, who were being gradually absorbed into the Papal sovereignty. Nor need we at present notice Savoy, Piemonte, and Saluzzo. Although these northwestern provinces were all-important through the period of Franco-Spanish wars, inasmuch as they opened the gate of Italy to French armies and supplied those armies with a base for military operations, the Duchy of Savoy had not yet become an exclusively Italian Power.

The kingdom of Naples, on the death of Alfonso the Magnanimous in 1458, had been separated from Sicily, and passed by testamentary appointment to his natural son Ferdinand. The bastard Aragonese dynasty was Italian in its tastes and interests, though unpopular both with the barons of the realm and with the people, who in their restlessness were ready to welcome any foreign deliverer from its oppressive yoke. This state of general discontent rendered the revival of the old Angevine party, and their resort to French aid, a source of peril to the monarchy. It also served as a convenient fulcrum for the ambitious schemes of conquest which the princes of the House of Aragon in Spain began to entertain. In territorial extent the kingdom of Naples was the most considerable parcel of the Italian community. It embraced the whole of Calabria, Apulia, the Abruzzi, and the Terra di Lavoro; marching on its northern boundary with the Papal States, and having no other neighbours. But though so large and so compact a State, the semi-feudal system of government which had obtained in Naples since the first conquest of the country by the Normans, the nature of its population, and the savage dynastic wars to which it had been constantly exposed, rendered it more backward in civilisation than the northern and central provinces.

The Papacy, after the ending of the schism and the settlement of Nicholas V. at Rome in 1447, gradually tended to become an Italian sovereignty. During the residence of the Popes at Avignon, and the weakness of the Papal See which followed in the period of the Councils (Pisa, Constance, and Basel), it had lost its hold not only on the immediate neighbourhood of Rome, but also on its outlying possessions in Umbria, the Marches of Ancona, and the Exarchate of Ravenna. The great Houses of Colonna and Orsini asserted independence in their principalities. Bologna and Perugia pretended to republican government under the shadow of noble families; Bentivogli, Bracci, Baglioni. Imola, Faenza, Forli, Rimini, Pesaro, Urbino, Camerino, Città di Castello, obeyed the rule of tyrants, who were practically lords of these cities though they bore the title of Papal vicars, and who maintained themselves in wealth and power by exercising the profession of *condottieri*. It was the chief object of the Popes, after they were freed from the pressing perils of General Councils, and were once more settled in their capital and recognised as sovereigns by the European Powers, to subdue their vassals and consolidate their provinces into a homogeneous kingdom. This plan was conceived and carried out by a succession of vigorous and unscrupulous Pontiffs—Sixtus IV., Alexander VI., Julius II., and Leo X.—throughout the period of distracting foreign wars which agitated Italy. They followed for the most part one line of policy, which was to place the wealth and authority of the Holy See at the disposal of their relatives, Riarios, Della Roveres, Borgias, and Medici. Their military delegates, among whom the most efficient captain was the terrible Cesare Borgia, had full power to crush the liberties of cities, exterminate the dynasties of despots, and reduce refractory districts to the Papal sway. For these services they were rewarded with ducal and princely titles, with the administration of their conquests, and with the investiture of fiefs as vassals of the Church. The system had its obvious disadvantages. It tended to indecent nepotism; and as Pope succeeded Pope at intervals of a few years, each bent on aggrandising his own family at the expense of those of his predecessors and the Church, the ecclesiastical States were kept in a continual ferment of expropriation and internal revolution. Yet it is difficult to conceive how a spiritual Power like the Papacy could have solved the problem set before it of becoming a substantial secular sovereignty, without recourse to this ruinous method. The Pope, a lonely man upon an ill-established throne, surrounded by rivals whom his elevation had disappointed, was compelled to rely on the strong arm of adventurers with whose interests his own were indissolubly connected. The profits of all these schemes of egotistical rapacity eventually accrued, not to the relatives of the Pontiffs (none of whom except the Della Roveres in Urbino founded a permanent dynasty at this period), but to the Holy See. Julius II., for example, on his election in 1503, entered into possession of all that Cesare Borgia had attempted to grasp for his own use. He found the Orsini and Colonna humbled, Romagna reduced to submission; and he carried on the policy of conquest by trampling out the liberties of Bologna and Perugia, recovering the cities held by Venice on the coast of Ravenna, and extending his sway over Emilia. The martial energy of Julius added Parma and Piacenza to the States of the Church, and detached Modena and Reggio from the Duchy of Ferrara. These new cities were gained by force; but Julius pretended that they formed part of the Exarchate of Ravenna, which had been granted to his predecessors by Pepin and Charles the Great. He pursued the Papal line of conquest in a nobler spirit than his predecessors, not seeking to advance his relatives so much as to reinstate the Church in her dominions. But he was reckless in the means employed to secure this object. Italy was devastated by wars stirred up, and by foreign armies introduced, in order that the Pope might win a point in the great game of ecclesiastical aggrandisement. That his successor, Leo X., reverted to the former plan of carving principalities for his relatives out of the possessions of their neighbours and the Church, may be counted among the most important causes of the final ruin of Italian independence.

Of the Duchy of Milan it is not necessary to speak at any great length, although the wars between France and Spain were chiefly carried on for its possession. It had been formed into a compact domain, of comparatively small extent, but of vast commercial and agricultural resources, by the two dynasties of Visconti and Sforza. In 1494 Lodovico Sforza, surnamed Il Moro, ruled Milan for his nephew, the titular Duke, whom he kept in gilded captivity, and whom he eventually murdered. In order to secure his usurped authority, this would-be Machiavelli thought it prudent to invite Charles VIII. into Italy. Charles was to assert his right to the throne of Naples. Lodovico was to be established in the Duchy of Milan. All his subsequent troubles arose from this transaction. Charles came, conquered, and returned to France, disturbing the political equilibrium of the Italian States and founding a disastrous precedent for future foreign interference. His successor in the French kingdom, Louis XII., believed he had a title to the Duchy of Milan through his grandmother Valentina, daughter of Gian Galeazzo Visconti. The claim was not a legal one; for in the investiture of the Duchy females were excluded. It sufficed, however, to inflame the cupidity of Louis; and while he was still but Duke of Orleans, with no sure prospect of inheriting the crown of France, he seems to have indulged the fancy of annexing Milan. No sooner had he ascended the French throne than he began to act upon this ambition. He descended into Lombardy, overran the Milanese, sent Lodovico Sforza to die in a French prison, and initiated the duel between Spain and France for mastery, which ended with the capture of Francis I. at Pavia and his final cession of all rights over Italy to Charles V. by the Treaty of Cambray (Paix des Dames).

Of all the republics which had conferred lustre upon Italy in its medieval period of prosperity Venice alone remained independent. She never submitted to a tyrant; and her government, though growing yearly more closely oligarchical, was acknowledged to be just and liberal. During the centuries of her greatest power Venice hardly ranked among Italian States. It had been her policy to confine herself to the lagoons and to the extension of her dominion over the Levant. In the fifteenth century, however, this policy was abandoned. Venice first possessed herself of Padua, by exterminating the despotic House of Carrara; next of Verona, by destroying the Scala dynasty. Subsequently, during the long dogeship of Francesco Foscari (1428-1457), she devoted herself in good earnest to the acquisition of territory upon the mainland. Then she entered as a Power of the first magnitude into the system of purely Italian politics. The Republic of S. Mark owned the sea coast of the Adriatic from Aquileia to the mouths of the Po; and her Lombard dependencies stretched as far as Bergamo westward. Her Italian neighbours were, therefore, the Duchy of Milan, the little Marquisate of Mantua, and the Duchy of Ferrara. When Constantinople fell in 1458, Venice was still more tempted to pursue this new policy of Italian aggrandisement. Meanwhile her growing empire seemed to menace the independence of less wealthy neighbours. The jealousy thus created and the cupidity which brought her into collision with Julius II. in 1508, exposed Venice to the crushing blow inflicted on her power by the combined forces of Europe in the war of the League of Cambray. From this blow, as well as from the simultaneous decline of their Oriental and Levantine commerce, the Venetians never recovered.

When we turn to the Florentines, we find that at the same epoch, 1494, their ancient republican constitution had been fatally undermined by the advances of the family of Medici towards despotism. Lorenzo de' Medici, who enjoyed the credit of maintaining the equilibrium of Italy by wise diplomacy, had lately died. He left his son Piero, a hot-headed and rash young man, to control the affairs of the commonwealth, as he had previously controlled them, with a show of burgherlike equality, but with the reality of princely power. Another of his sons, Giovanni, received the honour of the Cardinalship. The one was destined to compromise the ascendency of his family in Florence for a period of eighteen years; the other was destined to re-establish that ascendency on a new and more despotic basis. Piero had not his father's prudence, and could not maintain himself in the delicate position of a commercial and civil tyrant. During the disturbances caused by the invasion of Charles VIII.

he was driven with all his relatives into exile. The Medici were restored in 1512, after the battle of Ravenna, by Spanish troops, at the petition of the Cardinal Giovanni. The elevation of this man to the Papacy in 1513 enabled him to plant two of his nephews, as rulers, in Florence, and to pave the way whereby a third eventually rose to the dignity of the tiara. Clement VII. finally succeeded in rendering Florence subject to the Medici, by extinguishing the last sparks of republican opposition, and by so modifying the dynastic protectorate of his family that it was easily converted into a titular Grand Duchy.

The federation of these five Powers had been artificially maintained during the half-century of Italy's highest intellectual activity. That was the epoch when the Italians nearly attained to coherence as a nation, through common interests in art and humanism, and by the complicated machinery of diplomatic relations. The federation perished when foreign Powers chose Lombardy and Naples for their fields of battle. The disasters of the next thirty-three years (1494-1527) began in earnest on the day when Louis XII. claimed Milan and the Regno. He committed his first mistake by inviting Ferdinand the Catholic to share in the partition of Naples. That province was easily conquered; but Ferdinand retained the whole spoils for himself, securing a large Italian dependency and a magnificent basis of operations for the Spanish crown. Then Louis made a second mistake by proposing to the visionary Emperor Maximilian that he should aid France in subjugating Venice. We have few instances on record of short-sighted diplomacy to match the Treaties of Granada and Blois (1501 and 1504), through which this monarch, acting rather as a Duke of Milan than a King of France, complicated his Italian schemes by the introduction of two such dangerous allies as the Austrian Emperor and the Spanish sovereign, while the heir of both was in his cradle—that fatal child of fortune, Charles.

The stage of Italy was now prepared for a conflict which in no wise interested her prosperous cities and industrious population. Spain, France, Germany, with their Swiss auxiliaries, had been summoned upon various pretexts to partake of the rich prey she offered. Patriots like Machiavelli perceived too late the suicidal self-indulgence which, by substituting mercenary troops for national militia, and by accustoming selfish tyrants to rely on foreign aid, had exposed the Italians defenceless to the inroads of their warlike neighbours. Whatever parts the Powers of Italy might play, the game was really in the hands of French, Spanish, and German invaders. Meanwhile the mutual jealousies and hatreds of those Powers, kept in check by no tie stronger than diplomacy, prevented them from forming any scheme of common action. One great province (Naples) had fallen into Spanish hands; another (Milan) lay open through the passes of the Alps to France. The Papacy, in the centre, manipulated these two hostile foreign forces with some advantage to itself, but with ever-deepening disaster for the race. As in the days of Guelf and Ghibelline, so now again the nation was bisected. The contest between French and Spanish factions became cruel. Personal interests were substituted for principles; cross-combinations perplexed the real issues of dispute; while one sole fact emerged into distinctness—that, whatever happened, Italy must be the spoil of the victorious duellist.

The practical termination of this state of things arrived in the battle of Pavia, when Francis was removed as a prisoner to Madrid, and in the Sack of Rome, when the Pope was imprisoned in the Castle of S. Angelo. It was then found that the laurels and the profit of the bloody contest remained with the King of Spain. What the people suffered from the marching and countermarching of armies, from the military occupation of towns, from the desolation of rural districts, from ruinous campaigns and sanguinary battles, from the pillage of cities and the massacres of their inhabitants, can best be read in Burigozzo's 'Chronicle of Milan,' in the details of the siege of Brescia and the destruction of Pavia, in the 'Chronicle of Prato' and in the several annals of the Sack of Rome. The exhaustion of the country seemed complete; the spirit of the people was broken. But what soon afterwards became apparent, and what in 1527 might have been thought incredible, was that the single member of the Italian union which profited by these apocalyptic sufferings of the nation, was the Papacy. Clement VII., imprisoned in the Castle of S. Angelo, forced day and night to gaze upon his capital in flames and hear the groans of tortured Romans, emerged the only vigorous survivor of the five great Powers on whose concert Italian independence had been founded. Instead of being impaired, the position of the Papacy had been immeasurably improved. Owing to the prostration of Italy, there was now no resistance to the Pope's secular supremacy within the limits of his authorised dominion. The defeat of France and the accession of a Spanish monarch to the Empire guaranteed peace. No foreign force could levy armies or foment uprisings in the name of independence. Venice had been stunned and mutilated by the League of Cambray. Florence had been enslaved after the battle of Ravenna. Milan had been relinquished, outworn and depopulated, to the nominal ascendency of an impotent Sforza. Naples was a province of the Spanish monarchy. The feudal vassals and the subject cities of the Holy See had been ground and churned together by a series of revolutions unexampled even in the medieval history of the Italian communes. If, therefore, the Pope could come to terms with the King of Spain for the partition of supreme authority in the peninsula, they might henceforward share the mangled remains of the Italian prey at peace together. This is precisely what they resolved on doing. The basis of their agreement was laid in the Treaty of Barcelona in 1529. It was ratified and secured by the Treaty of Cambray in the same year. By the former of these compacts Charles and Clement swore friendship. Clement promised the Imperial crown and the investiture of Naples to the King of Spain. Charles agreed to reinstate the Pope in Emilia, which had been seized from Ferrara by Julius II.; to procure the restoration of Ravenna and Cervia by the Venetians; to subdue Florence to the House of Medici; and to bestow the hand of his natural daughter Margaret of Austria on Clement's bastard nephew Alessandro, who was already designated ruler of the city. By the treaty of Cambray Francis I. relinquished his claims on Italy and abandoned his Italian supporters without conditions, receiving in exchange the possession of Burgundy. The French allies who were sacrificed on this occasion by the Most Christian to the Most Catholic monarch consisted of the Republics of Venice and Florence, the Dukes of Milan and Ferrara, the princely Houses of Orsini and Fregosi in Rome and Genoa, together with the Angevine nobles in the realm of Naples. The Paix des Dames, as this act of capitulation was called (since it had been drawn up in private conclave by Louise of Savoy and Margaret of Austria, the mother and the aunt of the two signatories), was a virtual acknowledgment of the fact that French influence in Italy was at an end.[1]

The surrender of Italy by Francis made it necessary that Charles V. should put order in the vast estates to which he

[1] It is significant for the future of Italy that both the ladies who drew up this agreement were connected with Savoy. Louise, Duchess of Angoulême, was a daughter of the house. Margaret, daughter of Maximilian, was Duchess Dowager of Savoy.

now succeeded as sole master. He was, moreover, Emperor elect; and he judged this occasion good for assuming the two crowns according to antique custom. Consequently in July 1529 he caused Andrea Doria to meet him at Barcelona, crossed the Mediterranean in a rough passage of fourteen days, landed at Genoa on August 12, and proceeded by Piacenza, Parma and Modena to Bologna, where Clement VII. was already awaiting him. The meeting of Charles and Clement at Bologna was so solemn an event in Italian history, and its results were so important for the several provinces of the peninsula, that I may be excused for enlarging at some length upon this episode. With pomp and pageantry it closed an age of unrivalled intellectual splendour and of unexampled sufferings through war. By diplomacy and debate it prescribed laws for a new age of unexpected ecclesiastical energy and of national peace procured at the price of slavery. Illustrious survivors from the period of the Pagan Renaissance met here with young men destined to inaugurate the Catholic Revival. The compact struck between Emperor and Pope in private conferences, laid a basis for that firm alliance between Spain and Rome which seriously influenced the destinies of Europe. Finally, this was the last occasion upon which a modern Cæsar received the iron and the golden crowns in Italy from the hands of a Roman Pontiff. The fortunate inheritor of Spain, the Two Sicilies, Austria and the Low Countries, who then assumed them both at the age of twenty-nine, was not only the last who wielded the Imperial insignia with imperial authority, but was also a far more formidable potentate in Italy than any of his predecessors since Charles the Great had been.[1]

[1] In what follows regarding Charles V. at Bologna I am greatly indebted to Giordani's laboriously compiled volume: *Della Venuta e Dimora in Bologna del Sommo Pont. Clemente VII. &c.* (Bologna, 1882).

That Charles should have employed the galleys of Doria for the transhipment of his person, suite, and military escort from Barcelona, deserves a word of comment. Andrea Doria had been bred in the service of the French crown, upon which Genoa was in his youth dependent. He formed a navy of decisive preponderance in the Western Mediterranean, and in return for services rendered to Francis in the Neapolitan campaign of 1528, he demanded the liberation of his native city. When this was refused, Doria transferred his allegiance to the Spaniard, surprised Genoa and reinstated the republic, magnanimously refusing to secure its tyranny for himself or even to set the ducal cap upon his head. Charles invested him with the principality of Melfi and made him a Grandee of Spain. By this series of events Genoa was prepared to accept the yoke of Spanish influence and customs, which pressed so heavily in the succeeding century on Italy.

Charles had a body of 2,000 Spaniards already quartered at Genoa, as well as strong garrisons in the Milanese, and a force of about 7,000 troops collected by the Prince of Orange from the *débris* of the army which had plundered Rome. While he was on his road from Genoa to Bologna, this force was already moving upon Florence. He brought with him as escort some 10,000 men, counting horse and infantry. The total of the troops which obeyed his word in Italy might be computed at about 27,000, including Spanish cavalry and foot-soldiers, German lansknechts, and Italian mercenaries. This large army, partly stationed in important posts of defence, partly in movement, was sufficient to make every word of his a law. The French were in no position to interfere with his arrangements. His brother Ferdinand, King of Bohemia and Hungary, was engaged in a doubtful contest with Soliman before the gates of Vienna. He was himself the most considerable potentate in Germany, then distracted by the struggles of the Reformation. Italy lay crushed and prostrate, trampled down by armies, exhausted by imposts and exactions, terrorised by brutal violence. That Charles had come to speak his will and be obeyed was obvious.

To greet the King on his arrival at Genoa, Clement deputed two ambassadors, the Cardinals Ercole Gonzaga and Monsignor Gianmatteo Giberti, Bishop of Verona. Gonzaga was destined to play a part of critical importance in the Tridentine Council. Giberti had made himself illustrious in the Church by the administration of his diocese on a system which anticipated the coming ecclesiastical reforms, and was already famous in the world of letters by his generous familiarity with students.[1] Three other men of high distinction and of fateful future waited on their imperial master. Of these the first was Cardinal Alessandro Farnese, who succeeded Clement in the Papacy, opened the Tridentine Council, and added a new reigning family to the Italian princes. The others were the Pope's nephews, Alessandro de' Medici, Duke of Florence designate, and his cousin the Cardinal Ippolito de' Medici. Six years later, Ippolito died at Itri, poisoned by his cousin Alessandro, who was himself murdered at Florence in 1537 by another cousin, Lorenzino de' Medici.

It had been intended that Charles should travel to Bologna from Parma through Mantua, where the Marquis Federigo Gonzaga had made great preparations for his reception. But the route by Reggio and Modena was more direct; and, yielding to the solicitations of Alfonso, Duke of Ferrara, he selected this instead. One of the stipulations of the Treaty of Barcelona, it will be remembered, had been that the Emperor should restore Emilia—that is to say, the cities and territories of Modena, Reggio, and Rubbiera—to

[1] See *Italian Literature*, Vol. V. p. 313.

the Papacy. Clement regarded Alfonso as a contumacious vassal, although his own right to that province only rested on the force of arms by which Julius II. had detached it from the Duchy of Ferrara. It was therefore somewhat difficult for Charles to accept the duke's hospitality. But when he had once done so, Alfonso knew how to ingratiate himself so well with the arbiter of Italy, that on taking leave of his guest upon the confines of Bologna, he had already secured the success of his own cause.

Great preparations, meanwhile, were being made in Bologna. The misery and destitution of the country rendered money scarce, and cast a gloom over the people. It was noticed that when Clement entered the city on October 24, none of the common folk responded to the shouts of his attendants, *Viva Papa Clemente!* The Pope and his Court, too, were in mourning. They had but recently escaped from the horrors of the Sack of Rome, and were under a vow to wear their beards unshorn in memory of their past sufferings. Yet the municipality and nobles of Bologna exerted their utmost in these bad times to render the reception of the Emperor worthy of the lustre which his residence and coronation would confer upon them. Gallant guests began to flock into the city. Among these may be mentioned the brilliant Isabelle d' Este, sister of Duke Alfonso, and mother of the reigning Marquis of Mantua. She arrived on November 1 with a glittering train of beautiful women, and took up her residence in the Palazzo Manzoli. Her quarters obtained no good fame in the following months; for the ladies of her suite were liberal of favours. Jousts, masquerades, street-brawls and duels were of frequent occurrence beneath her windows—Spaniards and Italians disputing the honour of those light amours. On November 8 came Andrea Doria with his relative, the Cardinal Girolamo of that name. About the same time

Cardinal Lorenzo Campeggi, Bishop of Bologna, returned from his legation to England, where (as students of our history are well aware) he had been engaged upon the question of Henry VIII.'s divorce from Katharine of Aragon. Next day Charles arrived outside the gate, and took up his quarters in the rich convent of Certosa, which now forms the Campo Santo.

He was surrounded by a multitude of ambassadors and delegates from the Bolognese magistracy, by Cardinals and ecclesiastics of all ranks, some of whom had attended him from the frontier, while others were drawn up to receive him. November 5 was a Friday, and this day was reckoned lucky by Charles. He therefore passed the night of the 4th at the Certosa, and on the following morning made his solemn entry into the city. A bodyguard of Germans, Burgundians, Spaniards, halberdiers, lansknechts, men at arms and cannoneers, preceded him. High above these was borne the captain-general of the imperial force in Italy, the fierce and cruel Antonio de Leyva, under whose oppression Milan had been groaning. This ruthless tyrant was a martyr to gout and rheumatism. He could not ride or walk; and though he retained the whole vigour of his intellect and will, it was with difficulty that he moved his hands or head. He advanced in a litter of purple velvet, supported on the shoulders of his slaves. Among the splendid crowd of Spanish grandees who followed the troops, it is enough to mention the Grand Marshal, Don Alvaro Osorio, Marquis of Astorga, who carried a naked sword aloft. He was armed, on horseback; and his mantle of cloth of gold blazed with dolphins worked in pearls and precious stones. Next came Charles, mounted on a bay jennet, armed at all points, and holding in his hand the sceptre. Twenty-four pages, chosen from the nobles of Bologna, waited on his bridle and stirrups. The train was brought up by a multitude of secular and ecclesiastical princes too numerous to record in detail. Conspicuous among them for the historian were the Count of Nassau, Albert of Brandenburg, and the Marquis Bonifazio of Montferrat, the scion of the Eastern Paleologi. As this procession defiled through the streets of Bologna, it was remarked that Charles, with true Spanish haughtiness, made no response to the acclamations of the people, except once when, passing beneath a balcony of noble ladies, he acknowledged their salute by lifting the cap from his head.

Clement, surrounded by a troop of prelates, was seated to receive him on a platform raised before the Church of San Petronio in the great piazza. The king dismounted opposite the Papal throne, ascended the steps beneath his canopy of gold and crimson, and knelt to kiss the Pontiff's feet. When their eyes first met, it was observed that both turned pale; for the memory of outraged Rome was in the minds of both; and Cæsar, while he paid this homage to Christ's Vicar, had the load of those long months of suffering and insult on his conscience. Clement bent down, and with streaming eyes saluted him upon the cheek. Then, when Charles was still upon his knees, they exchanged a few set words referring to the purpose of their meeting and their common desire for the pacification of Christendom. After this the Emperor elect arose, seated himself for a while beside the Pope, and next, at his invitation, escorted him to the great portal of the church. On the way, he inquired after Clement's health; to which the Pope replied somewhat significantly that, after leaving Rome, it had steadily improved. He tempered this allusion to his captivity, however, by adding that his eagerness to greet his Majesty had inspired him with more than wonted strength and courage. At the doorway they parted; and the Emperor, having paid his devotions to the Sacrament and kissed the altar, was conducted to the apartments prepared for him in the Palazzo Pubblico. These were adjacent to the Pope's lodgings in the same palace, and were so arranged that the two potentates could confer in private at all times. It is worthy of remark that the negotiations for the settlement of Italy which took place during the next six months in those rooms, were conducted personally by the high contracting parties, and that none of their deliberations transpired until the result of each was made public.

The whole of November 5 had been occupied in these ceremonies. It was late evening when the Emperor gained his lodgings. The few next days were ostensibly occupied in receiving visitors. Among the first of these was the unfortunate ex-queen of Naples, Isabella, widow of Frederick of Aragon, the last king of the bastard dynasty founded by Alfonso. She was living in poverty at Ferrara, under the protection of her relatives, the Este family. On the 18th came the Prince of Orange and Don Ferrante Gonzaga, from the camp before Florence. The siege had begun, but had not yet been prosecuted with the strictest vigour. During the whole time of Charles's residence at Bologna, it must be borne in mind that the siege of Florence was being pressed. Superfluous troops detached from garrison duty in the Lombard towns were drafted across the hills to Tuscany. Whatever else the Emperor might decide for his Italian subjects, this at least was certain: Florence should be restored to the Medicean tyrants, as compensation to the Pope for Roman sufferings. The Prince of Orange came to explain the state of things at Florence, where government and people seemed prepared to resist to the death. Gonzaga had private business of his own to conduct, touching his engagement to the Pope's ward, Isabella, daughter and heiress of the wealthy Vespasiano Colonna.

Meanwhile, ambassadors from all the States and lordships

of Italy flocked to Bologna. Great nobles from the South—
Ascanio Colonna, Grand Constable of Naples; Alfonso
d' Avalos, Marquis of Vasto; Giovanni Luigi Caraffa, Prince
of Stigliano—took up their quarters in adjacent houses, or in
the upper story of the Public Palace. The Marquis of Vasto
arrests our gaze for a moment. He was nephew to the
Marquis of Pescara (husband of Vittoria Colonna), who had
the glory of taking Francis prisoner at Pavia, and afterwards
the infamy of betraying the unfortunate Girolamo Morone
and his master the Duke of Milan to the resentment of the
Spanish monarch. What part Pescara actually played in
that dark passage of plot and counterplot remains obscure.
But there is no doubt that he employed treachery, single if
not double, for his own advantage. His arrogance and
avowed hostility to the Italians caused his very name to be
execrated; nor did his nephew, the Marquis of Vasto, differ
in these respects from the more famous chief of his house.
This man was also destined to obtain an evil reputation when
he succeeded in 1532 to the government of Milan. Here too
may be noticed the presence at Bologna of Girolamo Morone's
son, who had been created Bishop of Modena in 1529. For
him a remarkable fate was waiting. Condemned to the
dungeons of the Inquisition as a heretic by Paul IV., rescued
by Pius IV., and taken into highest favour at that Pontiff's
Court, he successfully manipulated the closing of the Tridentine Council to the profit of the Papal See.

Negotiations for the settlement of Italian affairs were
proceeding without noise, but with continual progress, through
this month. The lodgings of ambassadors and lords were so
arranged in the Palazzo Pubblico that they, like their
Imperial and Papal masters, could confer at all times and
seasons. Every day brought some new illustrious visitor.
On the 22nd arrived Federigo Gonzaga, Marquis of Mantua,
who took up his quarters in immediate proximity to Charles

and Clement. His business required but little management. The House of Gonzaga was already well affected to the Spanish cause, and counted several captains in the imperial army. Charles showed his favour by raising Mantua to the rank of a Duchy. It was different with the Republic of Venice and the Duke of Milan. The Emperor elect had reasons to be strongly prejudiced against them both—against Venice, as the most formidable of the French allies in the last war; against Francesco Maria Sforza, as having been implicated, though obscurely, in Morone's conspiracy to drive the Spaniards from Italy and place the crown of Naples on Pescara's head. Clement took both under his protection. He had sufficient reasons to believe that the Venetians would purchase peace by the cession of their recent acquisitions on the Adriatic coast, and he knew that the pacification of Italy could not be accomplished without their aid. In effect, the Republic agreed to relinquish Cervia and Ravenna to the Pope, and their Apulian ports to Charles, engaging at the same time to pay a sum of 800,000 ducats and stipulating for an amnesty to all their agents and dependents. It is not so clear why Clement warmly espoused the cause of Sforza. That he did so is certain. He obtained a safe-conduct for the duke, and made it a point of personal favour that he should be received into the Emperor's grace. This stipulation appears to have been taken into account when the affairs of Ferrara were decided at a later date against the Papal interests.

Francesco Maria Sforza appeared in Bologna on the 22nd. This unfortunate bearer of one of the most coveted titles in Europe had lately lived a prisoner in his own Castello, while the city at his doors and the fertile country round it were being subjected to cruellest outrage and oppression from Spanish, French, Swiss, and German mercenaries. He was a man ruined in health as well as fortune. Six years before

this date, one of his chamberlains, Bonifazio Visconti, had
given him a slight wound in the shoulder with a poisoned
dagger. From this wound he never recovered; and it was
pitiable to behold the broken man, unable to move or stand
without support, dragging himself upon his knees to Cæsar's
footstool. Charles appears to have discerned that he had
nothing to fear and much to gain, if he showed clemency to
so powerless a suitor. Francesco was the last of his line.
His health rendered it impossible that he should expect heirs;
and although he subsequently married a princess of the
House of Denmark, he died childless in the autumn of 1535.
It was therefore determined, in compliance with the Pope's
request, that Sforza should be confirmed in the Duchy of
Milan. Pavia, however, was detached and given to the
terrible Antonio de Leyva for his lifetime. The garrisons of
Milan and Como were left in Spanish hands; and the duke
promised to wring 400,000 ducats as the price of his investiture, with an additional sum of 500,000 ducats to be paid in
ten yearly instalments, from his already blood-sucked people.
It will be observed that money figured largely in all these
high political transactions. Charles, though lord of many
lands, was, even at this early stage of his career, distressed for
want of cash. He rarely paid his troops, but commissioned
the captains in his service to levy contributions on the
provinces they occupied. The funds thus raised did not
always reach the pockets of the soldiers, who subsisted as
best they could by marauding. Having made these terms,
Francesco Maria Sforza was received into the Imperial favour.
He returned to Milan, in no sense less a prisoner than he had
previously been, and with the heartrending necessity of
extorting money from his subjects at the point of Spanish
swords. In exchange for the ducal title, he thus had made
himself a tax-collector for his natural enemies. Secluded in
the dreary chambers of his castle, assailed by the execrations

of the Milanese, he may well have groaned, like Marlowe's
Edward—

> But what are Kings, when regiment is gone,
> But perfect shadows in a sunshine day?
> My foemen rule; I bear the name of King;
> I wear the crown; but am controlled by them.

When he died he bequeathed his duchy to the crown of Spain.
It was detached from the Empire, and became the private
property of Charles and of his son, Philip II.

During the month of December negotiations for the terms
of peace in Italy went briskly forward. On the part of Venice,
two men of the highest distinction arrived as orators. These
were Pietro Bembo and Gasparo Contarini, both of whom
received the honours of the Cardinalate from Paul III. on his
accession. Of Bembo's place in Italian society, as the dictator
of literature at this epoch, I have already sufficiently spoken
in another part of my work on the Renaissance. Contarini
will more than once arrest our notice in the course of this
volume. Of all the Italians of the time, he was perhaps the
greatest, wisest, and most sympathetic. Had it been possible
to avert the breach between Catholicism and Protestantism,
to curb the intolerance of Inquisitors and the ambition of
Jesuits, and to guide the reform of the Church by principles
of moderation and liberal piety, Contarini was the man who
might have restored unity to the Church in Europe. Once,
indeed, at Regensburg in 1541, he seemed upon the very
point of effecting a reconciliation between the parties that
were tearing Christendom asunder. But his failure was
ever more conspicuous than his momentary semblance of
success. It was not in the temper of the times to accept
a Concordat founded on however philosophical, however
politic considerations. Contarini will be remembered as a
'beautiful soul,' born out of the due moment, and by no
means adequate to cope with the fierce passions that raged

round him. Among Protestants he was a Catholic, and they regarded his half-measures with contempt. Among Catholics he passed for a suspected Lutheran, and his writings were only tolerated after they had been subjected to rigorous castration at the hands of Papal Inquisitors.[1]

On Christmas eve the ambassadors and representatives of the Italian Powers met together in the chambers of Cardinal Gattinara, Grand Chancellor of the Empire, to subscribe the terms of a confederation and perpetual league for the maintenance of peace. From this important document the Florentines were excluded, as open rebels to the will of Charles and Clement. There was no justice in the rigour with which Florence was now treated. Her republican independence had hitherto been recognised, although her own internal discords exposed her to a virtual despotism. But Clement stipulated and Charles conceded, as a *sine qua non* in the project of pacification, that Florence should be converted into a Medicean duchy. For the Duke of Ferrara, whom the Pope regarded as a contumacious vassal, and whose affairs were still the subject of debate, a place was specially reserved in the treaty. He, as I have already observed, had been taken under the Imperial protection; and a satisfactory settlement of his claims was now a mere question of time. On the evening of the same day, the Pope bestowed on Charles the Sword of the Spirit, which it was the wont of Rome to confer on the best-beloved of her secular sons at this festival. The peace was publicly proclaimed, amid universal plaudits, on the last day of the year 1529.

The chief affairs to be decided in the new year were the reduction of Florence to submission and the coronation of the Emperor. The month of January was passed in jousts and pastimes; ceremonial privileges were conferred on the University of Bologna; magnificent embassies from the

[1] See Ranke, vol. i. p. 153, note.

Republic of S. Mark, glowing in senatorial robes of crimson silk, were entertained; and a singular deputation from the African Court of Prester John obtained audience of the Roman Pontiff. Amid these festivities there arrived, on January 16, three delegates from Florence, who spent some weeks in fruitless efforts to obtain a hearing from the arbiters of Italy. Clement refused to deal with them, because their commonwealth was still refractory. Charles repelled them, because he wished to gratify the Pope, and knew that Florence remained staunch in her devotion to the French crown. The old proverb 'Lilies with lilies,' the white lily of Florence united with the golden fleur-de-lys of France, had still political significance in this day of Italian degradation. Meanwhile Francis I. treated his faithful allies with lukewarm tolerance. The smaller fry of Italian potentates, worshippers of the rising sun of Spain, curried favour with their masters by insulting the republic's representatives. On their return to Florence, the ambassadors had to report a total diplomatic failure. But this, far from breaking the untamable spirit of the Signory and people, prompted them in February to new efforts of resistance and to edicts of outlawry against citizens whom they regarded as traitors to the State. Among the proscribed were Francesco Guicciardini, Roberto Acciaiuoli, Francesco Vettori, and Baccio Valori. Of these men Francesco Guicciardini, Francesco Vettori, and Baccio Valori were attendant at Bologna upon the Pope. They all adhered with fidelity to the Medicean party at this crisis of their country's fate, and all paid dearly for their loyalty. When Cosimo I., by their efforts, was established in the duchy, he made it one of his first cares to rid himself of these too faithful servants. Baccio Valori was beheaded after the battle of Montemurlo in 1537 for practice with the exiles of Filippo Strozzi's party. Francesco Guicciardini, Francesco Vettori, and Roberto Acciaiuoli died in disgrace before the year 1543—their only crime being that they had made themselves the ladder whereby a Medici had climbed into his throne, and which it was his business to upset when firmly seated. For the heroism of Florence at this moment it would be difficult to find fit words of panegyric. The republic stood alone, abandoned by France to the hot rage of Clement and the cold contempt of Charles, deserted by the Powers of Italy, betrayed by lying captains, deluged on all sides with the scum of armies pouring into Tuscany from the Lombard pandemonium of war. The situation was one of impracticable difficulty. Florence could not but fall. Yet every generous heart will throb with sympathy while reading the story of that final stand for independence, in which a handful of burghers persisted, though congregated princes licked the dust from feet of Emperor and Pontiff.

Charles had come to assume the iron and the golden crowns in Italy. He ought to have journeyed to Monza or to S. Ambrogio at Milan for the first, and to the Lateran in Rome for the second of these investitures. An Emperor of the Swabian House would have been compelled by precedent and superstition to observe this form. It is true that the coronation of a German prince as the successor of Lombard kings and Roman Augusti, had always been a symbolic ceremony rather than a rite which ratified genuine Imperial authority. Still the ceremony connoted many medieval aspirations. It was the outward sign of theories that had once exerted an ideal influence. To dissociate the twofold sacrament from Milan and from Rome was the same as robbing it of its main virtue, the virtue of a mystical conception. It was tantamount to a demonstration that the belief in Universal Monarchy had passed away. By breaking the old rules of his investiture, Charles notified the disappearance of the medieval order, and proclaimed new political ideals to the world. When asked whether he would not follow custom and seek the Lombard crown in Monza, he brutally replied that he was not wont to run after crowns, but to have crowns running after him. He trampled no less on that still more venerable *religio loci* which attached imperial rights to Rome. Together with this ancient piety, he swept the Holy Roman Empire into the dust-heap of archaic curiosities. By declaring his will to be crowned where he chose, he emphasised the modern state motto of *L'état, c'est moi*, and prepared the way for a Pope's closing of a General Council by the phrase *L'Eglise, c'est moi*. Charles had sufficient reasons for acting as he did. The Holy Roman Empire ever since the first event of Charles the Great's coronation, when it justified itself as a diplomatical expedient for unifying Western Christendom, had existed more or less as a shadow. Charles violated the duties which alone gave the semblance of a substance to that shadow. As King of Italy, he had desolated the Lombard realm of which he sought the title. As Emperor elect, he had ravished his bride, the Eternal City. As suitor to the Pope for both of his expected crowns, he stood responsible for the multiplied insults to which Clement had been so recently exposed. No Emperor had been more powerful since Charles the Great than this Charles V., the last who took his crowns in Italy. It was significant that the man in whose name Rome had suffered outrage, and who was about to detach Lombardy from the Empire, was by his own will invested at Bologna. The citizens of Monza were accordingly bidden to send the iron crown to Bologna. It arrived on February 20, and on the 22nd Charles received it from the hands of Clement in the chapel of the palace. The Cardinal who performed the ceremony of unction was a Fleming, William Hencheneor, who in the Sack of Rome had bought his freedom for the large sum of 40,000 crowns. On this auspicious occasion he cut off half the beard which he still wore in sign of mourning!

The Duke and Duchess of Urbino made their entrance into Bologna on the same day. Francesco Maria della Rovere, Duke of Urbino, Prefect of Rome, and Captain General of the armies of the Church, was one of the most noted warriors of that time. Yet victory had rarely crowned his brows with laurels. Imitating the cautious tactics of Braccio, and emulating the fame of Fabius Cunctator, he reduced the art of war to a system of manœuvres, and rarely risked his fortune in the field. It was chiefly due to his dilatory movements that the disaster of the Sack of Rome was not averted. He had been expelled by Leo X. from his duchy to make room for Lorenzo de' Medici, and report ran that a secret desire to witness the humiliation of a Medicean Pontiff caused him to withhold his forces from attacking the tumultuary troops of Bourbon. Francesco Maria was a man of violent temper; nineteen years before, he had murdered the Pope's Legate, Cardinal Francesco Alidosi, with his dagger, in the open streets of Bologna. His wife, Eleanora Ippolita Gonzaga, presided with grace over that brilliant and cultivated Court which Castiglione made famous by his 'Cortegiano.' The duke and duchess survive to posterity in two masterpieces of portraiture by the hand of Titian which now adorn the gallery of the Uffizzi.

February 24, which was the anniversary of Charles's birthday, had been fixed for his coronation as Emperor in San Petronio. This church is one of the largest Gothic buildings in Italy. Its façade occupies the southern side of the piazza. The western side, on the left of the church, is taken up by the Palazzo Pubblico. In order to facilitate the passage of the Pope and Emperor with their Courts and train of princes from the palace to the cathedral, a wooden bridge wide enough to take six men abreast was constructed from an opening in the Hall of the Ancients. The bridge descended by a gradual line to the piazza, broadened out into a platform before the front of San Petronio, and then again ascended through the nave to the high altar. It was covered with blue draperies, and so arranged that the vast multitudes assembled in the square and church to see the ceremony had free access to it on all sides. On the morning of the 24th, the solemn procession issued from the palace, and defiled in order down the gangway. Clement was borne aloft by Pontifical grooms in their red liveries. He wore the tiara and a cope of state fastened by Cellini's famous stud, in which blazed the Burgundian diamond of Charles the Bold. Charles walked in royal robes attended by the Count of Nassau and Don Pietro di Toledo, the Viceroy of Naples, who afterwards gave his name to the chief street in that city. Before him went the Marquis of Montferrat, bearing the sceptre; Philip, Duke of Bavaria, carrying the golden orb; the Duke of Urbino, with the sword; and the Duke of Savoy, holding the imperial diadem. This Duke of Savoy was uncle to Francis I. and brother-in-law to Charles—his wife, Beatrice, being a sister of the Empress, and his sister, Louise, mother of the French king. This double relationship made his position during the late wars a difficult one. Yet his territory had been regarded as neutral, and in the pacification of Italy he judged it wise to adhere without reserve to the victorious King of Spain. It was noticed that Ferrante di Sanseverino, Prince of Salerno, though known to be in Bologna, occupied no post of distinction in the Imperial train. He was closely related to the Emperor by his mother, Maria of Aragon, and had done good service in the recent campaigns against Lautrec. The reason for this neglect does not appear. But it may be mentioned that some years later he espoused the French cause, and was deprived of his vast hereditary fiefs. In his ruin the poet Bernardo, father of Torquato Tasso, was involved.

To enumerate all the nobles of Spain, Italy and Germany,

with the ambassadors from England, France, Scotland, Hungary, Bohemia and Portugal, who swelled the Imperial *cortège*; to describe the series of ceremonies by which Charles was first consecrated as a deacon, anointed, dressed and undressed, and finally conducted to the Pope for coronation; to narrate the breaking of the bridge at one point, and the squabbles between the Genoese and Sienese delegates for precedence, would be superfluously tedious. The day was well-nigh over when at length Charles received the Imperial insignia from the Pope's hands. *Accipe gladium sanctum, Accipe virgam, Accipe pomum, Accipe signum gloriæ!* As Clement pronounced these sentences, he gave the sword, the sceptre, the globe, and the diadem in succession to the Emperor, who knelt before him. Charles bent and kissed the Papal feet. He then rose and took his throne beside the Pope. It was placed two steps lower than that of Clement. The ceremony of coronation and inthronisation being now complete, Charles was proclaimed: *Romanorum Imperator semper augustus, mundi totius Dominus, universis Dominis, universis Principibus et Populis semper venerandus.* When Mass was over, Pope and Emperor shook hands. At the church-door, Charles held Clement's stirrup, and when the Pope had mounted, he led his palfrey for some paces, in sign of filial submission.

The month of March was distinguished by the arrival of illustrious visitors. The Duchess of Savoy, with an escort of eighteen lovely maids of honour, made her pompous entry on the 4th, and took up her quarters in the Palazzo Pepoli. On the 6th came the Duke of Ferrara, for whom Charles had procured a safe-conduct from the Pope. During the Emperor's stay at Bologna, Alfonso d' Este had been assiduous in paying him and his Court small attentions, sending excellent provisions for the household and furnishing the royal table with game and every kind of delicacy. The settlement of his dispute with the Holy See was the only important business that remained to be transacted. Charles prevailed upon both Clement and Alfonso to state their cases in writing and to place them in the hands of jurisconsults to report upon. There is little doubt that his own mind was already made up in favour of the duke; but he did not pass sentence until the following December, nor was the decision published before April in the year 1531. The substance of the final agreement was as follows. Modena, Reggio and Rubbiera were declared fiefs of the Empire, seeing that they had not been included in Pepin's gift of the Exarchate. Charles confirmed their investiture to Alfonso, in return for a considerable payment to the Imperial Chancery. He had previously conferred the town of Carpi, forfeited by Alberto Pio as a French adherent, on the duke. Ferrara remained a fief of the Church, and Clement consented to acknowledge Alfonso's tenure, upon his disbursement of 100,000 ducats. This decision saved Modena to the bastard line of Este, when Pope Clement VIII. seized Ferrara as a lapsed fief in 1598. In the sixty-seven years which passed between the date of Charles's coronation and the extinction of the duchy, Ferrara enjoyed the fame of the most brilliant Court in Italy, and shone with the lustre conferred on it by men like Tasso and Guarini.

The few weeks which now remained before Charles left Bologna were spent for the most part in jousts and tournaments, visits to churches, and social entertainments. Veronica Gambara threw her apartments open to the numerous men of letters who crowded from all parts of Italy to witness the ceremony of Charles's coronation. This lady was widow to the late lord of Correggio, and one of the two most illustrious women of her time.[1] She dwelt with princely state in a palace of the Marsili; and here might be

[1] See *Italian Literature*, Vol. V. p. 251.

seen the poets Bembo, Mauro, and Molza in conversation
with witty Berni, learned Vida, stately Trissino, and noble-
hearted Marcantonio Flaminio. Paolo Giovio and Francesco
Guicciardini, the chief historians of their time, were also to
be found there, together with a host of literary and diplomatic worthies attached to the Courts of Urbino and
Ferrara or attendant on the train of cardinals, who, like
Ippolito de' Medici, made a display of culture. Meanwhile
the Dowager Marchioness of Mantua and the Duchess of
Savoy entertained Italian and Spanish nobles with masqued
balls and carnival processions in the Manzoli and Pepoli
palaces. Frequent quarrels between hot-blooded youths
of the rival nations added a spice of chivalrous romance
to love-adventures in which the ladies of these Courts
played a too conspicuous part. What still remained to Italy
of Renaissance splendour, wit, and fashion, after the Sack of
Rome and the prostration of her wealthiest cities, was concentrated in this sunset blaze of sumptuous festivity at
Bologna. Nor were the arts without illustrious representatives. Francesco Mazzola, surnamed Il Parmigianino, before
whose altar-piece in his Roman studio the rough soldiers of
Bourbon's army were said to have lately knelt in adoration,
commemorated the hero of the day by painting Charles
attended by Fame who crowned his forehead, and an infant
Hercules who handed him the globe. Titian, too, was there,
and received the honour of several sittings from the Emperor.
His life-sized portrait of Charles in full armour, seated on a
white war-horse, has perished. But it gave such satisfaction
at the moment that the fortunate master was created knight
and count palatine, and appointed painter to the Emperor
with a fixed pension. Titian also painted portraits of
Antonio de Leyva and Alfonso d' Avalos, but whether upon
this occasion or in 1532, when he was again summoned to the
Imperial Court at Bologna, is not certain. From this assem-

blage of eminent personages we notice the absence of Pietro Aretino. He was at the moment out of favour with Clement VII. But independently of this obstacle, he may well have thought it imprudent to quit his Venetian retreat and expose himself to the resentment of so many princes whom he had alternately loaded with false praises and bemired with loathsome libels.

People observed that the Emperor in his excursions through the streets of Bologna usually wore the Spanish habit. He was dressed in black velvet, with black silk stockings, black shoes, and a black velvet cap adorned with black feathers. This sombre costume received some relief from jewels used for buttons; and the collar of the Golden Fleece shone upon the monarch's breast. So slight a circumstance would scarcely deserve attention, were it not that in a short space of time it became the fashion throughout Italy to adopt the subdued tone of Spanish clothing. The upper classes consented to exchange the varied and brilliant dresses which gave gaiety to the earlier Renaissance for the dismal severity conspicuous in Morone's masterpieces, in the magnificent gloom of the Genoese Brignoli, and in the portraits of Roman Inquisitors. It is as though the whole race had put on mourning for its loss of liberty, its servitude to foreign tyrants and ecclesiastical hypocrites. Nor is it fanciful to detect a note of moral sadness and mental depression corresponding to these black garments in the faces of that later generation. How different is Tasso's melancholy grace from Ariosto's gentle joyousness; the dried-up precision of Baroccio's Francesco Maria della Rovere from the sanguine joviality of Titian's first duke of that name! One of the most acutely critical of contemporary poets felt the change which I have indicated, and ascribed it to the same cause. Campanella wrote as follows:

> Black robes befit our age.   Once they were white ;
> Next many-hued ; now dark as Afric's Moor,
> Night-black, infernal, traitorous, obscure,
> Horrid with ignorance and sick with fright.
> For very shame we shun all colours bright,
> Who mourn our end—the tyrants we endure,
> The chains, the noose, the lead, the snares, the lure—
> Our dismal heroes, our souls sunk in night.

In the midst of this mirth-making there arrived on March 20 an embassy from England, announcing Henry VIII.'s resolve to divorce himself at any cost from Katharine of Aragon. This may well have recalled both Pope and Emperor to a sense of the gravity of European affairs. The schism of England was now imminent. Germany was distracted by Protestant revolution. The armies of Cæsar were largely composed of mutinous Lutherans. Some of these soldiers had even dared to overthrow a colossal statue of Clement VII. and grind it into powder at Bologna ; and this outrage, as it appears, went unpunished. The very troops employed in reducing rebellious Florence were commanded by a Lutheran general ; and Clement began to fear that, after Charles's departure, the Prince of Orange might cross the Apennines and expose the Papal person to the insults of another captivity in Bologna. Nor were the gathering forces of revolutionary Protestants alone ominous. Though Soliman had been repulsed before Vienna, the Turks were still advancing on the eastern borders of the Empire. Their fleets swept the Levantine waters, while the pirate dynasties of Tunis and Algiers threatened the whole Mediterranean coast with ruin. Charles, still uncertain what part he should take in the disputes of Germany, left Bologna for the Tyrol on March 28. Clement, on the last day of the month, took his journey by Loreto to Rome.

It will be useful, at this point, to recapitulate the net

results of Charles's administration of Italian affairs in 1530. The kingdom of the Two Sicilies, with the island of Sardinia and the Duchy of Milan, became Spanish provinces, and were ruled henceforth by viceroys. The House of Este was confirmed in the Duchy of Ferrara, including Modena and Reggio. The Duchies of Savoy and Mantua and the Marquisate of Montferrat, which had espoused the Spanish cause, were undisturbed. Genoa and Siena, both of them avowed allies of Spain, the former under Spanish protection, the latter subject to Spanish coercion, remained with the name and empty privileges of republics. Venice had made her peace with Spain, and though she was still strong enough to pursue an independent policy, she showed as yet no inclination, and had, indeed, no power, to stir up enemies against the Spanish autocrat. The Duchy of Urbino, recognised by Rome and subservient to Spanish influence, was permitted to exist. The Papacy once more assumed a haughty tone, relying on the firm alliance struck with Spain. This league, as years went by, was destined to grow still closer, still more fruitful of results.

Florence alone had been excepted from the articles of peace. It was still enduring the horrors of the memorable siege when Clement left Bologna at the end of May. The last hero of the republic, Francesco Ferrucci, fell fighting at Gavignana on August 2. Their general, Malatesta Baglioni, broke his faith with the citizens. Finally, on August 12, the town capitulated. Alessandro de' Medici, who had received the title of Duke of Florence from Charles at Bologna, took up his residence there in July 1531, and held the State by help of Spanish mercenaries under the command of Alessandro Vitelli. When he was murdered by his cousin in 1537, Cosimo de' Medici, the scion of another branch of the ruling family, was appointed Duke. Charles V. recognised his title and Cosimo soon showed that he determined to be master in

his own duchy. He crushed the exiled party of Filippo
Strozzi, who attempted a revolution of the State, exterminated its leaders, and contrived to rid himself of the powerful
adherents who had placed him on the throne. But he
remained a subservient though not very willing ally of Spain;
and when he expelled Alessandro Vitelli from the fortress
that commanded Florence, he admitted a Spaniard, Don
Juan de Luna, in his stead. During the petty wars of
1552-56 which Henri II. carried on with Charles V. in Italy,
Siena attempted to shake off the yoke of a Spanish garrison
established there in 1547 under the command of Don Hurtado
de Mendoza. The citizens appealed to France, who sent them
the great Marshal, Piero Strozzi, brother of Cosimo's vanquished enemy Filippo. Cosimo through these years supported
the Spanish cause with troops and money, hoping to guide
events in his own interest. At length, by the aid of Gian
Giacomo Medici, sprung from an obscure Milanese family, who
had been trained in the Spanish methods of warfare, he succeeded in subduing Siena. He now reaped the fruits of his
Spanish policy. In 1557 Philip II. conceded the Sienese territory, reserving only its forts, to the Duke of Florence, who in
1569 obtained the title of Grand Duke of Tuscany from Pope
Pius V. This title was confirmed by the Empire in 1575 to
his son Francesco.

Thus the republics of Florence and Siena were extinguished. The Grand Duchy of Tuscany was created. It
became an Italian power of the first magnitude, devoted to
the absolutist principles of Spanish and Papal sovereignty.
The further changes which took place in Italy after the year
1530, turned equally to the profit of Spain and Rome.
These were principally the creation of the Duchy of Parma
for the Farnesi (1545-1559), of which I shall have to speak
in the next chapter; the resumption of Ferrara by the
Papacy in 1597, which reduced the House of Este to the

smaller fiefs of Modena and Reggio; the acquisition of Montferrat by Mantua in 1586; the cession of Saluzzo to Savoy in 1598, and the absorption of Urbino into the Papal domains in 1631.

It was hoped when Charles and Clement proclaimed the pacification of Italy at Bologna on the last day of 1529, that the peninsula would no longer be the theatre of wars for supremacy between the French and Spaniards. This expectation proved delusive; for the struggle soon broke out again. The people, however, suffered less extensively than in former years; because the Spanish party, supported by Papal authority, was decidedly predominant. The Italian princes, whether they liked it or not, were compelled to follow in the main a Spanish policy. At length, in 1559, by the Peace of Cateau Cambresis signed between Henri II. and Philip II., the French claims were finally abandoned, and the Spanish hegemony was formally acknowledged. The later treaty of Vervins, in 1598, ceded Saluzzo to the Duchy of Savoy, and shut the gates of Italy to French interference.

Though the people endured far less misery from foreign armies in the period between 1530 and 1600 than they had done in the period from 1494 to 1527, yet the state of the country grew ever more and more deplorable. This was due in the first instance to the insane methods of taxation adopted by the Spanish viceroys, who held monopolies of corn and other necessary commodities in their hands, and who invented imposts for the meanest articles of consumption. Their example was followed by the Pope and petty princes. Alfonso II. of Ferrara, for instance, levied a tenth on all produce which passed his city gates, and on the capital engaged in every contract. He monopolised the sale of salt, flour, bread; and imposed a heavy tax on oil. Sixtus V. by exactions of a like description and by the sale of numberless offices, accumulated a vast sum of money, much of which bore heavy interest. He was so ignorant of the first principle of political economy as to lock up the accruing treasure in the Castle of S. Angelo. The rising of Masaniello in Naples was simply due to the exasperation of the common folk at having even fruit and vegetables taxed. In addition to such financial blunders, we must take into account the policy pursued by all princes at this epoch, of discouraging commerce and manufactures. Thus Cosimo I. of Tuscany induced the old Florentine families to withdraw their capital from trade, sink it in land, create entails in perpetuity on eldest sons, and array themselves with gimcrack titles which he liberally supplied. Even Venice showed at this epoch a contempt for the commerce which had brought her into a position of unrivalled splendour. This wilful depression of industry was partly the result of Spanish aristocratic habits, which now invaded Italian society. But it was also deliberately chosen as a means of extinguishing freedom. Finally, if war proved now less burdensome, the exhaustion of Italy and the decay of military spirit rendered the people liable to the scourge of piracy. The whole seacoast was systematically plundered by the navies of Barbarossa and Dragut. The inhabitants of the ports and inland villages were carried off into slavery, and many of the Italians themselves drove a brisk trade in the sale of their compatriots. Brigandage, following in the wake of agricultural depression and excessive taxation, depopulated the central provinces. All these miseries were exacerbated by frequent recurrences of plagues and famines.

It is characteristic of the whole tenor of Italian history that, in spite of the virtual hegemony which the Spaniards now exercised in the peninsula, the nation continued to exist in separate parcels, each of which retained a certain individuality. That Italy could not have been treated as a single province by the Spanish autocrat will be manifest, when we consider the European jealousy to which so summary an exhibition of force would have given rise. It is also certain that the Papacy, which had to be respected, would have resisted an openly declared Spanish despotism. But more powerful, I think, than all these considerations together, was the past prestige of the Italian States. Europe was not prepared to regard that brilliant and hitherto respected constellation of commonwealths, from which all intellectual culture, arts of life, methods of commerce, and theories of political existence had been diffused, as a single province of the Spanish monarchy. The Spaniards themselves were scarcely in a position to entertain the thought of reducing the peninsula to bondage, *vi et armis*. And if they had attempted any measure tending to this result, they would undoubtedly have been resisted by an alliance of the European Powers. What they sought, and what they gained, was a preponderating influence in each of the parcels which they recognised as nominally independent.

The intellectual and social life of the Italians, though much reduced in vigour, was therefore still, as formerly, concentrated in cities marked by distinct local qualities, and boastful of their ancient glories. The Courts of Ferrara and Urbino continued to form centres for literary and artistic coteries. Venice remained the stronghold of mental unrestraint and moral license, where thinkers uttered their thoughts with tolerable freedom, and libertines indulged their tastes unhindered. Rome early assumed novel airs of piety, and external conformity to austere patterns became the fashion here. Yet the Papal capital did not wholly cease to be the resort of students and of artists. The universities maintained themselves in a respectable position—far different, indeed, from that which they had held in the last century, yet not ignoble. Much was being learned on many lines of study divergent from those prescribed by earlier humanists. Padua, in particular, distinguished itself for medical researches. This was the flourishing time, moreover, of Academies, in which, notwithstanding nonsense talked and foolish tastes indulged, some solid work was done for literature and science. The names of the Cimento, Della Crusca, and Palazzo Vernio at Florence, remind us of not unimportant labours in physics, in the analysis of language, and in the formation of a new dramatic style of music. At the same time the resurgence of popular literature and the creation of popular theatrical types deserve to be particularly noticed. It is as though the Italian nation at this epoch, suffocated by Spanish etiquette, and poisoned by Jesuitical hypocrisy, sought to expand healthy lungs in free spaces of open air, indulging in dialectical niceties and immortalising street-jokes by the genius of masqued comedy.

This most ancient and intensely vital race had given Europe the Roman Republic, the Roman Empire, the system of Roman law, the Romance languages, Latin Christianity, the Papacy, and, lastly, all that is included in the art and culture of the Renaissance. It was time, perhaps, that it should go to rest a century or so, and watch uprising nations—the Spanish, English, French, and so forth—stir their stalwart limbs in common strife and novel paths of pioneering industry.

After such fashion let us, then, if we can contrive to do so, regard the Italians during their subjection to the Church and Austria. Were it not for these consolatory reflections, and for the present reappearance of the nation in a new and previously unapprehended form of unity, the history of the Counter-Reformation period would be almost too painful for investigation. What the Italians actually accomplished during this period in art, learning, science, and literature, was indeed more than enough to have conferred undying lustre on such races as the Dutch or Germans at the same epoch. But it would be ridiculous to compare Italians with either Dutchmen or Germans at a time when Italy was still so incalculably superior. Compared with their own standard, compared with what they might have achieved under more favourable conditions of national independence, the products of this age are saddening. The tragic elements of my present theme are summed up in the fact that Italy during the Counter-Reformation was inferior to Italy during the Renaissance, and that this inferiority was due to the interruption of vital and organic processes by reactionary forces.

It would not be just to condemn Spain and the Papacy because, being reactionary powers, they quenched for three centuries the genial light of Italy. We must rather bear in mind that both Spain and the Papacy were at that time cosmopolitan factors of the first magnitude, with perplexing world-problems confronting them. Charles bore upon his shoulders the concerns of the Empire, the burden of the German revolution, and the distracting anxiety of a duel with Islam. When his son bowed to the yoke of government, he had to meet the same perplexities, complicated with Netherlands in revolt, England in antagonism, and France in dubious ferment. A succession of Popes were hampered by painful European questions, which the instinct of self-preservation taught them to regard as paramount. They were fighting for existence; for the Catholic creed; for their own theocratic sovereignty. They held strong cards. But against them were drawn up the battalions of heresy, free thought, political insurgence in the modern world. The *Zeitgeist* that has made us what we are, had begun to organise stern opposition to the Church. It was natural enough that both the Spanish autocrat and the successor of S. Peter should at this crisis have regarded Italian affairs as subordinate in importance to wider matters which demanded their attention. Yet if we shift our point of view from this high vantage-ground of Imperial and Papal anxieties, and place ourselves in the centre of Italy as our post of observation, it will be apparent that nothing more ruinous for the prosperity of the Italian people could have been devised than the joint autocracy accorded at Bologna to two cosmopolitan but non-national forces in their midst. An alien monarchy greedy for gold, a panic-stricken hierarchy in terror for its life, warped the tendencies and throttled the energies of the most artistically sensitive, the most heroically innovating of the existing races. However we may judge the merits of the Spaniards, they were assuredly not those which had brought Italy into the first rank of European nations. The events of a single century proved that, far from being able to govern other peoples, Spain was incapable of self-government on any rational principle. Whatever may have been the policy thrust upon the chief of Latin Christianity in the desperate struggle with militant rationalism, the repressive measures which it felt bound to adopt were eminently pernicious to a race like the Italians, who showed no disposition for religious regeneration, and who were yet submitted to the tyranny of ecclesiastical discipline and intellectual intolerance at every point.

The settlement made by Charles V. in 1530, and the various changes which took place in the duchies between that date and the end of the century, had then the effect of rendering the Papacy and Spain omnipotent in Italy. These kindred autocrats were joined in firm alliance, except during the brief period of Paul IV.'s French policy, which ended in the Pope's complete discomfiture by Alva in 1557. They used their aggregated forces for the riveting of spiritual, political, and social chains upon the modern world. What they only partially effected in Europe at large, by means of S. Bartholomew massacres, exterminations of Jews in Toledo

and of Mussulmans in Granada, holocausts of victims in the
Low Countries, wars against French Huguenots and German
Lutherans, naval expeditions and plots against the state of
England, assassinations of heretic princes, and occasional
burning of free-thinkers, they achieved with plenary success
in Italy. The centre of the peninsula, from Ferrara to
Terracina, lay at the discretion of the Pope. The Two
Sicilies, Sardinia and the Duchy of Milan were absolute
dependencies of the Spanish crown. Tuscany was linked by
ties of interest, and by the stronger bonds of terrorism, to
Spain. The insignificant principalities of Mantua, Modena,
Parma could not do otherwise than submit to the same
predominant authority. It is not worth while to take into
account the tiny republics of Genoa and Lucca. Their
history through this period, though not so uneventful, is
scarcely less insignificant than that of San Marino. Venice
alone stood independent, still powerful enough to extinguish
Bedmar's Spanish conspiracy in silence, still proud enough to
resist the encroachments of Paul V. with spirit, yet sensible
of her decline and spending her last energies on warfare with
the Turk.

At the close of the century, by the Peace of Vervins in
1598 and two subsequent treaties, Spain and France settled
their long dispute. France was finally excluded from Italy
by the cession of Saluzzo to Savoy, while Savoy at the same
moment, through the loss of its Burgundian provinces, became
an Italian power. The old antagonism which, dating from
the Guelf and Ghibelline contentions of the thirteenth century,
had taken a new form after the Papal investiture of Charles
of Anjou with the kingdoms of Sicily and Naples, now ceased.
That antique antagonism of parties, alien to the home interests of Italy, had been exasperated by the rivalry of Angevine
and Aragonese princes; had assumed formidable intensity
after the invasion of Charles VIII. in 1494; and had expanded

under the reigns of Louis XII. and Francis I. into an open struggle between France and Spain for the supremacy of Italy. It now was finally terminated by the exclusion of the French and the acknowledged over-lordship of the Spaniard. But though peace seemed to be secured to a nation tortured by so many desolating wars of foreign armies, the Italians regarded the cession of Saluzzo with despondency. The partisans of national independence and political freedom had become, however illogically, accustomed to consider France as their ally.[1] They now beheld the gates of Italy closed against the French; they saw the extinction of their ancient Guelf policy of calling French arms into Italy. They felt that rest from strife was dearly bought at the price of prostrate servitude beneath Spanish and Austrian Hapsburgs, Spanish Bourbons, and mongrel princelings bred by crossing these stocks with decaying scions of Italian nobility. As a matter of fact, this was the destiny which lay before them for nearly two centuries after the signing of the Peace of Vervins.

Yet the cession of Saluzzo was really the first dawn of hope for Italy. It determined the House of Savoy as an Italian dynasty, and brought for the first time into the sphere of purely Italian interests that province from which the future salvation of the nation was to come. From 1598 until 1870 the destinies of Italy were bound up with the advance of Savoy from a duchy to a kingdom, with its growth in wealth, military resources and political self-consciousness, and with its ultimate acceptance of the task, accomplished in our days, of freeing Italy from foreign tyranny and forming a single nation out of many component elements. Those component elements by their diversity had conferred lustre on the race in the Middle Ages, by their jealousies had wrecked

---

[1] See, for instance, temp. Henri IV., Sarpi's *Letters*, vol. i. p. 233.

its independence in the Renaissance, and by their weakness had left it at the period of the Counter-Reformation a helpless prey to Papal and Spanish despotism.

The levelling down of the component elements of the Italian race beneath a common despotism, which began in the period I have chosen for this work, was necessary perhaps before Italy could take her place as a united nation gifted with constitutional self-government and independence. Except, therefore, for the sufferings and the humiliations inflicted on her people; except for their servitude beneath the most degrading forms of ecclesiastical and temporal tyranny; except for the annihilation of their beautiful Renaissance culture; except for the depression of arts, learning, science, and literature, together with the enfeeblement of political energy and domestic morality; except for the loathsome domination of hypocrites and persecutors and informers; except for the Jesuitical encouragement of every secret vice and every servile superstition which might emasculate the race and render it subservient to authority—except for these appalling evils, we have no right perhaps to deplore the settlement of Italy by Charles V. in 1530, or the course of subsequent events. For it is tolerably certain that some such levelling down as then commenced was needed to bring the constituent States of Italy into accord; and it is indubitable, as I have had occasion to point out, that the political force which eventually introduced Italy into the European system of federated nations, was determined in its character, if not created, then. None the less, the history of this period (1530–1600) in Italy is a prolonged, a solemn, an inexpressibly heartrending tragedy.

It is the tragic history of the eldest and most beautiful, the noblest and most venerable, the freest and most gifted of Europe's daughters, delivered over to the devilry that issued from the most incompetent and arrogantly stupid of the

European sisterhood, and to the cruelty, inspired by panic, of an impious theocracy. When we use these terms to designate the Papacy of the Counter-Reformation, it is not that we forget how many of those Popes were men of blameless private life and serious views for Catholic Christendom. When we use these terms to designate the Spanish race in the sixteenth century, it is not that we are ignorant of Spanish chivalry and colonising enterprise, of Spanish romance, or of the fact that Spain produced great painters, great dramatists, and one great novelist in the brief period of her glory. We use them deliberately, however, in both cases; because the Papacy at this period committed itself to a policy of immoral, retrograde, and cowardly repression of the most generous of human impulses under the pressure of selfish terror; because the Spaniards abandoned themselves to a dark fiend of religious fanaticism; because they were merciless in their conquests and unintelligent in their administration of subjugated provinces; because they glutted their lusts of avarice and hatred on industrious folk of other creeds within their borders; because they cultivated barren pride and self-conceit in social life; because at the great epoch of Europe's reawakening they chose the wrong side and adhered to it with fatal obstinacy. This obstinacy was disastrous to their neighbours and ruinous to themselves. During the short period of three reigns (between 1598 and 1700) they sank from the first to the third grade in Europe, and saw the sceptre passing in the New World from their hands to those of more normally constituted races. That the self-abandonment to sterilising passions and ignoble persecutions which marked Spain out for decay in the second half of the sixteenth century, and rendered her the curse of her dependencies, can in part be ascribed to the enthusiasm aroused in previous generations by the heroic conflict with advancing Islam, is a thesis capable of demonstration. Yet none the less is it true that her action at that period was calamitous to herself and little short of destructive to Italy.

After the year 1530 seven Spanish devils entered Italy. These were the devil of the Inquisition, with stake and torture-room, and war declared against the will and soul and heart and intellect of man; the devil of Jesuitry, with its sham learning, shameless lying, and casuistical economy of sins; the devil of vice-royal rule, with its life-draining monopolies and gross incapacity for government; the devil of an insolent soldiery, quartered on the people, clamorous for pay, outrageous in their lusts and violences; the devil of fantastical taxation, levying tolls upon the bare necessities of life, and drying up the founts of national well-being at their sources; the devil of petty-princedom, wallowing in sloth and cruelty upon a pinchbeck throne; the devil of effeminate hidalgoism, ruinous in expenditure, mean and grasping, corrupt in private life, in public ostentatious, vain of titles, cringing to its masters, arrogant to its inferiors. In their train these brought with them seven other devils, their pernicious offspring: idleness, disease, brigandage, destitution, ignorance, superstition, hypocritically sanctioned vice. These fourteen devils were welcomed, entertained, and voluptuously lodged in all the fairest provinces of Italy. The Popes opened wide for them the gates of outraged and depopulated Rome. Dukes and marquises fell down and worshipped the golden image of the Spanish Belial-Moloch—that hideous idol whose face was blackened with soot from burning human flesh, and whose skirts were dabbled with the blood of thousands slain in wars of persecution. After a tranquil sojourn of some years in Italy, these devils had everywhere spread desolation and corruption. Broad regions, like the Patrimony of S. Peter and Calabria, were given over to marauding bandits; wide tracts of fertile country, like the Sienese Maremma, were abandoned to malaria; wolves prowled through empty villages

round Milan; in every city the pestilence swept off its
hundreds daily; manufactures, commerce, agriculture, the
industries of town and rural district, ceased; the Courts
swarmed with petty nobles, who vaunted paltry titles, and
resigned their wives to cicisbei and their sons to sloth; art
and learning languished; there was not a man who ventured
to speak out his thought or write the truth; and over the
Dead Sea of social putrefaction floated the sickening oil of
Jesuitical hypocrisy.

CHAPTER II

THE PAPACY AND THE TRIDENTINE COUNCIL

The Counter-Reformation—Its Intellectual and Moral Character—Causes of the Gradual Extinction of Renaissance Energy—Transition from the Renaissance to the Catholic Revival—New Religious Spirit in Italy—Attitude of Italians toward German Reformation—Oratory of Divine Love—Gasparo Contarini and the Moderate Reformers—New Religious Orders—Paul III.—His early History and Education—Political Attitude between France and Spain—Creation of the Duchy of Parma—Imminence of a General Council—Review of previous Councils—Paul's Uneasiness—Opens a Council at Trent in 1542—Protestants virtually excluded, and Catholic Dogmas confirmed in the first Sessions—Death of Paul in 1549—Julius III.—Paul IV.—Character and Ruling Passions of G. P. Caraffa—His Futile Opposition to Spain—Tyranny of his Nephews—Their Downfall—Paul devotes himself to Church Reform and the Inquisition—Pius IV.—His Minister Morone—Diplomatic Temper of this Pope—His Management of the Council—Assistance rendered by his Nephew Carlo Borromeo—Alarming State of Northern Europe—The Council reopened at Trent in 1562—Subsequent History of the Council—It closes with a complete Papal Triumph in 1563—Place of Pius IV. in History—Pius V.—The Inquisitor Pope—Population of Rome—Social Corruption—Sale of Offices and Justice—Tridentine Reforms depress Wealth—Ascetic Purity of Manners becomes fashionable—Piety—The Catholic Reaction generates the Counter-Reformation—Battle of Lepanto—Gregory XIII.—His Relatives—Policy of Enriching the Church at Expense of the Barons—Brigandage in States of the Church—Sixtus V.—His Stern Justice—Rigid Economy—Great Public Works—Taxation—The City of Rome assumes its present Form—Nepotism in the Counter-Reformation Period—Various Estimates of the Wealth accumulated by Papal Nephews—Rise of Princely Roman Families.

IT is not easy to define the intellectual and moral changes which passed over Italy in the period of the Counter-

Reformation;[1] it is still less easy to refer those changes to distinct causes. Yet some analysis tending toward such definition is demanded from a writer who has undertaken to treat of Italian culture and manners between the years 1530 and 1600.

In the last chapter I attempted to describe the depth of servitude to which the States of Italy were severally reduced at the end of the wars between France and Spain. The desolation of the country, the loss of national independence, and the dominance of an alien race, can be counted among the most important of those influences which produced the changes in question. Whatever opinions we may hold regarding the connexion between political autonomy and mental vigour in a people, it can hardly be disputed that a sudden and universal extinction of liberty must be injurious to arts and studies that have grown up under free institutions.

But there were other causes at work. Among these a prominent place should be given to an alteration in the intellectual interests of the Italians themselves. The original impulses of the Renaissance, in scholarship, painting, sculpture, architecture, and vernacular poetry, had been exhausted. Humanism, after recovering the classics and forming a new ideal of culture, was sinking into pedantry and academic erudition. Painting and sculpture, having culminated in the great work of Michelangelo, tended toward a kind of empty mannerism. Architecture settled down into the types fixed by Palladio and Barozzi. Poetry seemed to have reached its

[1] I may here state that I intend to use this term Counter-Reformation to denote the reform of the Catholic Church, which was stimulated by the German Reformation, and which, when the Council of Trent had fixed the dogmas and discipline of Latin Christianity, enabled the Papacy to assume a militant policy in Europe, whereby it regained a large portion of the provinces that had previously lapsed to Lutheran and Calvinistic dissent,

highest point of development in Ariosto. The main motives supplied to art by medieval traditions and humanistic enthusiasm were worked out. Nor was this all. The Renaissance had created a critical spirit which penetrated every branch of art and letters. It was not possible to advance further on the old lines; yet painters, sculptors, architects, and poets of the rising generation had before their eyes the masterpieces of their predecessors, in their minds the precepts of the learned. All alike were rendered awkward and self-conscious by the sense of labouring at a disadvantage, and by the dread of academical censorship.

In truth, this critical spirit, which was the final product of the Renaissance in Italy, favoured the development of new powers in the nation: it hampered workers in the elder spheres of art, literature, and scholarship; but it set thinkers upon the track of those investigations which we call scientific. I shall endeavour, in a future chapter, to show how the Italians were now upon the point of carrying the ardour of the Renaissance into fresh fields of physical discovery and speculation, when their evolution was suspended by the Catholic Reaction. But here it must suffice to observe that formalism had succeeded by the operation of natural influences to the vigour and inventiveness of the national genius in the main departments of literature and fine art.

If we study the development of other European races, we shall find that each of them in turn, at its due season, passed through similar phases. The medieval period ends in the efflorescence of a new delightful energy, which gives a Rabelais, a Shakspere, a Cervantes to the world. The Renaissance riots itself away in Marinism, Gongorism, Euphuism, and the affectations of the Hôtel Rambouillet. This age is succeeded by a colder, more critical, more formal age of obedience to fixed canons, during which scholarly efforts are made to purify style and impose laws on taste. The ensuing period of sense is also marked by profounder inquiries into nature and more exact analysis of mental operations. The correct school of poets, culminating in Dryden and Pope, hold sway in England; while Newton, Locke, and Bentley extend the sphere of science. In France the age of Rabelais and Montaigne yields place to the age of Racine and Descartes. Germany was so distracted by religious wars, Spain was so downtrodden by the Inquisition, that they do not offer equally luminous examples.[1] It may be added that in all these nations the end of the eighteenth and the beginning of the nineteenth centuries are marked by a similar revolt against formality and common sense, to which we give the name of the Romantic movement.

Quitting this sphere of speculation, we may next point out that the European system had undergone an incalculable process of transformation. Powerful nationalities were in existence, who, having received their education from Italy, were now beginning to think and express thought with marked originality. The Italians stood no longer in a relation of uncontested intellectual superiority to these peoples, while they met them under decided disadvantages at all points of political efficiency. The Mediterranean had ceased to be the high road of commercial enterprise and naval energy. Charles V.'s famous device of the two columns, with its motto *Plus Ultra*, indicated that illimitable horizons had been opened, that an age had begun in which Spain, England and Holland should dispute the sovereignty of the Atlantic and Pacific Oceans. Italy was left, with diminished forces of resistance, to bear the brunt of Turk and Arab depredations. The point of gravity in the civilised world had shifted. The Occidental nations looked no longer toward the South of Europe.

[1] With regard to Germany, see Mr. T. E. Perry's acute and philosophical study, entitled *From Opitz to Lessing* (Boston).

While these various causes were in operation, Catholic Christianity showed signs of re-awakening. The Reformation called forth a new and sincere spirit in the Latin Church; new antagonisms were evoked, and new efforts after self-preservation had to be made by the Papal hierarchy. The centre of the world-wide movement which is termed the Counter-Reformation was naturally Rome. Events had brought the Holy See once more into a position of prominence. It was more powerful as an Italian State now, through the support of Spain and the extinction of national independence, than at any previous period of history. In Catholic Christendom its prestige was immensely augmented by the Council of Trent. At the same epoch, the foreigners who dominated Italy, threw themselves with the enthusiasm of fanaticism into this Revival. Spain furnished Rome with the militia of the Jesuits and with the engines of the Inquisition. The Papacy was thus able to secure successes in Italy which were elsewhere only partially achieved. It followed that the moral, social, political and intellectual activities of the Italians at this period were controlled and coloured by influences hostile to the earlier Renaissance. Italy underwent a metamorphosis, prescribed by the Papacy and enforced by Spanish rule. In the process of this transformation the people submitted to rigid ecclesiastical discipline, an adopted without assimilating the customs of a foreign troop of despots.

At first sight we may wonder that the race which had shone with such incomparable lustre from Dante to Ariosto, and which had done so much to create modern culture for Europe, should so quietly have accepted a retrogressive revolution. Yet, when we look closer, this is not surprising. The Italians were fatigued with creation, bewildered by the complexity of their discoveries, uncertain as to the immediate course before them. The Renaissance had been mainly the work of a select few. It had transformed society without permeating the masses of the people. Was it strange that the majority should reflect that, after all, the old ways are the best? This led them to approve the Catholic Revival. Was it strange that, after long, distracting, aimless wars, they should hail peace at any price? This lent popular sanction to the Spanish hegemony, in spite of its obvious drawbacks.

These may be reckoned the main conditions which gave a peculiar but not easily definable complexion of languor, melancholy, and dwindling vitality to nearly every manifestation of Italian genius in the second half of the sixteenth century, and which well-nigh sterilised that genius during the two succeeding centuries. In common with the rest of Europe, and in consequence of an inevitable alteration of their mental bias, they had lost the blithe spontaneity of the Renaissance. But they were at the same time suffering from grievous exhaustion, humiliated by the tyranny of foreign despotism, and terrorised by ecclesiastical intolerance. In their case, therefore, a sort of moral and intellectual atrophy becomes gradually more and more perceptible. The clear artistic sense of rightness and of beauty yields to doubtful taste. The frank audacity of the Renaissance is superseded by cringing timidity, lumbering dulness, somnolent and stagnant acquiescence in accepted formulæ. At first the best minds of the nation fret and rebel, and meet with the dungeon or the stake as the reward of contumacy. In the end everybody seems to be indifferent, satisfied with vacuity, enamoured of insipidity. The brightest episode in this dreary period is the emergence of modern music with incomparable sweetness and lucidity.

It must not be supposed that the change which I have adumbrated, passed rapidly over the Italian spirit. When Paul III. succeeded Clement on the Papal throne in 1534, some of the giants of the Renaissance still survived, and much of their great work was yet to be accomplished. Michelangelo had neither painted the Last Judgment nor planned the cupola which crowns S. Peter's. Cellini had not cast his Perseus for the Loggia de' Lanzi, nor had Palladio raised San Giorgio from the sea at Venice. Pietro Aretino still swaggered in lordly insolence; and though Machiavelli was dead, the 'silver histories' of Guicciardini remained to be written. Bandello, Giraldi and Il Lasca had not published their *Novelle*, nor had Cecchi given the last touch to Florentine comedy. It was chiefly at Venice, which preserved the ancient forms of her oligarchical independence, that the grand style of the Renaissance continued to flourish. Titian was in his prime; the stars of Tintoretto and Veronese had scarcely risen above the horizon. Sansovino was still producing masterpieces of picturesque beauty in architecture.

In order to understand the transition of Italy from the Renaissance to the Counter-Reformation manner, it will be well to concentrate attention on the history of the Papacy during the eight reigns of Paul III., Julius III., Paul IV., Pius IV., Pius V., Gregory XIII., Sixtus V., and Clement VIII.[1] In the first of these reigns we hardly notice that the Renaissance has passed away. In the last we are aware of a completely altered Italy. And we perceive that this alteration has been chiefly due to the ecclesiastical policy which brought the Council of Trent to a successful issue in the reign of Pius IV.

Before engaging in this review of Papal history, I must give some brief account of the more serious religious spirit which had been developed within the Italian Church; since the determination of this spirit toward rigid Catholicism in the second half of the sixteenth century decided the character of Italian manners and culture. Protestantism in the strict sense of the term took but little hold upon Italian society. It is true that the minds of some philosophical students were

[1] These eight reigns cover a space of time from 1534 to 1605

deeply stirred by the audacious discussion of theological principles in Germany. Such men had been rendered receptive of new impressions by the Platonising speculations of Ficino and Pico della Mirandola, as well as by the criticism of the Bible in its original languages which formed a subordinate branch of humanistic education. They had, furthermore, been powerfully affected by the tribulations of Rome at the time of Bourbon's occupation, and had grown to regard these as a divine chastisement inflicted on the Church for its corruption and ungodliness. Lutheranism so far influenced their opinions that they became convinced of the necessity of a return to the simpler elements of Christianity in creed and conduct. They considered a thoroughgoing reform of the hierarchy and of all Catholic institutions to be indispensable. They leant, moreover, with partiality to some of the essential tenets of the Reformation, notably to the doctrines of justification by faith and salvation by the merits of Christ, and also to the principle that Scripture is the sole authority in matters of belief and discipline. Thus both the Cardinals Morone and Contarini, the poet Flaminio, and the nobles of the Colonna family in Naples who imbibed the teaching of Valdes, fell under the suspicion of heterodoxy on these points. But it was characteristic of the members of this school that they had no will to withhold allegiance from the Pope as chief of Christendom. They shrank with horror from the thought of encouraging a schism or of severing themselves from the communion of Catholics. The essential difference between Italian and Teutonic thinkers on such subjects at this epoch seems to have been this : Italians could not cease to be Catholics without at the same time ceasing to be Christians. They could not accommodate their faith to any of the compromises suggested by the Reformation. Even when they left their country in a spirit of rebellion, they felt ill at ease both with

Lutherans and Calvinists. Like Bernardino Ochino and the Anti-Trinitarians of the Socinian sect, they wandered restlessly through Europe, incapable of settling down in communion with any one of the established forms of Protestantism. Calvin at Geneva instituted a real crusade against Italian thinkers, who differed from his views. He drove Valentino Gentile to death on the scaffold; and expelled Gribaldi, Simone, Biandrata, Alciati, Negro. Most of these men found refuge in Poland, Transylvania, even Turkey.[1]

There were bold speculators in Italy enough, who had practically abandoned the Catholic faith. But the majority of these did not think it worth their while to make an open rupture with the Church. Theological hair-splitting reminded them only of the medieval scholasticism from which they had been emancipated by classical culture. They were less interested in questions touching the salvation of the individual or the exact nature of the sacraments than in metaphysical problems suggested by the study of antique philosophers, or new theories of the material universe. The indifference of these men in religion rendered it easy for them to conform in all external points to custom. Their fundamental axiom was that a scientific thinker could hold one set of opinions as a philosopher, and another set as a Christian. Their motto was the celebrated *Foris ut moris, intus ut libet.*[2] Nor were ecclesiastical authorities dissatisfied with this attitude during the ascendency of humanistic culture. It was, indeed, the attitude of Popes like Leo, Cardinals like Bembo. And it only revealed its essential weakness when the tide of general opinion, under the blast of Teutonic revolutionary ideas, turned violently in favour of

[1] See Berti's *Vita di G. Bruno*, pp. 105-108.
[2] This maxim is ascribed to the materialistic philosopher Cremonini.

formal orthodoxy. Then indeed it became dangerous to adopt the position of a Pomponazzo.

The mental attitude of such men is so well illustrated by a letter written by Celio Calcagnini to Peregrino Morato, that I shall not hesitate to transcribe it here. It seems that Morato had sent his correspondent some treatise on the theological questions then in dispute; and Calcagnini replies:

'I have read the book relating to the controversies so much agitated at present. I have thought on its contents, and weighed them in the balance of reason. I find in it nothing which may not be approved and defended, but some things which, as mysteries, it is safer to suppress and conceal than to bring before the common people, inasmuch as they pertained to the primitive and infant state of the Church. Now, when the decrees of the Fathers and long usage have introduced other modes, what necessity is there for reviving antiquated practices which have long fallen into desuetude, especially as neither piety nor the salvation of the soul is concerned with them? Let us then, I pray you, allow these things to rest. Not that I disapprove of their being embraced by scholars and lovers of antiquity; but I would not have them communicated to the common people and those who are fond of innovations, lest they give occasion to strife and sedition. There are unlearned and unqualified persons who having, after long ignorance, read or heard certain new opinions respecting baptism, the marriage of the clergy, ordination, the distinction of days and food, and public penitence, instantly conceive that these things are to be stiffly maintained and observed. Wherefore, in my opinion, the discussion of these points ought to be confined to the initiated, that so the seamless coat of our Lord may not be rent and torn. . . . Seeing it is dangerous to treat such things before the multitude and in public discourses, I must deem it safest to " speak with the many and think with the few," and to keep in mind the advice of Paul, "Hast thou faith ? Have it to thyself before God."[1]

The new religious spirit which I have attempted to characterise as tinctured by Protestant opinions but disinclined for severance from Rome, manifested itself about the same time in several groups. One of them was at Rome, where a society named the Oratory of Divine Love, including from fifty to sixty members, began to meet as early as the reign of Leo X., in the Trastevere. This pious association included men of very various kinds. Sadoleto, Giberto, and Contarini were here in close intimacy with Gaetano di Thiene, the sainted founder of the Theatines, and with his friend Caraffa, the founder of the Roman Inquisition. Venice was the centre of another group, among whom may be mentioned Reginald Pole, Gasparo Contarini, Luigi Priuli, and Antonio Bruccioli, the translator of the Bible from the original tongues into Italian. The poet Marcantonio Flaminio became a member of both societies; and was furthermore the personal friend of the Genoese Cardinals Sauli and Fregoso, whom we have a right to count among thinkers of the same class. Flaminio, though he died in the Catholic communion, was so far suspected of heresy that his works were placed upon the Index of 1559. In Naples Juan Valdes made himself the leader of a similar set of men. His views, embodied in the work of a disciple, and revised by Marcantonio Flaminio, 'On the Benefits of Christ's Death,' revealed strong Lutheran tendencies, which at a later period would certainly have condemned him to perpetual imprisonment or exile. This book had a wide circulation in Italy, and was influential in directing the minds of thoughtful Christians to the problems of Justification. It was ascribed to Aonio Paleario, who suffered

[1] *C. Calcagnini Opera*, p. 195. I am indebted for the above version to McCrie's *Reformation in Italy*, p. 183.

martyrdom at Rome for maintaining doctrines similar to those of Valdes.[1] Round him gathered several members of the great Colonna family, notably Vespasiano, Duke of Palliano, and his wife, the star of Italian beauty, Giulia Gonzaga. Vittoria Colonna, Marchioness of Pescara, imbibed the new doctrines in the same circle ; and so did Bernardino Ochino. Modena could boast another association, which met in the house of Grillenzone ; while Ferrara became the headquarters of a still more pronounced reforming party under the patronage of the Duchess, Renée of France, daughter of Louis XII. These various societies and coteries were bound together by ties of friendship and literary correspondence, and were indirectly connected with less fortunate reforming theologians, with Aonio Paleario, Bernardino Ochino, Antonio dei Pagliaricci, Carnesecchi, and others, whose tragic history will form a part of my chapter on the Inquisition.

It does not fall within the province of this chapter to write an account of what has, not very appropriately, been called the Reformation in Italy. My purpose in the present book is, not to follow the fortunes of Protestantism, but to trace the sequel of the Renaissance, the merging of its impulse in new phases of European development. I shall therefore content myself with pointing out that at the opening of Paul III.'s reign, there was widely diffused throughout the chief Italian cities a novel spirit of religious earnestness and enthusiasm, which as yet had taken no determinate direction. This spirit burned most highly in Gasparo Contarini, who in 1541 was commissioned by the Pope to attend a conference at Rechensburg for the discussion

---

[1] Though as many as 40,000 copies were published, this book was so successfully stamped out that it seemed to be irrecoverably lost. The library of St. John's College at Cambridge, however, contains two Italian copies and one French copy. That of Laibach possesses an Italian and a Croat version. Cantù, *Gli Eretici*, vol. i. p. 360.

of terms of reconciliation with the Lutherans. He succeeded in drawing up satisfactory articles on the main theological points regarding human nature, original sin, redemption, and justification. These were accepted by the Protestant theologians at Rechensburg and might possibly have been ratified in Rome, had not the Congress been broken up by Contarini's total failure to accommodate differences touching the Pope's supremacy and the conciliar principle.[1] He made concessions to the Reformers, which roused the fury of the Roman Curia. At the same time political intrigues were set on foot in France and Germany to avert a reconciliation which would have immeasurably strengthened the Emperor's position. The moderate sections of both parties, Lutheran and Catholic, failed at Rechensburg. Indeed, it was inevitable that they should fail; for the breach between the Roman Church and the Reformation was not of a nature to be healed over at this date. Principles were involved which could not now be harmonised, and both parties in the dispute were on the point of developing their own forces with fresh internal vigour.

The Italians who desired reform of the Church were now thrown back upon the attempt to secure this object within the bosom of Catholicism. At the request of Paul III. they presented a memorial on ecclesiastical abuses, which was signed by Contarini, Caraffa, Sadoleto, Pole, Fregoso, Giberto, Cortese and Aleander. These Cardinals did not spare plain speech upon the burning problem of Papal misgovernment.

Meanwhile, the new spirit began to manifest itself in the foundation of orders and institutions tending to purification of Church discipline. The most notable of these was

---

[1] It should be observed, however, that Luther rejected the article on justification, and that Caraffa in Rome used his influence to prevent its acceptance by Paul III.

the order of Theatines established by Thiene and Caraffa. Its object was to improve the secular priesthood, with a view to which end seminaries were opened for the education of priests, who took monastic vows and devoted themselves to special observance of their clerical duties, as preachers, administrators of the sacraments, visitors of the poor and sick.

A Venetian, Girolamo Miani, at the same period founded a congregation, called the Somascan, for the education of the destitute and orphaned, and for the reception of the sick and infirm into hospitals. The terrible state in which Lombardy had been left by war rendered this institution highly valuable. Of a similar type was the order of the Barnabites, who were first incorporated at Milan, charged with the performance of acts of mercy, education, preaching, and other forms of Christian ministration. It may be finally added that the Camaldolese and Franciscan orders had been in part reformed by a spontaneous movement within their bodies.

If we compare the spirit indicated by these efforts in the first half of the sixteenth century with that of the earlier Renaissance, it will be evident that the Italians were ready for religious change. They sink, however, into insignificance beside two Spanish institutions which about the same period added their weight and influence to the Catholic revival. I mean, of course, the Inquisition and the Jesuit order. Paul III. empowered Caraffa in 1542 to re-establish the Inquisition in Rome upon a new basis resembling that of the Spanish Holy Office. The same Pope sanctioned and confirmed the Company of Jesus between the years 1540 and 1543. The establishment of the Inquisition gave vast disciplinary powers to the Church at the moment when the Council of Trent fixed her dogmas and proclaimed the absolute authority of the Popes. At the same time the Jesuits, devoted by their founder in blind obedience—*perinde ac cadaver*—to the service of the Papacy, penetrated Italy, Spain, France, Germany, and the transatlantic colonies. The Pope who succeeded Clement VII. in 1534 was in all ways fitted to represent the transition which I have indicated. Alessandro Farnese sprang from an ancient but decayed family in the neighbourhood of Bolsena, several of whose members had played a foremost part in the medieval revolutions of Orvieto. While still a young man of twenty-five, he was raised to the Cardinalate by Alexander VI. This advancement he owed to the influence of his sister Giulia, surnamed La Bella, who was then the Borgia's mistress. It is characteristic of an epoch during which the bold traditions of the fifteenth century still lingered, that the undraped statue of this Giulia (representing Vanity) was carved for the basement of Paul III.'s monument in the choir of S. Peter's. The old stock of the Farnesi, once planted in the soil of Papal corruption at its most licentious period, struck firm roots and flourished. Alessandro was born in 1468, and received a humanistic education according to the methods of the earlier Renaissance. He studied literature with Pomponius Laetus in the Roman Academy, and frequented the gardens of Lorenzo de' Medici at Florence. His character and intellect were thus formed under the influences of the classical revival and of the Pontifical Curia, at a time when pagan morality and secular policy had obliterated the ideal of Catholic Christianity. His sister was the Du Barry of the Borgian Court. He was himself the father of several illegitimate children, whom he acknowledged, and on whose advancement by the old system of Papal nepotism he spent the best years of his reign. Both as a patron of the arts and as an elegant scholar in the Latin and Italian languages, Alessandro showed throughout his life the effects of this early training. He piqued himself on choice expression, whenever he was called upon to use the pen in studied documents, or to answer ambassadors in public audiences. To his taste and love of splendour Rome owes the Farnese palace. He employed Cellini, and forced Michelangelo to paint the Last Judgment. On ascending the Papal throne he complained that this mighty genius had been too long occupied for Della Roveres and Medici. When the fresco was finished, he set the old artist upon his last great task of completing S. Peter's.

So far there was nothing to distinguish Alessandro Farnese from other ecclesiastics of the Renaissance. As Cardinal he seemed destined, should he ever attain the Papal dignity, to combine the qualities of the Borgian and Medicean Pontiffs. But before his elevation to that supreme height, he lived through the reigns of Julius II., Leo X., Adrian VI., and Clement VII. Herein lies the peculiarity of his position as Paul III. The pupil of Pomponius Laetus, the creature of Roderigo Borgia, the representative of Italian manners and culture before the age of foreign invasion had changed the face of Italy, Paul III. was called at the age of sixty-six to steer the ship of the Church through troubled waters and in very altered circumstances. He had witnessed the rise and progress of Protestant revolt in Germany. He had observed the stirrings of a new and sincere spirit of religious gravity, an earnest desire for ecclesiastical reform in his own country. He had watched the duel between France and Spain, during the course of which his predecessors Alexander V. and Julius II. restored the secular authority of Rome. He had seen that authority humbled to the dust in 1527, and miraculously rehabilitated at Bologna in 1580. He had learned by the example of the Borgias how difficult it was for any Papal family to found a substantial principality; and the vicissitudes of Florence and Urbino had confirmed this lesson. Finally, he had assisted at the coronation of Charles V.; and when he took the reins of power into his hands, he was well aware with what a formidable force he had to cope in the great Emperor.

Paul III. knew that the old Papal game of pitting France against Spain in the peninsula could not be played on the same grand scale as formerly. This policy had been pursued with results ruinous to Italy but favourable to the Church by Julius. It had enabled Leo and Clement to advance their families at the hazard of more important interests. But in the reign of the latter Pope it had all but involved the Papacy itself in the general confusion and desolation of the country. Moreover, France was no longer an effective match for Spain; and though their struggle was renewed, the issue was hardly doubtful. Spain had got too firm a grip upon the land to be cast off.

Yet Paul was a man of the elder generation. It could not be expected that a Pope of the Renaissance should suddenly abandon the medieval policy of Papal hostility to the Empire, especially when the Empire was in the hands of so omnipotent a master as Charles. It could not be expected that he should recognise the wisdom of confining Papal ambition to ecclesiastical interests, and of forming a defensive and offensive alliance with Catholic sovereigns for the maintenance of absolutism. It could not be expected that he should forego the pleasures and apparent profits of creating duchies for his bastards whereby to dignify his family and strengthen his personal authority as a temporal sovereign. It is true that the experience of the last half century had pointed in the direction of all these changes; and it is certain that the series of events connected with the Council of Trent, which began in Paul III.'s reign, rendered them both natural and necessary. Yet Paul, as a man of the elder generation, filling the Papal throne for fifteen years during a period of transition, adhered in the main to the policy of his predecessors. It was fortunate for him and for the Holy See that the basis of his character was caution combined with tough tenacity of purpose, capacity for dilatory action, diplomatic shiftiness and a political versatility that can best be described by the word trimming. These qualities enabled him to pass with safety through perils that might have ruined a bolder, a hastier, or a franker Pope, and to achieve the object of his heart's desire, where stronger men had failed, in the foundation of a solid duchy for his heirs.

Paul's jealousy of the Spanish ascendency in Italian affairs caused him to waver between the Papal and Imperial, Guelf and Ghibelline, parties. These names had lost much of their significance; but the habit of distinction into two camps was so rooted in Italian manners that each city counted its antagonistic factions, maintained by various forms of local organisation and headed by the leading families.[1] Burigozzo, under the year 1517, tells how the whole population of Milan was divided between Guelfs and Ghibellines, wearing different costumes; and it is not uncommon to read of petty nobles in the country at this period, who were styled Captains of one or the other party. The wars between France and Spain revived the almost obsolete dispute, which the despots of the fifteenth century and the diplomatic confederation of the five great powers had tended in large measure to erase. The Guelfs and Ghibellines were now partisans of France and Spain respectively. Thus a true political importance was regained for the time-honoured factions; and in the distracted state of Italy they were further intensified by the antagonism between exiles and the ruling families in cities. If Cosimo de' Medici, for example, was a Ghibelline or Spanish partisan, it followed as a matter of course that Filippo Strozzi was a Guelf and

---

[1] See Bruno's *Cena delle Ceneri*, ed. Wagner, vol. i. p. 133, for a humorous story illustrative of the state of things ensuing among the lower Italian classes.

stood for France. Paul III. managed to maintain himself by manipulating these factions and holding the balance between them for the advantage of his family and of the Church. He thus succeeded in creating the Duchy of Parma and Piacenza for his son, Pier Luigi Farnese, that outrageous representative of the worst vices and worst violences of the Renaissance. It will be remembered that Julius had detached these two cities from the Duchy of Milan, and annexed them to the Papal States, on the plea that they formed part of the old Exarchate of Ravenna. When Charles decided against this plea in the matter of Modena and Reggio, he left the Church in occupation of Parma and Piacenza. Paul created his son Duke of Nepi and Castro in 1587, and afterwards conferred the Duchy of Camerino on his grandson, Ottavio, who was then married to Margaret of Austria, daughter of Charles V., and widow of the murdered Alessandro de' Medici. The usual system of massacre, exile, and confiscation had reduced the signorial family of the Varani at Camerino to extremities. The fief reverted to the Church, and Paul induced the Cardinals to sanction his investiture of Ottavio Farnese with its rights and honours. He subsequently explained to them that it would be more profitable for the Holy See to retain Camerino and to relinquish Parma and Piacenza to the Farnesi in exchange. There was sense in this arrangement; for Camerino formed an integral part of the Papal States, while Parma and Piacenza were held under a more than doubtful title. Pier Luigi did not long survive his elevation to the dukedom of Parma. He was murdered by his exasperated subjects in 1547. His son, Ottavio, with some difficulty, maintained his hold upon this principality, until in 1559 he established himself and his heirs, with the approval of Philip II., in its perpetual enjoyment. The Farnesi repaid Spanish patronage by constant service, Alessandro, Prince of Parma, and son of Ottavio, being illustrious

in the annals of the Netherlands. It would not have been
worth while to enlarge on this foundation of the Duchy of
Parma, had it not furnished an excellent example of my
theme. By this act Paul III. proved himself a true and able
inheritor of those political traditions by which all Pontiffs
from Sixtus IV. to Clement VII. had sought to establish
their relatives in secular princedoms. It was the last eminent
exhibition of that policy, the last and the most brilliant
display of nepotistical ambition in a Pope. A new age had
opened, in which such schemes became impossible—when
Popes could no longer dare to acknowledge and legitimise
their bastards, and when they had to administer their
dominions exclusively for the temporal and ecclesiastical
aggrandisement of the tiara.

Nevertheless, Paul was living under the conditions which
brought this modern attitude of the Papacy into potent
actuality. He was surrounded by intellectual and moral
forces of recent growth but of incalculable potency. One of
the first acts of his reign was to advance six members of the
moderate reforming party—Sadoleto, Pole, Giberto, Federigo
Fregoso, Gasparo Contarini, and G. M. Caraffa—to the
Cardinalate. By this exercise of power he showed his willingness to recognise new elements of very various qualities in the
Catholic hierarchy. Five of these men represented opinions
which at the moment of their elevation to the purple had a
fair prospect of ultimate success. Imbued with a profound
sense of the need for ecclesiastical reform, and tinctured more
or less deeply with so-called Protestant opinions, they desired
nothing more intensely than a reconstitution of the Catholic
Church upon a basis which might render reconciliation with
the Lutherans practicable. They had their opportunity
during the pontificate of Paul III. It was a splendid one;
and, as I have already shown, the Conference of Rechensburg
only just failed in securing the end they so profoundly desired.

But the Papacy was not prepared to concede so much as they were anxious to grant; the German Reformers proved intractable; they were themselves impeded by their loyalty to antique Catholic traditions, and by their dread of a schism; finally, the militant expansive force of Spanish orthodoxy, expressing itself already in the concentrated energy of the Jesuit order, rendered attempts at fusion impossible. The victory in Rome remained with the faction of *intransigeant* Catholics; and this was represented, in Paul III.'s first creation of Cardinals, by Caraffa. Caraffa was destined to play a singular part in the transition period of Papal history which I am reviewing. He belonged as essentially to the future as Alessandro Farnese belonged to the past. He embodied the spirit of the Inquisition, and upheld the principles of ecclesiastical reform upon the narrow basis of Papal absolutism. He openly signalised his disapproval of Paul's nepotism; and when his time for ruling came, he displayed a remorseless spirit of justice without mercy in dealing with his own family. Yet he hated the Spanish ascendency with a hatred far more fierce and bitter than that of Paul III. His ineffectual efforts to shake off the yoke of Philip II. was the last spasm of the older Papal policy of resistance to temporal sovereigns, the last appeal made in pursuance of that policy to France by an Italian Pontiff.[1]

The object of this excursion into the coming period is to show in how deep a sense Paul III. may be regarded as the beginner of a new era, while he was at the same time the last continuator of the old. The Cardinals whom he promoted on his accession included the chief of those men who strove in

[1] Paul IV. as Pope was feeble compared with his predecessors, Julius II. and Leo X.; the Guises, on whom he relied for resuscitating the old French party in the South, were but half-successful adventurers, mere shadows of the Angevine invaders whom they professed to represent.

vain for a concordat between Rome and Reformation; it also included the man who stamped Rome with the impress of the Counter-Reformation. Yet Caraffa would not have had the fulcrum needed for this decisive exertion of power, had it not been for another act of Paul's reign. This was the convening of a Council at Trent. Paul's attitude toward the Council, which he summoned with reluctance, which he frustrated as far as in him lay, and the final outcome of which he was far from anticipating, illustrates in a most decisive manner his destiny as Pope of the transition.

The very name of a Council was an abomination to the Papacy. This will be apparent if we consider the previous history of the Church during the first half of the fifteenth century, when the conciliar authority was again invoked to regulate the Papal See and to check Papal encroachments on the realms and Churches of the Western nations. The removal of the Papal Court to Avignon, the great schism which resulted from this measure, and the dissent which spread from England to Bohemia at the close of the fourteenth century, rendered it necessary that the representative powers of Christendom should combine for the purpose of restoring order in the Church. Four main points lay before the powers of Europe, thus brought for the first time into deliberative and confederated congress to settle questions that vitally concerned them. The most immediately urgent was the termination of the schism, and the appointment of one Pope, who should represent the medieval idea of ecclesiastical face to face with imperial unity. The second was the definition of the indeterminate and ever-widening authority which the Popes asserted over the kingdoms and the Churches of the West. The third was the eradication of heresies which were rending Christendom asunder and threatening to destroy that ideal of unity in creed to which the Middle Ages clung with not unreasonable passion. The fourth was a reform of the

Church, considered as a vital element of Western Christendom, in its head and in its members.

The programme, very indistinctly formulated by the most advanced thinkers of the age, and only gradually developed by practice into actuality, was a vast one. It involved the embitterment of national jealousies, the accentuation of national characteristics, and the complication of antagonistic principles regarding secular and ecclesiastical government, which rendered a complete and satisfactory solution well-nigh impracticable. The effort to solve these problems had, however, important influence in creating conditions under which the politico-religious struggles of the sixteenth and seventeenth centuries were conducted.[1]

The first Council, opened at Pisa in 1409, was a congress of prelates summoned by Cardinals for the conclusion of the schism. It deposed two Popes, who still continued to assert their titles; it elected a third, Alexander V., who had no real authority. For the rest, it effected no reform, and cannot be said to have done much more than to give effect to those aspirations after Church-government by means of Councils which had been slowly forming during the continuance of the schism.

The second Council, opened at Constance in 1414, was a Council not convened by Cardinals, but by the universal demand of Europe that the advances of the Papacy toward tyranny should be checked, and that the innumerable abuses of the Church and Papal Curia should be reformed. It received a different complexion from that of Pisa, through the presidency of the Emperor and the attendance of representatives from the chief nations. At Constance the Papacy and the Roman Curia stood together, exposed to the hostile

---

[1] The best account of the Councils will be found in Professor Creighton's admirable *History of the Papacy during the Reformation* (2 vols. Longmans).

criticism of Europe. The authority of a General Council
was, after a sharp conflict, decreed superior to that of the
Bishop of Rome. Three Popes were forced to abdicate: and
a fourth, Martin V., was elected. The Council further
undertook to deal with heresy and with the reform of the
Church. It discharged the first of these offices by condemning Hus and Jerome of Prague to the stake. It left the
second practically untouched. Yet the question of reform had
been gravely raised, largely discussed, and fundamentally
examined. Two methods were posed at Constance for the
future consideration of earnest thinkers throughout Europe.
One was the way suggested by John Hus; that the Church
should be reconstituted, after a searching analysis of the real
bases of Christian conduct, an appeal to Scripture as the
final authority, and a loyal endeavour to satisfy the spiritual
requirements of individual souls and consciences. The second
plan was that of inquiry into the existing order of the Church
and detailed amendment of its flagrant faults, with preserva-
tion of the main system. The Council adopted satisfactory
measures of reform on neither of these methods. It contented
itself with stipulations and concordats, guaranteeing special
privileges to the Churches of the several nations. But in the
following century it became manifest that the Teutonic races
had declared for the method suggested by Hus; while the
Latin races, in the Council of Trent, undertook a purgation
of the Church upon the second of the two plans. The Reformation was the visible outcome of the one, the Counter-
Reformation of the other method.

The Council of Constance was thus important in causing
the recognition of a single Pope, and in ventilating the
divergent theories upon which the question of reform was
afterwards to be disputed. But perhaps the most significant
fact it brought into relief was the new phase of political
existence into which the European races had entered.

Nationality, as the main principle of modern history, was now established; and the diplomatic relations of sovereigns as the representatives of peoples were shown to be of overwhelming weight. The visionary medieval polity of Emperor and Pope faded away before the vivid actuality of full-formed individual nations, federally connected, controlled by common but reciprocally hostile interests.[1]

The Council of Basel, opened in 1431, was in appearance a continuation of the Council of Constance. But its method of procedure ran counter to the new direction which had been communicated to European federacy by the action of the Constance congress. There the votes had been taken by nations. At Basel they were taken by men, after the questions to be decided had been previously discussed by special congregations and committees deputed for preliminary deliberations. It soon appeared that the fathers of the Basel Council aimed at opposing a lawfully elected Pope, and sought to assume the administration of the Church into their own hands. Their struggle with Eugenius IV., their election of an antipope, Felix V., and their manifest tendency to substitute oligarchical for Papal tyranny in the Church, had the effect of bringing the conciliar principle itself into disfavour with the European powers. The first symptom of this repudiation of the Council by Europe was shown in the neutrality proclaimed by Germany. The attitude of other Courts and nations proved that the Western races were for the moment prepared to leave the Papal question open on the basis supplied by the Council of Constance.

The result of this failure of the conciliar principle at Basel was that Nicholas V. inaugurated a new age for the Papacy in Rome. I have already described the chief features

[1] See above, p. 2, for the special sense in which I apply the word federation to Italy before 1530, and to Europe at large in the modern period.

of the Papal government from his election to the death of
Clement VII. It was a period of unexampled splendour for
the Holy See, and of substantial temporal conquests. The
second Council of Pisa, which began its sittings in 1511
under French sanction and support, exercised no disastrous
influence over the restored powers and prestige of the Papacy.
On the contrary, it gave occasion for a counter-council, held
at the Lateran under the auspices of Julius II. and Leo X.,
in which the Popes established several points of ecclesiastical
discipline that were not without value to their successors.
But the leaven which had been scattered by Wyclif and Hus,
of which the Council of Constance had taken cognisance, but
which had not been extirpated, was spreading in Germany
throughout this period. The Popes themselves were doing
all in their power to propagate dissent and discontent. Well
aware of the fierce light cast by the new learning they had
helped to disseminate, upon the dark places of their own
ecclesiastical administration, they still continued to raise
money by the sale of pardons and indulgences, to bleed their
Christian flock by monstrous engines of taxation, and to
offend the conscience of an intelligent generation by their
example of ungodly living. The Reformation ran like wild-
fire through the North. It grew daily more obvious that
a new Council must be summoned for carrying out measures
of internal reform and for coping with the forces of belligerent
Protestantism. When things had reached this point, Charles V.
declared his earnest desire that the Pope should summon a
General Council. Paul III. now showed in how true a sense
he was the man of a transitional epoch. So long as possible
he resisted, remembering to what straits his predecessors had
been reduced by previous Councils, and being deeply conscious
of scandals in his own domestic affairs which might expose
him to the fate of a John XXIII. Reviewing the whole series
of events which have next to be recorded, we are aware that

Paul had no great cause for agitation. The Council he so much dreaded was destined to exalt his office, and to recombine the forces of Catholic Christendom under the absolute supremacy of his successors. The Inquisition and the Company of Jesus, both of which he sanctioned at this juncture, were to guard, extend, and corroborate that supreme authority. But this was by no means apparent in 1540. It is a character of all transitional periods that in them the cautious men regard past precedents of peril rather than sanguine expectations based on present chances. A hero, in such passes, goes to meet the danger, armed with his own cause and courage. A genius divines the future, and interprets it, and through interpretation tries to govern it. Paul was neither a hero nor a man of genius. Yet he did as much as either could have done; and he did it in a temper which perhaps the hero and the genius could not have commanded. He sent Legates to publish the opening of a Council at Trent in the spring of 1545; and he resolved to work this Council on the principles of diplomatical conservatism, reserving for himself the power of watching events and of enlarging or restricting its efficiency as might seem best to him.[1]

It is singular that the Council thus reluctantly conceded by Paul III. should, during its first sessions and while he yet

[1] The first official opening of the Council at Trent was in November 1542, by Cardinals Pole and Morone as Legates. It was adjourned in July 1543, on account of insufficient attendance. When it again opened in 1545, Pole reappeared as Legate. With him were associated two future Popes, Giov. Maria del Monte (Julius III.), and Marcello Cervini (Marcellus II.). The first session of the Council took place in December 1545, four Cardinals, four Archbishops, twenty-one Bishops, and five Generals of Orders attending. Among these were only five Spanish and two French prelates; no German, unless we count Cristoforo Madrazzo, the Cardinal Bishop of Trent, as one. No Protestants appeared; for Paul III. had successfully opposed their ultimatum, which demanded that final appeal on all debated points should be made to the sole authority of Holy Scripture.

reigned, have confirmed the dogmatic foundations of modern Catholicism, made reconciliation with the Teutonic Reformers impossible, and committed the secular powers which held with Rome to a policy that rendered the Papal supremacy incontestable.[1] Face to face with the burning question of the Protestant rebellion, the Tridentine fathers hastened to confirm the following articles. First, they declared that divine revelation was continuous in the Church of which the Pope was head; and that the chief written depository of this revelation—namely, the Scriptures—had no authority except in the version of the Vulgate. Secondly, they condemned the doctrine of Justification by Faith, adding such theological qualifications and reservations as need not, at this distance of time, and on a point devoid of present actuality, be scrupulously entertained. Thirdly, they confirmed the efficacy and the binding authority of the Seven Sacraments. It is thus clear that, on points of dogma, the Council convened by Pope and Emperor committed Latin Christianity to a definite repudiation of the main articles for which Luther had con-

---

[1] Throughout the sessions of the Council, Spanish, French, and German representatives, whether fathers or ambassadors, maintained the theory of Papal subjection to conciliar authority. The Spanish and French were unanimous in zeal for episcopal independence. The French and German were united in a wish to favour Protestants by reasonable concessions. Thus the Papal supremacy had to face serious antagonism, which it eventually conquered by the numerical preponderance of the Italian prelates, by the energy of the Jesuits, by diplomatic intrigues, and by manipulation of discords in the opposition. Though the Spanish fathers held with the French and German on the points of episcopal independence and conciliar authority, they disagreed whenever it became a question of compromise with Protestants upon details of dogma or ritual. The Papal Court persuaded the Catholic sovereigns of Spain and France and the Emperor that episcopal independence would be dangerous to their own prerogatives; and at every inconvenient turn in affairs, it was made clear that Catholic sovereigns, threatened by the Protestant revolution, could not afford to separate their cause from that of the Pope.

tended. Each of these points they successively traversed, foreclosing every loophole for escape into accommodation. It was in large measure due to Caraffa's energy and ability that these results were attained.

The method of procedure adopted by the Council, and the temper in which its business was conducted, were no less favourable to the Papacy than the authoritative sanction which it gave to dogmas. From the first, the presidency and right of initiative in its sessions were conceded to the Papal Legates; and it soon became customary to refer decrees, before they were promulgated, to his Holiness in Rome for approval. The decrees themselves were elaborated in three congregations, one appointed for theological questions, the second for reforms, the third for supervision and ratification. They were then proposed for discussion and acceptance in general sessions of the Council. Here each vote told; and as there was a standing majority of Italian prelates, it required but little dexterity to secure the passing of any measure upon which the Court of Rome insisted. The most formidable opposition to the Papal prerogatives during these manœuvres proceeded from the Spanish bishops, who urged the introduction of reforms securing the independence of the episcopacy.

We find a remarkable demonstration of Paul III.'s difficulties as Pope of the transition, in the fact that while the Council of Trent was waging this uncompromising war against Reformers, his dread of Charles V. compelled him to suspend its sessions, transfer it to Bologna, and declare himself the political ally of German Protestants. This transference took place in 1547. His Legates received orders to invent some decent excuse for a step which would certainly be resisted, since Bologna was a city altogether subject to the Holy See. The Legates, by the connivance of the physicians in Trent, managed to create a panic of contagious epidemic.[1]

[1] See Sarpi, p. 249.

Charles had won victories which seemed to place Germany at his discretion. His preponderance in Italy was thereby dangerously augmented. Paul, following the precedents of policy in which he had been bred, thought it at this crisis necessary to subordinate ecclesiastical to temporal interests. He interrupted the proceedings of the Council in order to hamper the Emperor in Germany. He encouraged the Northern Protestants in order that he might maintain an open issue in the loins of his Spanish rival. Nothing could more delicately illustrate the complications of European politics than the inverted attitude assumed by the Roman Pontiff in his dealings with a Catholic Emperor at this moment of time.[1]

The opposition of the Farnesi to Paul's scheme for restoring Parma to the Holy See in 1549, broke Paul III.'s health and spirits. He died on November 10, and was succeeded by the Cardinal Giovanni Maria del Monte, of whose reign little need be said. Julius III. removed the Council from Bologna to Trent in 1551, where it made some progress in questions touching the Eucharist and the administration of episcopal sees; but in the next year its sessions were suspended, owing to the disturbed state of Southern Germany and the presence of a Protestant army under Maurice of Saxony in the Tyrol.[2] This Pope passed his time agreeably and innocently enough in the villa which he built near the Porta del Popolo. His relatives were invested with several

---

[1] Charles, at this juncture, was checkmated by Paul through his own inability to dispense with the Pope's co-operation as chief of the Catholic Church. So long as he opposed the Reformation it was impossible for him to assume an attitude of violent hostility to Rome.

[2] During the brief and unimportant sessions at Bologna, Jesuit influences began to make themselves decidedly felt in the Council, where Lainez and Salmeron attended as Theologians of the Papal See. Up to this time the Dominicans had shaped decrees. Dogmatic orthodoxy was secured by their means. Now the Jesuits were to fight and win the battle of Papal Supremacy.

petty fiefs—that of their birthplace, Monte Sansovino, by Cosimo de' Medici; that of Novara by the Emperor, and that of Camerino by the Church. The old methods of Papal nepotism were not as yet abandoned. His successor, Marcello II., survived his elevation only three weeks; and in May 1555, Giovanni Pietro Caraffa was elected, with the title of Paul IV. We have already made the acquaintance of this Pope as a member of the Oratory of Divine Love, as a co founder of the Theatines, as the Organiser of the Roman Inquisition, and as a leader in the first sessions of the Tridentine Council. Paul IV. sprang from a high and puissant family of Naples. He was a man of fierce, impulsive and uncompromising temper, animated by two ruling passions—burning hatred for the Spaniards who were trampling on his native land, and ecclesiastical ambition intensified by rigid Catholic orthodoxy. The first act of his reign was a vain effort to expel the Spaniards from Italy by resorting to the old device of French assistance. The abdication of Charles V. had placed Philip II. on the throne of Spain, and the settlement whereby the Imperial crown passed to his brother Ferdinand had substituted a feeble for a powerful Emperor. But Philip's disengagement from the cares of Germany left him more at liberty to maintain his preponderance in Southern Europe. It was fortunate for Paul IV. that Philip was a bigoted Catholic and a superstitiously obedient son of the Church. These two potentates, who began to reign in the same year, were destined, after the settlement of their early quarrel, to lead and organise the Catholic Counter-Reformation. The Duke of Guise at the Pope's request marched a French army into Italy. Paul raised a body of mercenaries, who were chiefly German Protestants;[1] and opened negotiations with Soliman, entreating the Turk to

[1] Sarpi, quoted in his Life by Fra Fulgenzio, p. 83, says Paul called his Grisons mercenaries 'Angels sent from Heaven.'

make a descent on Sicily by sea. Into such a fantastically false position was the Chief of the Church, the most Catholic of all her Pontiffs, driven by his jealous patriotism. We seem to be transported back into the times of a Sixtus IV. or an Alexander VI. And in truth, Paul's reversion to the antiquated Guelf policy of his predecessors was an anachronism. That policy ceased to be efficient when Francis I. signed the Treaty of Cambray; the Church, too, had gradually assumed such a position that armed interference in the affairs of secular sovereigns was suicidal. This became so manifest that Paul's futile attack on Philip in 1556 may be reckoned the last war raised by a Pope. From it we date the commencement of a new system of Papal co-operation with Catholic powers.

The Duke of Alva put the forces at his disposal in the Two Sicilies into motion, and advanced to meet the Duke of Guise. But while the campaign dragged on, Philip won the decisive battle of S. Quentin. The Guise hurried back to France, and Alva marched unresisted upon Rome. There was no reason why the Eternal City should not have been subjected to another siege and sack. The will was certainly not wanting in Alva to humiliate the Pope, who never spoke of Spaniards but as renegade Jews, Marrani, heretics, and personifications of pride. Philip, however, wrote reminding his general that the date of his birth (1527) was that of Rome's calamity, and vowing that he would not signalise the first year of his reign by inflicting fresh miseries upon the capital of Christendom. Alva was ordered to make peace on terms both honourable and advantageous to his Holiness; since the King of Spain preferred to lose the rights of his own crown rather than to impair those of the Holy See in the least particular. Consequently, when Alva entered Rome in peaceful pomp, he did homage for his master to the Pope, who was generously willing to absolve him for his past offences. Paul IV. publicly exulted in the abasement of his conquerors, declaring that it would teach kings in future the obedience they owed to the Chief of the Church. But Alva did not conceal his discontent. It would have been better, he said, to have sent the Pope to sue for peace and pardon at Brussels, than to allow him to obtain the one and grant the other on these terms.

Paul's ambition to expel the Spaniards from Italy exposed him to the worst abuses of that Papal nepotism which he had denounced in others. He judged it necessary to surround himself with trusty and powerful agents of his own kindred.[1] With that view he raised one of his nephews, Carlo, to the Cardinalate, and bestowed on two others the principal fiefs of the Colonna family. The Colonnas were by tradition Ghibelline. This sufficed for depriving them of Palliano and Montebello. Carlo Caraffa, who obtained the scarlet, had lived a disreputable life which notoriously unfitted him for any ecclesiastical dignity. In the days of Sixtus and Alexander this would have been no bar to his promotion. But the Church was rapidly undergoing a change; and Carlo, complying with the hypocritical spirit of his age, found it convenient to affect a thorough reformation, and to make open show of penitence. Rome now presented the singular spectacle of an inquisitorial Pope, unimpeachable in moral conduct and zealous for Church reform, surrounded by nephews who were little better than Borgias. The Caraffas began to dream of principalities and sceptres. It was their ambition to lay hold on Florence, where Cosimo de' Medici, as a pronounced ally of Spain, had gained the bitter hatred of their uncle. But their various misdoings,

---

[1] New men—and Popes were always *novi homines*—are compelled to take this course, and suffer when they take it. We might compare their difficulties with those which hampered Napoleon when he aspired to the Imperial tyranny over French conquests in Europe.

acts of violence and oppression, avarice and sensuality, gradually reached the ears of the Pope. In an assembly of the Inquisition, held in January 1559, he cried aloud, 'Reform! reform! reform!' Cardinal Pacheco, a determined foe of the Caraffeschi, raised his voice, and said, 'Holy Father! reform must first begin with us.' Pallavicini adds the remark that Paul understood well who was meant by *us*. He immediately retired to his apartments, instituted a searching inquiry into the conduct of his nephews, and, before the month was out, deprived them of all their offices and honours, and banished them from Rome. He would not hear a word in their defence; and when Cardinal Farnese endeavoured to procure a mitigation of their sentence, he brutally replied, 'If Paul III. had shown the same justice, your father would not have been murdered and mutilated in the streets of Piacenza.' In open consistory, before the Cardinals and high officials of his realm, with tears streaming from his eyes, he exposed the evil life of his relatives, declared his abhorrence of them, and protested that he had dwelt in perfect ignorance of their crimes until that time. This scene recalls a similar occasion, when Alexander VI. bewailed himself aloud before his Cardinals after the murder of the Duke of Gandia by Cesare. But Alexander's repentance was momentary; his grief was that of a father for Absalom; his indignation gave way to paternal weakness for the fratricide. Paul, though his love for his relatives seems to have been fervent, never relaxed his first severity against them. They were buried in oblivion; no one uttered their names in the Pope's presence. The whole secular administration of the Papal States was changed; not an official kept his place. For the first time Rome was governed by ministers in no way related to the Holy Father.

Paul now turned his attention, with the fiery passion

that distinguished him, to the reformation of ecclesiastical abuses. On his accession he had published a Bull declaring that this would be a principal object of his reign. Nor had he in the midst of other occupations forgotten his engagement. A Congregation specially appointed for examining, classifying, and remedying such abuses had been established. It was divided into three committees, consisting of eight Cardinals, fifteen prelates, and fifty men of learning. At the same time the Inquisition was rigorously maintained. Paul extended its jurisdiction, empowered it to use torture, and was constant in his attendance on its meetings and 'acts of faith.'[1] But now that his plans for the expulsion of the Spaniards had failed, and his nephews had been hurled from their high station into the dust, there remained no other interest to distract his mind. Every day witnessed the promulgation of some new edict touching monastic discipline, simony, sale of offices, collation to benefices, church ritual, performance of clerical duties, and appointment to ecclesiastical dignities. It was his favourite boast that there would be no need of a Council to restore the Church to purity, since he was doing it.[2] And indeed his measures formed the nucleus of the Tridentine decrees upon this topic in the final sessions of the Council. Under this government Rome assumed an air of exemplary behaviour which struck foreigners with mute astonishment. Cardinals were compelled to preach in their basilicas. The Pope himself, who

---

[1] Pallavicini, in his history of the Council of Trent (Lib. xiv. ix. 5), specially commends Paul's zeal for the Holy Office. Speaking of his other pious institutions, he says : 'Fra esse d' eterna lode lo fa degno il tribunal dell' inquisizione, che dal zelo di lui e prima in autorità di consigliero e poscia in podestà di principe riconosce il presente suo vigor nell' Italia, e dal quale riconosce l' Italia la sua conservata integrità della fede : e per quest' opera salutare egli rimane ora tanto più benemerito ed onorabile quanto più allora ne fu mal rimeritato e disonorato.'

[2] See Luigi Mocenigo in *Rel. degli Amb. Veneti*, vol. x. p. 25.

was vain of his eloquence, preached. Gravity of manners, external signs of piety, a composed and contrite face, ostentation of orthodoxy by frequent confession and attendance at the Mass, became fashionable; and the Court adopted for its motto the *Si non caste tamen caute* of the Counter-Reformation.[1] Aretino, with his usual blackguardly pointedness of expression, has given a hint of what the new *régime* implied in the following satiric lines :—

> Caraffa, ipocrita infingardo,
> Che tien per coscienza spirituale
> Quando si mette del pepe in sul cardo.

Paul IV. brought the first period of the transition to an end. There were no attempts at dislodging the Spaniard, no Papal wars, no tyranny of Papal nephews converted into feudal princes, after his days. He stamped Roman society with his own austere and bigoted religion. That he was in any sense a hypocrite is wholly out of the question. But he made Rome hypocritical, and by establishing the Inquisition on a firm basis, he introduced a reign of spiritual terror into Italy. At his death the people rose in revolt, broke into the dungeons of the Inquisition, released the prisoners, and destroyed the archives. The Holy Office was restored, however; and its higher posts of trust soon came to be regarded as stepping-stones to the Pontifical dignity.

The successor of Paul IV. was a man of very different quality and antecedents. Giovanni Angelo Medici sprang, not from the Florentine house of Medici, but from an obscure Lombard stem. His father acquired some wealth by farming the customs in Milan; and his eldest brother, Gian Giacomo, pushed his way to fame, fortune and a title by piracy upon the Lake of Como.[2] Gian Giacomo estab-

---

[1] 'Roma a paragone delli tempi degli altri pontefici si poteva riputar come un onesto monasterio di religiosi' (*op. cit.* p. 41).

[2] In my *Sketches and Studies in Italy* I have narrated the romantic history of this filibuster.

lished himself so securely in his robber fortress of Musso that he soon became a power to reckon with. He then entered the Imperial service, was created Marquis of Marignano by the Duke of Milan, and married a lady of the Orsini house, a sister of the Duchess of Parma. At a subsequent period he succeeded in subduing Siena to the rule of Cosimo de' Medici, who then acknowledged a pretended consanguinity between the two families.[1] The younger brother, Giovanni Angelo, had meanwhile been studying law, practising as a jurist, and following the Court at Rome in the place of protonotary, which, as the custom then was, he purchased in 1527. Paul III. observed him, took him early into favour, and on the marriage of Gian Giacomo, advanced him to the Cardinalate. This was the man who assumed the title of Pius IV. on his election to the Papacy in 1559.

Paul IV. hated Cardinal Medici, and drove him away from Rome. It is probable that this antipathy contributed something to Giovanni Angelo's elevation. Of humble Lombard blood, a jurist and a worldling, pacific in his policy, devoted to Spanish interests, cautious and conciliatory in the conduct of affairs, ignorant of theology and indifferent to niceties of discipline, Pius IV. was at all points the exact opposite of the fiery Neapolitan noble, the Inquisitor and fanatic, the haughty trampler upon kings, the armed antagonist of Alva, the brusque impulsive autocrat, the purist of orthodoxy, who preceded him upon the Papal throne.[2] His trusted counsellor was Cardinal Morone, whom Paul had thrown into the dungeons of the Inquisition on a charge of favouring Lutheran opinions, and who was liberated

---

[1] Soranzo: Alberi, vol. x. p. 67. Pius IV. adopted the arms of the Florentine Medici, and spent 30,000 scudi on carving them about through Rome. See P. Tiepolo, *ib.* p. 174.

[2] 'Veramente quasi in ogni parte si può chiamare il rovescio dell' altro' (*op. cit.* p. 50).

by the rabble in their fury.[1] This in itself was significant of the new *régime* which now began in Rome. Morone, like his master, understood that the Church could best be guided by diplomacy and arts of peace. The two together brought the Council of Trent to that conclusion which left an undisputed sovereignty in theological and ecclesiastical affairs to the Papacy. It would have been impossible for a man of Caraffa's stamp to achieve what these sagacious temporisers and adroit managers effected.

Without advancing the same arrogant claims to spiritual supremacy as Paul had made, Pius was by no means a feeble Pontiff. He knew that the temper of the times demanded wise concessions; but he also knew how to win through these concessions the reality of power. It was he who initiated and firmly followed the policy of alliance between the Papacy and the Catholic sovereigns.[2] Instead of assert-

[1] Luigi Mocenigo says of him that Pius 'averlo per un angelo di paradiso, e adoperandolo per consiglio in tutte le sue cose importanti.' Alberi, vol. x. p. 40. The case made out against Morone during the pontificate of Paul IV. may be studied in Cantù, *op. cit.* vol. ii. pp. 171-192, together with his defence in full. It turned mainly on these articles:—unsound opinions regarding justification by faith, salvation by Christ's blood, good works, invocation of saints, reliques; dissemination of the famous book on the *Benefits of Christ's Death*; practice with heretics. He was imprisoned in the Castle of S. Angelo from June 1557 till August 1559. Suspicions no doubt fell on him through his friendship with several of the moderate reformers, and from the fact that his diocese of Modena was a nest of liberal thinkers—the Grillenzoni, Castelvetro, Filippo Valentini, Faloppio, Camillo Molza, Francesco da Porto, Egidio Foscarari, and others, all of whom are described by Cantù, *op. cit.* Disc. xxviii. The charges brought against these persons prove at once the mainly speculative and innocuous character of Italian heresy, and the implacable enmity which a Pope of Caraffa's stamp exercised against the slightest shadow of heterodoxy.

[2] Soranzo, *op. cit.* p. 75, says: 'Con li principi tiene modo affatto contrario al suo predecessore; perchè mentre quello usava dire, il grado dei pontefici esser per mettersi sotto i piedi gl' imperatori e i re, questo dice che senza l' autorità dei principi non si può conservare quella dei pontefici.'

ing the interests of the Church in antagonism to secular potentates, he undertook to prove that their interests were identical. Militant Protestantism threatened the civil no less than the ecclesiastical order. The episcopacy attempted to liberate itself from monarchical and pontifical authority alike. Pius proposed to the autocrats of Europe a compact for mutual defence, divesting the Holy See of some of its privileges, but requiring in return the recognition of its ecclesiastical absolutism. In all difficult negotiations he was wont to depend upon himself; treating his counsellors as agents rather than as peers, and holding the threads of diplomacy in his own hands. Thus he was able to transact business as a sovereign with sovereigns, and came to terms with them by means of personal correspondence. The reconstruction of Catholic Christendom, which took visible shape in the decrees of the Tridentine Council, was actually settled in the Courts of Spain, Austria, France, and Rome. The Fathers of the Council were the mouthpieces of royal and Papal cabinets. The Holy Ghost, to quote a profane satire of the time, reached Trent in the despatch-bags of couriers, in the sealed instructions issued to ambassadors and legates.

We observe throughout the negotiations which crowned the policy of this Pope with success, the operation not only of a pacific and far-seeing character, but also of the temper of a lawyer. Pius drew up the Tridentine decrees as an able conveyancer draws up a complicated deed, involving many trusts, recognising conflicting rights, providing for distant contingencies. It was in fact the marriage contract of eccclesiastical and secular absolutism, by which the estates of Catholic Christendom were put in trust and settlement for posterity. In formulating its terms the Pope granted points to which an obstinate or warlike predecessor, a Julius II. or a Paul IV., would never have subscribed his signature. In purely theological matters, such as the concession of the chalice to the laity and the marriage of the clergy, he was even willing to yield more for the sake of peace than his Court and clergy would agree to. But for each point he gave, he demanded a substantial equivalent, and showed such address in bargaining, that Rome gained far more than it relinquished. When the contract had been drafted, he ratified it by a full and ready recognition, and lawyer-like was punctual in executing all the terms to which he pledged himself.

We must credit Pius IV. with keen insight into the new conditions of Catholic Europe, and recognise him as the real founder of the modern as distinguished from the medieval Papacy. That transition which I have been describing in the present chapter remained uncertain in its issue up to his pontificate. Before his death the salvation of Catholicism, the integrity of the Catholic Church, the solidity of the Roman hierarchy, and the possibility of a vigorous Counter-Reformation were placed beyond all doubt.

It is noticeable that these substantial successes were achieved, not by a religious fanatic, but by a jurist; not by a saint, but by a genial man of the world; not by force of intellect and will, but by adroitness; not by masterful authority, but by pliant diplomacy; not by forcing, but by following the current of events. Since Gregory VII., no Pope had done so much as Pius IV. for bracing the ancient fabric of the Church and confirming the Papal prerogative. But what a difference there is between a Hildebrand and a Giovanni Angelo Medici! How Europe had changed, when a man of the latter's stamp was the right instrument of destiny for starting the weather-beaten ship of the Church upon a new and prosperous voyage.

Pius IV. was greatly assisted in his work by circumstances, of which he knew how to avail himself. Had it not been for the renewed spiritual activity of Catholicism to which I have alluded in this chapter, he might not have been able to carry that work through. He took no interest in theology, and felt no sympathy for the Inquisition.[1] But he prudently left that institution alone to pursue its function of policing the ecclesiastical realm. The Jesuits rendered him important assistance by propagating their doctrine of passive obedience to Rome. Spain supported him with the massive strength of a nation Catholic to the core; and when the Spanish prelates gave him trouble, he could rely for aid upon the Spanish crown. His own independence, as a prudent man of business, uninfluenced by bigoted prejudices or partialities for any sect, enabled him to manipulate all resources at his disposal for the main object of uniting Catholicism and securing Papal supremacy. He was also fortunate in his family relations, having no occasion to complicate his policy by nepotism. One of the first acts of his reign had been to condemn four of the Caraffeschi—Cardinal Caraffa, the Duke of Palliano, Count Aliffe and Leonardo di Cardine—to death; and this act of justice ended for ever the old forms of domestic ambition which had hampered the Popes of the Renaissance in their ecclesiastical designs. His brother, the Marquis of Marignano, died in 1555; and this event opened for him the path to the Papacy, which he would never have attained in the lifetime of so grasping and ambitious a man.[2] With his next brother, Augusto, who succeeded to the marquisate, he felt no sympathy.[3] His nephew Federigo Borromeo died in youth. His other nephew, Carlo Borromeo, the sainted Archbishop of Milan, remained close to his person in Rome.[4] But Carlo

---

[1] Soranzo, *op. cit.* p. 74.
[2] Soranzo, *op. cit.* p. 71, says: 'Il marchese suo fratello con la moglie gli diede il cappello, e con la morte il papato.'
[3] Mocenigo, *op. cit.* p. 52. Soranzo, *op. cit.* p. 93.
[4] Margherita Medici, sister of the Pope, had married Gilberto Borromeo.

Borromeo was a man who personified the new spirit of Catholicism. Sincerely pious, zealous for the faith, immaculate in conduct, unwearied in the discharge of diocesan duties, charitable to the poor, devoted to the sick, he summed up all the virtues of the Counter-Reformation. Nor had he any of the virtues of the Renaissance. A Venetian Ambassador described him as cold of political temperament, little versed in worldly affairs, and perplexed when he attempted to handle matters of grave moment.[1] His presence at the Papal Court, so far from being perilous, as that of an ambitious Cardinal Nipote would have been, or scandalous, as that of former Riarios, Borgias and Caraffas had undoubtedly been, was a source of strength to Pius. It imported into his immediate surroundings just what he himself lacked, and saved him from imputations of worldliness which in the altered temper of the Church might have proved inconvenient.[2] Truly, among all Pontiffs who have occupied S. Peter's Chair, Pius IV. deserved in the close of his life to be called fortunate. He had risen from obscurity, had entered Rome in humble office at the moment of Rome's deepest degradation. He had lived through troubled times, and for some years had felt the whole weight of Catholic concerns upon his shoulders. At the last, he was conscious of having opened a new era for the Church, and of being able to transmit a sceptre of undisputed authority to his successors. His death-bed was troubled with no remorse, with no ingratitude of relatives, with no political complications produced by family ambition or by the sacrifice of his official duties to personal aggrandisement.

Soon after the election of Pope Pius IV. the state of

[1] See Mocenigo, *op. cit.* p. 53. Soranzo, *op. cit.* p. 91.
[2] Gia. Soranzo (*op. cit.* p. 133) says of Carlo Borromeo, 'ch' egli solo faccia più profitto nella Corte di Roma che tutti i decreti del Concilio insieme.'

Europe made the calling of a General Council indispensable. Paul's impolitic pretensions had finally alienated England from the Roman Church. Scotland was upon the point of declaring herself Protestant. The Huguenots were growing stronger every year in France, the Queen Mother, Catherine de' Medici, being at that time inclined to favour them. The Confession of Augsburg had long been recognised in Germany. The whole of Scandinavia, with Denmark, was lost to Catholicism. The Low Countries, in spite of Philip, Alva, and the Inquisition, remained intractable. Bohemia, Hungary, and Poland were alienated, ripe for open schism. The tenets of Zwingli had taken root in German Switzerland. Calvin was gaining ground in the French cantons. Geneva had become a stationary fortress, the stronghold of belligerent reformers, whence heresy sent forth its missionaries and promulgated subversive doctrines through the medium of an ever-active press. Transformed by Calvin from its earlier condition of a pleasure-loving and commercial city, it was now what Deceleia under Spartan discipline had been to Athens in the Peloponnesian war—a permanent ἐπιτειχισμός, perpetually garrisoned and on guard to harry the flanks of Catholics. Faithful to the Roman See in a strict sense of the term, there remained only Spain, Portugal, and Italy. As the events of the next century proved, the disaffected nations still offered rallying-points for the Catholic cause, from which the tide of conquest was rolled back upon the Reformation. But in 1559 the outlook for the Church was very gloomy; no one could predict whether a General Council might not increase her difficulties by weakening the Papal power and sowing further seeds of discord among her few faithful adherents. Yet Pius, after an attempt to combine the Catholic nations in a crusade against Geneva, which was frustrated by the jealousy of Spain, the internal weakness of France and the respect inspired by Switzerland,[1] determined to cast his fortunes on the Council. He had several strong points in his favour. The reigning Emperor, Ferdinand, wielded a power insignificant when compared with that of Charles V. The Protestants, though formally invited, were certain not to attend a Council which had already condemned the articles of their Confession. The cardinal dogmas of Catholicism had been confirmed in the sessions of 1545-1552. It was to be hoped that, with skilful management, existing differences of opinion with regard to doctrine, church-management, and reformation of abuses, might be settled to the satisfaction of the Catholic powers.

The Pope accordingly sent five Legates, the Cardinals Gonzaga, Seripando, Simoneta, Hosius, and Puteo, to Trent, who opened the Council on January 15, 1562.[2] As had been anticipated, the Protestants showed strong disinclination to attend. The French prelates were unable to appear, pending negotiations with the Huguenots at Poissy and Pontoise. The German prelates intimated their reluctance to take part in the proceedings. The Court of France demanded that the chalice for the laity and the use of the vulgar tongue in religious services should be conceded. The Emperor also insisted on these points, making a further demand for the marriage of the clergy. Circumstances both in France and Germany seemed to render these conditions imperative, if the rapid spread of Protestant dissent were to be checked and the remnant of the Catholic population to be kept in obedience. Of ecclesiastics, only Spaniards and Italians, the latter in a large majority, appeared at Trent. The Courts of other nations were represented by ambassadors, who took no part in the deliberations of the Council.[3]

[1] See Sarpi, vol. ii. pp. 43, 44.
[2] Cardinal Puteo was soon replaced by a Papal nephew, the Cardinal d'Altemps (Mark of Hohen Ems).
[3] At the first session there were five Cardinals, one hundred and

In spite of this inauspicious commencement, Pius declared the Council a General Council, and further decreed that it should be recognised as a continuation of that Council which had begun at Trent in 1545. This rendered the co-operation of Protestants impossible, since they would have been compelled to accept the earlier dogmatic resolutions of the Fathers. It was decided that no proxies should be allowed to absentees; that the questions of doctrine and reform should be prepared for discussion in two separate congregations, and should be taken into consideration in full sessions simultaneously; finally that the Papal Legates should alone have the privilege of proposing resolutions to the fathers. This last point, by which the Court of Rome reserved to itself the control of all proceedings in the Council, was carried by a clever ruse. Until too late the Spanish prelates do not seem to have been aware of the immense power they had conferred on Rome by passing the words *Legatis proponentibus*.[1] The principle involved in this phrase continued to be hotly disputed all through the sessions of the Council. But Pius knew that so long as he stuck fast to it he always held the ace of trumps, and nothing would induce him to relinquish it.

Fortified in this position of superiority, Pius now proceeded to organise his forces and display his tactics. All through the sessions of the Council they remained the same; and as the method resulted in his final victory, it deserves to be briefly described. At any cost he determined to secure a numerical majority in the Synod. This was effected by drafting Italian prelates, as occasion required, to Trent.

four prelates, including Patriarchs, Archbishops and Bishops, four Abbots, and four Generals of Orders. These were all Italians, Spaniards, and Portuguese. And yet this Conciliabulum called itself a General Council, inspired by the Holy Ghost to legislate for the whole of Latin and Teutonic Christianity.

[1] See Sarpi, vol. ii. p. 87.

Many of the poorer sort were subsidised, and placed under the supervision of Cardinal Simoneta, who gave them orders how to vote. A small squadron of witty bishops was told off to throw ridicule on inconvenient speakers by satirical interpolations, or to hamper them by sophistical arguments. Spies were introduced into the opposite camps, who kept the Legates informed of what the French or Spaniards deliberated in their private meetings. The Legates meanwhile established a daily post of couriers, who carried the minutest details of the Council to the Vatican. When the resolutions of the congregations on which decrees were to be framed had been drawn up, they referred them to his Holiness. Without his sanction they did not propose them in a general session. In this fashion, by means of his standing majority, the exclusive right of his Legates to propose resolutions, and the previous reference of these resolutions to himself, Pius was enabled to direct the affairs of the Council. It soon became manifest that while the fathers were talking at Trent their final decisions were arranged in Rome. This not unnaturally caused much discontent. It began to be murmured that the Holy Ghost was sent from Rome to Trent in carpet-bags. A man of more imperious nature than Pius might, by straining his prerogatives, have produced an irreconcilable rupture. But he was aware that the very existence of the Papacy depended on circumspection. He therefore used all his advantages with caution, and resolved to win the day by diplomacy. With this object in view he introduced the further system of negotiating with the Catholic Courts through special agents. Instead of framing the decrees upon the information furnished by his Legates, he in his turn submitted them to Philip, Catherine de' Medici, and Ferdinand, agreed on terms of mutual concession, persuaded the princes that their interests were identical with his own, and then returned such measures to the Council as could be safely passed. In course of time the Holy Ghost was not packed up at Rome for Trent in carpet-bags before he had gone the round of Europe and made his bow in all the cabinets.

It must not, however, be thought that matters went smoothly for the Pope at first, or that so novel a method as that which I have described whereby the faith and discipline of Christendom were settled by negotiations between sovereigns, came suddenly into existence. In its first sessions the Council, to quote the Pope's own words, resembled the Tower of Babel rather than a Synod of Fathers. The Spanish prelates contended fiercely for two principles touching the episcopacy: one was that the residence of bishops in their dioceses had been divinely commanded; the other, that their authority is derived from Christ immediately. The first struck at the Pope's power to dispense from the duty of residence; and if it had been established without qualification, it would have ruined his capital. The second would have rendered the episcopacy independent of Rome, and have made the Holy Father one of a numerous oligarchy instead of the absolute chief of a hierarchy. Pius was able to show Philip that the independence of the bishops must inflict deep injuries on the crown of Spain. Philip therefore wrote to forbid insistence on this point. But the Spanish prelates, though coerced, were not silenced, and the storm which they had raised went grumbling on.

Difficulties of a no less serious nature arose when the French and Imperial ambassadors arrived at Trent in the spring. They demanded, as I have already stated, that the chalice should be conceded to the laity; nor is it easy to understand why this point might not have been granted. Pius himself was ready to make the concession; and the only valid argument against it was that it imperilled the uniformity of ritual throughout all Catholic countries.

The Germans further stipulated for the marriage of the clergy, which the Pope was also disposed to entertain, until he reflected that celibacy alone retained the clergy faithful to his interests and regardless of those of their own nations. At this juncture of affairs the Roman Court, which was strongly opposed to both concessions, received material aid from the dissensions of the Council. The Spaniards would hear nothing of the Eucharist under both forms. The marriage of the clergy was opposed by French and Spaniards alike. On the point of episcopal independence, the French supported the Spaniards; but Pius used the same arguments in France which he had used in Spain, with similar success. Thus there was no agreement on any of the disputed questions between Spaniards, Frenchmen and Germans; and since the ambassadors could neither propose nor vote, and the Italian prelates were in a permanent majority, Pius was able to defer and temporise at leisure.

Nevertheless, he began to feel the gravity of the situation. He saw that the embassies constituted dangerous centres of intrigue and national organisation at Trent. He was not entirely satisfied with his own Legate, the Cardinal Gonzaga, who supported the divine right of the episcopacy and quarrelled with his colleagues. The Spaniards, infuriated at having sacrificed the right of proposing measures, began to talk openly about the reform of the Papacy. Disagreeable messages reached Rome from France and Spain and Germany, complaining of the Pope's absolutism in Council, and demanding that the reform of the Church should be taken into serious and instant consideration. His devoted adherent, Lainez, General of the Jesuits, embittered opposition by passionately preaching the doctrine of passive obedience. Two dangers lay before him. One was that the Council should break up in confusion, with discredit to Rome and anarchy for the Catholic Church. The other was that it should be prolonged in its dissensions by the princes, with a view of depressing and enfeebling the Papal authority. Other perils of an incalculable kind threatened him in the announced approach of the mighty Cardinal of Lorraine, brother to the Duke of Guise, with a retinue of French bishops released from the Conference at Poissy. Though he kept on packing the Council with fresh relays of Italians, it was much to be apprehended that they might be unable to oppose a coalition between French and Spanish prelates, should that be now effected.

Pius, at this crisis, resolved on two important lines of policy, the energetic pursuit of which speedily brought the Council of Trent to a peaceful termination. The first was to meet the demand for a searching reformation of the Church with cheerful acquiescence; but to oppose a counter-demand that the secular States in all their ecclesiastical relations should at the same time be reformed. This implied a threat of alienating patronage and revenue from the princes; it also indicated plainly that the tiara and the crowns had interests in common. The second was to develop the diplomatic system upon which he had already tentatively entered.

The events of the spring, 1563, hastened the adoption of these measures by the Pope. Cardinal Lorraine had arrived with his French bishops;[1] and the Papal Legates found themselves involved at once in intricate disputes on questions touching the Huguenots and the interests of the Gallican Church. The Italians were driven in despair to epigrams: *Dalla scabie Spagnuola siamo caduti nel mal Francese.* Somewhat later, the Emperor despatched a bulky and verbose letter, announcing his intention to play the part which

[1] He reached Trent, November 13, 1562, with eighteen Bishops and three Abbots of France, charged by Charles IX. to demand purified ritual, reformed discipline of clergy, use of vernacular in church services, and finally, if possible, the marriage of the clergy.

Sigismund had assumed at the Council of Constance. He complained roundly of the evils caused by the reference of all resolutions to Rome, by the exclusive rights of the Legates to propose decrees, and by the intrigues of the Italian majority in the Synod. He wound up by declaring that the reformation of the Church must be accomplished in Trent, not left to the judgment of the Papal Curia; and threatened to arrive from Innsbruck by the Brenner. Though Ferdinand was in a position of ecclesiastical and political weakness, such an Imperial rescript could not be altogether contemned; especially as Cardinal Lorraine, soon after his arrival, had made the journey to Innsbruck on purpose to confer with the Emperor. It therefore behoved the Pope to act with decision; and an important event happened in the first days of March, which materially assisted him in doing so. This was the death of Cardinal Gonzaga, whom Pius determined to replace by the moderate and circumspect Morone.[1]

Through Ippolito d' Este, Cardinal of Ferrara, he opened negotiations with the French Court, showing that the wishes of the prelates in the Council on the question of episcopacy were no less opposed to the crown than to his own interests. Cardinal Simoneta urged the same point on the Marquis of Pescara, who governed Milan for Philip, and was well inclined to the Papal party. Cardinal Morone was sent on a special embassy to the Emperor.[2] By wise concessions, in which the prerogatives of the Imperial ambassadors at Trent were

[1] The confusion at Trent in the spring of 1563 is thus described by the Bishop of Alife: 'Methinks Antichrist has come, so greatly confounded are the perturbations of the Holy Fathers here.' Phillipson, p. 525.

[2] When Morone set out, he told the Venetian envoy in Rome that he was going on a forlorn hope. 'L' ill^{mo} Morone, quando partì per il Concilio, mi disse che andava a cura disperata e che *nulla spes erat* della religione Cattolica' (Soranzo, *op. cit.* p. 82). The Jesuit Canisius, by his influence with Ferdinand, secured the success of Morone's diplomacy.

considerably enlarged, and a searching reformation of the Church was promised, Morone succeeded in establishing a good working basis for the future. It came to be understood that while the Pope would allow no further freedom to the bishops, he was well disposed to let his Legates admit the envoys of the Catholic powers into their counsels. From this time forward the Synod may be said to have existed only as a mouthpiece for uttering the terms agreed on by the Pope and potentates. Morone returned to Trent, and the Emperor withdrew from Innsbruck toward the north.

The difficulty with regard to France and Germany consisted in this, that politics forced both King and Emperor to consider the attitude of their Protestant subjects. Yet both alike were unable to maintain their position as Catholic sovereigns, if they came to open rupture with the Papacy. Ferdinand, as we have just seen, had expressed himself contented with the situation of affairs at Trent. But the French prelates still remained in opposition, and the French Court was undecided. Cardinal Morone, upon his arrival at Trent, began to flatter the Cardinal of Lorraine, affecting to take no measures of importance without consulting him. This conduct, together with timely compliments to several Frenchmen of importance, smoothed the way for future agreement; while the couriers who arrived from France, brought the assurance that Ippolito d' Este's representations had not been fruitless. Pius, meanwhile, was playing the same conciliatory game in Rome, where Don Luigi d' Avila arrived as a special envoy from Philip. The ambassador obtained a lodging in the Vatican, and was seen in daily social intercourse with his Holiness.[1] But the climax of this policy was reached when Lorraine accepted the Pope's invitation, and undertook a journey to Rome. This happened

[1] Sarpi says that Don Luigi resided in the lodgings of Count Federigo Borromeo, a deceased nephew of the Pope.

in September. The French Cardinal was pompously received, entertained in the palace, and honoured with personal visits in his lodgings by the Pope. Weary of Trent and the tiresome intrigues of the Council, this unscrupulous prelate was still further inclined to negotiation after the murder of his brother, Duke of Guise. It must be remembered that the Guises in France were after all but a potent faction of semi-royal adventurers, who had risen to eminence by an alliance with Diane de Poitiers. The murder of the Duke shook the foundations of their power; and the Cardinal was naturally anxious to be back again in France. For the moment he basked in the indolent atmosphere of Rome, surrounded by those treasures of antique and Renaissance luxury which still remained after the Sack of 1527. Pius held out flattering visions of succession to the Papacy, and proved convincingly that nothing could sustain the House of Guise or base the Catholic faith in France except alliance with the Papal See. Lorraine, who had probably seen enough of episcopal *canaillerie* in the Council, and felt his inner self expand in the rich climate of pontifical Rome, allowed his ambition to be caressed, confessed himself convinced, and returned to Trent intoxicated with his visit, the devoted friend of Rome.

Menaces, meanwhile, had been astutely mingled with cajoleries. The French and the Imperial Courts were growing anxious on the subject of reform in secular establishments. Pius had threatened to raise the whole question of national Churches and the monarch's right of interfering in their administration. This was tantamount to flinging a burning torch into the powder-magazine of Huguenot and Lutheran grievances. In order to save themselves from the disaster of explosion, they urged harmonious action with the Papacy upon their envoys. The Spanish Court, through Pescara, De Luna, and D'Avalos, wrote despatches of like tenor. It was now debated whether a congress of crowned heads should not be held to terminate the Council in accordance with the Papal programme. This would have suited Pius. It was the point to which his policy had led. Yet no such measure could be lightly hazarded. A congress while the Council was yet sitting, would have been too palpable and cynical a declaration of the Papal game. As events showed, it was not even necessary. When Lorraine returned to Trent, the French opposition came to an end. The Spanish had been already neutralised by the firm persistent exhibition of Philip's will to work for Roman absolutism.[1] There was nothing left but to settle details, to formulate the terms of ecclesiastical reform, and to close the Council of Trent with a unanimous vote of confidence in his Holiness. The main outlines of dogma and discipline were quickly drawn. Numerous details were referred to the Pope for definition. The Council terminated in December with an act of submission, which placed all its decrees at the pleasure of the Papal sanction. Pius was wise enough to pass and ratify the decrees of the Tridentine fathers by a Bull dated on December 26, 1563, reserving to the Papal sovereign the sole right of interpreting them in doubtful or disputed cases. This he could well afford to do; for not an article had been penned without his concurrence, and not a stipulation had been made without a previous understanding with the Catholic powers. The very terms, moreover, by which his ratification was conveyed, secured his supremacy, and conferred upon his successors and himself the privileges of a court of ultimate appeal. At no previous period in the history of the Church had so wide, so undefined, and so

[1] Yet the Spanish bishops fought to the end, under the leadership of their chief Guerrero, for the principle of conciliar independence and the episcopal prerogatives. 'We had better not have come here, than be forced to stand by as witnesses,' says the Bishop of Orense. Phillipson, p. 577.

unlimited an authority been accorded to the See of Rome. Thus Pius IV. was triumphant in obtaining conciliar sanction for Pontifical absolutism, and in maintaining the fabric of the Roman hierarchy unimpaired, the cardinal dogmas of Latin Christianity unimpeached and after formal inquisition reasserted in precise definitions. A formidable armoury had been placed at the disposal of the Popes, who were fully empowered to use it, and who had two mighty engines for its application ready in the Holy Office and the Company of Jesus.[1]

After the termination of the Council there was nothing left for Pius but to die. He stood upon a pinnacle which might well have made him nervous—lest haply the Solonian

[1] The vague reference of all decrees passed by the Tridentine Council to the Pope for interpretation enabled him and his successors to manipulate them as they chose. It therefore happened, as Sarpi says ('Tratt. delle Mat. Ben.' *Opere*, vol. iv. p. 161), that no reform, with regard to the tenure of benefices, residence, pluralism, &c., which the Council had decided, was adopted without qualifying expedients which neutralised its spirit. If the continuance of benefices *in commendam* ceased, the device of *pensions* upon benefices was substituted; and a thousand pretexts put colossal fortunes extracted from Church property, now as before, into the hands of Papal nephews. Witness the contrivances whereby Cardinal Scipione Borghese enriched himself in the Papacy of Paul V. The Council had decreed the residence of bishops in their sees; but it had reserved to the Pope a power of dispensation; so that those whom he chose to exile from Rome were bound to reside, and those whom he desired to have about him were released from this obligation. On each and all delicate points the Papacy was more autocratic after than before the Council. One of Sarpi's letters (vol. i. p. 371) to Jacques Leschassier, dated December 22, 1609, should be studied by those who wish to penetrate the '*reserved altre arcane arti*,' the '*renunzie*,' '*pensioni*' and '*altri stratagemmi*,' by means of which the Papal Curia, during the half-century after the Tridentine Council, managed to evade its decrees, and to get such control over Church property in Italy that 'out of 500 benefices not one is conferred legally.' Compare the passage in the 'Trattato delle Materie Beneficiarie,' p. 163. There Sarpi says that five-sixths of Italian benefices are at the Pope's disposal, and that there is good reason to suppose that he will acquire the remaining sixth.

maxim, 'Call no man fortunate until his death,' should be verified in his person. During the two years of peace and retirement which he had still to pass, the unsuccessful conspiracy of Benedetto Accolti and Antonio Canossa against his life gave point to this warning. But otherwise, withdrawn from cares of state, which he committed to his nephew, Carlo Borromeo, he enjoyed the tranquillity that follows successful labour, and sank with undiminished prestige into his grave at the end of 1565. Those who believe in masterful and potent leaders of humanity may be puzzled to account for the triumph achieved by this commonplace arbiter of destiny. Not by strength but by pliancy of character he accomplished the transition from the medieval to the modern epoch of Catholicism. He was no Cromwell, Frederick the Great, or Bismarck; only a politic old man, contriving by adroit avoidance to steer the ship of the Church clear through innumerable perils. This scion of the Italian middle class, this moral mediocrity, placed his successors in S. Peter's Chair upon a throne of such supremacy that they began immediately to claim jurisdiction over kings and nations. Thirty-eight years before his death, when Clement VII. was shut up in S. Angelo, it seemed as though the Papal power might be abolished. Forty-five years after his death, Sarpi, writing to a friend in 1610, expressed his firm opinion that the one, the burning question for Europe was the Papal power.[1] Through him, poor product as he was of ordinary Italian circumstances, elected to be Pope because of his easy-going mildness by prelates worn to death in fiery Caraffa's reign, it happened that the flood of Catholic reaction was rolled over Europe. In a certain sense we may therefore regard him as a veritable *Flagellum Dei*, wielded by inscrutable fate. It seems that at momentous epochs of world-history no hero is needed to effect the purpose of the

[1] *Lettere*, vol. ii. p. 167.

Time-Spirit. A Gian Angelo Medici, agreeable, diplomatic, benevolent, and pleasure-loving, sufficed to initiate a series of events which kept the Occidental races in perturbation through two centuries. A great step had been taken in the Pontificate of Pius IV. That reform of the Church, which the success of Protestantism rendered necessary, and which the Catholic powers demanded, had been decreed by the Council of Trent. Pius showed no unwillingness to give effect to the Council's regulations; and the task was facilitated for him by his nephew, Carlo Borromeo, and the Jesuits. It still remained, however, to be seen whether a new Pope might not reverse the policy on which the Counter-Reformation had been founded, and impede the beneficial inner movement which was leading the Roman hierarchy into paths of sobriety. Should this have happened, it would have been impossible for Romanism to assume a warlike attitude of resistance toward the Protestants in Europe, or to have rallied its own spiritual forces. The next election was therefore a matter of grave import.

Nothing is more remarkable in the history of the Papacy at this epoch than the singular contrast offered by each Pontiff in succession to his predecessor. The conclave was practically uncontrolled in its choice by any external force of the first magnitude. Though a Duke of Florence might now, by intrigue, determine the nomination of a Pius IV., no commanding Emperor or King of France, as in the times of Otto the Great or Philip le Bel, could designate his own candidate. There was no strife, so open as in the Renaissance period, between Cardinals subsidised by Spain or Austria or France.[1] The result was that the deliberations of

---

[1] This does not mean that the Spanish crown had not a powerful voice in the elections. See the history of the conclaves which elected Urban VII., Gregory XIV., Innocent IX., Clement VIII., in Ranke, vol. ii. pp. 31–39. Yet it was noticed by those close observers,

the conclave were determined by motives of petty interests, personal jealousies, and local considerations, to such an extent that the election seemed finally to be the result of chance or inspiration. We find the most unlikely candidates, Caraffa and Peretti, attributing their elevation to the direct influence of the Holy Ghost, in the consciousness that they had slipped into S. Peter's Chair by the maladroitness of conflicting factions. The upshot, however, of these uninfluenced elections generally was to promote a man antagonistic to his predecessor. The clash of parties and the numerical majority of independent Cardinals excluded the creatures of the last reign, and selected for advancement one who owed his position to the favour of an antecedent Pontiff. This result was further secured by the natural desire of all concerned in the election to nominate an old man, since it was for the general advantage that a pontificate should, if possible, not exceed five years.

The personal qualities of Carlo Borromeo were of grave importance in the election of a successor to his uncle. He had ruled the Church during the last years of Pius IV.; and the newly appointed Cardinals were his dependents. Had he attempted to exert his power for his own election, he might have met with opposition. He chose to use it for what he considered the deepest Catholic interests. This unselfishness led to the selection of a man, Michele Ghislieri, whose antecedents rendered him formidable to the still corrupt members of the Roman hierarchy, but whose character was precisely of the stamp required for giving solidity to the new phase on which the Church had entered. As Pius IV. had been the exact opposite to Paul IV., so Pius V. was a complete contrast to Pius IV. He had passed the best years of

the Venetian envoys, that France and Spain had abandoned their former policy of subsidising the Cardinals who adhered to their respective factions.

his life as chief of the Inquisition. Devoted to theology and to religious exercises, he lacked the legal and mundane faculties of his predecessor. But these were no longer necessary. They had done their duty in bringing the Council to a favourable close, and in establishing the Catholic concordat. What was now required was a Pope who should, by personal example and rigid discipline, impress Rome with the principles of orthodoxy and reform. Carlo Borromeo, self-conscious, perhaps, of the political incapacity which others noticed in him, and fervently zealous for the Catholic Revival, devolved this duty on Michele Ghislieri, who completed the work of his two predecessors.

Paul IV. had laid a basis for the modern Roman Church by strengthening the Inquisition and setting internal reforms on foot. Pius IV., externally, by his settlement of the Tridentine Council, and by the establishment of the Catholic concordat, built upon this basis an edifice which was not as yet massive. Carlo Borromeo and the Jesuits during the last pontificate prepared the way for a Pope who should cement and gird that building, so that it should be capable of resisting the inroads of time and should serve as a fortress of attack on heresy. That Pope was Michele Ghislieri, who assumed the title of Pius V. in 1566.

Before entering on the matter of his reign, it will be necessary to review the state of Rome at this moment in the epoch of transition, when the medieval and Renaissance phases were fast merging into the phase of the Counter-Reformation. Old abuses which have once struck a deep root in any institution, die slowly. It is therefore desirable to survey the position in which the Papal Sovereign of the Holy City, as constituted by the Council of Trent, held sway there.

The population of Rome was singularly fluctuating. Being principally composed of ecclesiastics with their households and dependents; foreigners resident in the city as suitors or ambassadors; merchants, tradespeople and artists attracted by the hope of gain; it rose or fell according to the qualities of the reigning Pope and the greater or less train of life which happened to be fashionable. Noble families were rather conspicuous by their absence than by their presence; for those of the first rank, Colonna and Orsini, dwelt upon their fiefs and visited the capital only as occasion served. The minor aristocracy which gave solidity to social relations in towns like Florence and Bologna, never attained the rank of a substantial oligarchy in Rome. Nor was there an established dynasty round which a circle of peers might gather in permanent alliance with the Court. On the other hand, the frequent succession of Pontiffs chosen from various districts encouraged the growth of an ephemeral nobility who battened for a while upon the favour of their Papal kinsmen, flooded the city with retainers from their province, and disappeared upon the election of a new Pope, to make room for another flying squadron. Instead of a group of ancient Houses, intermarrying and transmitting hereditary rights and honours to their posterity, Rome presented the spectacle of numerous celibate establishments, displaying great pomp, it is true, but dispersing and disappearing upon the decease of the patrons who assembled them. The households of wealthy Cardinals were formed upon the scale of princely Courts. Yet no one, whether he depended on the mightiest or the feeblest prelate, could reckon on the tenure of his place beyond the lifetime of his master. Many reasons, again— among which may be reckoned the hostility of reigning Pontiffs to the creatures of their predecessors or to their old rivals in the conclave—caused the residence of the chief ecclesiastics in Rome to be precarious. Thus the upper stratum of society was always in a state of flux, its elements shifting according to laws of chronic uncertainty. Beneath it spread a rabble of inferior and dubious gentlefolk, living in idleness upon the favour of the Court, serving the Cardinals and bishops in immoral and dishonest offices, selling their wives, their daughters and themselves, all eager to rise by indirect means to places of emolument.[1] Lower down, existed the *bourgeoisie* of artists, bankers, builders, shop-keepers and artisans; and at the bottom of the scale came hordes of beggars. Rome, like all Holy Cities, entertained multitudes of eleemosynary paupers. Gregory XIII. is praised for having spent more than 200,000 crowns a year on works of charity, and for having assigned the district of San Sisto (in the neighbourhood of Trinità del Monte, one of the best quarters of the present city) to the beggars.[2]

Such being the social conditions of Rome, it is not surprising to learn that during the reign of so harsh a Pontiff as Paul IV., the population sank to a number estimated at between 40,000 and 50,000. It rose rapidly to 70,000, and touched 80,000 in the reign of Pius IV. Afterwards it gradually ascended to 90,000, and during the popular pontificate of Gregory XIII. it is said to have reached the high figure of 140,000. These calculations are based upon the reports of the Venetian ambassadors, and can be considered as impartial, although they may not be statistically exact.[3]

What rendered Roman society rotten to the core was universal pecuniary corruption. In Rome nothing could be had without payment; but men with money in their purse obtained whatever they desired. The office of the Datatario alone brought from ten to fourteen thousand crowns a month into the Papal treasury in 1560.[4] This large sum accrued

[1] See Mocenigo, *op. cit.* p. 85; Aretino's *Dialogo della Corte di Roma*; and the private history of the Farnesi.
[2] Giov. Carraro and Lor. Priuli, *op. cit.* pp. 275, 306.
[3] Alberi, vol. x. pp. 35, 83, 277.
[4] Mocenigo's computation, *op. cit.* p. 29.

from the composition of benefices and the sale of vacant offices. The Camera Apostolica, or Chamber of Justice, was no less venal. A price was set on every crime, for which its punishment could be commuted into cash-payment. Even so severe a Pope as Paul IV. committed to his nephew, by published and printed edict, the privilege of compounding with criminals by fines.[1] One consequence of this vile system, rightly called by the Venetian envoy 'the very strangest that could be witnessed or heard of in such matters,' was that wealthy sinners indulged their appetites at the expense of their families, and that innocent people became the prey of sharpers and informers.[2] Rome had organised a vast system of *chantage*. Another consequence was that acts of violence were frightfully common. Men could be hired to commit murders at sums varying from ten to four scudi; and on the death of Paul IV., when anarchy prevailed for a short while in Rome, an eyewitness asserts that several hundred assassinations were committed within the walls in a few days.[3]

It was not to be expected that a population so corrupt, accustomed for generations to fatten upon the venality and vices of the hierarchy, should welcome those radical reforms which were the best fruits of the Tridentine Council. They specially disliked the decrees which enforced the residence of prelates, and the limitation of benefices held by a single ecclesiastic. These regulations implied the withdrawal of wealthy patrons from Rome, together with an incalculable reduction in the amount of foreign money spent there. Nor were the measures for abolishing a simoniacal sale of offices, and the growing demand for decency in the administration of

[1] *Ibid.* p. 81.
[2] The true history of the Cenci, as written by Bertolotti, throws light upon these points.
[3] Mocenigo, *op. cit.* p. 88.

justice, less unpopular. The one struck at the root of private speculation in lucrative posts, and deprived the Court of revenues which had to be replaced by taxes. The other destroyed the arts of informers, checked lawlessness and license in the rich, and had the same lamentable effect of impoverishing the Papal treasury. In proportion as the Curia ceased to subsist upon the profits of simony, superstition, and sin, it was forced to maintain itself by imposts on the people, and by resuming, as Gregory XIII. attempted to do, its obsolete rights over fiefs and lands accorded on easy terms or held by doubtful titles. Meanwhile the retrenchment rendered necessary in all households of the hierarchy, and the introduction of severer manners, threatened many minor branches of industry with extinction.

These changes began to manifest themselves during the pontificate of Pius IV. The Pope himself was inclined to a liberal and joyous scale of living. But he was not remarkable for generosity; and the new severity of manners made itself felt by the example of his nephew Carlo Borromeo—a man who, while living in the purple, practised austerities that were apparent in his emaciated countenance. The Jesuits ruled him; and, through him, their influence was felt in every quarter of the city.[1] 'The Court of Rome,' says the Venetian envoy in the year 1565, ' is no longer what it used to be either in the quality or the numbers of the courtiers. This is principally due to the poverty of the Cardinals and the parsimony of the Popes. In the old days, when they gave away more iberally, men of ability flocked from all quarters. This reduction of the Court dates from the Council; for the bishops and beneficed clergy being now obliged to retire to their residences, the larger portion of the Court has left Rome. To the same cause may be ascribed a diminution in the numbers of those who serve the Pontiff, seeing that since only one

[1] Giac. Soranzo, *op. cit.* pp. 131-136.

benefice can now be given, and that involves residence, there
are few who care to follow the Court at their own expense and
inconvenience without hope of greater reward. The poverty
of the Cardinals springs from two causes. The first is that
they cannot now obtain benefices of the first class, as was
the case when England, Germany, and other provinces were
subject to the Holy See, and when moreover they could hold
three or four bishoprics apiece together with other places of
emolument, whereas they now can only have one apiece.
The second cause is that the number of the Cardinals has
been increased to seventy-five, and that the foreign powers
have ceased to compliment them with large presents and
benefices, as was the wont of Charles V. and the French
crown.' In the last of these clauses we find clearly indicated
one of the main results of the concordat established between
the Papacy and the Catholic sovereigns by the policy of
Pius IV. It secured Papal absolutism at the expense of the
College. Soranzo proceeds to describe the changes visible in
Roman society. 'The train of life at Court is therefore
mean, partly through poverty, but also owing to the good
example of Cardinal Borromeo, seeing that people are wont
to follow the manners of their princes. The Cardinal holds
in his hands all the threads of the administration; and living
religiously in the retirement I have noticed, indulging in
liberalities to none but persons of his own stamp, there is
neither Cardinal nor courtier who can expect any favour from
him unless he conform in fact or in appearance to his mode
of life. Consequently one observes that they have altogether
withdrawn, in public at any rate, from every sort of pleasures.
One sees no longer Cardinals in masquerade or on horseback,
nor driving with women about Rome for pastime, as the
custom was of late; but the utmost they do is to go alone in
close coaches. Banquets, diversions, hunting parties, splendid
liveries and all the other signs of outward luxury have been

abolished; the more so that now there is at Court no layman of high quality, as formerly when the Pope had many of his relatives or dependents around him. The clergy always wear their robes, so that the reform of the Church is manifested in their appearance. This state of things, on the other hand, has been the ruin of the artisans and merchants, since no money circulates. And while all offices and magistracies are in the hands of Milanese, grasping and illiberal persons, very few indeed can be still called satisfied with the present reign.'[1]

One chief defect of Pius IV., judged by the standard of the new party in the Church, had been his coldness in religious exercises. Paolo Tiepolo remarks that during the last seven months of his life he never once attended service in his chapel.[2] This indifference was combined with lukewarmness in the prosecution of reforms. The Datatario still enriched itself by the composition of benefices, and the Camera by the composition of crimes. Pius V., on the contrary, embodied in himself those ascetic virtues which Carlo Borromeo and the Jesuits were determined to propagate throughout the Catholic world. He never missed a day's attendance on the prescribed services of the Church, said frequent Masses, fasted at regular intervals, and continued to wear the coarse woollen shirt which formed a part of his friar's costume. In his piety there was no hypocrisy. The people saw streams of tears pouring from the eyes of the Pontiff bowed in ecstasy before the Host. A rigid reformation of the churches, monasteries and clergy was immediately set on foot throughout the Papal States. Monks and nuns complained, not without cause, that austerities were expected from them which were not included in the rules to which they vowed obedience. The severity of the Inquisition was

[1] Soranzo, *op. cit.* pp. 186-188.
[2] *Op. cit.* p. 171.

augmented, and the Index Expurgatorius began to exercise a stricter jurisdiction over books. The Pope spent half his time at the Holy Office, inquiring into cases of heresy of ten or twenty years' standing. From Florence he caused Carnesecchi to be dragged to Rome and burned; from Venice the refugee Guido Zanetti of Fano was delivered over to his tender mercies; and the excellent Carranza, Archbishop of Toledo, was sent from Spain to be condemned to death before the Roman tribunal. Criminal justice, meanwhile, was administered with greater purity, and the composition of crimes for money, if not wholly abolished, was moderated. In the collation to bishoprics and other benefices the same spirit of equity appeared; for Pius inquired scrupulously into the character and fitness of aspirants after office.

The zeal manifested by Pius V. for a thoroughgoing reform of manners may be illustrated by a curious circumstance related by the Venetian ambassador in the first year of the pontificate.[1] On July 26, 1566, an edict was issued, compelling all prostitutes to leave Rome within six days, and to evacuate the States of the Church within twelve days. The exodus began. But it was estimated that about 25,000 persons, counting the women themselves with their hangers-on and dependents, would have to quit the city if the edict were enforced.[2] The farmers of the customs calculated that they would lose some 20,000 ducats a year in consequence, and prayed the Pope for compensation. Meanwhile the roads across the Campagna began to be thronged by caravans, which were exposed to the attacks of robbers. The confusion became so great, and the public discontent was so openly expressed, that on August 17 Pius repealed his edict and

[1] Mutinelli, *Storia Arcana*, &c. vol. i. pp. 51-54.
[2] Assuming the population of Rome to have been about 90,000 at that date, this number appears incredible. Yet we have it on the best of all evidences, that of a resident Venetian envoy.

permitted the prostitutes to reside in certain quarters of the city.

Pius IV. had wasted the greater part of his later life in bed, neglecting business, entertaining his leisure with buffoons and good companions, eating much and drinking more. Pius V., on the contrary, carried the habits of the convent with him into the Vatican, and bestowed the time he spared from devotion upon the transaction of affairs. He was of choleric complexion, adust, lean, wasted, with sunken eyes and snow-white hair, looking ten years older than he really was.

Such a Pope changed the face of Rome, or rather stereotyped the change which had been instituted by Cardinal Borromeo. 'People, even if they are not really better, seem at least to be so,' says the Venetian envoy, who has supplied me with the details I have condensed.[1] Retrenchments in the Papal establishment were introduced; money was scarce; the Court grew meaner in appearance; and nepotism may be said to have been extinct in the days of Pius V. He did indeed advance one nephew, Michele Bonelli, to the Cardinalate; but he showed no inclination to enrich or favour him beyond due measure. A worn man, without ears, marked by the bastonado, frequented the palace, and stood near the person of the Pope, as Captain of the Guard. This was Paolo Ghislieri, a somewhat distant relative of Pius, who had passed his life in servitude to Barbary corsairs and had been ransomed by a merchant upon the election of his kinsman. No other members of the Papal family were invited to Rome.

Pius V., while living this exemplary monastic life upon the Papal throne, ruled Catholic Christendom more absolutely than any of his predecessors. As the Papacy recognised its dependence on the sovereigns, so the sovereigns in their turn

[1] Tiepolo, *op. cit.* p. 172.

perceived that religious conformity was the best safeguard of their secular authority. Therefore the Catholic States subscribed, one after the other, to the Tridentine Profession of Faith, and adopted one system in matters of Church discipline. A new Breviary and a new Missal were published with the Papal sanction. Seminaries were established for the education of ecclesiastics, and the Jesuits laboured in their propaganda. The Inquisition and the Congregation of the Index redoubled their efforts to stamp out heresy by fire and iron, and by the suppression or mutilation of books. A rigid uniformity was impressed on Catholicism. The Pope, to whom such power had been committed by the Council, stood at the head of each section and department of the new organisation. To his approval every measure in the Church was referred, and the Jesuits executed his instructions with punctual exactness.

It is not, therefore, to be wondered that Pius V. should have opened the era of active hostilities against Protestantism. Firmly allied with Philip II., he advocated attacks upon the Huguenots in France, the Protestants in Flanders, and the English crown. There is no evidence that he was active in promoting the Massacre of S. Bartholomew, which took place three months after his death; and the expedition of the Invincible Armada against England was not equipped until another period of fifteen years had elapsed. Yet the negotiations in which he was engaged with Spain, involving enterprises to the detriment of the English realm and the French Reformation, leave no doubt that both S. Bartholomew and the Armada would have met with his hearty approval. One glorious victory gave lustre to the reign of Pius V. In 1571 the navies of Spain, Venice and Rome inflicted a paralysing blow upon the Turkish power at Lepanto; and this success was potent in fanning the flame of Catholic enthusiasm.

The pontificates of Paul IV., Pius IV., and Pius V.

differing as they did in very important details, had achieved
a solid triumph for reformed Catholicism, of which both the
diplomatical and the ascetic parties in the Church, Jesuits
and Theatines, were eager to take advantage. A new spirit
in the Roman polity prevailed, upon the reality of which its
future force depended; and the men who embodied this spirit
had no mind to relax their hold on its administration. After
the death of Pius V. they had to deal with a Pope who
resembled his penultimate predecessor, Pius IV., more than
the last Pontiff. Ugo Buoncompagno, the scion of a *bourgeois*
family settled in Bologna, began his career as a jurist. He
took orders in middle life, was promoted to the Cardinalate,
and attained the supreme honour of the Holy See in 1572.
The man responded to his name. He was a good companion,
easy of access, genial in manners, remarkable for the facility
with which he cast off care and gave himself to sanguine
expectations.[1] In an earlier period of Church history he
might have reproduced the Papacy of Paul II. or Innocent
VIII. As it was, Gregory XIII. fell at once under the potent
influence of Jesuit directors. His confessor, the Spanish
Francesco da Toledo, impressed upon him the necessity of
following the footsteps of Paul IV. and Pius V. It was made
plain that he must conform to the new tendencies of the
Catholic Church; and in his neophyte's zeal he determined
to outdo his predecessors. The example of Pius V. was not
only imitated, but surpassed. Gregory XIII. celebrated three
Masses a week, built churches, and enforced parochial
obedience throughout his capital. The Jesuits in his reign
attained to the maximum of their wealth and influence.
Rome, 'abandoning her ancient license, displayed a moderate
and Christian mode of living; and in so far as the external
observance of religion was concerned, she showed herself not
far removed from such perfection as human frailties allow.'[2]

[1] Paolo Tiepolo, *op. cit.* p. 312.   [2] *Id., op. cit.* p. 214.

While he was yet a layman, Gregory became the father of one son, Giacomo. Born out of wedlock, he was yet acknowledged as a member of the Buoncompagno family, and admitted under this name into the Venetian nobility.[1] The Pope manifested paternal weakness in favour of his offspring. He brought the young man to Rome, and made him Governatore di Santa Chiesa with a salary of 10,000 ducats. The Jesuits and other spiritual persons scented danger. They persuaded the Holy Father that conscience and honour required the alienation of his bastard from the sacred city. Giacomo was relegated to honourable exile in Ancona. But he suffered so severely from this rebuff, that terms of accommodation were agreed on. Giacomo received a lady of the Sforza family in marriage, and was established at the Papal Court with a revenue amounting to about 25,000 crowns.[2] The ecclesiastical party, now predominant in Rome, took care that he should not acquire more than honorary importance in the government. Two of the Pope's nephews were promoted to the Cardinalate with provisions of about 10,000 crowns apiece. His old brother abode in retirement at Bologna under strict orders not to seek fortune or to perplex the Papal purity of rule in Rome.[3]

I have introduced this sketch of Gregory's relations in order to show how a Pope of his previous habits and personal proclivities was now obliged to follow the new order of the Church. It was noticed that the mode of life in Rome during his reign struck a just balance between license and austerity, and that general satisfaction pervaded society.[4] Outside the city this contentment did not prevail. Gregory

[1] The Venetians, when they inscribed his name upon the Libro d' Oro, called him 'a near relative of his Holiness.'
[2] This lady was a sister of the Count of Santa Fiora. For a detailed account of the wedding, see Mutinelli, *Stor. Arc.* vol. i. p. 112.
[3] Tiepolo, *op. cit.* pp. 213, 219–221, 263, 266.
[4] Giov. Corraro, *op. cit.* p. 277.

threw his States into disorder by reviving obsolete rights of the Church over lands mortgaged or granted with obscure titles. The petty barons rose in revolt, armed their peasants, fomented factions in the country towns, and filled the land with brigands. Under the leadership of men like Alfonso Piccolomini and Roberto Malatesta, these marauding bands assumed the proportion of armies. The neighbouring Italian States—Tuscany, Venice, Naples, Parma, all of whom had found the Pope arbitrary and aggressive in his dealings with them—encouraged the bandits by offering them an asylum and refusing to co-operate with Gregory for their reduction.

His successor, Sixtus V., found the whole Papal dominion in confusion. It was impossible to collect the taxes. Life and property were nowhere safe. By a series of savage enactments and stern acts of justice Sixtus swept the brigands from his States. He then applied his powerful will to the collection of money and the improvement of his provinces. In the four years which followed his election he succeeded in accumulating a round sum of four million crowns, which he stored up in the Castle of S. Angelo. The total revenues of the Papacy at this epoch were roughly estimated at 750,000 crowns, which in former reigns had been absorbed in current costs and the pontifical establishment. By rigorous economy and retrenchments of all kinds Sixtus reduced these annual expenses to a sum of 250,000, thus making a clear profit of 500,000 crowns.[1] At the same time he had already spent about a million and a half on works of public utility, including the famous Acqua Felice, which brought excellent water into Rome. Roads and bridges throughout the States of the Church were repaired. The Chiana of Orvieto and the Pontine Marsh were drained.

[1] See Giov. Gritti, *op. cit.* p. 333.

Encouragement was extended, not only to agriculture, but also to industries and manufactures. The country towns obtained wise financial concessions, and the unpopular resumption of lapsed lands and fiefs was discontinued. Rome meanwhile began to assume her present aspect as a city, by the extensive architectural undertakings which Sixtus set on foot. He loved building; but he was no lover of antiquity. For pagan monuments of art he showed a monastic animosity, dispersing or mutilating the statues of the Vatican and Capitol; turning a Minerva into an image of the Faith by putting a cross in her hand; surmounting the columns of Trajan and Antonine with figures of Peter and Paul; destroying the Septizonium of Severus, and wishing to lay sacrilegious hands on Caecilia Metella's tomb. To medieval relics he was hardly less indifferent. The old buildings of the Lateran were thrown down to make room for the heavy modern palace. But, to atone in some measure for these acts of vandalism, Sixtus placed the cupola upon S. Peter's and raised the obelisk in the great piazza which was destined to be circled with Bernini's colonnades. This obelisk he topped with a cross. Christian inscriptions, signalising the triumph of the Pontiff over infidel emperors, the victory of Calvary over Olympus, the superiority of Rome's saints and martyrs to Rome's old deities and heroes, left no doubt that what remained of the imperial city had been subdued to Christ and purged of paganism. Wandering through Rome at the present time, we feel in every part the spirit of the Catholic Revival, and murmur to ourselves those lines of Clough:

O ye mighty and strange, ye ancient divine ones of Hellas!
Are ye Christian too? To convert and redeem and renew you,
Will the brief form have sufficed, that a Pope has set up on the apex
Of the Egyptian stone that o'ertops you, the Christian symbol?
And ye, silent, supreme in serene and victorious marble,

Ye that encircle the walls of the stately Vatican chambers,
Are ye also baptized; are ye of the Kingdom of Heaven?
Utter, O some one, the word that shall reconcile Ancient and
 Modern.

Nothing was more absent from the mind of Sixtus than any attempt to reconcile Ancient and Modern. He was bent on proclaiming the ultimate triumph of Catholicism, not only over antiquity, but also over the Renaissance. His inscriptions, crosses, and images of saints are the enduring badges of serfdom set upon the monuments of ancient and renascent Italy, bearing which they were permitted by the now absolute Pontiff to remain as testimonies to his power.

Retrenchment alone could not have sufficed for the accumulation of so much idle capital, and for so extensive an expenditure on works of public utility. Sixtus therefore had recourse to new taxation, new loans, and the creation of new offices for sale. The Venetian envoy mentions eighteen imposts levied in his reign; a sum of 600,000 crowns accruing to the Camera by the sale of places; and extensive loans, or Monti, which were principally financed by the Genoese.[1] It was necessary for the Papacy, now that it had relinquished the larger part of its revenues derived from Europe, to live upon the proceeds of the Papal States. The complicated financial expedients on which successive Popes relied for developing their exchequer, have been elaborately explained by Ranke.[2] They were materially assisted in their efforts to support the Papal dignity upon the resources of their realm, by the new system of nepotism which now began to prevail. Since the Council of Trent, it was impossible for a Pope to acknowledge his sons, and few, if any, of the Popes after Pius IV. had sons to acknowledge.[3] The tendencies of the

[1] Giov. Gritti, *op. cit.* p. 337.
[2] *History of the Popes*, Book IV. section I.
[3] Giacomo Buoncompagno was born while Gregory XIII. was still a layman and a lawyer.

WEALTH OF PAPAL FAMILIES

Church rendered it also incompatible with the Papal position that near relatives of the Pontiff should be advanced, as formerly, to the dignity of independent princes. The custom was to create one nephew Cardinal, with such wealth derived from office as should enable him to benefit the Papal family at large. Another nephew was usually ennobled, endowed with capital in the public funds for the purchase of lands, and provided with lucrative places in the secular administration. He then married into a Roman family of wealth and founded one of the aristocratic houses of the Roman State. We possess some details respecting the incomes of the Papal nephews at this period, which may be of interest.[1] Carlo Borromeo was reasonably believed to enjoy revenues amounting to 50,000 scudi. Giacomo Buoncompagno's whole estate was estimated at 120,000 scudi; while the two Cardinal nephews of Gregory XIII. had each about 10,000 a year. At the same epoch Paolo Giordano Orsini, Duke of Bracciano, enjoyed an income of some 25,000, his estate being worth 60,000, but being heavily encumbered. These figures are taken from the Reports of the Venetian envoys. If we may trust them as accurate, it will appear by a comparison of them with the details furnished by Ranke, that Gregory's successors treated their relatives with greater generosity.[2] Sixtus V. enriched the Cardinal Montalto with an ecclesiastical income of 100,000 scudi. Clement VIII. bestowed

---

[1] Sarpi writes: 'In my times Pius V., during five years, accumulated 25,000 ducats for the Cardinal nephew; Gregory XIII., in thirteen years, 80,000 for one nephew, and 20,000 for another; Sixtus V., for his only nephew, 9,000; Clement VIII., in thirteen years, for one nephew, 8,000, and for the other, 3,000; and this Pope, Paul V., in four years, for one nephew alone, 40,000. To what depths are we destined to fall in the future?' (*Lettere*, vol. i. p. 281). This final question was justified by the event; for, after the Borghesi, came the Ludovisi and Barberini, whose accumulations equalled, if they did not surpass, those of any antecedent Papal families.

[2] The details may be examined in Ranke, vol. ii. pp. 303-311.

on two nephews—one Cardinal, the other layman—revenues of about 60,000 apiece in 1599. He is computed to have hoarded altogether for his family a round sum of 1,000,000 scudi. Paul V. was believed to have given to his Borghese relatives nearly 700,000 scudi in cash, 24,600 scudi in funds, and 268,000 in the worth of offices.[1] The Cardinal Ludovico Lodovisi, nephew of Gregory XV., had a reputed income of 200,000 scudi; and the Ludovisi family obtained 800,000 in *luoghi di monte* or funds. Three nephews of Urban VIII., the brothers Barberini, were said to have enjoyed joint revenues amounting to half a million scudi, and their total gains from the pontificate touched the enormous sum of 105,000,000. These are the families, sprung from obscurity or mediocre station, whose palaces and villas adorn Rome, and who now rank, though of such recent origin, with the aristocracy of Europe.

Sixtus V. died in 1590. To follow the history of his successors would be superfluous for the purpose of this book. The change in the Church which began in the reign of Paul III. was completed in his pontificate. About half a

---

[1] Sarpi's Letters supply some details relating to Paul V.'s nepotism. He describes the pleasure which this Pope took on one day of each week in washing his hands in the gold of the Datatario and the Camera (vol. i. p. 281), and says of him, 'attende solo a far danari' (vol. ii. p. 237). When Paul gave his nephew Scipione the Abbey of Vangadizza, with 12,000 ducats a year, Sarpi computed that the Cardinal held about 100,000 ducats of ecclesiastical benefices (vol. i. p. 219). When the Archbishopric of Bologna, worth over 16,000 ducats a year, fell vacant in 1610, Paul gave this to Scipione, who held it a short time without residence, and then abandoned it to Alessandro Ludovisi, retaining all its revenues, with the exception of 2,000 ducats, for himself as a *pension* (vol. ii. pp. 158, 300). In the year 1610 Sarpi notices the purchase of Sulmona and other fiefs by Paul for his family, at the expenditure of 160,000 ducats (vol. ii. p. 70). In another place he speaks of another sum of 100,000 spent upon the same object (vol. i. p. 249, note). Well might he exclaim, 'Il pontefice è atteso ad arrichir la sua casa' (vol. i. p. 294).

century, embracing seven tenures of the Holy Chair, had sufficed to develop the new phase of the Papacy as an absolute sovereignty, representing the modern European principle of absolutism, both as the acknowledged Head of Catholic Christendom, and also as a petty Italian power.

CHAPTER III

THE INQUISITION AND THE INDEX

Different Spirit in the Holy Office and the Company of Jesus—Both needed by the Counter-Reformation—Heresy in the Early Church—First Origins of the Inquisition in 1203—S. Dominic—The Holy Office becomes a Dominican Institution—Recognised by the Empire—Its early Organisation—The Spanish Inquisition—Founded in 1484—How it differed from the earlier Apostolical Inquisition—Jews, Moors, New Christians—Organisation and History of the Holy Office in Spain—Torquemada and his Successors—The Spanish Inquisition never introduced into Italy—How the Roman Inquisition organised by Caraffa differed from it—*Autos da fe* in Rome—Proscription of suspected Lutherans—The Calabrian Waldenses—Protestants at Locarno and Venice—Digression on the Venetian Holy Office—Persecution of Free Thought in Literature—Growth of the Index Librorum Prohibitorum—Sanction given to it by the Council of Trent—The Roman Congregation of the Index—Final Form of the Censorship of Books under Clement VIII.—Analysis of its Regulations—Proscription of Heretical Books—Correction of Texts—Purgation and Castration—Inquisitorial and Episcopal Licences—Working of the System of this Censorship in Italy—Its long Delays—Hostility to Sound Learning—Ignorance of the Censors—Interference with Scholars in their Work—Terrorism of Booksellers—Vatican Scheme for the Restoration of Christian Erudition—Frustrated by the Tyranny of the Index—Dishonesty of the Vatican Scholars—Biblical Studies rendered nugatory by the Tridentine Decree on the Vulgate—Decline of Learning in Universities—Miserable Servitude of Professors—Greek dies out—Muretus and Manutius in Rome—The Index and its Treatment of Political Works—Machiavelli—*Ratio Status*—Encouragement of Literature on Papal Absolutism—Sarpi's Attitude—Comparative Indifference of Rome to Books of Obscene or Immoral Tendency—Bandello and Boccaccio—Papal Attempts to control Intercourse of Italians with Heretics.

IN pursuing the plan of this book, which aims at showing how the spirit of the Catholic Revival penetrated every sphere

of intellectual activity in Italy, it will now be needful to
consider the two agents, both of Spanish origin, on whose
assistance the Church relied in her crusade against liberties
of thought, speech and action. These were the Inquisition
and the Company of Jesus. The one worked by extirpation
and forcible repression; the other by mental enfeeblement
and moral corruption. The one used fire, torture, imprisonment, confiscation of goods, the proscription of learning, the
destruction or emasculation of books. The other employed
subtle means to fill the vacuum thus created with spurious
erudition, sophistries, casuistical abominations and false
doctrines profitable to the Papal absolutism. Opposed in
temper and in method, the one fierce and rigid, the other
saccharine and pliant, these two bad angels of Rome contributed in almost equal measure to the triumph of Catholicism.

In the earlier ages of the Church, the definition of heresy
had been committed to episcopal authority. But the cognisance of heretics and the determination of their punishment
remained in the hands of secular magistrates. At the end of
the twelfth century the wide diffusion of the Albigensian
heterodoxy through Languedoc and Northern Italy alarmed
the chiefs of Christendom, and furnished the Papacy with
a good pretext for extending its prerogatives. Innocent III.
in 1203 empowered two French Cistercians, Pierre de Castelnau
and Raoul, to preach against the heretics of Provence. In the
following year he ratified this commission by a Bull, which
censured the negligence and coldness of the bishops, appointed
the Abbot of Citeaux Papal delegate in matters of heresy, and
gave him authority to judge and punish misbelievers. This
was the first germ of the Holy Office as a separate Tribunal.
In order to comprehend the facility with which the Pope
established so anomalous an institution, we must bear in
mind the intense horror which heresy inspired in the Middle

Ages. Being a distinct encroachment of the Papacy upon the episcopal jurisdiction and prerogatives, the Inquisition met at first with some opposition from the bishops. The people for whose persecution it was designed, and at whose expense it carried on its work, broke into rebellion; the first years of its annals were rendered illustrious by the murder of one of its founders, Pierre de Castelnau. He was canonised, and became the first Saint of the Inquisition. Two other Peters obtained the like honour through their zeal for the Catholic faith: Peter of Verona, commonly called Peter Martyr, the Italian saint of the Dominican order; and Peter Arbues, the Spanish saint, who sealed with his blood the charter of the Holy Office in Aragon.

In spite of opposition the Papal institution took root and flourished. Philip Augustus responded to the appeals of Innocent; and a crusade began against the Albigenses, in which Simon de Montfort won his sinister celebrity. During those bloody wars the Inquisition developed itself as a force of formidable expansive energy. Material assistance to the cause was rendered by a Spanish monk of the Augustine order, who settled in Provence on his way back from Rome in 1206. Domenigo de Guzman, known to universal history as S. Dominic, organised a new militia for the service of the orthodox Church between the years 1215 and 1219. His order, called the Order of the Preachers, was originally designed to repress heresy and confirm the faith by diffusing Catholic doctrine and maintaining the creed in its purity. It consisted of three sections: the Preaching Friars; nuns living in conventual retreat; and laymen, entitled the Third Order of Penitence or the Militia of Christ, who in after years were merged with the congregation of S. Peter Martyr, and corresponded to the familiars of the Inquisition. Since the Dominicans were established in the heat and passion of a crusade against heresy, by a rigid Spaniard who employed his energies in persecuting misbelievers, they assumed at the outset a belligerent and inquisitorial attitude. Yet it is not strictly accurate to represent S. Dominic himself as the first Grand Inquisitor. The Papacy proceeded with caution in its design of forming a tribunal dependent on the Holy See and independent of the bishops. Papal Legates with plenipotentiary authority were sent to Languedoc, and decrees were issued against the heretics, in which the Inquisition was rather implied than directly named; nor can I find that S. Dominic, though he continued to be the soul of the new institution until his death in 1221, obtained the title of Inquisitor.

Notwithstanding this vagueness, the Holy Office may be said to have been founded by S. Dominic; and it soon became apparent that the order he had formed was destined to monopolise its functions. The Emperor Frederick II. on his coronation, in 1221, declared his willingness to support a separate Apostolical tribunal for the suppression of heresy. He sanctioned the penalty of death by fire for obstinate heretics, and perpetual imprisonment for penitents—forms of punishment which became stereotyped in the proceedings of the Holy Office.[1] The tribunal, now recognised as a Dominican institution, derived its authority from the Pope. The bishops were suffered to sit with the Inquisitors, but only in

---

[1] See Cantù, *Gli Eretici d' Italia*, vol. i. Discorso 5, and the notes appended to it, for Frederick's edicts and letters to Gregory IX. upon this matter of heresy. The Emperor treats of *Heretica Pravitas* as a crime against society, and such, indeed, it then appeared according to the medieval ideal of Christendom united under Church and Empire. Yet Frederick himself, it will be remembered, died under the ban of the Church and was placed by Dante among the heresiarchs in the tenth circle of Hell. We now regard him justly as one of the precursors of the Renaissance. But at the beginning of his reign, in his peculiar attitude of Holy Roman Emperor, he had to proceed with rigour against freethinkers in religion. They were foes to the medieval order, of which he was the secular head.

such subordinate capacity as left to them a bare title of authority.[1] The secular magistracy was represented by an assessor, who, being nominated by the Inquisitor, became his servile instrument. The expenses of the Court in prosecuting, punishing and imprisoning heretics, together with the maintenance of the Inquisitors and their guards, were thrown upon the communes which they visited. Such was the organisation which the Popes, aided by S. Dominic, and availing themselves of the fanatical passions aroused in the Provençal wars, succeeded in creating for their own aggrandisement. It is strange to think that its ratification by the supreme secular power was obtained from an Emperor who died in contumacy, excommunicated and persecuted as an arch-heretic by the priests he had supported.

This Apostolical Inquisition was at once introduced into Lombardy, Romagna and the Marches of Treviso. The extreme rigour of its proceedings, the extortions of monks, and the violent resistance offered by the communes, led to some relaxation of its original constitution. More authority had to be conceded to the bishops; and the right of the Inquisitors to levy taxes on the people was modified. Yet it retained its true form of a Papal organ, superseding the episcopal prerogatives, and overriding the secular magistrates, who were bound to execute its biddings. As such it was admitted into Tuscany, and established in Aragon. Venice received it in 1289, with certain reservations that placed its proceedings under the control of Doge and Council. In Languedoc, the country of its birth, it remained rooted at Toulouse and Carcassonne; but the Inquisition did not extend its authority over central and northern France.[2] In Paris its functions were performed by the Sorbonne. Nor did it obtain a footing in England, although the statute 'De

---

[1] Sarpi, 'Dircorso dell' Origine,' &c. *Opere*, vol. iv. p. 6.
[2] See Christie's *Etienne Dolet*, chap. 21.

Haeretico Comburendo,' passed in 1401 at the instance of the higher clergy, sanctioned the principles on which it existed. The wide and ready acceptance of so terrible an engine of oppression enables us to estimate the profound horror which heresy inspired in the Middle Ages.[1] On the whole, the Inquisition performed the work for which it had been instituted. Those spreading sects, known as Waldenses, Albigenses, Cathari and Paterines, whom it was commissioned to extirpate, died away into obscurity during the fourteenth century; and through the period of the Renaissance the Inquisition had little scope for the display of energy in Italy. Though dormant, it was by no means extinct, however; and the spirit which created it, needed only external cause and circumstance to bring it once more into powerful operation. Meanwhile the Popes throughout the Renaissance used the imputation of heresy, which never lost its blighting stigma, in the prosecution of their secular ambition. As Sarpi has pointed out, there were few of the Italian princes with whom they came into political collision, who were not made the subject of such accusation.

The revival of the Holy Office on a new and far more murderous basis, took place in 1484. We have seen that hitherto there had been two types of inquisition into heresy. The first, which remained in force up to the year 1203, may be called the episcopal. The second was the Apostolical or Dominican; it transferred this jurisdiction from the bishops to the Papacy, who employed the order of S. Dominic for the special service of the tribunal instituted by the Imperial

[1] Visitors to Milan must have been struck with the equestrian statue to the Podestà Oldrado da Trezzeno in the Piazza de' Mercanti. Underneath it runs an epitaph containing among the praises of this man: *Catharos ut debuit ussit*. An Archbishop of Milan of the same period (middle of the thirteenth century), Enrico di Settala, is also praised upon his epitaph because *jugulavit haereses*. See Cantù, *Gli Eretici d' Italia*, vol. i. p. 108.

decrees of Frederick II. The third deserves no other name than Spanish, though, after it had taken shape in Spain, it was transferred to Portugal, applied in all the Spanish and Portuguese colonies, and communicated with some modifications to Italy and the Netherlands.[1] Both the second and the third types of inquisition into heresy were Spanish inventions, patented by the Roman Pontiffs and monopolised by the Dominican order. But the third and final form of the Holy Office in Spain distinguished itself by emancipation from Papal and Royal control, and by a specific organisation which rendered it the most formidable of irresponsible engines in the annals of religious institutions.

The crimes of which the second or Dominican Inquisition had taken cognisance were designated under the generic name of heresy. Heretics were either patent by profession of some heterodox cult or doctrine; or they were suspected. The suspected included witches, sorcerers, and blasphemers who invoked the devil's aid; Catholics abstaining from confession and absolution; harbourers of avowed heretics; legal defenders of the cause of heretics; priests who

[1] Sarpi estimates the number of victims in the Netherlands during the reign of Charles V. at 50,000; Grotius at 100,000. In the reign of Philip II. perhaps another 25,000 were sacrificed. Motley (*Rise of the Dutch Republic*, vol. ii. p. 155) tells how in February 1568 a sentence of the Holy Office, confirmed by royal proclamation, condemned all the inhabitants of the Netherlands, some three millions of souls, with a few specially excepted persons, to death. It was customary to burn the men and bury the women alive. In considering this institution as a whole, we must bear in mind that it was extended to Mexico, Lima, Carthagena, the Indies, Sicily, Sardinia, Oran, Malta. Of the working of the Holy Office in the Spanish and Portuguese colonies we possess but few authentic records. The *Histoire des Inquisitions* of Joseph Lavallée (Paris, 1809) may, however, be consulted. In vol. ii. pp. 5-9 of this work there is a brief account of the Inquisition at Goa written by one Pyrard; and pp. 45-157 extend the singularly detailed narrative of a Frenchman, Dellon, imprisoned in its dungeons. Some curious circumstances respecting delation, prison life, and *autos da fe* are here minutely recorded.

gave Christian burial to heretics; magistrates who showed lukewarmness in pursuit of heretics; the corpses of dead heretics, and books that might be taxed with heretical opinions. All ranks in the social hierarchy, except the Pope, his Legates and Nuncios, and the bishops, were amenable to this Inquisition. The Inquisitors could only be arraigned and judged by their peers. In order to bring the machinery of imprisonment, torture and final sentence into effect, it was needful that the credentials of the Inquisitor should be approved by the sovereign, and that his procedure should be recognised by the bishop. These limitations of the Inquisitorial authority safeguarded the crown and the episcopacy in a legal sense. But since both crown and episcopacy concurred in the object for which the Papacy had established the tribunal, the Inquisitor was practically unimpeded in his functions. Furnished with royal or princely letters patent, he travelled from town to town, attended by his guards and notaries, defraying current expenses at the cost of provinces and towns through which he passed. Where he pitched his camp, he summoned the local magistrates, swore them to obedience, and obtained assurance of their willingness to execute such sentences as he might pronounce. Spies and informers gathered round him, pledged to secresy and guaranteed by promises of State protection. The court opened; witnesses were examined; the accused were acquitted or condemned. Then sentence was pronounced, to which the bishop or his delegate, often an Inquisitor, gave a formal sanction. Finally, the heretic was handed over to the secular arm for the execution of justice. The extraordinary expenses of the tribunal were defrayed by confiscation of goods, a certain portion being paid to the district in which the crime had occurred, the rest being reserved for the maintenance of the Holy Office.

Such, roughly speaking, was the method of the Inquisition

before 1484; and it did not materially differ in Italy and Spain. Castile had hitherto been free from the pest. But the conditions of that kingdom offered a good occasion for its introduction at the date which I have named. During the Middle Ages the Jews of Castile acquired vast wealth and influence. Few families but felt the burden of their bonds and mortgages. Religious fanaticism, social jealousy, and pecuniary distress exasperated the Christian population; and as early as the year 1391, more than 5,000 Jews were massacred in one popular uprising. The Jews, in fear, adopted Christianity. It is said that in the fifteenth century the population counted some million of converts—called New Christians, or, in contempt, Marranos; a word which may probably be derived from the Hebrew Maranatha. These converted Jews, by their ability and wealth, crept into high offices of state, obtained titles of aristocracy, and founded noble houses. Their daughters were married with large dowers into the best Spanish families; and their younger sons aspired to the honours of the Church. Castilian society was being penetrated with Jews, many of whom had undoubtedly conformed to Christianity in externals only. Meanwhile a large section of the Hebrew race remained faithful to their old traditions; and a mixed posterity grew up, which hardly knew whether it was Christian or Jewish, and had opportunity for joining either party.

A fertile field was now opened for Inquisitorial energy. The orthodox Dominicans saw Christ's flock contaminated. Not without reason did earnest Catholics dread that the Church in Castile would suffer from this blending of the Jewish with the Spanish breed. But they had a fiery Catholic enthusiasm to rely upon in the main body of the nation. And in the crown they knew that there were passions of fear and cupidity, which might be used with overmastering effect. It sufficed to point out to Ferdinand that a persecution of the New Christians would flood his coffers with gold extorted from suspected misbelievers. No merely fabled El Dorado lay in the broad lands and costly merchandise of these imperfect converts to the faith. It sufficed to insist upon the peril to the state if an element so ill-assimilated to the nation were allowed to increase unchecked. At the same time, the Papacy was nothing loth to help them in their undertaking. Sixtus IV., one of the worst of Pontiffs, sat then on S. Peter's Chair. He readily discerned that a considerable portion of the booty might be indirectly drawn into his exchequer; and he knew that any establishment of the Inquisition on an energetic basis would strengthen the Papacy in its combat with national and episcopal prerogatives. The Dominicans on their side can scarcely be credited with a pure zeal for the faith. They had personal interests to serve by spiritual aggrandisement, by the elevation of their order, and by the exercise of an illimitable domination.

It was a Sicilian Inquisitor, Philip Barberis, who suggested to Ferdinand the Catholic the advantage he might secure by extending the Holy Office to Castile. Ferdinand avowed his willingness; and Sixtus IV. gave the project his approval in 1478. But it met with opposition from the gentler-natured Isabella. She refused at first to sanction the introduction of so sinister an engine into her hereditary dominions. The clergy now contrived to raise a popular agitation against the Jews, reviving old calumnies of impossible crimes, and accusing them of being treasonable subjects. Then Isabella yielded; and in 1481 the Holy Office was founded at Seville. It began its work by publishing a comprehensive edict against all New Christians suspected of Judaising, which offence was so constructed as to cover the most innocent observance of national customs. Resting from labour on Saturday; performing ablutions at

stated times; refusing to eat pork or puddings made of
blood; and abstaining from wine, sufficed to colour accusations of heresy. Men who had joined the Catholic communion after the habits of a lifetime had been formed, thus
found themselves exposed to peril of death by the retention
of mere sanitary rules.[1]

Upon the publication of this edict, there was an exodus of
Jews by thousands into the fiefs of independent vassals of the
crown—the Duke of Medina Sidonia, the Marquis of Cadiz,
and the Count of Arcos. All emigrants were *ipso facto*
declared heretics by the Holy Office. During the first year
after its foundation, Seville beheld 298 persons burned alive,
and 79 condemned to perpetual imprisonment. A large square
stage of stone, called the Quemadero, was erected for the
execution of those multitudes who were destined to suffer death
by hanging or by flame. In the same year, 2,000 were burned
and 17,000 condemned to public penitence, while even a larger
number were burned in effigy, in other parts of the kingdom.

While estimating the importance of these punishments,
we must remember that they implied confiscation of property.
Thus whole families were orphaned and consigned to penury.
Penitence in public carried with it social infamy, loss of civil
rights and honours, intolerable conditions of ecclesiastical

---

[1] See Lavallée, *Histoire des Inquisitions*, vol. ii. pp. 341–361, for the
translation of a process instituted in 1570 against a Mauresque female
slave. Suspected of being a disguised infidel, she was exposed to the temp-
tations of a Moorish spy, and convicted mainly on the evidence furnished by certain Mussulman habits to which she adhered. Llorente
reports a similar specimen case, vol. i. p. 442. The culprit was a tinker
aged 71, accused in 1528 of abstaining from pork and wine, and using
certain ablutions. He defended himself by pleading that, having been
converted at the age of 45, it did not suit his taste to eat pork or drink
wine, and that his trade obliged him to maintain cleanliness by
frequent washing. He was finally condemned to carry a candle at an
auto da fe in sign of penitence, and to pay four ducats, the costs of his
trial. His detention lasted from September 1529 till December 18,
1530.

surveillance, and heavy pecuniary fines. Penitents who had been reconciled, returned to society in a far more degraded condition than convicts released on ticket of leave. The stigma attached in perpetuity to the posterity of the condemned, whose names were conspicuously emblazoned upon church-walls as foemen to Christ and to the state.

It is not strange that the New Christians, wealthy as they were and allied with some of the best blood in Spain, should have sought to avert the storm descending on them by appeals to Rome. In person or by procurators, they carried their complaints to the Papal Curia, imploring the relief of private reconciliation with the Church, special exemption from the jurisdiction of the Holy Office, rehabilitation after the loss of civil rights and honours, dispensation from humiliating penances, and avocation of causes tried by the Inquisition to less prejudiced tribunals. The object of these petitions was to avoid perpetual infamy, to recover social status, and to obtain an impartial hearing in doubtful cases. The Papal Curia had anticipated the profits to be derived from such appeals. Sixtus IV. was liberal in briefs of indulgence, absolution and exemption, to all comers who paid largely. But when his suitors returned to Spain, they found their dearly purchased parchments of no more value than waste paper. The Holy Office laughed Papal Bulls of Privilege to scorn, and the Pope was too indifferent to exert such authority as he might have possessed.

Meanwhile, the Inquisition rapidly took shape. In 1483 Thomas of Torquemada was nominated Inquisitor General for Castile and Aragon. Under his rule a Supreme Council was established, over which he presided for life. The crown sent three assessors to this board; and the Inquisitors were strengthened in their functions by a council of jurists. Seville, Cordova, Jaen, Toledo became the four subordinate centres of the Holy Office, each with its own tribunal and its own right of performing acts of faith. Commission was sent out to all Dominicans, enjoining on them the prosecution of their task in every diocese.

In 1484 a General Council was held, and the constitution of the Inquisition was established by articles. In these articles four main points seem to have been held in view. The first related to the system of confiscation, fines, civil disabilities, losses of office, property, honours, rights, inheritances, which formed a part of the penitentiary procedure, and by which the crown and Holy Office made pecuniary gains. The second secured secrecy in the action of the tribunal, whereby a door was opened to delation, and accused persons were rendered incapable of rational defence. The third elaborated the judicial method, so as to leave no loophole of escape even for those who showed a wish to be converted, empowering the use of torture, precluding the accused from choosing their own counsel, and excluding the bishops from active participation in the sentence. The fourth multiplied the charges under which suspected heretics, even after their death, might be treated as impenitent or relapsed, so as to increase the number of victims and augment the booty.

The two most formidable features of the Inquisition as thus constituted were the exclusion of the bishops from its tribunal and the secrecy of its procedure. The accused was delivered over to a court that had no mercy, no common human sympathies, no administrative interest in the population. He knew nothing of his accusers; and when he died or disappeared from view no record of his case survived him.

The Inquisition rested on the double basis of ecclesiastical fanaticism and protected delation. The court was *prima facie* hostile to the accused; and the accused could never hope to confront the detectives upon whose testimony he was arraigned before it. Lives and reputations lay thus at the mercy of professional informers, private enemies, malicious calumniators. The denunciation was sometimes anonymous, sometimes signed, with names of two corroborative witnesses. These witnesses were examined, under a strict seal of secresy, by the Inquisitors, who drew up a form of accusation, which they submitted to theologians called Qualificators. The qualificators were not informed of the names of the accused, the delator, or the witnesses. It was their business to qualify the case of heresy as light, grave, or violent. Having placed it in one of these categories, they returned it to the Inquisitors, who now arrested the accused and flung him into the secret prisons of the Holy Office. After some lapse of time he was summoned for a preliminary examination. Having first been cautioned to tell the truth, he had to recite the Paternoster, Credo, Ten Commandments, and a kind of catechism. His pedigree was also investigated, in the expectation that some traces of Jewish or Moorish descent might serve to incriminate him. If he failed in repeating the Christian shibboleths, or if he was discovered to have infidel ancestry, there existed already a good case to proceed upon. Finally, he was questioned upon the several heads of accusation condensed from the first delation and the deposition of the witnesses. If needful at this point, he was put to the torture, again and yet again.[1] He never heard the names of his accusers, nor was he furnished with a full bill of the charges against him in writing. At this stage he was usually remanded, and the judicial proceedings were deliberately lengthened out with a view of crushing his spirit and bringing him to abject submission. For his defence he might select one advocate, but only from a list furnished by his judges; and this advocate in no case saw the original documents of the impeachment. It rarely happened, upon this one-sided method of trial, that

[1] The Supreme Council forbade the repetition of torture; but this hypocritical law was evaded in practice by declaring that the torture had been suspended. Llorente, vol. i. p. 307.

an accused person was acquitted altogether. If he escaped burning or perpetual incarceration, he was almost certainly exposed to the public ceremony of penitence, with its attendant infamy, fines, civil disabilities, and future discipline. Sentence was not passed upon condemned persons until they appeared, dressed up in a San Benito, at the place of punishment. This costume was a sort of sack, travestying a monk's frock, made of coarse yellow stuff, and worked over with crosses, flames, and devils, in glaring red. It differed in details according to the destination of the victim: for some ornaments symbolised eternal hell, and others the milder fires of purgatory. If sufficiently versed in the infernal heraldry of the Holy Office, a condemned man might read his doom before he reached the platform of the *auto*. There he heard whether he was sentenced to relaxation—in other words, to burning at the hands of the hangman—or to reconciliation by means of penitence. At the last moment, he might by confession *in extremis* obtain the commutation of a death sentence into life-imprisonment, or receive the favour of being strangled before he was burned. A relapsed heretic, however—that is, one who after being reconciled had once again apostatised, was never exempted from the penalty of burning. To make these holocausts of human beings more ghastly, the pageant was enhanced by processions of exhumed corpses and heretics in effigy. Artificial dolls and decomposed bodies, with grinning lips and mouldy foreheads, were hauled to the huge bonfire, side by side with living men, women, and children. All of them alike—*fantoccini*, skeletons, and quick folk—were enveloped in the same grotesquely ghastly San Benito, with the same hideous yellow mitres on their pasteboard, worm-eaten, or palpitating foreheads. The procession presented an ingeniously picturesque discord of ugly shapes, an artistically loathsome dissonance of red and yellow hues, as it defiled, to the infernal music of growled psalms and screams and moanings, beneath the torrid blaze of Spanish sunlight.

Spaniards—such is the barbarism of the Latinised Iberian nature—delighted in these shows as they did and do in bull-fights. Butcheries of heretics formed the choicest spectacles at royal christenings and bridals.

At Seville the Quemadero was adorned with four colossal statues of prophets, to which some of the condemned were bound, so that they might burn to death in the flames arising from the human sacrifice between them.

In the autumn of 1484 the Inquisition was introduced into Aragon; and Saragossa became its headquarters in that State. Though the Aragonese were accustomed to the institution in its earlier and milder form, they regarded the new Holy Office with just horror. The Marranos counted at that epoch the Home Secretary, the Grand Treasurer, a Protonotary, and a Vice-Chancellor of the realm among their members; and they were allied by marriage with the purest aristocracy. It is not, therefore, marvellous that a conspiracy was formed to assassinate the Chief Inquisitor, Peter Arbues. In spite of a coat-of-mail and an iron skullcap worn beneath his monk's dress, Arbues was murdered one evening while at prayer in church. But the revolt, notwithstanding this murder, flashed like an ill-loaded pistol in the pan. Jealousies between the old and new Christians prevented any common action; and the Inquisition took a bloody vengeance upon all concerned. It even laid its hand on Don James of Navarre, the Infant of Tudela.

The Spanish Inquisition was now firmly grounded. Directed by Torquemada, it began to encroach upon the crown, to insult the episcopacy, to defy the Papacy, to grind the Commons, and to outrage by its insolence the aristocracy. Ferdinand's avarice had overreached itself by creating an ecclesiastical power dangerous to the best interests of the

realm, but which fascinated a fanatically pious people, and
the yoke of which could not be thrown off. The Holy Office
grew every year in pride, pretensions, and exactions. It
arrogated to its tribunal crimes of usury, bigamy, blas-
phemous swearing, and unnatural vice, which appertained by
right to the secular courts. It depopulated Spain by the
extermination and banishment of at least three million
industrious subjects during the first 139 years of its existence.
It attacked princes of the blood, archbishops, fathers of the
Tridentine Council.[1] It filled every city in the kingdom, the
convents of the religious, and the palaces of the nobility, with
spies. The Familiars, or lay brethren devoted to its service,
lived at charges of the communes, and debauched society by
crimes of rapine, lust and violence.[2] Ignorant and blood-
thirsty monks composed its provincial tribunals, who, like
the horrible Lucero el Tenebroso, at Cordova, paralysed whole
provinces with a veritable reign of terror.[3] Hated and
worshipped, its officers swept through the realm in the
guise of powerful *condottieri*. The Grand Inquisitor maintained a bodyguard of fifty mounted Familiars and two
hundred infantry; his subordinates were allowed ten horse-
men and fifty archers apiece. Where these black guards
appeared, city gates were opened; magistrates swore fealty
to masters of more puissance than the king; the resources
of flourishing districts were placed at their disposal. Their
arbitrary acts remained unquestioned, their mysterious sentences irreversible. Shrouded in secrecy, amenable to no
jurisdiction but their own, they revelled in the license of

[1] Llorente, in his Introduction to the *History of the Inquisition*,
gives a long list of illustrious Spanish victims.

[2] See Llorente, vol. i. p. 349, for their outrages on women.

[3] For the history of Lucero's tyranny, read Llorente, vol. i. pp.
345-353. When at last he had to be deposed, it was not to a dungeon
or the scaffold, but to his bishopric of Almeria that this miscreant was
relegated.

irresponsible dominion. Spain gradually fell beneath the charm of their dark fascination. A brave though cruel nation drank delirium from the poison-cup of these vile medicine-men, whose Moloch-worship would have disgusted cannibals.

Torquemada was the genius of evil who created and presided over this foul instrument of human crime and folly. During his eighteen years of administration, reckoning from 1480 to 1498, he sacrificed, according to Llorente's calculation, above 114,000 victims, of whom 10,220 were burned alive 6,860 burned in effigy, and 97,000 condemned to perpetual imprisonment or public penitence.[1] He, too, it was who in 1492 compelled Ferdinand to drive the Jews from his dominions. They offered 30,000 ducats for the war against Granada, and promised to abide in Spain under heavy social disabilities, if only they might be spared this act of national extermination. Then Torquemada appeared before the king, and, raising his crucifix on high, cried: 'Judas sold Christ for thirty pieces of silver. Look ye to it, if ye do the like!' The edict of expulsion was issued on the last of March. Before the last of July all Jews were sentenced to depart, carrying no gold or silver with them. They disposed of their lands, houses, and goods for next to nothing, and went forth to die by thousands on the shores of Africa and Italy. Twelve who were found concealed at Malaga in August were condemned to be pricked to death by pointed reeds.[2]

The exodus of the Jews was followed in 1502 by a similar exodus of Moors from Castile, and in 1524 by an exodus of Mauresques from Aragon. To compute the loss of wealth and population inflicted upon Spain by these mad edicts, would be impossible. We may wonder whether the followers of Cortes, when they trod the teocallis of Mexico and gazed

---

[1] Llorente, vol. i. p. 229. The basis for these and following calculations is explained ib. pp. 272-281.

[2] Llorente, vol. i. p. 263.

with loathing on the gory elf-locks of the Aztec priests, were not reminded of the Torquemada they had left at home. His cruelty became so intolerable that even Alexander VI. was moved to horror. In 1494 the Borgia appointed four assessors, with equal powers, to restrain the blood-thirst of the fanatic.

After Torquemada, Diego Deza reigned as second Inquisitor General from 1498 to 1507. In these years, according to the same calculation, 2,592 were burned alive, 896 burned in effigy, 34,952 condemned to prison or public penitence.[1] Cardinal Ximenez de Cisneros followed between 1507 and 1517. The victims of this decade were 3,564 burned alive, 1,232 burned in effigy, 48,059 condemned to prison or public penitence.[2] Adrian, Bishop of Tortosa, tutor to Charles V. and afterwards Pope, was Inquisitor General between 1516 and 1525. Castile, Aragon, and Catalonia, at this epoch, simultaneously demanded a reform of the Holy Office from their youthful sovereign. But Charles refused, and the tale of Adrian's administration was 1,620 burned alive, 560 burned in effigy, 21,845 condemned to prison or public penitence.[3] The total, during forty-three years, between 1481 and 1525, amounted to 234,526, including all descriptions of condemned heretics.[4] These figures are of necessity vague, for the Holy Office left but meagre records of its proceedings. The vast numbers of cases brought before the Inquisitors rendered their method of procedure almost as summary as that of Fouquier-Tinville, while policy induced them to bury the memory of their victims in oblivion.[5]

[1] Llorente, vol. i. p. 341.   [2] *Ib.* p. 360.
[3] *Ib.* p. 406.   [4] *Ib.* p. 407.
[5] I know that Llorente's calculations have been disputed: as, for instance, in some minor details by Prescott (*Ferd. and Isab.* vol. iii. p. 492). The truth is that no data now exist for forming a correct census of the victims of the Spanish Moloch; and Llorente, though he writes with the moderation of evident sincerity, and though he had access to

Sometimes, while reading the history of the Holy Office in Spain, we are tempted to imagine that the whole is but a grim unwholesome nightmare, or the fable of malignant calumny. That such is not the case, however, is proved by a jubilant inscription on the palace of the Holy Office at Seville, which records the triumphs of Torquemada. Of late years, too, the earth herself has disgorged some secrets of the Inquisition. 'A most curious discovery,' writes Lord Malmesbury in his Memoirs,[1] 'has been made at Madrid. Just at the time when the question of religious liberty was being discussed in the Cortes, Serrano had ordered a piece of ground to be levelled, in order to build on it, and the workmen came upon large quantities of human bones, skulls, lumps of blackening flesh, pieces of chains, and braids of hair. It was then recollected that the *autos da fe* used to take place at that spot in former days. Crowds of people rushed to the place, and the investigation was continued. They found layer upon layer of human remains, showing that hundreds had been inhumanly sacrificed. The excitement and indignation this produced among the people was tremendous, and the party for religious freedom taking advantage of it, a Bill on the subject was passed by an enormous majority.' Let modern Spain remember that a similar Aceldama lies hidden in the precincts of each of her chief towns!

the archives of the Inquisition, does not profess to do more than give an estimate based upon certain fixed data. However, it signifies but little whether we reckon by thousands or by fifteen hundreds. That foul monster spawned in the unholy embracements of perverted religion with purblind despotism cannot be defended by discounting five or even ten per cent. Let its apologists write for every 1,000 of Llorente 100 and for every 100 of Llorente 10, and our position will remain unaltered. The Jesuit historian of Spain, Mariana, records the burning of 2,000 persons in Andalusia alone in 1482. Bernaldez mentions 700 burned in the one town of Seville between 1482 and 1489. An inscription carved above the portals of the Holy Office in Seville stated that about 1,000 had been burned between 1492 and 1524.

[1] Vol. ii. p. 399.

I have enlarged upon the details of the Spanish Inquisition for two reasons. In the first place it strikingly illustrates the character of the people who now had the upper hand in Italy. In the second place, its success induced Paul III., acting upon the advice of Giov. Paolo Caraffa, to remodel the Roman office on a similar type in 1542. It may at once be said that the real Spanish Inquisition was never introduced into Italy.[1] Such an institution, claiming independent jurisdiction and flaunting its cruelties in the light of day, would not have suited the Papal policy. As temporal and spiritual autocrats, the Popes could not permit a tribunal of which they were not the supreme authority. It was their interest to consult their pecuniary advantage rather than to indulge insane fanaticism; to repress liberty of thought by cautious surveillance rather than by public terrorism and open acts of cruelty. The Italian temperament was, moreover, more humane than the Spanish; nor had the refining culture of the Renaissance left no traces in the nation. Furthermore, the necessity for so Draconian an institution was not felt. Catholicism in Italy had not to contend with Jews and Moors, Marranos and Moriscoes. It was, indeed, alarmed by the spread of Lutheran opinions. Caraffa complained to Paul III. that 'the whole of Italy is infected with the Lutheran heresy, which has been embraced not only by statesmen but also by many ecclesiastics.'[2] Pius V. was so panic-stricken by the prevalence of heresy in Faenza that he seriously meditated destroying the town and dispersing its inhabitants.[3] Yet, after a few years of active persecution, this peril proved to be unreal. The Reformation had not taken root so deep and wide in Italy that it could not be eradicated. When, therefore, the Spanish

---

[1] Naples and Milan passionately and successfully opposed its introduction by the Spanish viceroys. But it ruled in Sicily and Sardinia.
[2] McCrie, p. 186.   [3] Mutinelli, *Storia Arcana*, vol. i. p. 79.

viceroys sought to establish their national Inquisition in Naples and Milan, the rebellious people received protection and support from the Papacy; and the Holy Office, as remodelled in Rome, became a far less awful engine of oppression than that of Seville.

It was sufficiently severe, however. 'At Rome,' writes a resident in 1568, 'some are daily burned, hanged, or beheaded; the prisons and places of confinement are filled, and they are obliged to build new ones.'[1] This general statement may be checked by extracts from the dispatches of Venetian ambassadors in Rome, which, though they are not continuous, and cannot be supposed to give an exhaustive list of the victims of the Inquisition, enable us to judge with some degree of accuracy what the frequency of executions may have been.[2] On September 27, 1567, a session of the Holy Office was held at S. Maria sopra Minerva. Seventeen heretics were condemned. Fifteen of these were sentenced to perpetual imprisonment, the galleys for life, fines or temporary imprisonment, according to the nature of their offences. Two were reserved for capital punishment—namely, Carnesecchi and a friar from Cividale di Belluno. They were beheaded and burned upon the bridge of S. Angelo on October 4. On May 28, 1569, there was an Act of the Inquisition at the Minerva, twenty Cardinals attending. Four impenitent heretics were condemned to the stake. Ten penitents were sentenced to various punishments of less severity. On August 2, 1578, occurred a singular scandal touching some Spaniards and Portuguese of evil manners, all of whom were burned with the exception of those who contrived to escape in time. On August 5, 1581, an English Protestant was burned for grossly insulting the Host. On February 20, 1582,

[1] McCrie, p. 272.
[2] Mutinelli's *Storia Arcana*, &c. vol. i., is the source from which I have drawn the details given above.

after an Act of the Inquisition in due form, seventeen heretics were sentenced, three to death, and the rest to imprisonment &c. We must bear in mind that Mutinelli, who published the extracts from the Venetian despatches which contain these details, does not profess to aim at completeness. Gaps of several years occur between the documents of one envoy and those of his successor. Nor does it appear that the writers themselves took notice of more than solemn and ceremonial proceedings, in which the Acts of the Inquisition were published with Pontifical and Curial pomp.[1] Still, when these considerations have been weighed, it will appear that the victims of the Inquisition, in Rome, could be counted, not by hundreds, but by units. After illustrious examples, like those of Aonio Paleario, Pietro Carnesecchi, Giordano Bruno, who were burned for Protestant or Atheistical opinions, the names of distinguished sufferers are few. Wary heretics, a Celio Secundo Curio, a Galeazzo Caracciolo, a Bernardino Ochino, a Pietro Martire Vermigli, a Pietro Paolo Vergerio, a Lelio Socino, escaped betimes to Switzerland and carried on their warfare with the Church by means of writings.[2] Others, tainted with heresy, like Marco Antonio Flaminio, managed to satisfy the Inquisition by timely concessions. The Protestant Churches, which had sprung up in Venice, Lucca, Modena, Ferrara, Faenza, Vicenza, Bologna, Naples, and Siena, were easily dispersed.[3] Their pastors fled or submitted. The flocks conformed to Catholic orthodoxy. Only in a few

[1] It is singular that only one contemporary writes from Rome about Bruno's execution in 1600; whence, I think, we may infer that such events were too common to excite much attention.

[2] The main facts about these men may be found in Cantù's *Gli Eretici d' Italia*, vol. ii. This work is written in no spirit of sympathy with Reformers. But it is superior in learning and impartiality to McCrie's.

[3] For the repressive measures used at Lucca, see *Archivio Storico*, vol. x. pp. 162-185. They include the prohibition of books, regulation of the religious observances of Lucchese citizens abroad in France or

cases was extreme rigour displayed. A memorable massacre took place in the year 1561 in Calabria within the province of Cosenza. Here at the end of the fourteenth century a colony of Waldensians had settled in some villages upon the coast. They preserved their peculiar beliefs and ritual, and after three centuries numbered about 4,000 souls. Nearly the whole of these, it seems, were exterminated by sword, fire, famine, torture, noisome imprisonment, and hurling from the summits of high cliffs.[1] A few of the survivors were sent to work upon the Spanish galleys. Some women and children were sold into slavery. At Locarno, on the Lago Maggiore, a Protestant community of nearly 800 persons was driven into exile in 1555 : and at Venice, in 1560-7, a small sect, holding reformed opinions, suffered punishment of a peculiar kind. We read of five persons by name, who, after being condemned by the Holy Office, were taken at night from their dungeons to the Porto del Lido beyond the Due Castelli, and there set upon a plank between two gondolas. The gondolas rowed asunder: and one by one the martyrs fell and perished in the waters.[2]

Flanders, and proscription of certain heretics, with whom all intercourse was forbidden.

[1] An eye-witness gives a heart-rending account of these persecutions; sixty thrown from the tower of Guardia, eighty-eight butchered like beasts in one day at Montalto, seven burned alive, one hundred old women tortured and then slaughtered. *Arch. Stor.* vol. ix. pp 193-195.

[2] McCrie, *op. cit.* pp. 232-236. The five men were Giulio Gherlandi of Spresiano, near Treviso (executed in 1562), Antonio Rizzetto of Vicenza (in 1566), Francesco Sega of Rovigo (sentenced in 1566), Francesco Spinola of Milan (in 1567), and Fra Baldo Lupatino (1556). McCrie bases his report upon the *Histoire des Martyrs* (Genève, 1597), and De Porta's *Historia Reformationis Rhæticarum Ecclesiarum* Thinking these sources somewhat suspicious, I applied to my friend Mr. H. F. Brown, whose researches in the Venetian archives are becoming known to students of Italian history. He tells me that all the above cases, except that of Spinola, exist in the Frari. Lupatino was condemned as a Lutheran ; the others as Anabaptists. In passing

The position of the Holy Office in Venice was so far peculiar as to justify a digression upon its special constitution. Always jealous of ecclesiastical interference, the Republic insisted on the Inquisition being made dependent on the State. Three nobles of senatorial rank were chosen to act as Assessors of the Holy Office in the capital; and in the subject cities this function was assigned to the Rectors, or lieutenants of S. Mark. It was the duty of these lay members to see that justice was impartially dealt by the ecclesiastical tribunal, to defend the State against clerical encroachments, and to refer dubious cases to the Doge in Council. They were forbidden to swear oaths of allegiance or of secresy to the Holy Office, and were bound to be present at all trials, even in the case of ecclesiastical offenders. No causes could be avocated to Rome, and no crimes except heresy were held to lie within the jurisdiction of the court. The State reserved to itself

sentence on Lupatino, the Chief Inquisitor remarked that he could not condemn him to death by fire in Venice, but must consign him to a watery grave. This is characteristic of Venetian state policy. It appears that, of the above-named persons, Sega, though sentenced to death by drowning, recanted at the last moment, saying, 'Non voglio esser negato, ma voglio redirmi et morir buon Christiano.' Mr. Brown adds that there is nothing in the archives to prove that he was executed; but there is also nothing to show that his sentence was commuted. Two other persons involved in this trial, viz. Nic. Bucello of Padua and Alessio of Bellinzona, upon recantation, were subjected to public penances and confessions for different terms of years. Sega's fate must, therefore, be considered doubtful; since the fact that no commutation of sentence is on record lends some weight to the hypothesis that he withdrew his recantation, and submitted to martyrdom. I will close this note by expressing my hope that Mr. Brown, who is already engaged upon the papers of the Venetian Holy Office, will make them shortly the subject of a special publication. Considering how rare are the full and authentic records of any Inquisition, this would be of incalculable value for students of history. The series of trials in the Frari extends from 1541 to 1794, embracing 1,562 *processi* for the sixteenth century, 1,469 for the seventeenth, 541 for the eighteenth, and 25 of no date. Nearly all the towns and districts of the Venetian State are involved.

witchcraft, profane swearing, bigamy and usury; allowed no interference with Jews, infidels, and Greeks; forbade the confiscation of goods in which the heirs of condemned persons had interest; and made separate stipulations with regard to the Index of Prohibited Books. It precluded the Inquisition from extending its authority in any way, direct or indirect, over trades, arts, guilds, magistrates and communal officials.[1] The tenor of this system was to repress ecclesiastical encroachments on the State prerogatives, and to secure equity in the proceedings of the Holy Office. Had practice answered to theory in the Venetian Inquisition, by far the worst abuses of the institution would have been avoided. But as a matter of fact, causes were not unfrequently transferred to Rome; confiscations were permitted; and the lists of the condemned include Mussulmans, witches, conjurers, men of scandalous life, &c., showing that the jurisdiction of the Holy Office extended beyond heresy in Venice.[2]

The truth is that the Venetians, though they were willing to risk an open rupture with Rome, remained at heart sound Churchmen devoted to the principles of the Catholic Reaction. The Republic conceded the fact of Inquisitorial authority, while it reserved the letter of State-supervision. Venetian decadence was marked by this hypocrisy of pride; and so long as appearances were saved, the Holy Office exercised its functions freely. The nobles who acted as assessors had no sympathy with religious toleration, being themselves under the influence of confessors and directors.

How little the subjects of S. Mark at this epoch trusted the good faith of laws securing liberty of thought in Venice, may be gathered from what happened immediately after the

[1] See Sarpi's 'Discourse on the Inquisition.' *Opere*, vol. iv.
[2] I owe to Mr. H. F. Brown details about the register of criminals condemned by the Holy Office, which substantiate my statement regarding the various types of cases in its jurisdiction.

publication of the Index Expurgatorius in 1596. From an
official report upon the decline of the printing trade in
Venice, it appears that within the space of a few months the
number of presses fell from 125 to 40.[1] Printers were afraid
to undertake either old or new works, and the trade languished
for lack of books to publish. Yet an edict had been issued
announcing that by the terms of the Concordat with Clement
VIII., the Venetian press would only be subject to State
control and not to the Roman tribunals.[2] The truth is that,
in regard both to the Holy Office and to the Index, Venice
was never strong enough to maintain the independence which
she boasted. By cunning use of the confessional and by
unscrupulous control of opinion, the Church succeeded in
doing there much the same as in any other Italian city.
Successive Popes made, indeed, a show of respecting the
liberties of the Republic. On material points, touching
revenue and State-administration, they felt it wise to concede
even more than complimentary privileges; and when Paul V.
encroached upon these privileges, the Venetians were ready
to resist him. Yet the quarrels between the Vatican and
San Marco were, after all, but family disputes. The Venetians
at the close of the sixteenth century proved themselves
no better friends to spiritual freedom than were the Grand
Dukes of Tuscany. Their political jealousies, commercial
anxieties, and feints of maintaining a power that was rapidly
decaying, denoted no partiality for the opponents of Rome—
unless, like Sarpi, these wore the livery of the State and
defended with the pen its secular prerogatives. Therefore,
when the Signory published Clement VIII.'s Index, when
copies of that Index were sown broadcast, while only an

[1] The document in question, prepared for the use of the Signoria,
exists in MS. in the Marcian Library, Misc. Eccl. et Civ. Class. VII.
Cod. MDCCLXI.
[2] This edict is dated August 24, 1596.

edition of sixty was granted to the Concordat, authors and publishers felt, and felt rightly, that their day had passed. The art of printing sank at once to less than a third of its productivity. The city where it had flourished so long, and where it had effected so much of enduring value for European culture, was gagged in scarcely a less degree than Rome. We have full right to insist upon these facts, and to draw from them a stringent corollary. If Venice allowed the trade in books, which had brought her so much profit and such honour in the past, to be paralysed by Clement's Index, what must have happened in other Italian towns? The blow which maimed Venetian literature, was mortal elsewhere; and the finest works of genius in the first half of the seventeenth century had to find their publishers in Paris.[1] But these reflections have led me to anticipate the proper development of the subject of this chapter.

In Italy at large the forces of the Inquisition were directed, not as in Spain against heretics in masses, but against the leaders of heretical opinion, and less against personalities than against ideas. Italy during the Renaissance had been the workshop of ideas for Europe. It was the business of the Counter-Reformation to check the industry of that *officina scientiarum*, to numb the nervous centres which had previously emitted thought of pregnant import for the modern world, and to prevent the reflux of ideas, elaborated by the northern races in fresh forms, upon the intelligence which had evolved them. To do so now was comparatively easy. It only needed to put the engine of the Index Librorum Prohibitorum into working order in concert with the Inquisition.

Throughout the Middle Ages it had been customary to burn heretical writings. The bishops, the universities, and the Dominican Inquisitors exercised this privilege; and by

[1] This will be apparent when I come to treat of Marino and Tassoni.

their means, in the age of manuscripts, the life of a book was soon extinguished. Whole libraries were sometimes sacrificed at one fell swoop, as in the case of the 6,000 volumes destroyed at Salamanca in 1490 by Torquemada, on a charge of sorcery.[1] After the invention of printing it became more difficult to carry on this warfare against literature, while the rapid diffusion of Protestant opinions through the press rendered the need for their extermination urgent. Sixtus IV. laid a basis for the Index by prohibiting the publication of any books which had not previously been licensed by ecclesiastical authority. Alexander VI. by a brief of 1501 confirmed this measure, and placed books under the censorship of the episcopacy and the Inquisition. Finally, the Lateran Council, in its tenth session, held under the auspices of Leo X., gave solemn ecumenical sanction to these regulations.

The censorship having been thus established, the next step was to form a list of books prohibited by the Inquisitors appointed for that purpose. The Sorbonne in Paris drew one up for their own use, and even presented a petition to Francis I. that publication through the press should be forbidden altogether.[2] A royal edict to this effect was actually promulgated in 1535. Charles V. commissioned the University of Louvain in 1539 to furnish a similar catalogue, proclaiming at the same time the penalty of death for all who read or owned the works of Luther in his realms.[3] The University printed their catalogue with Papal approval in 1549. These lists of the Sorbonne and Louvain formed the nucleus of the Apostolic Index, which, after the close of the Council of Trent, became binding upon Catholics. When the Inquisition had been established in Rome, Caraffa, who was then at its head, obtained the sanction of Paul III. for

---

[1] Llorente, vol. i. p. 281.
[2] Christie's *Etienne Dolet*, pp. 220-224.
[3] Llorente, vol. i. p. 463.

submitting all books, old or new, printed or in manuscript, to the supervision of the Holy Office. He also contrived to place booksellers, public and private libraries, colporteurs and officers of customs, under the same authority; so that from 1543 forward it was a penal offence to print, sell, own, convey or import any literature, of which the Inquisition had not first been informed, and for the diffusion or possession of which it had not given its permission. Giovanni della Casa, who was sent in 1546 to Venice with commission to prosecute P. Paolo Vergerio for heresy, drew up a list of about seventy prohibited volumes, which was printed in that city.[1] Other lists appeared, at Florence in 1552, and at Milan in 1554. Philip II. at last, in 1558, issued a royal edict commanding the publication of one catalogue which should form the standard for such Indices throughout his States.[2] These lists, revised, collated, and confirmed by Papal authority, were reprinted, in the form which ever afterwards obtained, at Rome by command of Paul IV. in 1559. The Tridentine Council ratified the regulations of the Inquisition and the Index concerning prohibited books, and referred the execution of them in detail to the Papacy. A congregation was appointed at Rome, which, though technically independent of the Holy Office, worked in concert with it. This Congregation of the Index brought the Tridentine decrees into harmony with the practice that had been developed by Caraffa as Inquisitor and Pope. Their list was published in 1564 with the authority of Pius IV. Finally, in 1595 the decrees embodying the statutes of the Church upon this topic were issued in print, together with a largely augmented catalogue of interdicted books. This document will form the basis of what I have to say with regard to the Catholic crusade against literature.

[1] In the year 1548. The MS. cited above (p. 150) mentions another Index of the Venetian Holy Office published in 1554.
[2] Sarpi, *Ist. del Conc. Trid.* vol. ii. p. 90.

Not without reason did Aonio Paleario call this engine of the Index 'a dagger drawn from the scabbard to assassinate letters' —*sica districta in omnes scriptores*.[1] Not without reason did Sarpi describe it as 'the finest secret which has ever been discovered for applying religion to the purpose of making men idiotic.'[2] Paul IV. designated in his Index Expurgatorius sixty-one printing firms by name, all of whose publications were without exception prohibited, adding a similar prohibition for the books edited by any printer who had published the writings of any heretic; so that in fine, as Sarpi says, 'there was not a book left to read.' Truly he might well exclaim in another passage that the Church was doing its best to extinguish sound learning altogether.[3]

In order to gain a clear conception of the warfare carried on by Rome against free literature, it will be well to consider first the rules for the Index of Prohibited Books, sketched out by the fathers delegated by the Tridentine Council, published by Pius IV., augmented by Sixtus V., and reduced to their final form by Clement VIII. in 1595.[4] Afterwards I shall proceed to explain the operation of the system, and to illustrate by details the injury inflicted upon learning and enlightenment

[1] In his *Oratio pro se ipso ad Senenses*. Printed by Gryphius at Lyons in 1552.

[2] *Ist. del Conc. Trid.* vol. ii. p. 91. The passage deserves to be transcribed. 'Sotto colore di fede e religione sono vietati con la medesima severità e dannati gli autori de' libri da' quali l' autorità del principe e magistrati temporali è difesa dalle usurpazioni ecclesiastiche; dove l' autorità de' Concilj e de' Vescovi è difesa dalle usurpazioni della Corte Romana; dove le ipocrisie o tirannidi con le quali sotto pretesto di religione il popolo è ingannato o violentato sono manifestate. In somma non fu mai trovato più bell' arcano per adoperare la religione a far gli uomini insensati.'

[3] *Discorso sopra l' Inq.* vol. iv. p. 54.

[4] These rules form the Preface to modern editions of the Index. The one I use is dated Naples, 1862. They are also printed in vol. iv. of Sarpi's works.

THE INDEX OF CLEMENT VIII. 155

The preambles to this document recite the circumstances under which the necessity for digesting an Index or Catalogue of Prohibited Books arose. These were the diffusion of heretical opinions at the epoch of the Lutheran schism, and their propagation through the press. The Council of Trent decreed that a list of writings 'heretical, or suspected of heretical pravity, or injurious to manners and piety,' should be drawn up. This charge they committed to prelates chosen from all nations, who, when the catalogue had been completed, referred it for sanction and approval to the Pope. He nominated a congregation of eminent ecclesiastics, by whose care the catalogue was perfected, and rules were framed, defining the use that should be made of it in future. It was issued officially, as I have already stated, in 1564, the fifth year of the pontificate of Pius IV. with warning to all universities and civil and ecclesiastical authorities that any person of what grade or condition soever, whether clerk or layman, who should read or possess one or more of the proscribed volumes, would be accounted *ipso jure* excommunicate, and liable to prosecution by the Inquisition on a charge of heresy.[1] Booksellers, printers, merchants, and custom-house officials received admonition that the threat of excommunication and prosecution concerned them specially.

The first rules deal with the acknowledged writings of Protestant heresiarchs. Those of Luther, Zwingli, and Calvin, whether in their original languages or translated, are condemned absolutely and without exception. Next follow regulations for securing the monopoly of the Vulgate, considered as the sole authorised version of the Holy Scriptures. Translations of portions of the Bible made by learned men in Latin may be used by scholars with permission of a bishop, provided it be understood that they are never appealed to as the inspired text. Translations into

[1] Paulus Manutius Aldus printed this Index at Venice in 1564.

any vernacular idiom are strictly excluded from public use and circulation, but may, under exceptional circumstances, be allowed to students who have received license from a bishop or Inquisitor at the recommendation of their parish priest or confessor. Compilations made by heretics, in the form of dictionaries, concordances, &c., are to be prohibited until they have been purged and revised by censors of the press. The same regulation extends to polemical and controversial works touching on matters of doctrine in dispute between Catholics and Protestants. Next follow regulations concerning books containing lascivious or obscene matter, which are to be rigidly suppressed. Exception is made in favour of the classics, on account of their style; with the proviso that they are on no account to be given to boys to read. Treatises dealing professedly with occult arts, magic, sorcery, predictions of future events, incantation of spirits, and so forth, are to be proscribed; due reservation being made in favour of scientific observations touching navigation, agriculture, and the healing art, in which prognostics may be useful to mankind. Having thus broadly defined the literature which has to be suppressed or subjected to supervision, rules are laid down for the exercise of censure. Books, whereof the general tendency is good, but which contain passages savouring of heresy, superstition or divination, shall be reserved for the consideration of Catholic theologians appointed by the Inquisition; and this shall hold good also of prefaces, summaries, or annotations. All writings printed in Rome must be submitted to the judgment of the Vicar of the Pope, the Master of the Sacred Palace, or a person nominated by the Pontiff. In other cities the bishop, or his delegate, and the Inquisitor of the district shall be responsible for examining printed or manuscript works previous to publication; and without their license it shall be illegal to circulate them. Inquisitorial visits shall from time to time be made, under the authority of the bishop and the Holy Office, in book-shops or printing-houses, for the removal and destruction of prohibited works. Colporteurs of books across the frontiers, heirs and executors who have become depositaries of books, collectors of private libraries, as well as editors and booksellers, shall be liable to the same jurisdiction, bound to declare their property by catalogue, and to show license for the use, transmission, sale, or possession of the same.

With regard to the correction of books, it is provided that this duty shall fall conjointly on bishops and Inquisitors, who must appoint three men distinguished for learning and piety to examine the text and make the necessary changes in it. Upon the report of these censors, the bishops and Inquisitors shall give license of publication, provided they are satisfied that the work of emendation has been duly performed. The censor must submit not only the body of a book to scrupulous analysis; but he must also investigate the notes, summaries, marginal remarks, indexes, prefaces, and dedicatory epistles, lest haply pestilent opinions lurk there in ambush. He must keep a sharp look-out for heretical propositions, and arguments savouring of heresy; insinuations against the established order of the sacraments, ceremonies, usages and ritual of the Roman Church; new turns of phrase insidiously employed by heretics, with dubious and ambiguous expressions that may mislead the unwary; plausible citations of Scripture, or passages of holy writ extracted from heretical translations; quotations from the authorised text, which have been adduced in an unorthodox sense; epithets in honour of heretics, and anything that may redound to the praise of such persons; opinions savouring of sorcery and superstition; theories that involve the subjection of the human will to fate, fortune, and fallacious portents, or that imply paganism; aspersions upon ecclesiastics and princes; impugnments of the liberties, immunities, and jurisdiction of the Church; political doctrines in favour of antique virtues, despotic government, and the so-called Reason of State, which are in opposition to the evangelical and Christian law; satires on ecclesiastical rites, religious orders, and the state, dignity, and persons of the clergy; ribaldries or stories offensive and prejudicial to the fame and estimation of one's neighbours, together with lubricities, lascivious remarks, lewd pictures, and capital letters adorned with obscene images. All such peccant passages are to be expunged, obliterated, removed or radically altered, before the license for publication be accorded by the ordinary.

No book shall be printed without the author's name in full, together with his nationality, upon the title-page. If there be sufficient reason for giving an anonymous work to the world, the censor's name shall stand for that of the author. Compilations of words, sentences, excerpts, &c., shall pass under the name of the compiler. Publishers and booksellers are to take care that the printed work agrees with the MS. copy as licensed, and to see that all rules with regard to the author's name and his authority to publish have been observed. They are, moreover, to take an oath before the Master of the Sacred Palace in Rome, or before the bishop and Inquisitor in other places, that they will scrupulously follow the regulations of the Index. The bishops and Inquisitors are held responsible for selecting as censors men of approved piety and learning, whose good faith and integrity they shall guarantee, and who shall be such as will obey no promptings of private hatred or of favour, but will do all for the glory of God and the advantage of the faithful. The approbation of such censors, together with the license of the bishop and Inquisitor, shall be printed at the opening of every published book. Finally, if any work composed by a condemned author shall be licensed after due purgation and castration, it shall bear his name upon the title-page, together with the note of condemnation, to the end that, though the book itself be accepted, the author be understood to be rejected. Thus, for example, the title shall run as follows: 'The Library, by Conrad Gesner, a writer condemned for his opinions, which work was formerly published and proscribed, but is now expurgated and licensed by superior authority.'

The Holy Office was made virtually responsible for the censorship of books. But, as I have already stated, there existed a Congregation of prelates in Rome to whom the final verdict upon this matter was reserved. If an author in some provincial town composed a volume, he was bound in the first instance to submit the MS. to the censor appointed by the bishop and Inquisitor of his district. This man took time to weigh the general matter of the work before him, to scrutinise its propositions, verify quotations, and deliberate upon its tendency. When the license of the ordinary had been obtained, it was referred to the Roman Congregation of the Index, who might withhold or grant their sanction. So complicated was the machinery, and so vast the pressure upon the officials who were held responsible for the expurgation of every book imprinted or reprinted in all the Catholic presses, that even writers of conspicuous orthodoxy had to suffer grievous delays. An archbishop writes to Cardinal Sirleto about a book which had been examined thrice, at Rome, at Venice and again at Rome, and had obtained the Pope's approval, and yet the licence for reprinting it is never issued.[1] The censors were not paid; and in addition to being overworked and overburdened with responsibility, they were rarely men of adequate learning. In a letter from Bartolommeo de Valverde, chaplain to Philip II., under date 1584, we read plain-spoken complaints against these subordinates.[2] 'Unacquainted with literature, they discharge the function of

[1] Dejob, *De l'Influence*, &c. p. 60.   [2] *Id. op. cit.* p. 76.

condemning books they cannot understand. Without knowledge of Greek or Hebrew, and animated by a prejudiced hostility against authors, they take the easy course of proscribing what they feel incapable of judging. In this way the works of many sainted writers and the useful commentaries made by Jews have been suppressed.' A memorial to Sirleto, presented by Cardinal Gabriele Paleotti, points out the negligence of the Index-makers and their superficial discharge of onerous duties, praying that in future men of learning and honesty should be employed, and that they should receive payment for their labours.[1] These are the expostulations addressed by faithful Catholics, engaged in literary work demanded by the Vatican, to a Cardinal who was the soul and mover of the Congregation. They do not question the salutary nature of the Index, but only call attention to the incapacity and ignorance of its unpaid officials. Meanwhile, it was no easy matter to appoint responsible and learned scholars to the post. The inefficient censors proceeded with their work of destruction and suppression. A commentator on a Greek Father or the Psalms was corrected by an ignoramus who knew neither Greek nor Hebrew, anxious to discover petty collisions with the Vulgate, and eager to create annoyances for the author. Latino Latini, one of the students employed by the Vatican, refused his name to an edition of Cyprian which he had carefully prepared with far more than the average erudition, because it had been changed throughout by the substitution of bad readings for good, in defiance of MS. authority, with a view of preserving a literal agreement with the Vulgate.[2] Sigonius, another of the Vatican students, was instructed to prepare certain text-books by Cardinal Paleotti. These were an Ecclesiastical History, a treatise on the Hebrew Commonwealth, and an edition of Sulpicius Severus. The MSS. were

[1] Dejob, *op. cit* p. 78.   [2] *Id. op. cit.* p. 74.

returned to him, accused of unsound doctrine, and scrawled over with such remarks as 'false,' 'absurd.'[1] In addition to the intolerable delays of the Censure, and the arrogant inadequacy of its officials, learned men suffered from the pettiest persecution at the hands of informers. The Inquisitors themselves were often spies and persons of base origin. 'The Roman Court,' says Sarpi, 'being anxious that the office of the Inquisition should not suffer through negligence in its ministers, has confided these affairs to individuals without occupation, and whose mean estate renders them proud of their official position.'[2] It was not to be expected that such people should discharge their duties with intelligence and scrupulous equity. Pius V., himself an incorruptible Inquisitor, had to condemn one of his lieutenants for corruption or extortion of money by menaces.[3] There was still another source of peril and annoyance to which scholars were exposed. Their comrades, engaged in similar pursuits, not unfrequently wreaked private spite by denouncing them to the Congregation.[4] Van Linden indicated heresies in Osorius, Giovius, Albertus Pighius. The Jesuit Francesco Torres accused Maës, and threatened Latini. Sigonius obtained a licence for his 'History of Bologna,' but could not print it, owing to the delation of secret enemies. Baronius, when he had finished his 'Martyrology,' found that a cabal had raised insuperable obstacles in the way of its publication. I have been careful to select only examples of notoriously Catholic authors, men who were in the pay and under the special protection of the Vatican. How it fared with less-favoured scholars, may be left to the imagination. We are not astonished to find a man like Latini writing thus from Rome to

[1] Dejob, *op. cit.* p. 54.
[2] 'Discorso dell' Origine, &c. dell' Inquisizione.' *Opp* vol. iv. p. 34.
[3] Mutinelli, *Storia Arcana*, vol. i. p. 277
[4] Dejob, *op. cit.* pp. 53-57.

Maës during the pontificate of Paul IV.:[1] 'Have you not heard of the peril which threatens the very existence of books? What are you dreaming of, when now that almost every published book is interdicted, you still think of making new ones? Here, as I imagine, there is no one who for many years to come will dare to write except on business or to distant friends. An Index has been issued of the works which none may possess under pain of excommunication; and the number of them is so great that very few indeed are left to us, especially of those which have been published in Germany. This shipwreck, this holocaust of books will stop the production of them in your country also, if I do not err, and will teach editors to be upon their guard. As you love me and yourself, sit and look at your bookcases without opening their doors, and beware lest the very cracks let emanations come to you from those forbidden fruits of learning.' This letter was written in 1559, when Paul proscribed sixty-one presses, and prohibited the perusal of any work that issued from them. He afterwards withdrew this interdict. But the Index did not stop its work of extirpation.

Another embarrassment which afflicted men of learning, was the danger of possessing books by heretics and the difficulty of procuring them.[2] Yet they could not carry on their Biblical studies without reference to such authors as, for example, Erasmus or Reuchlin. The universities loudly demanded that books of sound erudition by heretics should at

[1] Dejob, *op. cit.* p. 75.
[2] Sarpi's Letters abound in useful information on this topic. Writing to French correspondents, he complains weekly of the impossibility even in Venice of obtaining books. See, for instance, *Lettere*, vol. i. pp. 286, 287, 360, vol. ii. p. 13. In one passage he says that the importation of books into Italy is impeded at Innsbruck, Trento, and throughout the Tyrolese frontiers (vol. i. p. 74). In another he warns his friends not to send them concealed in merchandise, since they will fall under so many eyes in the custom-houses and lazzaretti (vol. i. p. 303).

least be expurgated and republished. Yet the process of disfiguring their arguments, effacing the names of authors, expunging the praises of heretics, altering quotations and retouching them all over, involved so much labour that the demand was never satisfied. The strict search instituted at the frontiers stopped the importation of books,[1] and carriers refused to transmit them. In their dread of the Inquisition, these folk found it safer to abstain from book traffic altogether. Public libraries were exposed to intermittent raids, nor were private collections safe from such inspection. The not uncommon occurrence of old books in which precious and interesting passages have been erased with printer's ink, or pasted over with slips of opaque paper, testifies to the frequency of these inquisitorial visitations.[2] Any casual acquaintance, on leaving a man's house, might denounce him as the possessor of a proscribed volume; and everybody who owned a bookcase was bound to furnish the Inquisitors with a copy of his catalogue. Bookstalls lay open to the malevolence of informers. We possess an insolent letter of Antonio Possevino to Cardinal Sirleto, telling him that he had noticed a forbidden book by Filiarchi on a binder's counter, and bidding him to do his duty by suppressing it.[3] When this Cardinal's library was exposed for sale after his death, the curious observed that it contained 1,872 MSS. in Greek and Latin, 580 volumes of printed Greek books, and 8,939 volumes of Latin, among which 89 were on the Index.

[1] It was usual at this epoch to send Protestant publications from beyond the Alps in bales of cotton or other goods. This appears from the Lucchese proclamations against heresy published in *Arch. Stor.* vol. x.

[2] I may mention that having occasion to consult Savonarola's works in the Public Library of Perugia, which has a fairly good collection of them, I found them useless for purposes of study by reason of these erasures and Burke-plasters.

[3] Dejob, *op. cit.* p. 43.

But charity suggested that the Cardinal had retained these last for censure.

During the period of the Counter-Reformation it was the cherished object of the Popes to restore ecclesiastical and theological learning. They gathered men of erudition round them in the Vatican, and established a press for the purpose of printing the Fathers and diffusing Catholic literature. But they were met in the pursuance of this project by very serious difficulties. Their own policy tended to stifle knowledge and suppress criticism. The scholars whom they chose as champions of the faith worked with tied hands. Baronio knew no Greek; Latini knew hardly any; Bellarmino is thought to have known but little. And yet these were the apostles of Catholic enlightenment, the defenders of the infallible Church against students of the calibre of Erasmus, Casaubon, Sarpi! An insuperable obstacle to sacred studies of a permanently useful kind was the Tridentine decree which had declared the Vulgate inviolable. No codex of age or authority which displayed a reading at variance with the inspired Latin version might be cited. Sirleto, custodian of the Vatican Library, refused lections from its MSS. to learned men, on the ground that they might seem to impugn the Vulgate.[1] For the same reason, the critical labours of all previous students, from Valla to Erasmus, on the text of the Bible were suppressed, and the best MSS. of the Fathers were ruthlessly garbled, in order to bring their quotations into accordance with Jerome's translation. Galesini takes credit to himself in a letter to Sirleto for having withheld a clearly right reading in his edition of the Psalms, because it explained a mistake in the Vulgate.[2] We have seen how Latini's 'Cyprian' suffered from the censure; and there is a lamentable history of the Vatican edition of Ambrose, which was so mutilated that the Index had to protect it from confrontation

[1] Dejob, *op. cit.* p. 50. Also his *Muret*, pp. 223-227.
[2] Dejob, *De l'Influence*, p. 49.

with the original codices.[1] This dishonest dealing not only discouraged students and paralysed the energy of critical investigation, but it also involved the closing of public libraries to scholars. The Vatican could not afford to let the light of science in upon its workshop of forgeries and sophistications. A voice of reasonable remonstrance was sometimes raised by even the most incorruptible children of the Church. Thus Bellarmino writes to Cardinal Sirleto, suggesting a doubt whether it is obligatory to adhere to the letter of the Tridentine decree upon the Vulgate.[2] Is it rational, he asks, to maintain that every sentence in the Latin text is impeccable? Must we reject those readings in the Hebrew and the Greek which elucidate the meaning of the Scriptures, in cases where Jerome has followed a different and possibly a corrupt authority? Would it not be more sensible to regard the Vulgate as the sole authorised version for use in universities, pulpits, and divine service, while admitting that it is not an infallible rendering of the inspired original? He also touches, in a similar strain of scholar-like liberality, upon the Septuagint, pointing out that this version cannot have been the work of seventy men in unity, since the translator of Job seems to have been better acquainted with Greek than Hebrew, while the reverse is true of the translator of Solomon. Such remonstrances were not, however, destined to make themselves effectively heard. Instead of relaxing its severity after the pontificate of Pius IV., the Congregation of the Index grew, as we have seen, more rigid, until, in the rules digested by Clement VIII., it enforced the strictest letter of the law regarding the Vulgate, and ratified all the hypocrisies and subterfuges which that implied.

Under the conditions which I have attempted to describe,

[1] *Id. op. cit.* pp. 96–98.
[2] This very interesting and valuable letter is printed by Dejob in the work I have so often cited, p. 391.

it was impossible that Italy should hold her place among the nations which encouraged liberal studies. Rome had one object in view—to gag the revolutionary free voice of the Renaissance, to protect conservative principles, to establish her own supremacy, and to secure the triumph of the Counter-Reformation. In pursuance of this policy, she had to react against the learning and the culture of the classical revival; and her views were seconded not only by the overwhelming political force of Spain in the Peninsula, but also by the petty princes who felt that their existence was imperilled.

Independence of judgment was rigorously proscribed in all academies and seats of erudition. New methods of education and new text-books were forbidden. Professors found themselves hampered in their choice of antique authors. Only those classics which were sanctioned by the Congregation of the Index could be used in lecture rooms. On the one hand, the great republican advocates of independence had incurred suspicion. On the other hand, the poets were prohibited as redolent of paganism. To mingle philosophy with rhetoric was counted a crime. Thomas Aquinas had set up Pillars of Hercules beyond which the reason might not seek to travel. Roman law had to be treated from the orthodox scholastic standpoint. Woe to the audacious jurist who made the Pandects serve for disquisitions on the rights of men and nations! Scholars like Sigonius found themselves tied down in their class-rooms to a wearyful routine of Cicero and Aristotle. Aonio Paleario complained that a professor was no better than a donkey working in a mill; nothing remained for him but to dole out commonplaces, avoiding every point of contact between the authors he interpreted and the burning questions of modern life. Muretus, who brought with him to Italy from France a ruined moral reputation with a fervid zeal for literature, who sold his soul to praise the Massacre of

S. Bartholomew and purge by fulsome panegyrics of great public crimes the taint of heresy that clung around him, found his efforts to extend the course of studies in Rome thwarted.[1] He was forbidden to lecture on Plato, forbidden to touch jurisprudence, forbidden to consult a copy of Eunapius in the Vatican Library. It cost him days and weeks of pleading to obtain permission to read Tacitus to his classes. Greek, the literature of high thoughts, noble enthusiasms, and virile sciences, was viewed with suspicion. As the monks of the Middle Ages had written on the margins of their MSS.: *Græca sunt, ergo non legenda*, so these new obscurantists exclaimed: *Græca sunt, periculosa sunt, ergo non legenda*. 'I am forced,' he cries in this extremity, 'to occupy myself with Latin and to abstain entirely from Greek.' And yet he knew that 'if the men of our age advance one step further in their neglect of Greek, doom and destruction are impending over all sound arts and sciences.' 'It is my misery,' he groans, 'to behold the gradual extinction and total decay of Greek letters, in whose train I see the whole body of refined learning on the point of vanishing away.'[2]

A vigorous passage from one of Sarpi's letters directly bearing on these points may here be cited (vol. i. p. 170): 'The revival of polite learning undermined the foundations of Papal monarchy. Nor was this to be wondered at. This monarchy began and grew in barbarism; the cessation of barbarism naturally curtailed and threatened it with extinction. This we already see in Germany and France; but Spain and Italy are still subject to barbarism. Legal studies sink daily from bad to worse. The Roman Curia opposes every branch of learning which savours of polite literature, while it defends its barbarism with tooth and nail. How can it do otherwise? Abolish those books on Papal

[1] See Dejob's Life of Muret, pp. 231, 238, 274, 320.
[2] *Id. op. cit.* pp. 262, 481.

Supremacy, and where shall they find that the Pope is another God, that he is almighty, that all rights and laws are closed within the cabinet of his breast, that he can shut up folk in hell, in a word that he has power to square the circle? Destroy that false jurisprudence, and this tyranny will vanish; but the two are reciprocally supporting, and we shall not do away with the former until the latter falls, which will only happen at God's good pleasure.'

The jealousy with which liberal studies were regarded by the Church bred a contempt for them in the minds of students. Benci, a professor of humane letters at Rome, says that his pupils walked about the class-room during his lectures. With grim humour he adds that he does not object to their sleeping, so long as they abstain from snoring.[1] But it is impossible, he goes on to complain, 'that I should any longer look upon the place in which I do my daily work as an academy of learning; I go to it rather as to a mill in which I must grind out my tale of worthless grain.' Muretus, when he had laboured twenty years in the chair of rhetoric at Rome, begged for dismissal. His memorial to the authorities presents a lamentable picture of the insubordination and indifference from which he had suffered.[2] 'I have borne immeasurable indignities from the continued insolence of these students, who interrupt me with cries, whistlings, hisses, insults, and such opprobrious remarks that I sometimes scarcely know whether I am standing on my head or heels.' 'They come to the lecture-room armed with poignards, and when I reprove them for their indecencies, they threaten over and over again to cut my face open if I do not hold my tongue.' The walls, he adds, are scrawled over with obscene emblems and disgusting epigrams,

---

[1] Dejob, *Marc Antoine Muret*, p. 349.
[2] The original is printed by Dejob, *Marc Antoine Muret*, pp. 487-489.

so that this haunt of learning presents the aspect of the lowest brothel; and the professor's chair has become a more intolerable seat than the pillory, owing to the missiles flung at him and the ribaldry with which he is assailed. The manners and conversation of the students must have been disgusting beyond measure, to judge by a letter of complaint from a father detailing the contamination to which his son was exposed in the Roman class-rooms, and the immunity with which the lewdest songs were publicly recited there.[1] But the total degradation of learning at this epoch in Rome is best described in one paragraph of Vittorio de' Rossi, setting forth the neglect endured by Aldo Manuzio, the younger. This scion of an illustrious family succeeded to the professorship of Muretus in 1588. 'Then,' says Rossi, ' might one marvel at, or rather mourn over, the abject and down-trodden state of the liberal arts. Then might one perceive with tears how those treasures of humane letters, which our fathers exalted to the heavens, were degraded in the estimation of youth. In the good old days men crossed the seas, undertook long journeys, traversed the cities of Greece and Asia, in order to obtain the palm of eloquence and salute the masters of languages and learning, at whose feet they sat entranced by noble words. But now these fellows poured scorn upon an unrivalled teacher of both

[1] The original letter, printed by Dejob, *op. cit.* p. 491, is signed by Giustiniano Finetti, who seems to have been a professor of medicine in the Roman University. His son, a youth of sixteen, complained that the students had demanded and obtained leave to recite a certain 'lettione che era carnavalesca d' ano et de priapo,' adding that they were in the habit of holding debates upon the thesis that 'res sod^{om} erant praeferendae veneri naturali, et reprobabant rem veneream cum feminis ac laudabant masturbationem.' The dialogue which the students obtained leave publicly to recite was probably similar to one that might still be heard some years ago in spring upon the quays of Naples, and which appeared to have descended from immemorial antiquity.

Greek and Latin eloquence, whose services were theirs for the asking, theirs without the fatigue of travel, without expense, without exertion. Though he freely offered them his abundance of erudition in both learned literatures, they shut their ears against him. At the hours when his lecture-room should have been thronged with multitudes of eager pupils you might see him, abandoned by the crowd, pacing the pavement before the door of the academy with one, or may be two, for his companions.'[1]

To accuse the Church solely and wholly for this decay of humanistic learning in Italy would be uncritical and unjust. We must remember that after a period of feverish energy there comes a time of languor in all epochs of great intellectual excitement. Nor was it to be expected that the enthusiasm of the fifteenth century for classical studies should have been prolonged into the second half of the sixteenth century. But we are justified in blaming the ecclesiastical and civil authorities of the Counter-Reformation for their determined opposition to the new direction which that old enthusiasm for the classics was now manifesting. They strove to force the stream of learning backward into scholastic and linguistic channels, when it was already ploughing for itself a fresh course in the fields of philosophical and scientific discovery. They made study odious, because they attempted to restrain it to the outworn husks of pedantry and rhetoric These, they thought, were innocuous. But what the intellectual appetite then craved, the pabulum that it required to satisfy its yearning, was rigidly denied it. Speculations concerning the nature of man and of the world, metaphysical explorations into the regions of dimly apprehended mysteries, physics, political problems, religious questions touching the great matters in

[1] The Latin text is printed in Renouard's *Imprimerie des Aldes*, p. 473.

dispute through Europe, all the storm and stress of modern life, the ferment of the modern mind and will and conscience, were excluded from the schools, because they were antagonistic to the Counter-Reformation. Italy was starved and demoralised in order to avert a revolution; and learning was asphyxiated by confinement to a narrow chamber filled with vitiated and exhausted air.[1]

Similar deductions may be drawn from the life of Paolo Manuzio in Rome. He left Venice in 1561 at the invitation of Pius IV., who proposed to establish a press 'for the publication of books printed with the finest type and the utmost accuracy, and more especially of works bearing upon sacred and ecclesiastical literature.'[2] Paolo's engagement was for twelve years; his appointments were fixed at 300 ducats for travelling expenses, 500 ducats of yearly salary, a press maintained at the Pontifical expense, and a pension secured upon his son's life. The scheme was a noble one. Paolo was to print all the Greek and Latin Fathers, and to furnish the Catholic world with an arsenal of orthodox learning. Yet, during his residence in Rome, no Greek book issued from his press.[3] Of the Latin Fathers he gave the Epistles of Jerome, Salvian, and Cyprian to the world. For the rest, he published the decrees of the Tridentine Council ten times, the Tridentine Catechism eight times, the 'Breviarium Romanum' four times, and spent the greater part of his leisure in editing minor translations, commentaries, and polemical or educational treatises. The result was miserable, and the man was ruined.

[1] As Sarpi says: 'Of a truth the extraordinary rigour with which books are hunted out for extirpation, shows how vigorous is the light of that lantern which they have resolved to extinguish.' *Lettere*, vol. i. p. 328.
[2] See Renouard, *op. cit.* pp. 442-459, for Paulus Manutius's life at Rome.
[3] *Op. cit.* pp. 184-216.

It remains to notice the action of the Index with regard to secular books in the modern languages. I will first repeat a significant passage in its statutes touching upon political philosophy and the so-called *Ratio Status* : 'Item, let all propositions, drawn from the digests, manners, and examples of the Gentiles, which foster a tyrannical polity and encourage what they falsely call the reason of state, in opposition to the law of Christ and of the Gospel, be expunged.' This, says Sarpi in his 'Discourse on Printing,' is aimed in general against any doctrine which impugns ecclesiastical jurisdiction over the civil sphere of princes and magistrates and the economy of the family.[1] Theories drawn from whatever source to combat Papal and ecclesiastical encroachments and to defend the rights of the sovereign in his monarchy or of the father in his household, are denominated and denounced as *Ratio Status*. The impugner of Papal absolutism in civil as well as ecclesiastical affairs is accounted *ipso facto* a heretic.[2] It would appear at first sight as though the clause in question had been specially framed to condemn Machiavelli and his school. The works of Machiavelli were placed upon the Index in 1559, and a certain Cesare of Pisa who had them in his library was put to the torture on this account in 1610. It was afterwards proposed to correct and edit them without his name; but his heirs very properly refused to sanction this proceeding, knowing that he would be made to utter the very reverse of what he meant in all that touched upon the Roman Church. This paragraph in the statutes of the Index had, however, a further and far more ambitious purpose than

---

[1] Sarpi's Works, vol. iv. p. 4.
[2] Sarpi, *Discorso*, vol. iv. p. 25, on Bellarmino's doctrine. Sarpi's *Letters*, vol. i. pp. 138, 243. Sarpi says that he and Gillot had both had their portraits painted in a picture of Hell and shown to the common folk as foredoomed to eternal fire, because they opposed doctrines of Papal omnipotence. *Ibid.* p. 151.

the suppression of Machiavelli, Guicciardini, and Sarpi. By assuming to condemn all political writings of which she disapproved, and by forbidding the secular authorities to proscribe any works which had received her sanction, the Church obtained a monopoly of popular instruction in theories of government. She interdicted every treatise that exposed her own ambitious interference in civil affairs or which maintained the rights of temporal rulers.[1] She protected and propagated the works of her servile ministers, who proclaimed that the ecclesiastical was superior in all points to the civil power; that nations owed their first allegiance to the Pope, who was divinely appointed to rule over them, and their second only to the Prince, who was a delegate from their own body; and that tyrannicide itself was justifiable when employed against a contumacious or heretical sovereign. Such were the theories of the Jesuits—of Allen and Parsons in England, Bellarmino in Italy, Suarez and Mariana in Spain, Boucher in France. In his critique of this monstrous unfairness Sarpi says: 'There are not wanting men in Italy, pious and of sound learning, who hold the truth upon such topics; but these can neither write nor send their writings to the press.'[2] The best years and the best energies of

---

[1] On this point, again, Sarpi's *Letters* furnish valuable details. He frequently remarks that a general order had been issued by the Congregation of the Index to suppress all books against the writings of Baronius, who was treated as a saint (vol. i. pp. 3, 147, ii. p. 35). He relates how the Jesuits had procured the destruction of a book written to uphold aristocracy in states, without touching upon ecclesiastical questions, as being unfavourable to their theories of absolution (vol. i. p. 122). He tells the story of a confessor who refused the sacraments to a nobleman, because he owned a treatise written by Quirino in defence of the Venetian prerogatives (vol. i. p. 113). He refers to the suppression of James I.'s *Apologia* and De Thou's *Histories* (vol. i. pp. 286, 287, 383).

[2] In the Treatise on the Inquisition, *Opere*, vol. iv. p. 58. Sarpi, in a passage of his *Letters* (vol. ii. p. 163), points out why the secular

Sarpi's life were spent, as is well known, in combating the arrogance of Rome and in founding the relations of State to Church upon a basis of sound common sense and equity. More than once he narrowly escaped martyrdom as the reward of his temerity; and when the poignard of an assassin struck him, his legend relates that he uttered the celebrated epigram: *Agnosco stilum Curiæ Romanæ.*

Sarpi protested, not without good reason, that Rome was doing her best to extinguish sound learning in Italy. But how did she deal with that rank growth of licentious literature which had sprung up during the Renaissance period? This is the question which should next engage us. We have seen that the Council of Trent provided amply for the extirpation of lewd and obscene publications. Accordingly, as though to satisfy the sense of decency, some of the most flagrantly immoral books, including the 'Decameron,' the 'Priapeia,' the collected works of Aretino, and certain medieval romances, were placed upon the Index. Berni was proscribed in 1559; but the interdict lasted only a short time, probably because it was discovered that his poems, though licentious, were free from the heresies which Pier Paolo Vergerio had sought to fix upon him. Meanwhile no notice was taken of the 'Orlando Furioso' and a multitude of novelists, of Beccadelli's and Pontano's verses, of Molza and Firenzuola, of the whole mass of mundane writers in short who had done so much to reveal the corruption of Italian manners. It seemed as though the Church cared less to ban obscenity than to burke those authors who had spoken freely of her vices. When we come to examine the expurgated editions of notorious authors, we shall see that this was literally the case. A castrated version of Bandello, revised by Ascanio Centorio degli Ortensi, was pub-

authorities were ill fitted to retaliate in kind upon these Papal proscriptions.

lished in 1560.¹ It omitted the dedications and preambles, suppressed some disquisitions which palliated vicious conduct, expunged the novels that brought monks or priests into ridicule, but left the impurities of the rest untouched. A reformed version of Folengo's 'Baldus' appeared in 1561. The satires on religious orders had been erased. Zambellus was cuckolded by a layman instead of a priest. Otherwise the filth of the original received no cleansing treatment. When Cosimo de' Medici requested that a revised edition of the 'Decameron' might be licensed, Pius V. entrusted the affair to Thomas Manrique, Master of the Sacred Palace. It was published by the Giunti in 1573 under the auspices of Gregory XIII., with the approval of the Holy Office and the Florentine Inquisition, fortified by privileges from Spanish and French kings, dukes of Tuscany, Ferrara, and so forth. The changes which Boccaccio's masterpiece had undergone were these; passages savouring of doubtful dogma, sarcasms on monks and clergy, the names of saints, allusions to the devil and hell, had disappeared. Ecclesiastical sinners were transformed into students and professors, nuns and abbesses into citizens' wives. Immorality in short was secularised. But the book still offered the same allurements to a prurient mind. Sixtus V. expressed his disapproval of this recension, and new editions were licensed in 1582 and 1588 under the revision of Lionardo Salviati and Luigi Groto. Both preserved the obscenities of the 'Decameron,' while they displayed more rigour with regard to satires on ecclesiastical corruption. It may be added, in justice to the Roman Church, that the 'Decameron' stands still upon the Index with the annotation *donec expurgetur*.² Therefore we must presume that the work of purification is not yet accomplished, though the Jesuits have used parts of it as a text-book in their

[1] See Dejob, *De l'Influence*, &c. chapter iii.
[2] *Index*, Naples, Pelella, 1862, p. 87.

schools, while Panigarola quoted it in his lectures on sacred eloquence.

It would weary the reader to enlarge upon this process of stupid or hypocritical purgation, whereby the writings of men like Doni and Straparola were stripped of their reflections on the clergy, while their indecencies remained untouched; or to show how Ariosto's Comedies were sanctioned, when his Satires, owing to their free speech upon the Papal Court, received the stigma.[1] But I may refer to the grotesque attempts which were made in this age to cast the mantle of spirituality over profane literature. Thus Hieronimo Malipieri rewrote the 'Canzoniere' of Petrarch, giving it a pious turn throughout; and the 'Orlando Furioso' was converted by several hands into a religious allegory.[2]

The action of Rome under the influence of the Counter-Reformation was clearly guided by two objects: to preserve Catholic dogma in its integrity, and to maintain the supremacy of the Church. She was eager to extinguish learning and to paralyse intellectual energy. But she showed no unwillingness to tolerate those pleasant vices which enervate a nation. Compared with unsound doctrine and audacious speculation, immorality appeared in her eyes a venial weakness. It was true that she made serious efforts to reform the manners of her ministers, and was fully alive to the necessity of enforcing decency and decorum. Yet a radical purification of society seemed of less importance to her than the conservation of Catholic orthodoxy and the inculcation of obedience to ecclesiastical authority. When we analyse the

[1] This treatment of Ariosto is typical. Men of not over-scrupulous nicety may question whether his Comedies are altogether wholesome reading. But not even a Puritan could find fault with his Satires on the score of their morality. Yet Rome sanctioned the Comedies and forbade the Satires.

[2] Curious details on this topic are supplied by Dejob, *op. cit.* pp. 179-181, and p. 184.

Jesuits' system of education, and their method of conducting the care of souls, we shall see to what extent the deeply seated hypocrisy of the Counter-Reformation had penetrated the most vital parts of the Catholic system. It will suffice, at the close of this chapter, to touch upon one other repressive measure adopted by the Church in its panic. Magistrates received strict injunctions to impede the journeys of Italian subjects into foreign countries where heresies were known to be rife, or where the rites of the Roman Church were not regularly administered.[1] In 1595 Clement VIII. reduced these admonitions to Pontifical law in a Bull, whereby he forbade Italians to travel without permission from the Holy Office, or to reside abroad without annually remitting a certificate of confession and communion to the Inquisitors. To ensure obedience to this statute would have been impossible without the co-operation of the Jesuits. They were, however, diffused throughout the nations of North, East, South, and West. When an Italian arrived, the Jesuit Fathers paid him a visit, and unless they received satisfactory answers with regard to his licence of travel and his willingness to accept their spiritual direction, these serfs of Rome sent a delation to the central Holy Office, upon the ground of which the Inquisitors of his province instituted an action against him in his absence. Merchants, who neglected these rules, found themselves exposed to serious impediments in their trading operations and to the peril of prosecution involving confiscation of property at home. Sarpi, who composed a vigorous critique of this abuse, points out what

[1] Any correspondence with heretics was accounted sufficient to implicate an Italian in the charge of heresy. Sarpi's *Letters* are full of matter on this point. He always used cypher, which he frequently changed, addressed his letters under feigned names, and finally resolved on writing in his own hand to no heretic. See *Lettere*, vol. ii. pp. 2, 151, 242, 248, 437. See also what Dejob relates about the timidity of Muretus, *Muret*, pp. 229 231.

injury was done to commerce by the system.[1] We may still further censure it as an intolerable interference with the liberty of the individual; as an odious exercise of spiritual tyranny on the part of an ambitious ecclesiastical power which aimed at nothing less than universal domination.

[1] 'Treatise on the Inquisition,' *Opere*, vol. iv. p. 45.

CHAPTER IV

THE COMPANY OF JESUS

Vast Importance of the Jesuits in the Counter-Reformation—Ignatius Loyola—His Youth—Retreat at Manresa—Journey to Jerusalem—Studies in Spain and Paris—First Formation of his Order at Sainte Barbe—Sojourn at Venice—Settlement at Rome—Papal Recognition of the Order—Its Military Character—Absolutism of the General—Devotion to the Roman Church—Choice of Members—Practical and Positive Aims of the Founder—Exclusion of the Ascetic, Acceptance of the Worldly Spirit—Review of the Order's Rapid Extension over Europe—Loyola's Dealings with his Chief Lieutenants—Propaganda—The Virtue of Obedience—The 'Exercitia Spiritualia'—Materialistic Imagination—Intensity and Superficiality of Religious Training—The Status of the Novice—Temporal Coadjutors—Scholastics—Professed of the Three Vows—Professed of the Four Vows—The General—Control exercised over him by his Assistants—His Relation to the General Congregation—Espionage a Part of the Jesuit System—Advantageous Position of a Contented Jesuit—The Vow of Poverty—Houses of the Professed and Colleges—The Constitutions and Declarations—Problem of the *Monita Secreta*—Reciprocal Relations of Rome and the Company—Characteristics of Jesuit Education—Direction of Consciences—Moral Laxity—Sarpi's Critique—Casuistry—Interference in Affairs of State—Instigation to Regicide and Political Conspiracy—Theories of Church Supremacy—Insurgence of the European Nations against the Company.

WE have seen in the preceding chapters how Spain became dominant in Italy, superseding the rivalry of confederated states by the monotony of servitude, and lending its weight to Papal Rome. The internal changes effected in the Church by the Tridentine Council, and the external power conferred on it, were due in no small measure to Spanish influence or sanction. A Spanish institution, the Inquisition, modified to suit Italian requirements, lent revived Catholicism weapons of repression and attack. We have now to learn by what means a partial vigour was communicated to the failing body of Catholic beliefs, how the Tridentine creed was propagated, the spiritual realm of the Roman Pontiff policed, and his secular authority augmented. A Spanish Order rose at the right moment to supply that intellectual and moral element of vitality without which the Catholic Revival might have remained as inert as a stillborn child. The devotion of the Jesuits to the Papacy was in reality the masterful Spanish spirit of that epoch masking its world-grasping ambition under the guise of obedience to Rome. This does not mean that the founders and first organisers of the Company of Jesus consciously pursued one object while they pretended to have another in view. The impulse which moved Loyola was spontaneous and romantic. The world has seen few examples of disinterested self-devotion equal to that of Xavier. Yet the fact remains that Jesuitry, taking its germ and root in the Spanish character, persisting as an organism within the Church but separate from the ecclesiastical hierarchy, devised the doctrine of Papal absolutism, and became the prime agent of that Catholic policy in Europe which passed for Papal during the Counter-Reformation. The indissoluble connexion between Rome, Spain, and the Jesuits, was apparent to all unprejudiced observers. For this triad of reactionary and belligerent forces Sarpi invented the name of the Diacatholicon, alluding under the metaphor of a drug to the virus which was being instilled in his days into all the States of Europe.[1]

[1] For Sarpi's use of this phrase see his *Lettere*, vol. ii. pp. 72, 80, 92. He clearly recognised the solidarity between the Jesuits and Spain. 'The Jesuit is no more separable from the Spaniard than the accident from the substance.' 'The Spaniard without the Jesuit is not worth

The founder of the Jesuit order was the thirteenth child of a Spanish noble, born in 1491 at his father's castle of Loyola in the Basque province of Guipuzcoa.[1] His full name was Iñigo Lopez de Recalde; but he is better known to history as Saint Ignatius Loyola. Ignatius spent his boyhood as page in the service of King Ferdinand the Catholic, whence he passed into that of the Duke of Najara, who was the hereditary friend and patron of his family. At this time he thought of nothing but feats of arms, military glory, and romantic adventures. He could boast but little education; and his favourite reading was in 'Amadis of Gaul.' That romance appeared during the boy's earliest childhood, and Spain was now devouring its high-flown rhapsodies with rapture. The peculiar admixture of mystical piety, Catholic enthusiasm, and chivalrous passion, which distinguishes 'Amadis,' exactly corresponded to the spirit of the Spaniards at an epoch when they had terminated their age-long struggle with the Moors, and were combining propagandist zeal with martial fervour in the conquest of the New World. Its pages inflamed the imagination of Ignatius. He began to compose a romance in honour of S. Peter, and chose a princess of blood royal for his Oriana. Thus, in the first days of youth,

more than lettuce without oil.' 'For the Jesuits to deceive Spain, would be tantamount to deceiving themselves.' *Ibid.* vol. i. pp. 203, 384, vol. ii. p. 48. Compare passages in vol. i. pp. 184, 189. He only perceived a difference in the degrees of their noxiousness to Europe. Thus ' the worst Spaniard is better than the least bad of the Jesuits ' (vol. i. p. 212).

[1] Study of the Jesuits must be founded on *Institutum Societatis Jesu*, 7 vols. Avenione; Orlandino, *Hist. Soc. Jesu*; Crétineau-Joly, *Histoire de la Compagnie de Jésus*; Ribadaneira, *Vita Ignatii*; Genelli's Life of Ignatius in German or the French translation; the Jesuit work, *Imago Primi Sæculi*; Ranke's account in his *History of the Popes*, and the three chapters assigned to this subject in Philippson's *La Contre-Révolution Religieuse*. The latter will be found a most valuable summary.

while his heart was still set on love and warfare, he revealed the three leading features of his character—soaring ambition, the piety of a devotee, and the tendency to view religion from the point of fiction.

Ignatius was thirty years of age when the events happened which determined the future of his life and so powerfully affected the destinies of Catholic Christendom. The French were invading Navarre; and he was engaged in the defence of its capital, Pampeluna. On May 20, 1521, a bullet shattered his right leg, while his left foot was injured by a fragment of stone detached from a breach in the bastion. Transported to his father's castle, he suffered protracted anguish under the hands of unskilled medical attendants. The badly set bone in his right leg had twice to be broken; and when at last it joined, the young knight found himself a cripple. This limb was shorter than the other; the surgeons endeavoured to elongate it by machines of iron, which put him to exquisite pain. After months of torture, he remained lame for life.

During his illness Ignatius read such books as the castle of Loyola contained. These were a 'Life of Christ' and the 'Flowers of the Saints' in Spanish. His mind, prepared by chivalrous romance, and strongly inclined to devotion, felt a special fascination in the tales of Dominic and Francis. Their heroism suggested new paths which the aspirant after fame might tread with honour. Military glory and the love of women had to be renounced; for so ambitious a man could not content himself with the successes of a cripple in these spheres of action. But the legends of saints and martyrs pointed out careers no less noble, no less useful, and even more enticing to the fancy. He would become the spiritual Knight of Christ and Our Lady. To S. Peter, his chosen protector, he prayed fervently; and when at length he rose from the bed of sickness, he firmly believed that his life had been saved by the intercession of this patron, and that it must be henceforth consecrated to the service of the faith. The world should be abandoned. Instead of warring with the enemies of Christ on earth, he would carry on a crusade against the powers of darkness. They were first to be met and fought in his own heart. Afterwards, he would form and lead a militia of like-hearted champions against the strongholds of evil in human nature.

It must not be thought that the scheme of founding a Society had so early entered into the mind of Ignatius. What we have at the present stage to notice is that he owed his adoption of the religious life to romantic fancy and fervid ambition, combined with a devotion to Peter, the saint of orthodoxy and the Church. Animated by this new enthusiasm, he managed to escape from home in the spring of 1522. His friends opposed themselves to his vocation; but he gave them the slip, took vows of chastity and abstinence, and began a pilgrimage to our Lady of Montserrat near Barcelona. On the road he scourged himself daily. When he reached the shrine he hung his arms up as a votive offering, and performed the vigil which chivalrous custom exacted from a squire before the morning of his being dubbed a knight. This ceremony was observed point by point, according to the ritual he had read in 'Amadis of Gaul.' Next day he gave his raiment to a beggar, and assumed the garb of a mendicant pilgrim. By self-dedication he had now made himself the Knight of Holy Church.

His first intention was to set sail for Palestine, with the object of preaching to the infidels. But the plague prevented him from leaving port; and he retired to a Dominican convent at Manresa, a little town of Catalonia, north-west of Barcelona. Here he abandoned himself to the cruellest self-discipline. Feeding upon bread and water, kneeling for seven hours together rapt in prayer, scourging his flesh thrice daily, and reducing sleep to the barest minimum, Ignatius sought by austerity to snatch that crown of sainthood which he felt to be his due. Outraged nature soon warned him .that he was upon a path which led to failure. Despair took possession of his soul, sometimes prompting him to end his life by suicide, sometimes plaguing him with hideous visions. At last he fell dangerously ill. Enlightened by the expectation of early death, he then became convinced that his fanatical asceticism was a folly. The despair, the dreadful phantoms which had haunted him, were ascribed immediately to the devil. In those rarer visitings of brighter visions, which sometimes brought consolation, bidding him repose upon God's mercy, he recognised angels sent to lead him on the pathway of salvation. God's hand appeared in these dealings; and he resolved to dedicate his body as well as his soul to God's service, respecting both as instruments of the divine will, and entertaining both in efficiency for the work required of them.

The experiences of Manresa proved eminently fruitful for the future method of Ignatius. It was here that he began to regard self-discipline and self-examination as the needful prelude to a consecrated life. It was here that he learned to condemn the asceticism of anchorites as pernicious or unprofitable to a militant Christian. It was here that, while studying the manual of devotion written by Garcia de Cisneros, he laid foundations for those famous 'Exercitia,' which became his instrument for rapidly passing neophytes through spiritual training similar to his own. It was here that he first distinguished two kinds of visions, infernal and celestial. Here also he grew familiar with the uses of concrete imagination; and understood how the faculty of sensuous realisation might be made a powerful engine for presenting the past of sacred history or the dogmas of orthodox theology under shapes of fancy to the mind.

Finally, in all the experiences of Manresa, he tried the temper of his own character, which was really not that of a poet or a mystic, but of a sagacious man of action, preparing a system calculated to subjugate the intelligence and will of millions. Tested by self-imposed sufferings and by diseased hallucinations, his sound sense, the sense of one destined to control men, gathered energy and grew in solid strength: yet enough remained of his fanaticism to operate as a motive force in the scheme which he afterwards developed; enough survived from the ascetic phase he had surmounted, to make him comprehend that some such agony as he had suffered should form the vestibule to a devoted life. We may compare the throes of Ignatius at Manresa with the contemporary struggles of Luther at Wittenberg and in the Wartzburg. Our imagination will dwell upon the different issues to which two heroes distinguished by practical ability were led through their contention with the powers of spiritual evil. Protagonists respectively of Reformation and Counter-Reformation, they arrived at opposite conclusions; the one championing the cause of spiritual freedom in the modern world, the other consecrating his genius to the maintenance of Catholic orthodoxy by spiritual despotism. Yet each alike fulfilled his mission by having conquered mysticism at the outset of his world-historical career.

Ignatius remained for the space of ten months at Manresa. He then found means to realise his cherished journey to the Holy Land. In Palestine he was treated with coldness as an ignorant enthusiast, capable of subverting the existing order of things, but too feeble to be counted on for permanent support. His motive ideas were still visionary; he could not cope with conservatism and frigidity established in comfortable places of emolument. It was necessary that he should learn the wisdom of compromise. Accordingly he returned to Spain, and put himself to school. Two years spent in preparatory studies at Barcelona, another period at Alcala, and another at Salamanca, introduced him to languages, grammar, philosophy, and theology. This man of noble blood and vast ambition, past the age of thirty, sat with boys upon the common benches. This self-consecrated saint imbibed the commonplaces of scholastic logic. It was a further stage in the evolution of his iron character from romance and mysticism into political and practical sagacity. It was a further education of his stubborn will to pliant temper. But he could not divest himself of his mission as a founder and apostle. He taught disciples, preached, and formed a sect of devotees. Then the Holy Office attacked him. He was imprisoned, once at Alcala for forty-two days, once at Salamanca for three weeks, upon charges of heresy. Ignatius proved his innocence. The Inquisitors released him with certificates of acquittal; but they sentenced him to four years' study of theology before he should presume to preach. These years he resolved to spend at Paris. Accordingly he performed the journey on foot, and arrived in the capital of France upon February 2, 1528. He was then thirty-seven years old.

At Paris he had to go to school again from the beginning. The alms of well-wishers, chiefly devout women at Barcelona, amply provided him with funds. These he employed not only in advancing his own studies, but also in securing the attachment of adherents to his cause. At this epoch he visited the towns of Belgium and London during his vacations. But the main outcome of his residence at Paris was the formation of the Company of Jesus. Those long years of his novitiate and wandering were not without their uses now. They had taught him, while clinging stubbornly to the main projects of his life, prudence in the choice of means, temperance in expectation, sagacity in the manipulation of fellow-workers selected for the still romantic ends he had in view.

His first two disciples were a Savoyard, Peter Faber or Le Fèvre, and Francis Xavier of Pampeluna. Faber was a poor student, whom Ignatius helped with money. Xavier sprang from a noble stock, famous in arms through generations, for which he was eager to win the additional honours of science and the Church. Ignatius assisted him by bringing students to his lectures. Under the personal influence of their friend and benefactor, both of these men determined to leave all and follow the new light. Visionary as the object yet was, the firm will, fervent confidence, and saintly life of Loyola inspired them with absolute trust. That the Christian faith, as they understood it, remained exposed to grievous dangers from without and from within, that millions of souls were perishing through ignorance, that tens of thousands were falling away through incredulity and heresy, was certain. The realm of Christ on earth needed champions, soldiers devoted to a crusade against Satan and his hosts. And here was a leader, a man among men, a man whose words were as a fire, and whose method of spiritual discipline was salutary and illuminative; and this man bade them join him in the Holy War. He gained them in a hundred ways, by kindness, by precept, by patience, by persuasion, by attention to their physical and spiritual needs, by words of warmth and wisdom, by the direction of their conscience, by profound and intense sympathy with souls struggling after the higher life. The means he had employed to gain Faber and Xavier were used with equal success in the case of seven other disciples. The names of these men deserve to be recorded; for some of them played a part of importance in European history, while all of them contributed to the foundation of the Jesuits. They were James Lainez, Alfonzo Salmeron, and Nicholas Bobadilla, three Spaniards; Simon Rodriguez d'Azevedo, a Portuguese; two Frenchmen, Jean Codure and Brouet; and Claude le Jay, a Savoyard. All these neophytes were subjected by Ignatius to rigid discipline, based upon his 'Exercitia.' They met together for prayer, meditation, and discussion, in his chamber at the College of S. Barbe. Here he unfolded to them his own plans, and poured out on them his spirit. At length, upon August 15, 1534, the ten together took the vows of chastity and poverty in the church of S. Mary at Montmartre, and bound themselves to conduct a missionary crusade in Palestine, or, if this should prove impracticable, to place themselves as devoted instruments, without conditions and without remuneration, in the hands of the Sovereign Pontiff.

The society was thus established, although its purpose remained indecisive. The founder's romantic dream of a crusade in Holy Land, though never realised, gave an object of immediate interest to the associated friends. Meanwhile two main features of its historical manifestation, the propaganda of the Catholic faith and unqualified devotion to the cause of the Roman See, had been clearly indicated. Nothing proves the mastery which Ignatius had now acquired over his own enthusiasm, or the insight he had gained into the right method of dealing with men, more than the use he made of his authority in this first instance. The society was bound to grow and to expand; and it was fated to receive the lasting impress of his genius. But, as though inspired by some prophetic vision of its future greatness, he refrained from circumscribing the still tender embryo within definite limits which might have been pernicious to its development.

The associates completed their studies at Paris, and in 1535 they separated, after agreeing to meet at Venice in the first months of 1537. Ignatius meanwhile travelled to Spain, where he settled his affairs by bestowing such property as he possessed on charitable institutions. He also resumed preaching with a zeal that aroused enthusiasm and extended his personal influence. At the appointed time the ten came

LOYOLA AT VENICE

together at Venice, ostensibly bent on carrying out their project of visiting Palestine. But war was now declared between the Turks and the Republic of S. Mark. Ignatius found himself once more accused of heresy, and had some trouble in clearing himself before the Inquisition. It was resolved in these circumstances to abandon the mission to Holy Land as impracticable for the moment, and to remain in Venice waiting for more favourable opportunities. We may believe that the romance of a crusade among the infidels of Syria had already begun to fade from the imagination of the founder, in whose career nothing is more striking than his gradual abandonment of visionary for tangible ends, and his progressive substitution of real for shadowy objects of ambition.

Loyola's first contact with Italian society during this residence in Venice exercised decisive influence over his plans. He seems to have perceived with the acute scent of an eagle that here lay the quarry he had sought so long. Italy, the fountain-head of intellectual enlightenment for Europe, was the realm which he must win. Italy alone offered the fulcrum needed by his firm and limitless desire of domination over souls. It was with Caraffa and the Theatines that Ignatius obtained a home. They were now established in the States of S. Mark through the beneficence of a rich Venetian noble, Girolamo Miani, who had opened religious houses and placed these at their disposition. Under the direction of their founder, they carried on their designed function of training a higher class of clergy for the duties of preaching and the priesthood, and for the repression of heresy by educational means. Caraffa's scheme was too limited to suit Ignatius; and the characters of both men were ill adapted for co-operation. One zeal for the faith inspired both. Here they agreed. But Ignatius was a Spaniard; and the second passion in Caraffa's breast was a Neapolitan's hatred for that nation. Ignatius, moreover, contemplated a vastly more expansive and elastic machinery for his workers in the vineyard of the faith than the future Pope's coercive temper could have tolerated. These two leaders of the Counter-Reformation, equally ambitious, equally intolerant of opposition, equally bent upon a vast dominion, had to separate. The one was destined to organise the Inquisition and the Index. The other evolved what is historically known as Jesuitry. Nevertheless we know that Ignatius learned much from Caraffa. The subsequent organisation of his Order showed that the Theatines suggested many practical points in the method he eventually adopted for effecting his designs.

Some of his companions, meanwhile, journeyed to Rome. There they obtained from Paul III. permission to visit Palestine upon a missionary enterprise, together with special privileges for their entrance into sacerdotal orders. Those of the ten friends who were not yet priests were ordained at Venice in June 1537. They then began to preach in public, roaming the streets with faces emaciated by abstinence, clad in ragged clothes, and using a language strangely compounded of Italian and Spanish. Their obvious enthusiasm, and the holy lives they were known to lead, brought them rapidly into high reputation of sanctity. Both the secular and the religious clergy of Italy could show but few men at that epoch equal to these brethren. It was settled in the autumn that they should all revisit Rome, travelling by different routes, and meditating on the form which the Order should assume. Palestine had now been definitely, if tacitly, abandoned. As might have been expected, it was Loyola who baptized his Order and impressed a character upon the infant institution. He determined to call it the Company of Jesus, with direct reference to those Companies of Adventure which had given irregular organisation to restless military spirits in the past. The new Company was to be a 'cohort or century combined for combat against spiritual foes; men-at-arms devoted, body and soul, to our Lord Jesus Christ and to His true and lawful Vicar upon earth.'[1] An Englishman of the present day may pause to meditate upon the grotesque parallel between the nascent Order of the Jesuits and the Salvation Army, and can draw such conclusions from it as may seem profitable.

Loyola's withdrawal from all participation in the nominal honour of his institution, his enrolment of the militia he had levied under the name of Jesus, and the combative functions which he ascribed to it, were very decided marks of originality. It stamped the body with impersonality from the outset, and indicated the belligerent attitude it was destined to assume. There was nothing exactly similar to its dominant conception in any of the previous religious orders. These had usually received their title from the founder, had aimed at a life retired from the world, had studied the sanctification of their individual members, and had only contemplated an indirect operation upon society. Ignatius, on the contrary, placed his community under the protection of Christ, and defined it at the outset as a militant and movable legion of auxiliaries, dedicated, not to retirement or to the pursuit of salvation, but to freely avowed and active combat in defence of their Master's vicegerent upon earth. It was as though he had divined the deficiencies of Catholicism at that epoch, and had determined to supplement them by the creation of a novel and a special weapon of attack. Some institutions of medieval chivalry, the Knights of the Temple and S. John, for instance, furnished the closest analogy to his foundation. Their spirit he transferred from the sphere of physical combat with visible forces, infidel and Mussulman, to the sphere of intellectual warfare against heresy, unbelief, insubordination in the Church. He had refined upon the crude enthusiasm of romance which inspired

[1] These phrases occur in the *Deliberatio primorum patrum.*

him at Montserrat. Without losing its intensity, this had become a motive force of actual and political gravity.

The Company of Jesus was far from obtaining the immediate approval of the Church. Paul III. indeed, perceived its utility, and showed marked favour to the associates when they arrived in Rome about the end of 1537. The people, too, welcomed their ministration gladly, and recognised the zeal which they displayed in acts of charity and their exemplary behaviour. But the Curia and higher clergy organised an opposition against them. They were accused of heresy and attempts to seduce the common folk. Ignatius demanded full and public inquiry, which was at first refused him. He then addressed the Pope in person, who ordered a trial, out of which the brethren came with full acquittal. After this success, they obtained a hold upon religious instruction in many schools of Rome. Adherents flocked around them; and they saw that it was time to give the society a defined organisation and to demand its official recognition as an Order. It was resolved to add the vow of obedience to their former vows of chastity and poverty. Obedience had always been a prime virtue in monastic institutions; but Ignatius conceived of it in a new and military spirit. The obedience of the Jesuits was to be absolute, extending even to the duty of committing sins at a superior's orders. The General, instead of holding office for a term of years, was to be elected for life, with unlimited command over the whole Order in its several degrees. He was to be regarded as Christ present and personified. This autocracy of the General might have seemed to menace the overlordship of the Holy See, but for a fourth vow which the Company determined to adopt. It ran as follows: ' That the members will consecrate their lives to the continual service of Christ and of the Popes, will fight under the banner of the Cross, and will serve the Lord and the Roman Pontiff as

God's vicar upon earth, in such wise that they shall be bound to execute immediately and without hesitation or excuse all that the reigning Pope or his successors may enjoin upon them for the profit of souls or for the propagation of the faith, and shall do so in all provinces whithersoever he may send them, among Turks or any other infidels, to furthest Ind, as well as in the region of heretics, schismatics, or believers of any kind.'

Loyola himself drew up these constitutions in five chapters, and had them introduced to Paul III., with the petition that they might be confirmed. This was in September 1539, and it is singular that the man selected to bring them under the Pope's notice should have been Cardinal Contarini. Paul had no difficulty in recognising the support which this new Order would bring to the Papacy in its conflict with Reformers and its diplomatic embarrassments with Charles V. He is even reported to have said, 'The finger of God is there!' Yet he could not confirm the constitutions without the previous approval of three Cardinals appointed to report on them. This committee condemned Loyola's scheme; and nearly a year passed in negotiations with foreign princes and powerful prelates, before a reluctant consent was yielded to the Pope's avowed inclination. At length the Bull of Sept. 27, 1540, 'Regimini militantis Ecclesiae,' launched the Society of Jesus on the world. Ignatius became the first General of the Order; and the rest of his life, a period of sixteen years, was spent in perfecting the machinery and extending the growth of this institution, which in all essentials was the emanation of his own mind.

It may be well at this point to sketch the organisation of the Jesuits, and to describe the progress of the Society during its founder's lifetime, in order that a correct conception may be gained of Loyola's share in its creation. Many historians of eminence, and among them so acute an observer as Paolo Sarpi, have been of the opinion that Jesuitry in its later developments was a deflection from the spirit and intention of Ignatius. It is affirmed that Lainez and Salmeron, rather than Loyola, gave that complexion to the Order which has rendered it a mark for the hatred and disgust of Europe. Aquaviva, the fifth General, has been credited with its policy of interference in affairs of states and nations. Yet I think it can be shown that the Society, as it appeared in the seventeenth century, was a logical and necessary development of the Society as Ignatius framed it in the sixteenth.[1] Lainez, who succeeded the founder as General, digested the constitutions and supplied them with a commentary or Directorium. He defined, formulated, and stereotyped the system; but the essential qualities of Jesuitry, its concentration upon political objects, its unscrupulousness in choice of means to ends, the worldliness which lurked beneath the famous motto *Ad Majorem Dei Gloriam*, were implicit in Loyola's express words and in his actual administration. The framework of the Order, as he fixed it, was so firmly traced and so cunningly devised for practical efficiency, that it admitted of no alteration except in the direction of more rigid definition. Lainez may, indeed, have emphasised its tendency to become a political machine, and may have weakened its religious tone, by his rules for the interpretation of the constitutions; but we have seen that the development of Loyola's own ideas ran in this direction. The real strength as well as the worst vices of Jesuitry were inherent in the system from the first; and in it we have perhaps the most remarkable instance on record

[1] Sarpi, though he expressed an opinion that the Jesuits of his day had departed from the spirit of their founders, spoke thus of Loyola's worldly aims (*Lettere*, vol. i. p. 224): 'Even Father Ignatius, Founder of the Company, as his biography attests, based himself in such wise upon human interest as though there were none divine to think about.'

LOYOLA'S ADMINISTRATION

of the evolution of a cosmopolitan and world-important organism from the embryo of one man's conception.

The Bull 'Regimini militantis Ecclesiae' restricted the number of the Jesuits to sixty. If Ignatius did not himself propose this limit, the restriction may perhaps have suggested his policy of reserving the full privileges of the Society for a small band of selected members—the very essence of the body, extracted by processes which will be afterwards described. Anyhow, it is certain that, though the Papal limitation was removed in 1548, and though candidates flowed on the tide of fashion toward the Order, yet the representative and responsible Fathers remained few in numbers. These were distributed as the General thought fit. He stayed in Rome; for Rome was the chosen headquarters of the Society, the nucleus of their growth, and the fulcrum of their energy. From Rome, as from a centre, Ignatius moved his men about the field of Europe. We might compare him under one metaphor to a chess-player directing his pieces upon the squares of the political and ecclesiastical chessboard: under another, to a spider spinning his web so as to net the greatest number of profitable partisans. The fathers were kept in perpetual motion. To shift them from place to place, to exclude them from their native soil, to render them cosmopolitan and pliant was the first care of the founder. He forbade the follies of ascetic piety, inculcated the study of languages and exact knowledge, and above all things recommended the acquisition of those social arts which find favour with princes and folk of high condition. 'Prudence of an exquisite quality,' he said, 'combined with average sanctity, is more valuable than eminent sanctity and less of prudence.' Also he bade them keep their eyes open for neophytes 'less marked by pure goodness than by firmness of character and ability in conduct of affairs, since men who are not apt for public business do not suit the requirements of the Company.' Orlandino tells us that though Ignatius felt drawn to men who showed eminent gifts for erudition, he preferred, in the difficulties of the Church, to choose such as knew the world well and were distinguished by their social station. The fathers were to seek out youths 'of good natural parts, adapted to the acquisition of knowledge and to practical works of utility.' Their pupils were, if possible, to have physical advantages and manners that should render them agreeable. These points had more of practical value than a bare vocation for piety. In their dealings with tender consciences, they were to act like 'good fishers of souls, passing over many things in silence as though these had not been observed, until the time came when the will was gained, and the character could be directed as they thought best.'[1] Loyola's dislike for the common forms of monasticism appears in his choice of the ordinary secular priest's cassock for their dress, and in his emancipation of the members from devotional exercises and attendance in the choir. The aversion he felt for ascetic discipline is evinced in a letter he addressed to Francis Borgia in 1548. It is better, he writes, to strengthen your stomach and other faculties, than to impair the body and enfeeble the intellect by fasting. God needs both our physical and mental powers for His service; and every drop of blood you shed in flagellation is a loss. The end in view was to serve the Church by penetrating European society, taking possession of its leaders in rank and hereditary influence, directing education, assuming the control of the confessional, and preaching the faith in forms adapted to the foibles and the fancies of the age. The interests of the Church were paramount: 'If she teaches that what seems to us white is black, we must declare it to be black upon the spot.' There were other precepts added. These, for instance, seem worth commemoration: 'The workers in the Lord's vineyard should

[1] See Philippson, *op. cit.* pp. 61, 62.

have but one foot on earth, the other should be raised to travel forward.' 'The abnegation of our own will is of more value than if one should bring the dead to life again.' 'No storm is so pernicious as a calm, and no enemy is so dangerous as having none.' It will be seen that what is known as Jesuitry, in its mundane force and in its personal devotion to a cause, emerges from the precepts of Ignatius. We may wonder how the romances of the mountain-keep of Loyola, the mysticism of Montserrat, and the struggles of Manresa should have brought the founder of the Jesuits to these results. Yet, if we analyse the problem, it will yield a probable solution. What survived from that first period was the spirit of enthusiastic service to the Church, the vast ambition of a man who felt himself a destined instrument for shoring up the crumbling walls of Catholicity, the martial instinct of a warrior fighting at fearful odds with nations ruining toward infidelity. He had no doubt where the right lay. He was a Spaniard, a servant of S. Peter; and for him the creed enounced by Rome was all in all. But his commerce with the world, his astute Basque nature, and his judgment of the European situation, taught him that he must use other means than those which Francis and Dominic had employed. He had to make his Company, that forlorn hope of Catholicism, the exponent of a decadent and rotten faith. He had to adapt it to the necessities of Christendom in dissolution, to constitute it by a guileful and sagacious method. He had to render it wise in the wisdom of the world, in order that he might catch the powers of this world by their interests and vices for the Church. He was like Machiavelli, endeavouring to save a corrupt state by utilising corruption for ends acknowledged sound. And, like Machiavelli, he was mistaken, because it will not profit man to trust in craft or the manipulation of evil. Luther was stronger in his weakness than the creator of the Jesuit machinery, wiser in his simplicity than the deviser of that subtle engine. But Luther had the onward forces of humanity upon his side. Ignatius could but retard them by his ingenuity. We may be therefore excused if we admire Ignatius for the virile effort which he made in a failing cause, and for the splendid gifts of organising prudence which he devoted to a misplaced object.

Under his direction, the members of the Society spread themselves over Europe, and always with similar results. Wherever they went, hundreds of adherents joined the Order. Paul III. and Julius III. heaped privileges upon it, seeing what a power it had become in warfare with heresy. Ignatius spared no pains to secure his position in Rome, paying court to cardinals and prelates, visiting ambassadors and princes, soliciting their favours and offering the service of his brethren in return. Profitable negotiations were opened with the King of Spain and the Duke of Bavaria, which, under cover of reforming convents, led to a partition of ecclesiastical property between the Jesuits and the State. Good reasons seemed to justify such acts of spoliation; for the old Orders were sunk in sloth and immorality beyond redemption, while the Company kept alive all that was sound in Catholic discipline, preaching, and instruction. In Italy the Jesuits made rapid progress from the first. Lainez occupied the Venetian territory, opposing Protestant opinions in Venice itself, at Brescia, and among the mountains of the Valtelline. Le Jay combated the forces of Calvin and Renée of France at Ferrara. Salmeron took possession of Naples and Sicily. Piacenza, Modena, Faenza, Bologna, and Montepulciano received the fathers with open arms. The Farnesi welcomed them in Parma. Wherever they went, they secured the good will of noble women, and gained some hold on universities. Colleges were founded in the chief cities of the peninsula, where they not only taught gratis, but used methods superior to those previously in vogue. Rome, however, remained the stronghold of the Company. Here Ignatius founded its first house in 1550. This was the Collegium Romanum; and in 1555 some hundred pupils, who had followed a course of studies in Greek, Latin, Hebrew, and theology, issued from its walls. In 1557 he purchased the palace Salviati, on the site of which now stands the vast establishment of the Gesù. In 1552 he started a separate institution, Collegium Germanicum, for the special training of young Germans. There was also a subordinate institution for the education of the sons of nobles. These colleges afforded models for similar schools throughout Europe: some of them intended to supply the Society with members, and some to impress the laity with Catholic principles. Uniformity was an object which the Jesuits always held in view.

They did not meet at first with like success in all Catholic countries. In Spain, Charles V. treated them with suspicion as the sworn men of the Papacy; and the Dominican Order, so powerful through its hold upon the Inquisition, regarded them justly as rivals. Though working for the same end, the means employed by Jesuits and Dominicans were too diverse for these champions of orthodoxy to work harmoniously together. The Jesuits belonged to the future, to the party of accommodation and control by subterfuge. The Dominicans were rooted in the past; their dogmatism admitted of no compromise; they strove to rule by force. There was therefore, at the outset, war between the kennels of the elder and the younger dogs of God in Spain. Yet Jesuitism gained ground. It had the advantage of being a native and a recent product. It was powerful by its appeals to the sensuous imagination and carnal superstitions of that Iberian-Latin people. It was seductive by its mitigation of oppressive orthodoxy and inflexible prescriptive law. Where the Dominican was steel, the Jesuit was reed; where the Dominican breathed fire and faggots, the Jesuit suggested casuistical distinctions; where the Dominican raised difficulties, the Jesuit solved scruples; where the Dominican presented theological abstractions, the Jesuit offered stimulative or agreeable images; where the Dominican preached dogma, the Jesuit retailed romance. It only needed one illustrious convert to plant the Jesuits in Spain. Him they found in Francis Borgia, Duke of Gandia, Viceroy of Catalonia, and subsequently the third General of the Order and a saint. This man placed the university, which he had founded, in their hands; and about the same time they gained a footing in the University of Salamanca. Still they continued to retain their strongest hold upon the people, who regarded them as saviours from the tyranny and ennui of the established Dominican hierarchy.

Portugal was won at a blow. Xavier and Rodriguez planted the Company there under the affectionate protection of King John III. When Xavier started on his mission to the Indies in 1541, Rodriguez took the affairs of the realm into his hands, controlled the cabinet, and formed the heir-apparent to their will.

With France they had more trouble. Both the University and the Parliament of Paris opposed their settlement. The Sorbonne even declared them 'dangerous in matters of the faith, fit to disturb the peace of the Church, and to reverse the order of monastic life; more adapted to destroy than to build.' The Gallican Church scented danger in these bondsmen of the Papacy; and it was only when they helped to organise the League that the influence of the Guises gave them a foothold in the kingdom. Even then their seminaries at Reims, Douai, and S. Omer must be rather regarded as outposts ($\dot{\epsilon}\pi\iota\tau\epsilon\iota\chi\iota\sigma\mu o\iota$) against England and Flanders than as nationally French establishments. In France they long remained a seditious and belligerent faction.[1]

[1] It was not till the epoch of Maria de' Medici's Regency that the Jesuits obtained firm hold on France.

They had the same partial and clandestine success in the Low Countries, where their position was at first equivocal, though they early gained some practical hold upon the University of Louvain. We are perhaps justified in attributing the evil fame of Reims, Douai, S. Omer, and Louvain to the incomplete sympathy which existed between the Jesuits and the countries where they made these settlements. Not perfectly at home, surrounded by discontent and jealousy, upon the borderlands of the heresies they were bound to combat, their system assumed its darkest colours in those hotbeds of intrigue and feverish fanaticism. In time, however, the Jesuits fixed their talons firmly upon the Netherlands, through the favour of Anne of Austria; and the year 1562 saw them comfortably ensconced at Antwerp, Louvain, Brussels, and Lille, in spite of the previous antipathy of the population. Here, as elsewhere, they pushed their way by gaining women and people of birth to their cause, and by showily meritorious services to education. Faber achieved ephemeral success as lecturer at Louvain.

To take firm hold on Germany had been the cherished wish of Ignatius; 'for there,' to use his own words, 'the pest of heresy exposed men to graver dangers than elsewhere.' The Society had scarcely been founded when Faber, Le Jay, and Bobadilla were sent north. Faber made small progress, and was removed to Spain. But Bobadilla secured the confidence of William, Duke of Bavaria; while Le Jay won that of Ferdinand of Austria. In both provinces they avowed their intention of working at the reformation of the clergy and the improvement of popular education—ends, which in the disorganised condition of Germany, seemed of highest importance to those princes. Through the influence of Bavaria, Bobadilla succeeded in rendering the Interim proclaimed by Charles V. nugatory; while Le Jay founded the college of the Order at Vienna. In this important post he was soon succeeded by Canisius, Ferdinand's confessor, through whose co-operation Cardinal Morone afterwards brought this Emperor into harmony with the Papal plan for winding up the Council of Trent. It should be added that Ingolstadt in Bavaria became the second headquarters of the Jesuit propaganda in Germany.

The methods adopted by Ignatius in dealing with his three lieutenants, Bobadilla, Le Jay, and Canisius, are so characteristic of Jesuit policy that they demand particular attention. Checkmated by Bobadilla in the matter of the Interim, Charles V. manifested his resentment. He was already ill-affected toward the Society, and its founder felt the need of humouring him. The highest grade of the Order was therefore ostentatiously refused to Bobadilla, until such time as the Emperor's attention was distracted from the cause of his disappointment. With Le Jay and Canisius the case stood differently. Ferdinand wished to make the former Bishop of Trieste and the latter Archbishop of Vienna. Ignatius opposed both projects, alleging that the Company of Jesus could not afford to part with its best servants, and that their vows of obedience and poverty were inconsistent with high office in the Church. He discerned the necessity of reducing each member of the Society to absolute dependence on the General, which would have been impracticable if any one of them attained to the position of a prelate. A law was therefore passed declaring it mortal sin for Jesuits to accept bishoprics or other posts of honour in the Church. Instead of assuming the mitre, Canisius was permitted to administer the See of Vienna without usufruct of its revenues. To the world this manifested the disinterested zeal of the Jesuits in a seductive light; while the integrity of the Society, as an independent self-sufficing body, exacting the servitude of absolute devotion from its members, was secured. Another instance of the same adroitness may be mentioned. The

Emperor in 1552 offered a Cardinal's hat to Francis Borgia, who was by birth the most illustrious of living Jesuits. Ignatius refrained from rebuffing the Emperor and insulting the Duke of Gandia by an open prohibition; but he told the former to expect the Duke's refusal, while he wrote to the latter expressing his own earnest hope that he would renounce an honour injurious to the Society. This diplomacy elicited a grateful but firm answer of *Nolo Episcopari* from the Duke, who thus took the responsibility of offending Charles V. upon himself. Meanwhile the missionary objects of the Company were not neglected. Xavier left Portugal in 1541 for that famous journey through India and China, the facts of which may be compared for their romantic interest with Cortes' or Pizarro's exploits. Brazil, the transatlantic Portugal, was abandoned to the Jesuits, and they began to feel their way in Mexico. In the year of Loyola's death, 1556, thirty-two members of the Society were resident in South America; one hundred in India, China, and Japan; and a mission was established in Ethiopia. Even Ireland had been explored by a couple of fathers, who returned without success, after undergoing terrible hardships. At this epoch the Society counted in round numbers one thousand men. It was divided in Europe into thirteen provinces: seven of these were Portuguese and Spanish; three were Italian (namely, Rome, Upper Italy, and Sicily); one was French; two were German. Castile contained ten colleges of the Order; Aragon, five Andalusia, five. Portugal was penetrated through and through with Jesuits. Rome displayed the central Roman and Teutonic colleges. Upper Italy had ten colleges. France could show only one college. In Upper Germany the Company held firm hold on Vienna, Prag, Munich, and Ingolstadt. The province of Lower Germany, including the Netherlands, was still undetermined. This expansion of the Order during the first sixteen years of its existence enables us to form some conception of the intellectual vigour and commanding will of Ignatius. He lived, as no founder of an Order, as few founders of religions, ever lived, to see his work accomplished and the impress of his genius stereotyped exactly in the forms he had designed upon the most formidable social and political organisation of modern Europe.

In his administration of the Order, Ignatius was absolute and autocratic. We have seen how he dealt with aspirants after ecclesiastical honours, and how he shifted his subordinates, as he thought best, from point to point upon the surface of the globe. The least attempt at independence on the part of his most trusted lieutenants was summarily checked by him. Simon Rodriguez, one of the earliest disciples of the College of S. Barbe at Paris, ruled the kingdom of Portugal through the ascendency which he had gained over John III. Elated by the vastness of his victory, Rodriguez arrogated to himself the right of private judgment, and introduced that ascetic discipline into the houses of his province which Ignatius had forbidden as inexpedient. Without loss of time, the General superseded him in his command; and, after a sharp struggle, Rodriguez was compelled to spend the rest of his days under strict surveillance at Rome. Lainez, in like manner, while acting as Provincial of Upper Italy, thought fit to complain that his best coadjutors were drawn from the colleges under his control to Rome. Ignatius wrote to this old friend, the man who best understood the spirit of its institution, and who was destined to succeed him in his headship, a cold and terrible epistle. 'Reflect upon your conduct. Let me know whether you acknowledge your sin, and tell me at the same time what punishment you are ready to undergo for this dereliction of duty.' Lainez expressed immediate submission in the most abject terms; he was ready to resign his post, abstain from preaching, confine his studies to the Breviary, walk as a beggar to Rome, and there teach grammar to children or perform menial offices. This was all Ignatius wanted. If he were the Christ of the Society, he well knew that Lainez was its S. Paul. He could not prevent him from being his successor, and he probably was well aware that Lainez would complete and supplement what he must leave unfinished in his life-work. The grovelling apology of such an eminent apostle, dictated as it was by hypocrisy and cunning, sufficed to procure his pardon, and remained among the archives of the Jesuits as a model for the spirit in which obedience should be manifested by them.

Obedience was, in fact, the cardinal and dominant quality of the Jesuit Order. To call it a virtue, in the sense in which Ignatius understood it, is impossible. The *Exercitia*, the Constitutions, and the Letter to the Portuguese Jesuits, all of which undoubtedly explain Loyola's views, reveal to us the essence of historical Jesuitry, the *fons et origo* of that long-continued evil which impested modern society. Let us examine some of his precepts on this topic. 'I ought to desire to be ruled by a superior who endeavours to subjugate my judgment and subdue my understanding.'—'When it seems to me that I am commanded by my superior to do a thing against which my conscience revolts as sinful, and my superior judges otherwise, it is my duty to yield my doubts to him, unless I am constrained by evident reasons.'—'I ought not to be my own, but His who created me, and his too through whom God governs me.'—'I ought to be like a corpse which has neither will nor understanding, like a crucifix that is turned about by him that holds it, like a staff in the hands of an old man who uses it at will for his assistance or pleasure.'—'In our Company the person who commands must never be regarded in his own capacity, but as Jesus Christ in him.'—'I desire that you strive and exercise yourselves to recognise Christ our Lord in every Superior.'

—'He who wishes to offer himself wholly up to God, must make the sacrifice not only of his will but of his intelligence.' —'In order to secure the faithful and successful execution of a Superior's orders, all private judgment must be yielded up.'—'A sin, whether venial or mortal, must be committed, if it is commanded by the Superior in the name of our Lord Jesus Christ or in virtue of obedience.' Of such nature was the virtue of obedience within the Order.[1] It rendered every member a tool in the hands of his immediate Superior, and the whole body one instrument in the hand of the General. The General's responsibility for the oblique acts and evasions of moral law, committed in the name of this virtue, was covered by the sounding phrase, 'Unto the greater glory of God.' He had also his own duty of obedience, which was to Holy Church. 'In making the sacrifice of our own judgment, the mind must keep itself ever whole and ready for obedience to the spouse of Christ, our Holy Mother, the Church orthodox, apostolic and hierarchical.'[2] Not a portion of the Catholic creed, of Catholic habits, of Catholic institutions, of Catholic superstitions, but must be valiantly defended. 'It is our duty loudly to uphold reliques, the cult of saints, stations, pilgrimages, indulgences, jubilees, the candles which are lighted before altars.' To criticise the clergy, even though notoriously corrupt, is a sin. The philosophy of the Church, as expressed by S. Thomas Aquinas, S. Bonaventura, and others, must be recognised as equal in authority with Holy Writ. It follows that just as a subordinate was enjoined to

---

[1] The letter addressed by Ignatius to the Portuguese Jesuits, March 22, 1553, on the virtue of obedience, the Constitutions and the glosses on them called Declarations, and the last chapter of the *Exercitia*, furnish the above sentences. See, too, Philippson, *op. cit.* pp. 60, 120–124.

[2] Read in the *Exercitia* (*Inst. Soc. Jesu*, vol. iv. pp. 167–173) the Rules for right accord with the Orthodox Church. What follows above is taken from that chapter.

sin, if sin were ordered by his Superior, so the whole Company were bound to lie, and do the things they disapproved, and preach the mummeries in which they disbelieved, in virtue of obedience to the Church. They may not even trust their senses; for 'If the Church pronounces a thing which seems to us white to be black, we must immediately say that it is black.'[1] The Jesuits were enrolled as an army, in an hour of grave peril for the Church, to undertake her defence. They pledged themselves, by this vow of obedience, to perform that duty with their eyes shut. It was not their mission to reform or purify or revivify Catholicism, but to maintain it intact with all its intellectual anachronisms. How well they succeeded may be judged from the issue of the Council of Trent, in which Lainez and Salmeron played so prominent a part. That rigid enforcement of every jot and tittle in the Catholic hierarchical organisation, in Catholic ritual, in the Catholic cult of saints and images, in the Catholic interpretation of Sacraments, in Catholic tradition as of equal value with the Bible, and lastly in the theory of Papal Supremacy, which was the astounding result of a Council convened to alter and reform the Church, can be attributed in no small measure to Jesuit persistency.

Ignatius attained his object. Obedience, blind, servile, unquestioning, unscrupulous, became the distinguishing feature of the Jesuits. But he condemned his Order to mediocrity. No really great man in any department of human knowledge or activity has arisen in the Company of Jesus. In course of time it became obvious to anyone of independent character and original intellect that their ranks were not the place for him. And if youths of real eminence

---

[1] *Exercitia*, ibid. p. 171. In this spirit a Jesuit of the present century writing on astronomy develops the heliocentric theory while he professes his submission to the geocentric theory as maintained by the Church.

entered it before they perceived this truth, their spirit was crushed. The machine was powerful enough for good and evil; but it remained an aggregate of individual inferiorities. Its merit and its perfection lay in this, that so complex an instrument could be moved by a single finger of the General in Rome. He consistently employed its delicate system of wheels and pulleys for the aggrandisement of the Order in the first place, in the second place for the control of the Catholic Church, and always for the subjugation and cretinisation of the mind of Europe.

The training of a Jesuit began with study of the *Exercitia Spiritualia*.[1] This manual had been composed by Loyola himself at intervals between 1522 and 1548, when it received the imprimatur of Pope Paul III. He based it on his own experiences at Manresa, and meant it to serve as a perpetual introduction to the mysteries of the religious life. It was used under the direction of a father, who prescribed a portion of its text for each day's meditation, employing various means to concentrate attention and enforce effect. The whole course of this spiritual drill extended over four weeks, during which the pupil remained in solitude. Light and sound and all distractions of the outer world were carefully excluded from his chamber. He was bidden to direct his soul inward upon itself and God, and was led by graduated stages to realise in the most vivid way the torments of the damned and the scheme of man's salvation. The first week was occupied in an examination of the conscience; the second in contemplation of Christ's Kingdom upon earth; the third in meditation on the Passion; the fourth in an ascent to the glory of the risen Lord. Materialism of the crudest type mingled with the indulgence of a reverie in this long spiritual journey. At every step the neophyte employed his five

[1] *Inst. Soc. Jesu*, vol. iv. The same volume contains the Directorium or rules for the use of the *Exercitia*.

senses in the effort of intellectual realisation. Prostrate upon the ground, gazing with closed eyelids in the twilight of his cell upon the mirror of imagination, he had to *see* the boundless flames of hell and souls encased in burning bodies, to *hear* the shrieks and blasphemies, to *smell* their sulphur and intolerable stench, to *taste* the bitterness of tears and *feel* the stings of ineffectual remorse. He had to localise each object in the camera obscura of the brain. If the Garden of Gethsemane, for instance, were the subject of his meditation, he was bound to place Christ here and the sleeping apostles there, and to form an accurate image of the angel and the cup. He gazed and gazed until he was able to handle the raiment of the Saviour, to watch the drops of bloody sweat beading his forehead and trickling down his cheeks, to grasp the chalice with the fingers of the soul. As each carefully chosen and sagaciously suggested scene was presented, he had to identify his very being, soul, will, intellect, and senses, with the mental vision. He lived again, so far as this was possible through fancy, the facts of sacred history. If the director judged it advisable, symbolic objects were placed before him in the cell; at one time skulls and bones, at another fresh sweet-smelling flowers. Fasting and flagellation, peculiar postures of the body, groanings and weepings, were prescribed as mechanical aids in cases where the soul seemed sluggish. The sphere traversed in these exercises was a narrow one. The drill aimed at intensity of discipline, at a concentrated and concrete impression, not at width of education or at intellectual enlightenment. Speculation upon the fundamental principles of religion was excluded. God's dealings with mankind revealed in the Old Testament found no place in this theory of salvation. Attention was riveted upon a very few points in the life of Christ and Mary, such as every Catholic child might be supposed to be familiar with. But it was fixed in such a way as to bring the terrors and raptures of the mystics, of a S. Catherine or a S. Teresa, within the reach of all; to place spiritual experience à la portée de tout le monde. The vulgarity is only equalled by the ingenuity and psychological adroitness of the method. The soul inspired with carnal dread of the doom impending over it, passed into almost physical contact with the incarnate Saviour. The designed effect was to induce a vivid and varied hypnotic dream of thirty days, from the influence of which a man should never wholly free himself. The end at which he arrived upon this path of self-scrutiny and materialistic realisation, was the conclusion that his highest hope, his most imperative duty, lay in the resignation of his intellect and will to spiritual guidance, and in blind obedience to the Church. Thousands and thousands of souls in the modern world have passed through this discipline; and those who responded to it best, have ever been selected, when this was possible, as novices of the Order. The director had ample opportunity of observing at each turn in the process whether his neophyte displayed a likely disposition.

When the 'Exercitia' had been performed, there was an end of asceticism. Ignatius, as we have seen, dreaded nothing more than the intrusion of that dark spirit into his Company; he aimed at nothing more earnestly than at securing agreeable manners, a cheerful temper, and ability for worldly business in its members.

The novice, when first received into one of the Jesuit houses, was separated so far as possible for two years from his family, and placed under the control of a master, who inspected his correspondence and undertook the full surveillance of his life. He received cautiously restricted information on the constitutions of the Society, and was recommended, instead of renouncing his worldly possessions, to reserve his legal rights and make oblation of them when he took the vows. It was not then made clear to him that what he gave would never under any circumstances be restored, although the Society might send him forth at will a penniless wanderer into the world. Yet this was the hard condition of a Jesuit's existence. After entering the Order he owned nothing, and he had no power to depart if he repented. But the General could cashier him by a stroke of the pen, condemning him to destitution in every land where Jesuits held sway, and to suspicion in every land where Jesuits were loathed. Before the end of two years, the novice generally signed an obligation to assume the vows. He was then drafted into the secular or spiritual service. Some novices became what is called Temporal Coadjutors; their duty was to administer the property of the Society, to superintend its houses, to distribute alms, to work in hospitals, to cook, garden, wash, and act as porters. They took the three vows of poverty, chastity, and obedience. Those, on the other hand, who showed some aptitude for learning, were classified as Scholastics, and were distributed among the colleges of the Order. They studied languages, sciences, and theology, for a period of five years; after which they taught in schools for another period of five or six years; and when they reached the age of about thirty, they might be ordained priests with the title of Spiritual Coadjutors. From this body the Society drew the rectors and professors of its colleges, its preachers, confessors, and teachers in schools for the laity. They were not yet full members, though they had taken the three vows and were irrevocably devoted to the service of the Order. The final stage of initiation was reached toward the age of forty-five, after long and various trials. Then the Jesuit received the title of Professed. He was either a professed of the three vows, or a professed of the four vows; having in the latter case dedicated his life to the special service of the Papacy in missions or in any other cause. The professed of four vows constituted the veritable Company of Jesus, the kernel of the organisation. They were never numerous. At Loyola's death they numbered thirty-five out of a thousand; and it has been calculated that their average proportion to the whole body is as two to a hundred.[1] Even these had no indefeasible tenure of their place in the Society. They might be dismissed by the General without indemnification.

The General was chosen for life from the professed of four vows by the General Congregation, which consisted of the provincials and two members of each province. He held the whole Society at his discretion; for he could deal at pleasure with each part of its machinery. The constitutions, strict as they appeared, imposed no barriers upon his will; for almost unlimited power was surrendered to him of dispensing with formalities, freeing from obligations, shortening or lengthening the periods of initiation, retarding or advancing a member in his career. Ideal fixity of type, qualified by the utmost elasticity in practice, formed the essence of the system. And we shall see that this principle pervaded the Jesuit treatment of morality. The General resided at Rome, consecrated solely to the government of the Society, holding the threads of all its complicated affairs in his hands, studying the personal history of each of its members in the minute reports which he constantly received from every province, and acting precisely as he chose with the highest as well as the lowest of his subordinates. Contrary to all precedents of previous religious orders, Ignatius framed the Company of Jesus upon the lines of a close aristocracy with autocratic authority confided to an elected chief. Yet the General of the Jesuits. like the Doge of Venice, had his hands tied by subtly powerful though almost invisible fetters. He was subjected at every hour of the day and night to the surveillance of five sworn spies, especially appointed to prevent him from altering the type or neglecting the concerns of the

[1] Philippson, *op. cit.* p. 142.

Order. The first of these functionaries, named the Administrator, who was frequently also the confessor of the General, exhorted him to obedience, and reminded him that he must do all things for the glory of God. Obedience and the glory of God, in Jesuit phraseology, meant the maintenance of the Company. The other four were styled Assistants. They had under their charge the affairs of the chief provinces; one overseeing the Indies, another Portugal and Spain, a third France and Germany, a fourth Italy and Sicily. Together with the Administrator, the Assistants were nominated by the General Congregation and could not be removed or replaced without its sanction. It was their duty to regulate the daily life of the General, to control his private expenditure on the scale which they determined, to prescribe what he should eat and drink, and to appoint his hours for sleep, and religious exercises, and the transaction of public business. If they saw grave reasons for his deposition, they were bound to convene the General Congregation for that purpose. And since the Founder knew that guardians need to be guarded, he provided that the Provincials might convene this assembly to call in question the acts of the Assistants. The General himself had no power to oppose its convocation.

The Company of Jesus was thus based upon a system of mutual and pervasive espionage. The novice on first entering had all his acts, habits, and personal qualities registered. As he advanced in his career, he was surrounded by jealous brethren, who felt it their duty to report his slightest weakness to a superior. The superiors were watched by one another and by their inferiors. Masses of secret intelligence poured into the central cabinet of the General; and the General himself ate, slept, prayed, worked, and moved about the world beneath the fixed gaze of ten vigilant eyes. Men accustomed to domesticity and freedom may wonder that life should have been tolerable upon these terms. Yet we must remember that from the moment when a youth had undergone the 'Exercitia' and taken the vows, he became no less in fact than in spirit *perinde ac cadaver* in the hands of his superior. The Company replaced for him both family and state; and in spite of the fourth vow, it is very evident that the Black Pope, as the General came to be nicknamed, owned more of his allegiance than the White Pope, who filled the chair of S. Peter. He could, indeed, at any moment be expelled and ruined. But if he served the Order well, he belonged to a vast, incalculably potent organism, of which he might naturally, after such training as he had received, be proud. The sacrifice of his personal volition and intelligence made him part of an indestructible corporation, which seemed capable of breaking all resistance by its continuity of will and effecting all purposes by its condensed sagacity. Nor was he in the hands of rigid disciplinarians. His peccadilloes were condoned, unless the credit of the Order came in question. His natural abilities obtained free scope for their employment; for it suited the interest of the Company to make the most of each member's special gifts. He had no tedious duties of the regular monastic routine to follow. He was encouraged to become a man of the world, and to mix freely with society. And thus, while he resigned himself, he lived the large life of a complex microcosm. Nor were men of resolute ambition without the prospect of eventually swaying an authority beyond that possessed by princes; for anyone of the professed might rise to the supreme power in the Order.

Something must be said about Loyola's interpretation of the vow of poverty. During his lifetime the Company acquired considerable wealth; and after his death it became a large owner of estates in Europe. How was this consistent with the observance of that vow, so strictly inculcated by the Founder on his first disciples, and so pompously proclaimed in their constitutions? The professed and all their houses, as well as their churches, were bound to subsist on alms; they preached, administered the sacraments of the Church, and educated gratis. They could inherit nothing, and were not allowed to receive money for their journeys. But here appeared the wisdom of restricting the numbers of the professed to a small percentage of the whole Society. The same rigid prohibition with regard to property was not imposed upon the houses of novices, colleges, and other educational establishments of the Jesuits; while the secular coadjutors were specially appointed for the administration of wealth which the professed might use but could not own.[1] In like manner, as they lived on alms, there was no objection to a priest of the Order receiving valuable gifts in cash or kind from grateful recipients of his spiritual bounty. A separate article of the constitutions furthermore reserved for the General the right of accepting any donation whatsoever made in favour of the whole Company, and of assigning capital or revenue as he judged wisest. Scholastics, even after they had taken the vow of poverty, were not obliged to relinquish their private possessions. Sooner or later, it was hoped that these would become the property of the order. In a word, the principle of this solemn obligation was so manipulated as to facilitate the acquisition and accumulation of wealth by the Jesuit like any other corporation. Only no individual Jesuit owned anything. He was rich or poor, he wore the clothes of princes or the rags of a mendicant, he lived sumptuously or begged in the street, he travelled with a following of servants or he walked on foot, according as it seemed good to his superiors. The vow of poverty, thus interpreted in practice, meant a total disengagement from temporalities on the part of every member, an absolute dependence of each subordinate upon his superiority in the hierarchy.

[1] Quinet calculates that at the close of the sixteenth century there were twenty-one houses of the professed (incapable of owning property) to 293 colleges (free from this inability).

Having thus far treated the organisation of the Jesuits as implicit in Loyola's own conception and administration, I ought to add that it received definite form from his successor, Lainez. The founder pronounced the Constitutions in 1553. But they were thoroughly revised after his death in 1558, at which date they first issued from the press. Lainez, again, supplemented these laws with a perpetual commentary which is styled the Declarations. These contain the bulk of those easements and indulgent interpretations, whereby the strictness of the original rules was explained away, and an almost unbounded elasticity was communicated to the system.

It would be rash to pronounce a decided opinion upon the much disputed question, whether, in addition to their Constitutions and Declarations, the Jesuits were provided with an esoteric code of rules known as 'Monita Secreta.'[1] The existence of such a manual, which was supposed to contain the very pith of Jesuitical policy, has been confidently asserted and no less confidently denied. In the absence of direct evidence, it may be worth quoting two passages from Sarpi's Letters, which prove that this keen-sighted observer believed the Society to be governed in its practice by statutes inaccessible to all but its most trusted members. 'I have always admired the policy of the Jesuits,' he writes in 1608, 'and their method of maintaining secrecy. Their Constitutions are in print, and yet one cannot set eyes upon a copy. I do not mean their Rules, which are published at Lyons, for those are mere puerilities, but the digest of laws which guide their conduct of the Order, and which they keep concealed. Every day many members leave, or are expelled from the Company; and yet their artifices are not exposed to view.'[2] In another letter, of the date 1610, Sarpi returns to

---

[1] A book with this title was published in 1612 at Cracow. It was declared a forgery at Rome by a congregation of Cardinals.

[2] *Lettere*, vol. i. p. 100.

the same point. 'The Jesuits before this Aquaviva was elected General were saints in comparison with what they afterwards became. Formerly they had not mixed in affairs of state or thought of governing cities. Since then they have indulged a hope of controlling the whole world. And I am sure that the least part of their Cabala is in the Ordinances and Constitutions of 1570. All the same, I am very glad to possess even these. Their true Cabala they never communicate to any but men who have been well tested and proved by every species of trial; nor is it possible for those who have been initiated into it, to think of retiring from the Order, since the congregation, through their excellent management of its machinery, know how to procure the immediate death of any such initiated member who may wish to leave their ranks.'[1] Probably the mistake which Sarpi and the world made, was in supposing that the Jesuits needed a written code for their most vital action. Being a potent and life-penetrated organism, the secret of their policy was not such as could be reduced to rule. It was not such as, if reduced to rule, could have been plastic in the affairs of public importance which the Company sought to control. Better than rule or statute, it was biological function. The supreme deliberative bodies of the Order created, transmitted, and continuously modified its tradition of policy. This tradition some member, partially initiated into their counsels, may have reduced to precepts in the published 'Monita Secreta' of 1612. But the quintessential flame which breathed a breath of life into the fabric of the Jesuits through two centuries of organic activity, was far too vivid and too spiritual to be condensed in any charter. A friar and a jurist, like Sarpi, expected to discover some controlling code. The public, grossly ignorant of evolutionary laws in the formation of social organisms, could not comprehend the non-existence of

[1] *Lettere*, vol. ii. p. 174.

this code. Adventurers supplied the demand from their knowledge of the ruling policy. But like the 'Liber Trium Impostorum' we may regard the 'Monita Secreta' of the Jesuits as an *ex post facto* fabrication.

There is no need to trace the further history of the Jesuits. Their part in the Counter-Reformation has rather been exaggerated than insufficiently recognised. Though it was incontestably considerable, we cannot now concede, as Macaulay in his random way conceded to this Company, the *spolia opima* of down-beaten Protestantism. Without the ecclesiastical reform which originated in the Tridentine Council; without the gold and sword of Spain; without the stakes and prisons of the Inquisition; without the warfare against thought conducted by the Congregation of the Index; the Jesuits alone could not have masterfully governed the Catholic revival. That revival was a movement of world-historical importance, in which they participated. It was their fortune to find forces in the world which they partially understood; it was their merit to know how to manipulate those forces; it was their misfortune and their demerit that they proved themselves incapable of diverting those forces to any wholesome end. In Italy a succession of worldly Popes, Paul III., Julius III., Pius IV., and Gregory XIII., heaped favours and showered wealth upon the Order. The Jesuits incarnated the political spirit of the Papacy at this epoch; they lent it a potency for good and evil which the decrepit but still vigorous institution arrogated to itself. They adapted its anachronisms with singular adroitness to the needs of modern society. They transfused their throbbing blood into its flaccid veins, until it became doubtful whether the Papacy had been absorbed into the Jesuits, or whether the Jesuits had remodelled the Papacy for contemporary uses. But this tendency in the aspiring Order to identify itself with Rome, this ambition to command the prestige of Rome as leverage for carrying out its own designs, stirred the resentment of haughty and *intransigeant* Pontiffs. The Jesuits were not beloved by Paul IV., Pius V., and Sixtus V.

It remains, however, to inquire in what the originality, the effective operation, and the modifying influence of the Jesuit Society consisted during the period with which we are concerned. It was their object to gain control over Europe by preaching, education, the direction of souls, and the management of public affairs. In each of these departments their immediate success was startling; for they laboured with zeal, and they adapted their methods to the requirements of the age. Yet, in the long run, art, science, literature, religion, morality and politics, all suffered from their interference. By preferring artifice to reality, affectation to sincerity, shams and subterfuges to plain principle and candour, they confused the conscience and enfeebled the intellect of Catholic Europe. When we speak of the Jesuit style in architecture, rhetoric and poetry, of Jesuit learning and scholarship, of Jesuit casuistry and of Jesuit diplomacy, it is either with languid contempt for bad taste and insipidity, or with the burning indignation which systematic falsehood and corruption inspire in honourable minds.

In education, the Jesuits, if they did not precisely innovate, improved upon the methods of the grammarians which had persisted from the Middle Ages through the Renaissance. They spared no pains in training a large and competent body of professors, men of extensive culture, formed upon one uniform pattern, and exercised in the art of popularising knowledge. These teachers were distributed over the Jesuit colleges; and in every country their system was the same. New catechisms, grammars, primers, manuals of history, enabled their pupils to learn with facility in a few months what it had cost years of painful labour to acquire under pompous pedants of the old *régime*. The mental and physical

aptitudes of youths committed to their charge were carefully
observed; and classes were adapted to various ages and
degrees of capacity. Hours of recreation alternated with
hours of study, so that the effort of learning should be neither
irksome nor injurious to health. Nor was religious education
neglected. Attendance upon daily Mass, monthly confession,
and instruction in the articles of the faith, formed an indispensable part of the system. When we remember that these
advantages were offered gratuitously to the public, it is not
surprising that people of all ranks and conditions should have
sent their boys to the Jesuit colleges. Even Protestants
availed themselves of what appeared so excellent a method;
and the Jesuits obtained the reputation of being the best
instructors of youth.[1] It soon became the mark of a good
Catholic to have frequented Jesuit schools; and in after life a
pupil who had studied creditably in their colleges, found himself everywhere at home. Yet the Society took but little
interest in elementary or popular education. Their object
was to gain possession of the nobility, gentry, and upper
middle class. The proletariate might remain ignorant; it
was the destiny of such folk to be passive instruments in
the hands of spiritual and temporal rulers. Nor were they
always scrupulous in the means employed for taking hold on
young men of distinction. One instance of the animosity
they aroused even in Italy at an early period of their activity
will suffice. Tuscany was thrown into commotion by the
discovery of their designs upon the boys they undertook to
teach. 'They were so madly bent,' says Galluzzi, 'upon
filling the ranks of their Company with individuals of wealth

[1] See Sarpi's *Letters*, vol. i. p. 352, for Protestant pupils of Jesuits.
Sarpi's *Memorial to the Signory of Venice on the Collegio de' Greci in
Rome* exposes the fallacy of their being reputed the best teachers of
youth, by pointing out how their aim is to withdraw their pupils'
allegiance from the nation, the government and the family, to themselves.

and birth that in 1584, in the single city of Siena, under the pretence of devotion, they seduced thirty youths of the noblest and richest houses, not without great injury to their families and grief to their parents. The most notorious of these cases was that of two sons of Pandolfo Petrucci, whose name indicates his high position in the aristocracy of Siena. These young men they got into their power by inducing them to commit a theft, and then compelled them to pledge fealty to the Society. Escaping by night in the direction of Rome, the lads were arrested by the city guards, and confessed that they had agreed to meet two Jesuits who were waiting to conduct them on their journey.'[1] It was, indeed, not the propagation of sound principles or liberal learning, but the aggrandisement of the Order and the enforcement of Catholic usages, at which the Jesuits aimed in their scheme of education. This was noticeable in their attitude toward literature and science. Michelet has described their method in a brilliant and exact metaphor, as the attempt to counteract the poison of free thought and stimulative studies by means of vaccination. They taught the classics in expurgated editions, history in drugged epitomes, science in popular lectures. Instead of banning what M. Renan is wont to style *études fortes*, they undertook to emasculate these and render them innocuous. While Bruno was burned by the Inquisition for proclaiming what the Copernican discovery involved for faith and metaphysic, Father Koster at Cologne vulgarised it into something pretty and agreeable. While Scaliger and Casaubon used the humanities as a propædeutic of the virile reason, the Jesuits contrived to sterilise and mechanise their influences by insipid rhetoric. Everywhere through Europe, by the side of stalwart thinkers, crept plausible Jesuit professors, following the light of learning like its shadow, mimicking the accent of the gods like parrots, and mocking their gestures like apes. Their

[1] *Storia del Granducato di Toscana*, vol. iv. p. 275.

adroit admixture of falsehood with truth in all departments of knowledge, their substitution of veneer for solid timber, and of pinchbeck for sterling metal, was more profitable to the end they had in view than the torture-chamber of the Inquisition or the quarantine of the Index. Mediocrities and respectabilities of every description—that is to say, the majority of the influential classes—were delighted with their method. What could be better than to see sons growing up, good Catholics in all external observances, devoted to the order of society and Mother Church, and at the same time showy Latinists, furnished with a cyclopædia of current knowledge, glib at speechifying, ingenious in the construction of an epigram or compliment? If some of the more sensible sort grumbled that Jesuit learning was shallow and Jesuit morality of base alloy, the reply, like that of an Italian draper selling palpable shoddy for broadcloth, came easily and cynically to the surface: *Imita bene!* The stuff is a good match enough! What more do you want? To produce plausible imitations, to save appearances, to amuse the mind with tricks, was the last resort of Catholicism in its warfare against rationalism. And such is the banality of human nature as a whole, that the Jesuits, those monopolists of Brummagem manufactures, achieved eminent success. Their hideous churches, daubed with plaster painted to resemble costly marbles, encrusted with stucco polished to deceive the eye, loaded with gewgaws and tinsel and superfluous ornament and frescoes turning flat surfaces into cupolas and arcades, passed for masterpieces of architectonic beauty. The conceits of their pulpit oratory, its artificial cadences and flowery verbiage, its theatrical appeals to gross sensations, wrought miracles and converted thousands. Their sickly Ciceronian style, their sentimental books of piety, 'the worse for being warm,' the execrable taste of their poetry, their flimsy philosophy and disingenuous history, infected the taste of Catholic

Europe like a slow seductive poison, flattering and accelerating the diseases of mental decadence. Sound learning died down beneath the tyranny of the Inquisition, the Index, the Council of Trent, Spain and the Papacy. A rank growth of unwholesome culture arose and flourished on its tomb under the forcing-frames of Jesuitry. But if we peruse the records of literature and science during the last three centuries, few indeed are the eminences even of a second order which can be claimed by the Company of Jesus.

The same critique applies to Jesuit morality. It was the Company's aim to control the conscience by direction and confession, and especially the conscience of princes, women, youths in high position. To do so by plain speaking and honest dealing was clearly dangerous. The world had had enough of Dominican austerity and dogmatism. To do so by open toleration and avowed cynicism did not suit the temper of the time. A reform of the monastic orders and the regular clergy had been undertaken by the Church. Pardoners, palmers, indulgence-mongers, jolly Franciscan confessors, and such-like folk were out of date. But the Jesuits were equal to the exigencies of the moment. We have seen how Ignatius recommended fishers of souls to humour queasy consciences. His successors expanded and applied the hint.—You must not begin by talking about spiritual things to people immersed in worldly interests. That is as simple as trying to fish without bait. On the contrary, you must insinuate yourself into their confidence by studying their habits, and spying out their propensities. You must appear to notice little at the first, and show yourself a good companion. When you become acquainted with the bosom sins and pleasant vices of folk in high position, you can lead them on the path of virtue at your pleasure. You must certainly tell them then that indulgence in sensuality, falsehood, fraud, violence, covetousness and tyrannical oppression is unconditionally wrong.

Make no show of compromise with evil in the gross; but refine away the evil by distinctions, reservations, hypothetical conditions, until it disappears. Explain how hard it is to know whether a sin be venial or mortal, and how many chances there are against its being in any strict sense a sin at all. Do not leave folk to their own blunt sense of right and wrong, but let them admire the finer edge of your scalpel, while you shred up evil into morsels they can hardly see. A ready way may thus be opened for the satisfaction of every human desire without falling into theological faults. The advantages are manifest. You will be able to absolve with a clear conscience. Your penitent will abound in gratitude and open out his heart to you. You will fulfil your function as confessor and counsellor. He will be secured for the sacred ends of our Society, and will contribute to the greater glory of God.—It was thus that the Jesuit labyrinth of casuistry, with its windings, turnings, secret chambers, whispering galleries, blind alleys, issues of evasion, came into existence; the whole vicious and monstrous edifice being crowned with the saving virtue of obedience and the theory of ends justifying means. After the irony of Pascal, the condensed rage of La Chalotais, and the grave verdict of the Parlement of Paris (1762), it is not necessary now to refute the errors or to expose the abominations of this casuistry in detail.[1] Yet it cannot be

[1] Having mentioned the names of these illustrious Frenchmen, I feel bound to point out how accurately their criticism of the Jesuits was anticipated by Paolo Sarpi. His correspondence between the years 1608 and 1622 demonstrates that this body of social corrupters had been early recognised by him in their true light. Sarpi calls them 'sottilissimi maestri in mal fare,' 'donde esce ogni falsità e bestemmia,' 'il vero morbo Gallico,' 'peste pubblica,' 'peste del mondo' (*Letters*, vol. i. pp. 142, 183, 245, ii. 82, 109). He says that they 'hanno messo l' ultima mano a stabilire una corruzione universale' (*ib.* vol. i. p. 304). By their equivocations and mental reservations 'fanno essi prova di gabbare Iddio' (*ib.* vol. ii. p. 82). 'La menzogna non iscusano soltanto ma lodano' (*ib.* vol. ii. p. 106). So far, the utterances

wholly passed in silence here; for its application materially favoured the influence of Jesuits in modern Europe.
which I have quoted might pass for the rhetoric of mere spite. But the portrait gradually becomes more definite in details limned from life· 'The Jesuits have so many loopholes for escape, pretexts, colours of insinuation, that they are more changeful than the Sophist of Plato; and when one thinks to have caught them between thumb and finger, they wriggle out and vanish ' (*ib.* vol. i. p. 230). ' The Jesuit fathers have methods of acquiring in this world, and making their neophytes acquire, heaven without diminution, or rather with augmentation, of this life's indulgences' (*ib.* vol. i. p. 313). 'The Jesuit fathers used to confer Paradise; they now have become dispensers of fame in this world' (*ibid.* p. 363). ' When they seek entrance into any place, they do not hesitate to make what promises may be demanded of them, possessing as they do the art of escape by lying with equivocations and mental reservations' (*ib.* vol. ii. p, 147). ' The Jesuit is a man of every colour; he repeats the marvel of the chameleon' (*ibid.* p. 105). ' When they play a losing game, they yet rise winners from the table. For it is their habit to insinuate themselves upon any condition demanded, having arts enough whereby to make themselves masters of those who bind them by prescribed rules. They are glad to enter in the guise of galley-slaves with irons on their ankles; since, when they have got in, they will find no difficulty in loosing their own bonds and binding others' (*ibid.* p. 134). ' They command two arts : the one of escaping from the bonds and obligations of any vow or promise they shall have made, by means of equivocation, tacit reservation, and mental restriction; the other of insinuating, like the hedgehog, into the narrowest recesses, being well aware that when they unfold their piercing bristles, they will obtain the full possession of the dwelling and exclude its master' (*ibid.* p. 144). 'Everybody in Italy is well aware how they have wrought confession into an art. They never receive confidences under that seal without disclosing all particulars in the conferences of their Society; and that with the view of using confession to the advantage of their Order and the Church. At the same time they preach the doctrine that the seal of the confessional precludes a penitent from disclosing what the confessor may have said to him, albeit his utterances have had no reference to sins or to the safety of the soul' (*ib.* vol. ii. p. 108). ' Should the Jesuits in France get hold of education, they will dominate the university, and eradicate sound letters. Yet why do I speak of healthy literature? I ought to have said good and wholesome doctrine, the which is verily mortal to that Company' (*ibid.* p. 162). 'Every species of vice finds its patronage in them. The avaricious trust their maxims, for trafficking in spiritual commodities; the superstitious, for substituting kisses upon images for the exercise of Christian

The working of the Company, as we have seen, depended upon a skilful manipulation of apparently hard-and-fast principles. The Declarations explained away the Constitutions; and an infinite number of minute exceptions and distinctions volatilised vows and obligations into ether. Transferring the same method to the sphere of ethics, they so wrought upon the precepts of the moral law, whether expressed in holy writ, in the ecclesiastical decrees, or in civil jurisprudence, as to deprive them of their binding force. The

virtues; the base fry of ambitious upstarts, for cloaking every act of scoundreldom with a veil of holiness. The indifferent find in them a palliative for their spiritual deadness; and whoso fears no God has a visible God ready made for him, whom he may worship with merit to his soul. In fine, there is nor perjury, nor sacrilege, nor parricide, nor incest, nor rapine, nor fraud, nor treason, which cannot be masked as meritorious beneath the mantle of their dispensation' (*ibid.* p. 330). 'I apprehend the difficulty of attacking their teachings; seeing that they merge their own interests with those of the Papacy, and that not only in the article of Pontifical authority, but in all points. At present they stand for themselves upon the ground of equivocations. But believe me, they will adjust this also, and that speedily; forasmuch as they are omnipotent in the Roman Court, and the Pope himself fears them' (*ibid.* p. 333). 'Had S. Peter known the creed of the Jesuits, he could have found a way to deny our Lord without sinning ' (*ibid.* p. 353). 'The Roman Court will never condemn Jesuit doctrine; for this is the secret of its empire—a secret of the highest and most capital importance, whereby those who openly refuse to worship it are excommunicated, and those who would do so if they dared are held in check' (*ibid.* p. 105). The object of this lengthy note is to vindicate for Sarpi a prominent and early place among those candid analysts of Jesuitry who now are lost in the great light of Pascal's genius. Sarpi's *Familiar Letters* have for my mind even more weight than the famous *Lettres Provinciales* of Pascal. They were written with no polemical or literary bias, at a period when Jesuitry was in its prime; and their force as evidence is strengthened by their obvious spontaneity. A book of some utility was published in 1703 at Salzburg (?), under the title of *Artes Jesuiticae* by Christianus Aletophilus. This contains a compendium of those passages in casuistical writings on which Pascal based his brilliant satires. Paul Bert's modern work, *La Morale des Jésuites* (Paris: Charpentier, 1881), is intended to prove that recent casuistical treatises of the school repeat those ancient perversions of sound morals.

subtlest elasticity had been gained for the machinery of the order by casuistical interpretation. A like elasticity was secured for the control and government of souls by an identical process. It was no wonder that the Jesuits became rapidly fashionable as confessors. The plainest prohibitions were as wax in their hands. The Decalogue laid down as rules for conduct: 'Thou shalt not steal;' 'Thou shalt not kill;' 'Thou shalt not commit adultery.' Christ spiritualised these rules into their essence: 'Thou shalt love thy neighbour as thyself;' 'Whosoever looketh on a woman to lust after her hath committed adultery already with her in his heart.' It is manifest that both the old and the new covenant, upon which modern Christianity is supposed to rest, suffered no transactions in matters so clear to the human conscience. Jesus himself refined upon the legality of the Mosaic code by defining sin as egotism or concupiscence. But the Company of Jesus took pains in their casuistry to provide attenuating circumstances for every sin in detail. By their doctrines of the invincible erroneous conscience, of occult compensation, of equivocation, of mental reservation, of probabilism, and of philosophical sin, they afforded loopholes for the gratification of every passion and for the commission of every crime. Instead of maintaining that any injury done to a neighbour is wrong, they multiplied instances in which a neighbour may be injured. Instead of holding firm to Christ's verdict that sexual vice is implicit in licentious desire, they analysed the sensual modes of crude voluptuousness, taxed each in turn at arbitrary values, and provided plausible excuses for indulgence. Instead of laying it down as a broad principle that men must keep their word, they taught them how to lie with spiritual impunity and with credit to their reputation as sons of the Church. Thus the inventive genius of the casuist, bent on dissecting immorality and reducing it to classes; the interrogative ingenuity of the confessor, pruriently inquisitive into private experience; the apologetic subtlety of the director, eager to supply his penitent with salves and anodynes; were all alike and all together applied to anti-social contamination in matters of lubricity, and to anti-social corruption in matters of dishonesty, fraud, falsehoods, illegality and violence. The single doctrine of probabilism, as Pascal abundantly proved, facilitates the commission of crime; for there is no perverse act which some casuist of note has not plausibly excused.

It may be urged that confession and direction, as adopted by the Catholic Church, bring the abominations of casuistry logically in their train. Priests who have to absolve sinners must be familiar with sin in all its branches. In the confessional they will be forced to listen to recitals, the exact bearings of which they cannot understand unless they are previously instructed. Therefore the writings of Sanchez, Diana, Liguori, Burchard, Billuard, Rousselot, Gordon, Gaisson, are put into their hands at an early age—works which reveal more secrets of impudicity than Aretino has described, or Commodus can have practised—works which recommend more craft and treachery and fraud and falsehood than Machiavelli accorded to his misbegotten Saviour of Society. In these writings men vowed to celibacy probe the foulest labyrinths of sexual impurity; men claiming to stand outside the civil order and the state imbibe false theories upon property and probity and public duty.

The root of the matter is wrong indubitably. It is contrary to good government that a sacerdotal class, by means of confession and direction, should be placed in a position of deciding upon conduct. It is revolting to human dignity that this same class, without national allegiance and without domestic ties, should have the opportunity of infecting young minds by unhealthy questionings and dishonourable suggestions. But this wrong, which is inherent in the modern

Catholic system, becomes an atrocity when it is employed, as the Jesuits employed it, as an instrument for moulding and controlling society in their own interest. While the Jesuits rendered themselves obnoxious to criticism by their treatment of the individual in his private and social capacity, they speedily became what Hallam cautiously styles 'rather dangerous supporters of the See of Rome' in public and political affairs. The ultimate failure of their diplomacy and intrigue over the whole field of modern statecraft inclines historians of the present epoch to underrate their mechanics of obstruction, and to underestimate the many occasions on which they did successfully retard the progress of civil government and intellectual freedom. It were wiser to regard them in the same light as fanatics laying stones upon a railway, or of dynamiters blowing up an emperor or a corner of Westminster Hall. The final end of the nefarious traffic may not be attained. But credit can be claimed by those who took their part in it, for the wreck of express trains, the perturbation of cities, and the mourning of peaceable families. And thus it was with the Jesuits. Though the results of their political intrigues have not corresponded to their hopes, they yet worked appreciable mischief by the organisation of the League in France, and the Thirty Years' War in Germany, and by their revolutionary theories which infected Europe with conspiracy and murder. Their method was not original. Machiavelli had expounded the doctrines they put in practice. He taught that in a desperate state of the nation men may have recourse to treachery and violence. The nation of the Jesuits was a hybrid between their Order and Catholicism. The peril to the Church was imminent; its decadence demanded desperate remedies. They invoked regicide, revolt, and treason, to effect an impossible cure.

The political theory of the Jesuits was deduced from their

fundamental principle of obedience to the Church. They maintained that the ecclesiastical is *jure divino* superior to the secular power. The Pope through God's commission and appointment sways the Church; the Church takes rank above the State, as the soul above the body. Consequently, the first allegiance of a Christian nation, together with its secular rulers, belongs of right to the Supreme Pontiff. The people is the real sovereign; and kings are delegates from the people, with authority which they can only justly exercise so long as they remain in obedience to Rome. It follows from these positions that every nation must refuse fealty to an irreligious or contumacious ruler. In the last resort they may lawfully remove him by murder; and they are *ipso facto* in a state of mortal sin if they elect or recognise a heretic as sovereign. This theory sprang from the writings of the English Jesuits, Allen and Parsons. It was elaborated in Rome by Cardinal Bellarmino, applied in Spain by Suarez and Mariana, and openly preached in France by Jean Boucher. The best energies of Paolo Sarpi were devoted to combating the main position of ecclesiastical supremacy. His works had a salutary effect by delimiting the relations of the Church to the State, and by demonstrating even to Catholics the pernicious results of acknowledging a Papal overlordship in temporal affairs. At the same time the boldly democratic principle of the sovereignty of the people, which the Jesuits advanced in order to establish their doctrine of ecclesiastical superiority, provoked opposition. It led to the contrary hypothesis of the Divine Right of sovereigns, which found favour in Protestant kingdoms and especially in England under the Stuart dynasty. When the French Catholics resolved to terminate the discords of their country by the recognition of Henri IV., they had recourse to this argument for justifying their obedience to a heretic. It was felt by all sound thinkers and by every patriot in Europe that the Papal prerogatives claimed by the Jesuits were too inconsistent with national liberties to be tolerated. The zeal of the Society had clearly outrun its discretion; and the free discussion of the theory of government which their insolent assumptions stimulated, weakened the cause they sought to strengthen. Their ingenuity overreached itself.

This, however, was as nothing compared with the hostility evoked by their unscrupulous application of these principles in practice. There was hardly a plot against established rule in Protestant countries with which they were not known or believed to be connected. The invasion of Ireland in 1579, the judicial murder of the Regent Morton in Scotland, and Babington's conspiracy against Elizabeth, emanated from their councils. They were held responsible for the attempted murder of the Prince of Orange in 1580, and for his actual murder in 1584. They loudly applauded Jacques Clément, the assassin of Henri III. in 1589, as 'the eternal glory of France.'[1] Numerous unsuccessful attacks upon the life of Henri IV., culminating in that of Jean Chastel in 1594, caused their expulsion from France. When they returned in 1608, they set to work again[2]; and the assassin Ravaillac, who succeeded in removing the obnoxious champion of European independence in 1610, was probably inspired by their doctrine.[3] They had a hand in the Gunpowder Plot

---

[1] See Mariana, *De Rege*, lib. i. cap. 6. This book, be it remembered, was written for the instruction of the heir-apparent, afterwards Philip III.

[2] Henri IV. let them return to France in mere dread of their machinations against him. See Sully, vol. v. p. 113.

[3] Sarpi, who was living at the time of Henri's murder, and who saw his best hopes for Italy and the Church of God extinguished by that crime, at first credited the Jesuits with the deliberate instigation of Ravaillac. He gradually came to the conclusion that, though they were not directly responsible, their doctrine of regicide had inflamed the fanatic's imagination. See, in succession, *Letters*, vol. ii. pp. 78, 79, 81, 83, 86 91, 105, 121, 170, 181, 192.

of 1605, and were thought by some to have instigated the
Massacre of S. Bartholomew. They fomented the League of
the Guises, which had for its object a change in the French
dynasty. They organised the Thirty Years' War, and they
procured the revocation of the Edict of Nantes. If it is not
possible to connect them immediately with all and each of
the criminal acts laid to their charge, the fact that a Jesuit
in every case was lurking in the background, counts by the
force of cumulative evidence heavily against them, and
explains the universal suspicion with which they came to
be regarded as factious intermeddlers in the concerns of
nations. Moreover, their written words accused them; for
the tyrannicide of heretics was plainly advocated in their
treatises on government. So profound was the conviction of
their guilt, that the death of Sixtus V. in 1590, predicted by
Bellarmino, the sudden death of Urban VII. in the same
year, and the death of Clement VIII. in 1605, also predicted
by Bellarmino—these three Popes being ill-affected toward the
Order—were popularly ascribed to their agency. But of their
practical intervention there is no proof. Old age and fever
must be credited, in these as in other cases, with the decease
of Roman Pontiffs supposed to have been poisoned.

It is not, however, to be wondered that sooner or later the
Jesuits made themselves insupportable by their intrigues in
all the countries where they were established.[1] Even to the
Papacy itself they proved too irksome to be borne. The
Company showed plainly that what they meant by obedience
to Rome was obedience to a Rome controlled and fashioned
by themselves. It was their ambition to stand in the same

---

[1] Expelled from Venice in 1606, from Bohemia in 1618, from Naples
and the Netherlands in 1622, from Russia in 1676, from Portugal in
1759, from Spain in 1767, from France in 1764. Suppressed by the
Bull of Clement XIV. in 1773. Restored in 1814, as an instrument
against the Revolution.

RELATION OF JESUITS TO ROME

relation to the Pope as the Shogûn to the Mikado of Japan. Nor does the analysis of their opinions fail to justify the condemnation passed upon them by the Parlement of Paris in 1762. 'These doctrines tend to destroy the natural law, that rule of manners which God Himself has imprinted on the hearts of men, and in consequence to sever all the bonds of civil society, by the authorisation of theft, falsehood, perjury, the most culpable impurity, and in a word each passion and each crime of human weakness; to obliterate all sentiments of humanity by favouring homicide and parricide; and to annihilate the authority of sovereigns in the State.'

Great psychological and pathological interest attaches to the study of the Jesuit Order. To withhold our admiration from the zeal, energy, self-devotion and constructive ability of its founders, would be impossible. Equally futile would it be to affect indifference before the sinister spectacle of so world-embracing an organism, persistently maintained in action for an anti-social end. There is something Roman in the colossal proportions of Loyola's idea, something Roman in the durability of the structure which perpetuates it. Yet the philosopher cannot but agree with the vulgar in his final judgment on the odiousness of these sacerdotal despots, these unflinching foes not merely to the heroes of the human intellect and to the champions of right conduct, but also to the very angels of Christianity. That the Jesuits should claim to have been founded by Him who preached the Sermon on the Mount, that they should flaunt their motto, A.M.D.G., in the sight of Him who spake from Sinai, is one of those practical paradoxes in which the history of decrepit religions abounds.

CHAPTER V

SOCIAL AND DOMESTIC MORALS : PART I

How did the Catholic Revival affect Italian Society?—Difficulty of Answering this Question—Frequency of Private Crimes of Violence—Homicides and Bandits—Savage Criminal Justice—Paid Assassins—Toleration of Outlaws—Honourable Murder—Example of the Lucchese Army -State of the Convents—The History of Virginia de Leyva—Lucrezia Buonvisi—The True Tale of the Cenci—The Brothers of the House of Massimo—Vittoria Accoramboni—The Duchess of Palliano—Wife-Murders—The Family of Medici.

WE are naturally led to inquire what discernible effect the Catholic Revival and the Counter-Reformation had upon the manners and morals of the Italians as a nation. Much has been said about the contrast between intellectual refinement and almost savage license which marked the Renaissance. Yet it can with justice be maintained that, while ferocity and brutal sensuality survived from the Middle Ages, humanism, by means of the new ideal it introduced, tended to civilise and educate the race. Now, however, the Church was stifling culture and attempting to restore that ecclesiastical conception of human life which the Renaissance had superseded. Did, then, her resuscitated Catholicism succeed in permeating the Italians with the spirit of Christ and of the Gospel? Were the nobles more quiet in their demeanour, less quarrelsome and haughty, more law-abiding and less given to acts of violence, than they had been in the previous period? Were the people more contented and less torn by factions, happier in their homes, less abandoned to the insanities of baleful superstitions?

It is obviously difficult to answer these questions with either completeness or accuracy. In the first place, we have no right to expect that the religious revival, signalised by the Tridentine Council, should have made itself immediately felt in the sphere of national conduct. In the second place, it was not, like the German Reformation, a renewal of Christianity at its sources, but a resuscitation of medieval Catholicity, in direct antagonism to the intellectual tendencies of the age. The new learning among northern races disintegrated that system of ideas upon which medieval society rested; but it also introduced religious and moral conceptions more vital than those ideas in their decadence. In Italy the disintegrating process had been no less thorough, nay far more subtle and pervasive. Yet the new learning had not led the nation to attempt a reconstruction of primitive Christianity. The Catholic Revival gave nothing vital or enthusiastic to the conscience of the race. It brought the old creeds, old cult, old superstitions, old abuses back, with stricter discipline and under a *régime* of terror. Meanwhile, it resolutely ranged its forces in opposition to what had been salutary and life-giving in the mental movement of the Renaissance. It compelled people who had watched the dawning of a new light, to shut their eyes upon that dayspring. It extinguished the studies of the Classical Revival; bade philosophers return to Thomas of Aquino; threatened thinkers with the dungeon or the stake who should presume to pass the Pillars of Hercules, when a whole Atlantic of knowledge had been opened to their curiosity. Under these circumstances it was impossible that a revolution, so retrograde in its nature, checking the tide of national energy in full flow, should have exercised a healthy influence over the Italian temperament at large. We have a right to expect, what in fact we find, the advent of hypocrisy and ceremonial observances, but little actual amendment in

manners. In the third place, the question is still further
complicated by the Catholic Revival having been effected con-
currently with the establishment of the Spanish Hegemony.
At the end of the first chapter of this volume I pointed out
the evils brought on Italy by her servitude to a foreign and
unsympathetic despot: the decline of commercial activity,
the multiplication of slothful lordlings, the depression of
industry, the diminution of wealth, and the suffering of the
lower classes from pirates, bandits, and tax-gatherers. These
conditions were sufficient to demoralise a people. And
medieval Catholicism, restored by edict, enforced by the Inquisition, propagated by Jesuits, was not of the fine enthusiastic quality to counteract them. Servile in its conception,
it sufficed to bridle and benumb a race of serfs, but not to
soften or to purify their brutal instincts.[1]

In this chapter I shall not attempt a general survey of
Italian society.[2] I shall content myself with supplying
materials for the formation of a judgment by narrating some
of the most remarkable domestic tragedies of the second half
of the sixteenth century, choosing those only which rest upon
well-sifted documentary evidence, and which bring the social
conditions of the country into strong relief. Before engaging
in these historical romances, it will be well to preface them

[1] The last section of Loyola's *Exercitia* is an epitome of post-
Tridentine Catholicism, though penned before the opening of the Council. In its last paragraph it inculcates the fear of God : 'neque porro
is timor solum, quem filialem appellamus, qui pius est ac sanctus
maxime; verum etiam alter, servilis dictus' (*Inst. Soc. Jesu*, vol. iv. p.
173).

[2] An interesting survey of this wider kind has been attempted by
U. A. Canello for the whole sixteenth century in his *Storia della Lett.
It. nel Secolo XVI.* (Milano: Vallardi, 1880). He tries to demonstrate
that, in the sphere of private life, Italian society gradually refined the
brutal lusts of the Middle Ages, and passed through fornication to a
true conception of woman as man's companion in the family. The
theme is bold ; and the author seems to have based it upon too slight
acquaintance with the real conditions of the Middle Ages.

with a few general remarks upon the state of manners they will illustrate.

The first thing which strikes a student of Italy between 1580 and 1600 is that crimes of violence, committed by private individuals for personal ends, continued steadily upon the increase.[1] Compared with the later Middle Ages, compared with the Renaissance, this period is distinguished by extraordinary ferocity of temper and by an almost unparalleled facility of bloodshed.[2] The broad political and religious contests which had torn the country in the first years of the sixteenth century, were pacified. Foreign armies had ceased to dispute the provinces of Italy. The victorious powers of Spain, the Church, and the protected principalities, seemed secure in the possession of their gains. But those international quarrels which kept the nation in unrest through a long period of municipal wars, ending in the horrors of successive invasions, were now succeeded by an almost universal discord between families and persons. Each province, each city, each village became the theatre of private feuds and assassinations. Each household was the scene of homicide and empoisonment. Italy presented the spectacle of a nation armed against itself, not to decide the issue of antagonistic political principles by civil strife, but to gratify lawless passions—cupidity, revenge, resentment—by deeds of personal high-handedness. Among the common people of the country and the towns, crimes of brutality and bloodshed were of daily occurrence; every man bore weapons for self-defence

[1] Galluzzi, in his *Storia del Granducato di Toscana*, vol. iv. p. 84, estimates the murders committed in Florence alone during the eighteen months which followed the death of Cosimo I., at 186.

[2] In drawing up these paragraphs I am greatly indebted to a vigorous passage by Signor Salvatore Bonghi in his *Storia di Lucrezia Buonvisi*, pp. 7-9, of which I have made free use, translating his words when they served my purpose, and interpolating such further details as might render the picture more complete.

and for attack upon his neighbour. The aristocracy and the upper classes of the *bourgeoisie* lived in a perpetual state of mutual mistrust, ready upon the slightest occasion of fancied affront to blaze forth into murder. Much of this savagery was due to the false ideas of honour and punctilio which the Spaniards introduced. Quarrels arose concerning a salute, a title, a question of precedence, a seat in church, a place in the prince's ante-chamber, a meeting in the public streets. Noblemen were ushered on their way by servants, who measured distances and took the height of daïs or of bench, before their master committed his dignity by advancing a step beyond the minimum that was due. Love-affairs and the code of honour with regard to women opened endless sources of implacable jealousies, irreconcileable hatreds, and offences that could only be wiped out with blood. On each and all of these occasions, the sword was ready to the right hand; and where this generous weapon would not reach, the harquebuss and knife of paid assassins were employed without compunction.[1] We must not, however, ascribe this condition of society wholly or chiefly to Spanish influences. It was in fact a survival of medieval habits under altered circumstances. During the municipal wars of the thirteenth century, and afterwards during the struggle of the despots for ascendency, the nation had become accustomed to internecine contests which set party against party, household against household, man against man. These humours in the cities, as Italian historians were wont to call them, had been partially suppressed by the confederation of the five great Powers at the close of the fifteenth century, and also by a prevalent urbanity of manners.

[1] The lax indulgence accorded by the Jesuit casuists to every kind of homicide appears in the extracts from those writers collected in *Artes Jesuiticae* (Salisburgi, 1703, pp. 75-83). Tamburinus went so far as to hold that if a man mixed poison for his enemy, and a friend came in and drank it up before his eyes, he was not bound to warn his friend, nor was he guilty of his friend's death (*ib.* p. 135, Art. 651).

At that epoch, moreover, they were systematised and controlled by the methods of *condottiere* warfare, which offered a legitimate outlet to the passions of turbulent young men. But when Italy sank into the sloth of pacification after the settlement of Charles V. at Bologna in 1530, when there were no longer *condottieri* to levy troops in rival armies, when political parties ceased in the cities, the old humours broke out again under the aspect of private and personal feuds. Though the names of Guelf and Ghibelline had lost their meaning, these factions reappeared, and divided Milan, the towns of Romagna, the villages of the Campagna. In the place of *condottieri* arose brigand chiefs, who, like Piccolomini and Sciarra, placed themselves at the head of regiments and swept the country on marauding expeditions. Instead of exiles driven by victorious parties in the state to seek precarious living on a foreign soil, bandits proscribed for acts of violence abounded. Thus the habits which had been created through centuries of political ferment, subsisted when the nation was at rest in servitude, assuming baser and more selfish forms of ferocity. The end of the sixteenth century witnessed the final degeneration and corruption of a medieval state of warfare, which the Renaissance had checked, but which the miseries of foreign invasions had resuscitated by brutalising the population, and which now threatened to disintegrate society in aimless anarchy and private lawlessness.

It must not be imagined that governments and magistracies were slack in their pursuit of criminals. Repressive statutes, proclamations of outlawry, and elaborate prosecutions succeeded one another with unwearied conscientiousness. The revenues of states were taxed to furnish blood-money and to support spies. Large sums were invariably offered for the capture or assassination of escaped delinquents; and woe to the wretches who became involved in criminal proceedings! Witnesses were tortured with infernal cruelty. Convicted culprits suffered horrible agonies before their death, or were condemned to languish out a miserable life in pestilential dungeons. But the very inhumanity of this judicial method, without mercy for the innocent from whom evidence could be extorted, and frequently inequitable in the punishments assigned to criminals of varying degrees of guilt, taught the people to defy justice and encouraged them in brutality. They found it more tolerable to join the bands of brigands who preyed upon their fields and villages, than to assist rulers who governed so unequally and cruelly. We know, for instance, that a robber chief, Marianazzo, refused the Pope's pardon, alleging that the profession of brigandage was more lucrative and offered greater security of life than any trade within the walls of Rome. Thus the bandits of that generation occupied the specious attitude of opposition to oppressive governments. There were, moreover, many favourable chances for a homicide. The Church was jealous of her rights of sanctuary. Whatever may have been her zeal for orthodoxy, she showed herself an indulgent mother to culprits who demanded an asylum. Feudal nobles prided themselves on protecting refugees within their fiefs and castles. There were innumerable petty domains left, which carried privileges of signorial courts and local justice. Cardinals, ambassadors, and powerful princes claimed immunity from common jurisdiction in their palaces, the courts and basements of which soon became the resort of escaped criminals. No extradition treaties subsisted between the several and numerous states into which Italy was then divided, so that it was only necessary to cross a frontier in order to gain safety from the law. The position of an outlaw in that case was tolerably secure, except against private vengeance or the cupidity of professional cutthroats, who gained an honest livelihood by murdering bandits with a good price on their heads. Condemned for the most part in their absence, these homicides entered a recognised and not dishonourable class. They were tolerated, received, and even favoured by neighbouring princes, who generally had some grudge against the state from which the outlaws fled. After obtaining letters of safe-conduct and protection, they enrolled themselves in the militia of their adopted country, while the worst of them became spies or secret agents of police. No government seems to have regarded crimes of violence with severity, provided these had been committed on a foreign soil. Murders for the sake of robbery or rape were indeed esteemed ignoble. But a man who had killed an avowed enemy, or had shed blood in the heat of a quarrel, or had avenged his honour by the assassination of a sister convicted of light love, only established a reputation for bravery which stood him in good stead. He was likely to make a stout soldier, and he had done nothing socially discreditable. On the contrary, if he had been useful in ridding the world of an outlaw some prince wished to kill, this murder made him a hero. In addition to the blood-money, he not unfrequently received lucrative office or a pension for life.

A very curious state of things resulted from these customs. States depended in large measure for the execution of their judicial sentences in cases of manslaughter and treason, upon foreign murderers and traitors. Towns were full of outlaws, each with a price upon his head, mutually suspicious, individually desirous of killing some fellow-criminal and thereby enriching his own treasury. If he were successful, he received a fair sum of money, with privileges and immunities from the state which had advertised the outlaw; and not unfrequently he obtained the further right of releasing one or more bandits from penalties of death or prison. It may be imagined at what cross-purposes the outlaws dwelt together, with crimes in many states accumulated on their shoulders; and what peril might ensue to society should they combine together, as indeed they tried to do in Bedmar's conspiracy against Venice. Meanwhile, the states kept this floating population of criminals in check by various political and social contrivances, which grew up from the exigencies and the habits of the moment. Instead of recruiting soldiers from the stationary population, it became usual, when a war was imminent, to enrol outlaws. Thus, when Lucca had to make an inroad into Garfagnana in 1613, the Republic issued a proclamation promising pardon and pay to those of its own bandits who should join its standard. Men to the number of 591 answered this call, and the little war which followed was conducted with more than customary fierceness.[1] Even the ordinary police and guards of cities were composed of fugitives from other states, care being taken to select by preference those who came stained only with honourable bloodshed. In 1593 the guard of the palace of Lucca was reinforced by the addition of forty-three men, among whom four were bandits for wounds inflicted upon enemies in open fight; twelve for homicide in duel sword to sword; five for the murder of more than one person in similar encounters; one for the murder of a sister and the wounding of her seducer; two for mutilating an enemy in the face; one for unlawful recruiting; one for wounding; one for countenancing bandits; and sixteen simple refugees.[2] The phrases employed to describe these men in the official report are sufficiently illustrative of contemporary moral standards. Thus we read ' Banditi per omicidi semplici *da buono a buono*, a sangue caldo, da spada a spada, *o di nemici*.' ' Per omicidio d' una sorella *per causa d' onore*.' To murder an enemy or a sister who had misbehaved herself was accounted excusable.

The prevalence of lawlessness encouraged a domestic custom which soon grew into a system. This was the

[1] See Salvatore Bonghi, *op. cit.* p. 159.
[2] Bonghi, *op. cit.* p. 159, note.

maintenance of so-called *bravi* by nobles and folk rich enough to afford so expensive a luxury. The outlaws found their advantage in the bargain which they drew with their employers; for besides being lodged, fed, clothed and armed, they obtained a certain protection from the spies and professional murderers who were always on the watch to kill them. Their masters used them to defend their persons when a feud was being carried on, or directed them against private enemies whom they wished to injure. It is not uncommon in the annals of these times to read: 'Messer So-and-so, having received an affront from the Count of V, employed the services of three *bravi*, valiant fellows up to any mischief, with whom he retired to his country house.' Or again: 'The Marquis, perceiving that his neighbour had a grudge against him on account of the Signora Lucrezia, thought it prudent to increase his body-guard, and therefore added Pepi and Lo Scarabone, bandits from Tuscany for murders of a priest and a citizen, to his household.' Or again: 'During the vacation of the Holy See the Baron X had, as usual, engaged men-at-arms for the protection of his palace.'

In course of time it became the mark of birth and wealth to lodge a rabble of such rascals. They lived on terms of familiarity with their employer, shared his secrets, served him in his amours, and executed any devil's job he chose to command. Apartments in the basement of the palace were assigned to them, so that a nobleman's house continued to resemble the castle of a medieval baron. But the *bravi*, unlike soldiery, were rarely employed in honourable business. They formed a permanent element of treachery and violence within the social organism. Not a little singular were the relations thus established. The community of crime, involving common interests and common perils, established a peculiar bond between the noble and his *bravo*. This was complexioned by a certain sense of 'honour rooted in dishonour,' and by a faint reflection from elder retainership. The compact struck between landowner and bandit parodied that which drew feudal lord and wandering squire together. There was something ignobly noble in it, corresponding to the confused conscience and perilous conditions of the epoch.

While studying this organised and half-tolerated system of social violence, we are surprised to observe how largely it was countenanced and how frequently it was set in motion by the Church. In a previous chapter on the Jesuits I have adverted to their encouragement of assassination for ends which they considered sacred. In a coming chapter upon Sarpi I shall show to what extent the Roman prelacy was implicated in more than one attempt to take away his life. The chiefs of the Church, then, instead of protesting against this vice of corrupt civilisation in Italy, lent the weight of their encouragement to what strikes us now, not only as eminently unchristian, but also as pernicious to healthy national conditions of existence. We may draw two conclusions from these observations: first, that religions, except in the first fervour of their growth and forward progress, recognise the moral conventions of the society which they pretend to regulate; secondly, that it is well-nigh impossible for men of one century to sympathise with the ethics of a past and different epoch. We cannot comprehend the regicidal theories of the Jesuits or the murderous intrigues of a Borghese Pontiff's Court, without admitting that priests, specially dedicated to the service of Christ and to the propagation of his gospel, felt themselves justified in employing the immoral and unchristian means which social custom placed at their disposal for ridding themselves of inconvenient enemies. This is at the same time their defence as human beings in the sixteenth century and their indictment as self-styled and professed successors of the Founder who rebuked Peter in the Garden of Gethsemane.

STATE OF CONVENTS

To make general remarks upon the state of sexual morality at this epoch, is hardly needful. Yet there are some peculiar circumstances which deserve to be noticed, in order to render the typical stories which I mean to relate intelligible. We have already seen that society condoned the murder of a sister by a brother, if she brought dishonour on her family; and the same privilege was extended to a husband in the case of a notoriously faithless wife. Such homicides did not escape judicial sentence, but they shared in the conventional toleration which was extended to murders in hot blood or in the prosecution of a feud. The state of the Italian convents at this period gave occasion to crimes in which women played a prominent part. After the Council of Trent reforms were instituted in religious houses. But they could not be immediately carried out; and, meanwhile, the economical changes which were taking place in the commercial aristocracy, filled nunneries with girls who had no vocation for a secluded life. Less money was yearly made in trade; merchants became nobles, investing their capital in land, and securing their estates on their eldest sons by entails. It followed that they could not afford to marry all their daughters with dowries befitting the station they aspired to assume. A large percentage of well-born women, accustomed to luxury and vitiated by bad examples in their homes, were thus thrown on a monastic life. Signor Bonghi reckons that at the end of the sixteenth century, more than five hundred girls, who had become superfluous in noble families, crowded the convents in the single little town of Lucca. At a later epoch there would have been no special peril in this circumstance. But at the time with which we are now occupied, an objectionable license still survived from earlier ages. The nunneries obtained evil notoriety as houses of licentious pleasure, to which soldiers and youths of dissolute habits resorted by preference.[1] There appears to have been a specific profligate fanaticism, a well-marked morbid partiality for these amours with cloistered virgins. The young men who prosecuted them, obtained a nickname indicative of their absorbing passion.[2] The attraction of mystery and danger had something, no doubt, to do with this infatuation; and the fascination that sacrilege has for depraved natures, may also be reckoned into the account. To enjoy a lawless amour was not enough; but to possess a woman who alternated between transports of passion and torments of remorse, added zest to guilty pleasure. For men who habitually tampered with magic arts and believed firmly in the devil, this raised romance to rapture. It was a common thing for debauchees to seek what they called *peripetezie di nuova idea*, or novel and exciting adventures stimulative of a jaded appetite, in consecrated places. At any rate, as will appear in the sequel of this chapter, convent intrigues occupied a large space in the criminal annals of the day.

[1] In support of this assertion I translate a letter addressed (Milan, September 15, 1622) by Cardinal Federigo Borromeo to the Prioress of the Convent of S. Margherita at Monza (Dandolo, *Signora di Monza*, p. 132). 'Experience of similar cases has shown how dangerous to your holy state is the vicinity of soldiers, owing to the correspondence which young and idle soldiers continually try to entertain with monasteries, sometimes even under fair and honourable pretexts. . . . Wherefore we have heard with much displeasure that in those places of our diocese where there are convents of nuns and congregations of virgins, ordinary lodgings for the soldiery have been established, called lonely houses (*case erme*), where they are suffered or obliged to dwell through long periods.' The Bishop commands the Prioress to admit no soldier, on any plea of piety, devotion or family relationship, into her convent; to receive no servant or emissary of a soldier; to forbid special services being performed in the chapel at the instance of a soldier; and, finally, to institute a more rigorous system of watch and ward than had been formerly practised.

[2] In Venice, for example, they were called *Monachini*. But the name varied in various provinces.

The Lady of Monza.

VIRGINIA MARIA DE LEYVA was a descendant of Charles V.'s general, Antonio de Leyva, who through many years administered the Duchy of Milan and died loaded with wealth and honours.[1] For his military service he was rewarded with the principality of Ascoli, the feudal lordship of the town of Monza, and the life-tenure of the city of Pavia. Virginia's father was named Martino, and upon his death her cousin succeeded to the titles of the house. She, for family reasons, entered the convent of S. Margherita at Monza, about the year 1595. Here she occupied a place of considerable importance, being the daughter of the Lord of Monza, of princely blood, wealthy, and allied to the great houses of the Milanese. S. Margherita was a convent of the Umiliate, dedicated to the education of noble girls, in which, therefore, considerable laxity of discipline prevailed.[2] Sister Virginia dwelt at ease within its walls, holding a kind of little court, and exercising an undefined authority in petty affairs which was conceded to her rank. Among her favourite companions at the time of the events I am about to narrate, were numbered the Sisters Ottavia Ricci, Benedetta Homata, Candida Brancolina, and Silvia Casata; she was waited on by a converse sister, Caterina da Meda. Adjoining the convent stood the house and garden of a certain Gianpaolo Osio, who plays the principal part in Virginia's tragedy. He must have been a young man of distinguished appearance; for when Virginia first set eyes upon him from a window overlooking his grounds, she ex-

[1] The following abstract of the history of Virginia Maria de Leyva is based on Dandolo's *Signora di Monza* (Milano, 1855). Readers of Manzoni's *I Promessi Sposi*, and of Rosini's tiresome novel, *La Signora di Monza*, will be already familiar with her in romance under the name of Gertrude.

[2] Carlo Borromeo found it necessary to suppress the Umiliati. But he left the female establishment of S. Margherita untouched.

claimed: 'Is it possible that one could ever gaze on anything
more beautiful?' He attracted her notice as early as the
year 1599 or 1600, under circumstances not very favourable
to the plan he had in view. His hands were red with the
blood of Virginia's bailiff, Giuseppe Molteno, whom he had
murdered for some cause unknown to us. During their first
interview (Virginia leaning from the window of her friend
Candida's cell, and Osio standing on his garden-plot beneath),
the young man courteously excused himself for this act of
violence, adding that he would serve her even more devotedly
than the dead Molteno, and begging to be allowed to write
her a letter. When the letter came, it was couched in terms
expressive of a lawless passion. Virginia's noble blood
rebelled against the insult, and she sent an answer back,
rebuffing her audacious suitor. The go-betweens in the
correspondence which ensued were the two nuns Ottavia and
Benedetta, and a certain Giuseppe Pesen, who served as
letter-carrier. Osio did not allow himself to be discouraged
by a first refusal, but took the hazardous step of opening
his mind to the confessor of the convent, Paolo Arrigone, a
priest of San Maurizio in Milan. Arrigone at once lent himself to the intrigue, and taught Osio what kind of letters he
should write Virginia. They were to be courteous, respectful,
blending pious rhetoric with mystical suggestions of romantic
passion. It seems that the confessor composed these
documents himself, and advised his fair penitent that there
was no sin in perusing them. From correspondence, Osio
next passed to interviews. By the aid of Arrigone he gained
access to the parlour of the convent, where he conversed with
Virginia through the bars. In their earlier meetings the lover
did not venture beyond compliments and modest protestations
of devotion. But as time went on, he advanced to kisses and
caresses, and once he made Virginia take a little jewel into
her mouth. This was a white loadstone, blessed by Arrigone,

and intended to operate like a love-charm. The girl, in fact, began to feel the influence of her seducer. In the final confession which she made, she relates how she fought against temptation. 'Some diabolical force compelled me to go to the window overlooking his garden; and one day when Sister Ottavia told me that Osio was standing there, I fainted from the effort to restrain myself. This happened several times. At one moment I flew into a rage and prayed to God to help me; at another I felt lifted from the ground and forced to go and gaze on him. Sometimes when the fit was on me, I tore my hair; I even thought of killing myself.' Virginia was surrounded by persons who had an interest in helping Osio. Not only the confessor, who was a man of infamous character, but her friends among the nuns, themselves accustomed to intrigue of a like nature, led her down the path to ruin. False keys were made, and one or other of the faithless sisters introduced the young man into the convent at night. When Virginia resisted and enlarged upon the sacrilege of breaking cloister, Arrigone supplied her with a printed book of casuistry, in which it was written that, though it might be sinful for a nun to leave her convent, there was no sin in a man entering it. At last she fell; and for seven years she lived in close intimacy with her lover, passing the nights with him, either in his own house or in one of the cells of S. Margherita. On one occasion, when he had to fly from justice, the girls concealed him in their rooms for fifteen days. The first fruit of this amour was a stillborn child; after giving birth to which Virginia sold all the silver she possessed, and sent a votive tablet to Our Lady of Loreto, on which she had portrayed a nun and baby, kneeling and weeping. 'Twice again I sent the same memorial to our Lady, imploring the grace of liberation from this passion. But the sorceries with which I was surrounded, prevailed. In my bed were found the bones of the dead, hooks of iron, and many other things of which the nuns were well informed. Nay, I would fain have given up my life to save my soul; and so great were my afflictions that in despair I went to throw myself into the well, but was restrained by the image of the Virgin at the bottom of the garden, for which I had a special devotion.' In course of time she gave birth to a little girl, named Francesca, who frequented the convent, and whom Osio legitimated as his child.

It was impossible that a connexion of long standing, known to several accomplices, and corroborated by the presence of the child Francesca, should remain hidden from the world. People began to speak about the fact in Monza. A druggist, named Reinaro Soncini, gossiped somewhat too openly. Osio had him shot one night by a servant in his pay. And now the lovers were engaged in a career of crime, which brought them finally to justice. Virginia's waiting-woman Caterina fell into disgrace with her mistress, and was shut up in a kind of prison by her orders. The girl declared that she would bring the whole bad affair before the superior authorities, and would do so immediately, seeing that Monsignor Barca, the visitor of S. Margherita, was about to make one of his official tours of inspection. This threat cost Caterina her life. About midnight, while a thunderstorm was raging, Virginia, accompanied by her usual associates, Ottavia, Benedetta, Silvia, and Candida, entered the room where the girl was confined. They were followed by Osio, holding in his hand a heavy instrument of wood and iron, called *piede di bicocca*, which he had snatched up in the convent outhouse. He found Caterina lying face downward on the bed, and smashed her skull with a single blow. The body was conveyed by him and the nuns into the fowlhouse of the sisters, whence he removed it on the following night, by the aid of Benedetta, into his own dwelling. From evidence which afterwards transpired, Osio decapitated the corpse, concealed the body in a sort of cellar, and flung the head into an empty well at Velate.

The disappearance of Caterina just before the visitation of Monsignor Barca, roused suspicion; and, though a murder was not immediately apprehended, the guilty associates felt that the cord of fate was being drawn around them. In the autumn of 1607 the tempest broke upon their heads. Virginia was removed from Monza to the convent called Del Bocchetto at Milan; and on November 27 the depositions of the abbess, prioress, and other members of S. Margherita were taken regarding Osio's intrigues, the assassination of Soncini, and the disappearance of Caterina. Among the nuns who had abetted Osio, the two most criminally implicated were Ottavia and Benedetta. Their evidence, if closely scrutinised, must reveal each secret of the past. It was much to Osio's interest, therefore, that they should not fall into the hands of justice; nor had he any difficulty in persuading them to rely on his assistance for contriving their escape to some convent in the Bergamasque territory. We may wonder, by the way, what sort of discipline was then maintained in nunneries, if two so guilty sisters counted upon safe entrance into an asylum, provided only they could leave the diocese of Milan for another.[1] On the night of Thursday, November 30, 1607, Osio came to the wall of the convent garden, and began to break a hole in it, through which Ottavia and Benedetta crept. The three then prowled along the city wall of Monza, till they found a breach wide enough for exit. Afterwards they took a path beside the river Lambro, and stopped for awhile at the church of the Madonna delle Grazie. Here the sisters prayed for assistance from our Lady in their journey, and recited the 'Salve Regina' seven times. Then

[1] In ecclesiastical affairs the diocese of Milan exercised jurisdiction over that of Bergamo, although Bergamo was subject in civil affairs to Venice. This makes the matter more puzzling.

they resumed their walk along the Lambro, and at a certain
point Ottavia fell into the river. In her dying depositions
she accused Osio of having pushed her in; and there seems
little doubt that he did so; for while she was struggling in
the water, he disengaged his harquebuss from his mantle
and struck her several blows upon the head and hands. She
pretended to be dead, and was carried down the stream to a
place where she contrived to crawl to land. Some peasants
came by, whose assistance she implored. But they, observing
that she was a nun of S. Margherita by her dress, refused to
house her for the rest of the night. They gave her a staff to
lean on, and after a painful journey she regained the church of
the Grazie at early dawn. Ottavia's wounds upon the head,
face, and right hand, inflicted by the stock of Osio's gun,
were so serious that, after making a clean breast to her
judges, she died of them upon December 26, 1607.

When Osio had pushed Ottavia into the Lambro, and
had tried to smash her brains out with his harquebuss, he
resumed his midnight journey with Sister Benedetta. They
reached an uninhabited house in the country about five or
six miles distant from Monza. Here Osio shut Benedetta up
in an empty room with a stone bench running along the
wall. She remained there all Friday, visited once by her
dreaded companion, who brought her bread, cheese, and wine.
She abstained from touching any of this food, in fear of
poison. About nine in the evening he returned, and bade
her prepare to march. They set out again together in the
dark; and after walking about three miles they came to a
well, down which Osio threw her. The well was deep and
had no water in it. Benedetta injured her left side in the
fall; and when she had reached the bottom, her would-be
murderer flung a big stone on her, which broke her right
leg. She contrived to protect her head by gathering stones
around it, and lay without moaning or moving, in the fear

that Osio would attempt fresh violence unless he thought her dead. From the middle of Friday night until Sunday morning she remained thus, exploring with her eyes the surface of her dungeon. It was dry and strewn with bones. In one corner lay a round black object which bore the aspect of a human skull. As it eventually turned out, this was the head of Caterina, whom Benedetta herself had helped to murder, and which Osio had thrown there. On Sunday, during Mass, the men of the village of Velate were in church, when they heard a voice from outside calling out, 'Help, help! I am at the bottom of this well!' The well, as it happened, was distant some dozen paces from the church door, and Benedetta had timed her call for assistance at a lucky moment. The villagers ran to the spot, and drew her out by means of a man who went down with a rope. She was then taken to the house of a gentleman, Signor Alberico degli Alberici, who, when no one else was charitable enough to receive her, opened his doors to the exhausted victim of that murderous outrage. It may be remarked that the same surgeon who had been employed to report on Ottavia's wounds, now appeared to examine Benedetta. His name was Ambrogio Vimercati. Benedetta was taken to the convent of S. Orsola, where her friend Ottavia lay dying; and after making a full confession, she eventually recovered her health and suffered life-long incarceration in her old convent.

Osio was still at large. On December 20, he addressed a long letter to the Cardinal Federigo Borromeo, in which he vainly attempted to defend himself and throw the blame on his associates. It is a loathsome document, blending fulsome protestations and fawning phrases with brutal denouncements of his victims and treacherous insinuations. One passage deserves notice. 'Who was it,' he says, 'who suggested my correspondence with Virginia? The priest Paolo Arrigone, that ruin of the monastery! The Canon Pisnato, who is now

confessor to the nuns of Meda; in his house you will find
what will never be discovered in mine, presents from nuns,
incitements to amours, and other such things. The priest
Giacomo Bertola, confessor of the nuns of S. Margherita;
who was his devotee? Sacha!—and he stayed there all the
day through. These men, being priests, are not prosecuted;
they are protected by their cloth, forsooth! It is only of
poor Osio that folk talk. Only he is persecuted, only he is
a malefactor, only he is the traitor!' Arrigone, as a matter
of fact, was tried, and condemned to two years' labour
at the galleys, after the expiration of which term he was not
to return to Monza or its territory. This seems a slight
sentence; for the judges found him guilty, not only of
promoting Osio's intrigue with Virginia by conducting the
correspondence and watching the door during their interviews in the parlour, but also of pursuing the Signora herself
with infamous proposals.

In his absence Osio was condemned to death on the gibbet.
His goods were confiscated to the State. His house in
Monza was destroyed, and a pillar of infamy recording his
crimes was erected on its site. A proclamation of outlawry
was issued on April 5, 1608, under the seal of Don Pietro de
Acevedo, Count of Fuentes, and governor of the State of
Milan, which offered 'to any person not himself an outlaw,
or to any commune, that shall consign Gianpaolo Osio to the
hands of justice, the reward of a thousand scudi from the
royal ducal treasury, together with the right to free four
bandits condemned for similar or less offences; and in case
of his being delivered dead, even though he shall be slain in
foreign parts, then the half of the aforesaid sum of money,
and the freedom of two bandits as above. And if the person
who shall consign him alive be himself an outlaw for similar
or less offences he shall receive, besides the freedom of himself and two other bandits, the half of the aforesaid sum of

money; and in the case of his consignment after death, the freedom of himself and of two other bandits as aforesaid.' I have recited this *Bando*, because it is a good instance of the procedure in use under like conditions. Justice preferred to obtain the culprit alive, and desired to receive him at honest hands. But there was an expectation of getting hold of him through less reputable agents. Therefore they offered free pardon to a bandit and a couple of accomplices, who might undertake the capture or the murder of the proscribed outlaw in concert, and in the event of his being produced alive a sum of money down. Osio, apparently, spent some years in exile, changing place and name and dress, living as he could from hand to mouth, until the rumour spread abroad that he was dead. He then returned to his country, and begged for sanctuary from an old friend. That friend betrayed him, had his throat cut in a cellar, and exposed his head upon the public market place.

Virginia was sentenced to perpetual incarceration in the convent of S. Valeria at Milan. She was to be 'inclosed within a little dungeon, the door of which shall be walled up with stones and mortar, so that the said Virginia Maria shall abide there for the term of her natural life, immured both day and night, never to issue thence, but shall receive food and other necessaries through a small hole in the wall of the said chamber, and light and air through an aperture or other opening.' This sentence was carried into effect. But at the expiration of many years, her behaviour justified some mitigation of the penalty. She was set at large, and allowed to occupy a more wholesome apartment, where the charity of Cardinal Borromeo supplied her with comforts befitting her station and the reputation she acquired for sanctity. Her own family cherished implacable sentiments of resentment against the woman who had brought disgrace upon them. Ripamonte, the historian of Milan, says that in his own time

she was still alive : ' a bent old woman, tall of stature, dried
and fleshless, but venerable in her aspect, whom no one could
believe to have been once a charming and immodest beauty.'
Her associates in guilt, the nuns of S. Margherita, were consigned to punishments resembling hers. Sisters Benedetta,
Silvia, and Candida suffered the same close incarceration.

Lucrezia Buonvisi.

The tale of Lucrezia Buonvisi presents some points of
similarity to that of the Signora di Monza.[1] Her father was
a Lucchese gentleman, named Vincenzo Malpigli, who passed
the better portion of his life at Ferrara as treasurer to Duke
Alfonso II. He had four children ; one son, Giovan Lorenzo,
and three daughters, of whom Lucrezia, born at Lucca in
1572, was probably the youngest. Vincenzo's wife sprang
from the noble Lucchese family of Buonvisi, at that time by
their wealth and alliances the most powerful house of the
Republic. Lucrezia spent some years of her girlhood at
Ferrara, where she formed a romantic friendship for a nobleman of Lucca named Massimiliano Arnolfini. This early
attachment was not countenanced by her parents. They
destined her to be the wife of one of Paolo Buonvisi's
numerous sons, her relatives upon the mother's side. In consequence of this determination, she was first affianced to an
heir of that house, who died; again to another, who also
died; and in the third place to their brother, called Lelio,
whom she eventually married in the year 1591. Lelio was
then twenty-five years of age, and Lucrezia nineteen. Her
beauty was so distinguished that in poems written on the
ladies of Lucca it received this celebration in a madrigal :—

---

[1] *Storia di Lucrezia Buonvisi*, by Salvatore Bonghi, Lucca 1864.
This is an admirably written historical monograph, based on accurate
studies and wide researches, containing a mine of valuable information
for a student of those times.

> Like the young maiden rose
> Which at the opening of the dawn,
> Still sprinkled with heaven's gracious dew,
> Her beauty and her bosom on the lawn
> Doth charmingly disclose,
> For nymphs and amorous swains with love to view;
> So delicate, so fair, Lucrezia yields
> New pearls, new purple to our homely fields,
> While Cupid plays and Flora laughs in her fresh hue.

Less than a year after her marriage with Lelio Buonvisi, Lucrezia resumed her former intimacy with Massimiliano Arnolfini. He was scarcely two years her elder, and they had already exchanged vows of fidelity in Ferrara. Massimiliano's temper inclined him to extreme courses; he was quick and fervent in all the disputes of his age, ready to back his quarrels with the sword, and impatient of delay in any matter he had undertaken. Owing to a feud which then subsisted between the families of Arnolfini and Boccella, he kept certain *bravi* in his service, upon whose devotion he relied. This young man soon found means to open a correspondence with Lucrezia, and arranged meetings with her in the house of some poor weavers who lived opposite the palace of the Buonvisi. Nothing passed between them that exceeded the limits of respectful courtship. But the situation became irksome to a lover so hot of blood as Massimiliano was. On the evening of June 5, in 1593, his men attacked Lelio Buonvisi, while returning with Lucrezia from prayers in an adjacent church. Lelio fell, stabbed with nineteen thrusts of the poignard, and was carried lifeless to his house. Lucrezia made her way back alone; and when her husband's corpse was brought into the palace, she requested that it should be laid out in the basement. A solitary witness of this act of violence, Vincenzo di Coreglia, deposed to having raised the dying man from the ground, put earth into his mouth by way of Sacrament, and urged him to forgive his enemies before he breathed his last. The weather had been very bad that day, and at nightfall it was thundering incessantly.

Inquisition was made immediately into the causes of Lelio's death. According to Lucrezia's account, her husband had reproved some men upon the road for singing obscene songs, whereupon they turned and murdered him. The corpse was exposed in the Church of the Servi, where multitudes of people gathered round it; and there an ancient dame of the Buonvisi house, flinging herself upon her nephew's body, vowed vengeance, after the old custom of the *Vocero*, against his murderers. Other members of the family indicated Massimiliano as the probable assassin; but he meantime had escaped, with three of his retainers, to a villa of his mother's at S. Pancrazio, whence he managed to take the open country and place himself in temporary safety.

During this while the judicial authorities of Lucca were not idle. The Podestà issued a proclamation inviting evidence under the menace of decapitation and confiscation of goods for whomsoever should be found to have withheld information. To this call a certain Orazio Carli, most imprudently, responded. He confessed to having been aware that Massimiliano was plotting the assassination of somebody—not Lelio; and said that he had himself facilitated the flight of the assassins by preparing a ladder, which he placed in the hands of a *bravo* called Ottavio da Trapani. This revelation delivered him over, bound hand and foot, to the judicial authorities, who at the same time imprisoned Vincenzo da Coreglia, the soldier present at the murder.

Massimiliano and his men meanwhile had made their way across the frontier to Garfagnana. Their flight and the suspicions which attached to them, rendered it tolerably certain that they were the authors of the crime. But justice demanded more circumstantial information, and the Podestà decided to work upon the two men already in his clutches. On June 4

Carli was submitted to the torture. The rack elicited nothing new from him, but had the result of dislocating his arms. He was then placed upon an instrument called the 'she-goat,' a sharp wooden trestle, to which the man was bound with weights attached to his feet, and where he sat for nearly four hours. In the course of this painful exercise, he deposed that Massimiliano and Lucrezia had been in the habit of meeting in the house of Vincenzo del Zoppo and Pollonia his wife, where the *bravi* also congregated and kept their arms. Grave suspicion was thus cast on Lucrezia. Had she perchance connived at her husband's murder? Was she an accomplice in the tragedy?

Lucrezia's peril now became imminent. Her brother, Giovan Lorenzo Malpigli, who remained her friend throughout, thought it best for her to retire as secretly as possible into a convent. The house chosen was that of S. Chiara in the town of Lucca. On June 5, she assumed the habit of S. Francis, cut her hair, changed her name from Lucrezia to Umilia, and offered two thousand crowns of dower to this monastery. Only four days had elapsed since her husband's assassination. But she, at all events, was safe from immediate peril; for the Church must now be dealt with; and the Church neither relinquished its suppliants, nor disgorged the wealth they poured into its coffers. The Podestà, when news of this occurrence reached him, sent at once to make inquiries. His messenger, Ser Vincenzo Petrucci, was informed by the Abbess that Lucrezia had just arrived and was having her hair shorn. At his request, the novice herself appeared—'a young woman, tall and pale, dressed in a nun's habit, with a crown upon her head.' She declared herself to be 'Madonna Lucretiina Malpigli, widow of Lelio Buonvisi.' The priest who had conducted her reception affirmed that 'the gentle lady, immediately upon her husband's death, conceived this good prompting of the spirit, and obeyed it on the spot.'

For the moment Lucrezia, whom in future we must call Sister Umilia, had to be left unmolested. The judges returned to the interrogation of their prisoners. Vincenzo del Zoppo and his wife Pollonia, in whose house the lovers used to meet, were tortured; but nothing that implied a criminal correspondence transpired from their evidence. Then the unlucky Carli was once more put to the strappado. He fell into a deep swoon, and was with difficulty brought to life again. Next his son, a youth of sixteen years, was racked with similar results. On June 7, they resolved to have another try at Vincenzo da Coreglia. This soldier had been kept on low diet in his prison during the last week, and was therefore ripe, according to the judicial theories of those times, for salutary torments. Having been strung up by his hands, he was jerked and shaken in the customary fashion until he declared his willingness to make a full confession. He had been informed, he said, that Massimiliano intended to assassinate Lelio by means of his three bravi, Pietro da Castelnuovo, Ottavio da Trapani, and Niccolo da Pariana. He engaged to stand by and cover the retreat of these men. It was Carli, and not Massimiliano, who had made overtures to him. On being once more tortured, he only confirmed this confession. Carli was again summoned, and set upon the 'she-goat,' with heavy weights attached to his feet. The poor wretch sat for two hours on this infernal machine, the sharp edges and spikes of which were so contrived as to press slowly and deeply upon the tenderest portions of his body.[1] But he endured this agony without uttering a word,

[1] Campanella, who was tortured in this way at Naples, says that on one occasion a pound and a half of his flesh was macerated, and ten pounds of his blood shed. 'Perduravi horis quadraginta, funiculis arctissimis ossa usque secantibus ligatus, pendens manibus retro contortis de fune super acutissimum lignum qui (?) carnis sextertium (?) in posterioribus mihi devoravit et decem sanguinis libras tellus ebibit.' Preface to *Atheismus Triumphatus*.

until the judges perceived that he was at the point of death. Next day, the 8th of June, Coreglia was again summoned to the justice-chamber. Terrified by the prospect of future torments, and wearied out with importunities, he at last made a clean breast of all he knew. It was not Carli, but Massimiliano himself, who had engaged him; and he had assisted at the murder of Lelio, which was accomplished by two of the *bravi*, Ottavio and Pietro. Coreglia said nothing to implicate Sister Umilia. On the contrary, he asserted that she seemed to lose her senses when she saw her husband fall.

The General Council, to whom the results of these proceedings were communicated, published an edict of outlawry against Massimiliano and his three *bravi*. A price of 500 crowns was put upon the head of each, wherever he should be killed; and 1,000 crowns were offered to anyone who should kill Massimiliano within the city or state of Lucca. At the same time they sent an envoy to Rome, requesting the Pope's permission to arrest Umilia, on the ground that she was gravely suspected of being privy to the murder and of entering the convent to escape justice. A few days afterwards, the miserable witnesses, Carli and Coreglia, were beheaded in their prison.

The Chancellor, Vincenzo Petrucci, left Lucca on June 12, and reached Rome on the 14th. He obtained an audience from Clement VIII. upon the 15th. When the Pope had read the letter of the Republic, he struck his palm down on his chair, and cried: 'Jesus! This is a grave case! It seems hardly possible that a woman of her birth should have been induced to take share in the murder of her husband.' After some conversation with the envoy, he added: 'It is certainly an ugly business. But what can we do now that she has taken the veil?' Then he promised to deliberate upon the matter and return an answer later. Petrucci soon perceived that the Church did not mean to relinquish its privileges, and

that Umilia was supported by powerful friends at court.
Cardinal Castrucci remarked in casual conversation: 'She is
surely punished enough for her sins by the life of the cloister.'
A second interview with Clement on June 21, confirmed him
in the opinion that the Republic would not obtain the dispensation they requested. Meanwhile the Signory of Lucca
prepared a schedule of the suspicions against Umilia, grounded
upon her confused evidence, her correspondence with Massimiliano, the fact that she had done nothing to rescue Lelio
by calling out, and her sudden resort to the convent. This
paper reached the Pope, who, on July 8, expressed his view
that the Republic ought to be content with leaving Umilia
immured in her monastery; and again, upon the 28rd, he
pronounced his final decision that 'the lady, being a nun and
tonsured and prepared for the perfect life, is not within the
jurisdiction of your Signory. It is further clear that, finding
herself exposed to the calumnies of those two witnesses and
injured in her reputation, she took the veil to screen her
honour.' On August 18, Petrucci returned to Lucca.

Clement conceded one point. He gave commission to the
Bishop of Lucca to inquire into Umilia's conduct within the
precincts of the monastery. But the Council refused this
intervention, for they were on bad terms with the Bishop and
resented ecclesiastical interference in secular causes. Moreover, they judged that such an inquisition, without torture
used and in a place of safety, would prove worse than useless.
Thus the affair dropped.

Meanwhile we may relate what happened to Massimiliano
and his *bravi*. They escaped, through Garfagnana and Massa,
into the territory of Alfonso Malaspina, Marquis of Villafranca
and Tresana. This nobleman, who delighted in protecting
outlaws, placed the four men in security in his stronghold of
Tresana. Pietro da Castelnuovo was an outlaw from Tuscany
for the murder of a Carmelite friar, which he had committed

at Pietrasanta a few days before the assassination of Lelio. Seventeen years after these events he was still alive and wanted for grave crimes committed in the Duchy of Modena. History knows no more about him, except that he had a wife and family. Of Niccolo da Pariana nothing has to be related. Ottavio da Trapani was caught at Milan, brought back to Lucca, and hanged there on June 13, 1604, after being torn with pincers. Massimiliano is said to have made his way to Flanders, where the Lucchese enjoyed many privileges, and where his family had probably hereditary connexions.[1] Like all outlaws, he lived in perpetual peril of assassination. Remorse and shame invaded him, especially when news arrived that the mistress, for whom he had risked all, was turning to a dissolute life (as we shall shortly read) in her monastery. His reason gave way; and, after twenty-two years of wandering, he returned to Lucca, and was caught. Instead of executing the capital sentence which had been pronounced upon him, the Signory consigned him to perpetual prison in the tower of Viareggio, which was then an insalubrious and fever-stricken village on the coast. Here, walled up in a little room, alone, deprived of light and air and physical decency, he remained forgotten for ten years from 1615 to 1625. At the latter date report was made that he had refused food for three days and was suffering from a dangerous hemorrhage. When the authorities proposed to break the wall of his dungeon and send a priest and surgeon to relieve him, he declared that he would kill himself if they intruded on his misery. Nothing more was heard of him until 1629, when he was again reported to be at the point of death. This time he requested the assistance of a priest; and it is probable that he then died at the age of sixty-nine, having

[1] I may here allude to a portrait in our National Gallery of a Lucchese Arnolfini and his wife, painted by Van Eyck.

survived the other actors in this tragedy and expiated the passion of his youth by life-long sufferings.

When we return to Sister Umilia, and inquire how the years had worn with her, a new chapter in the story opens. In 1606 she was still cloistered in S. Chiara, which indeed remained her home until her death. She had now reached the age of thirty-four. Suspicion meanwhile fell upon the conduct of the nuns of S. Chiara; and on January 9, in that year, a rope-ladder was discovered hanging from the garden wall of the convent. Upon inquiry, it appeared that certain men were in the habit of entering the house and holding secret correspondence with the sisters. Among these the most notorious were Piero Passari, a painter, infamous for vulgar profligacy, and a young nobleman of Lucca, Tommaso Samminiati. Both of them contrived to evade justice, and were proclaimed, as usual, outlaws. In the further course of investigation the strongest proofs were brought to light, from which it appeared that the chief promoter of these scandals was a man of high position in the state, advanced in years, married to a second wife, and holding office of trust as Protector of the Nunnery of S. Chiara. He was named Giovanbattista Dati, and represented an ancient Lucchese family mentioned by Dante. While Dati carried on his own intrigue with Sister Cherubina Mei, he did his best to encourage the painter in promiscuous debauchery, and to foster the passion which Samminiati entertained for Sister Umilia Malpigli. Dati was taken prisoner and banished for life to the island of Sardinia; but his papers fell into the hands of the Signory, who extracted from them the evidence which follows touching Umilia and Samminiati. This young man was ten years her junior; yet the quiet life of the cloister had preserved Umilia's beauty, and she was still capable of inspiring enthusiastic adoration. This transpires in the letters which Samminiati addressed to her through Dati from his asylum in Venice. They reveal, says Signor Bonghi, a strange confusion of madness, crime, and love.[1] Their style is that of a delirious rhetorician. One might fancy they had been composed as exercises, except for certain traits which mark the frenzy of genuine exaltation. Threats, imprecations, and blasphemies alternate with prayers, vows of fidelity and reminiscences of past delights in love. Samminiati bends before ' his lady ' in an attitude of respectful homage, offering upon his knees the service of awe-struck devotion. At one time he calls her ' his most beauteous angel,' at another ' his most lovely and adored enchantress.' He does not conceal his firm belief that she has laid him under some spell of sorcery; but entreats her to have mercy and to liberate him, reminding her how a certain Florentine lady restored Giovan Lorenzo Malpigli to health after keeping him in magic bondage till his life was in danger.[2] Then he swears unalterable fealty; heaven and fortune shall not change his love. It is untrue that at Florence or at Venice he has cast one glance on any other woman. Let lightning strike him, if he deserts Umilia. But she has caused him jealousy by stooping to a base amour. To this point he returns with some persistence. Then he entreats her to send him her portrait, painted in the character of S. Ursula. At another time he gossips about the nuns, forwarding messages, alluding to their several love-affairs, and condoling with them on the loss of a compliant confessor. This was a priest, who, when the indescribable corruptions of S. Chiara had been clearly proved, calmly remarked that there was no reason to make such a fuss—they were only

[1] Here again I have very closely followed the text of Signor Bonghi's monograph, pp. 112–115.
[2] It appears that violent passion for a person was commonly attributed at that epoch to enchantment. See above, the confession of the Lady of Monza, p. 249.

affairs of gentlefolk, *cose di gentilhuomini*. The rival of whom Samminiati was jealous seems to have been the painter Pietro, who held the key to all the scandals of the convent in his hand. Umilia, Dati, and Samminiati at last agreed 'to rid their neighbourhood of that pest.' The man had escaped to Rovigo, whither Samminiati repaired from Venice, 'attended by two good fellows thoroughly acquainted with the district.' But Pietro got away to Ferrara, his enemy following and again missing him. Samminiati writes that he is resolved to hunt 'that rascal' out, and make an end of him. Meanwhile Umilia is commissioned to do for Calidonia Burlamacchi, a nun who had withdrawn from the company of her guilty sisters and knew too many of their secrets. Samminiati sends a white powder and a little phial containing a liquid, both of which, he informs Umilia, are potent poisons, with instructions how to use them and how to get Calidonia to swallow the ingredients. Then 'if the devil does not help her, she will pass from this life in half a night's time, and without the slightest sign of violence.'

It may be imagined what disturbance was caused in the General Council by the reading of this correspondence. Nearly all the noble families of Lucca were connected by ties of blood or marriage with one or other of the culprits; and when the relatives of the accused had been excluded from the session, only sixty members were left to debate on further measures. I will briefly relate what happened to the three outlaws. Venice refused to give up Samminiati at the request of the Lucchese, saying that 'the Republic of S. Mark would not initiate a course of action prejudicial to the hospitality which every sort of person was wont to enjoy there.' But the young man was banished to Candia, whither he obediently retired. Pietro, the painter, was eventually permitted to return to the territory but not the town of Lucca. Dati surrounded himself with armed men, as was the custom of rich criminals

CONCLUSION OF LUCREZIA'S STORY

on whose head a price was set. After wandering some time, he submitted and took up his abode in Sardinia, whence he afterwards removed, by permission of the Signory, to France. There he died. With regard to the nuns, it seemed at first that the ends of justice would be defeated through the jealousies which divided the civil and ecclesiastical authorities in Lucca. The Bishop was absent, and his Vicar refused to institute a criminal process. Umilia remained at large in the convent, and even began a new intrigue with one Simo Menocchi. At last, in 1609, the Vicar prepared his indictment against the guilty nuns, and forwarded it to Rome. Their sentence was as follows: Sister Orizia condemned to incarceration for life and loss of all her privileges; Sister Umilia, to the same penalties for a term of seven years; Sisters Paola, Cherubina, and Dionea, received a lighter punishment. Orizia, it may be mentioned, had written a letter with her own blood to some lover; but nothing leads us to suppose that she was equally guilty with Umilia, who had entered into the plot to poison Sister Calidonia.

Umilia was duly immured, and bore her punishment until the year 1616, at which time the sentence expired. But she was not released for another two years; for she persistently refused to humble herself, or to request that liberation as a grace which was her due in justice. Nor would she submit to the shame of being seen about the convent without her monastic habit. Finally, in 1618, she obtained freedom and restoration to her privileges as a nun of S. Chiara. It may be added, as a last remark, that, when the convent was being set to rights, Umilia's portrait in the character of S. Ursula was ordered to be destroyed or rendered fit for devout uses by alterations. Any nun who kept it in her cell incurred the penalty of excommunication. In what year Umilia died remains unknown.

The Cenci.

Shifting the scene to Rome, we light upon a group of notable misdeeds enacted in the last half of the sixteenth century, each of which is well calculated to illustrate the conditions of society and manners at that epoch. It may be well to begin with the Cenci tragedy. In Shelley's powerful drama, in Guerrazzi's tedious novel and Scolari's digest, the legend of Beatrice Cenci has long appealed to modern sympathy. The real facts, extracted from legal documents and public registers, reduce its poetry of horror to comparatively squalid prose.[1] Yet, shorn of romantic glamour, the bare history speaks significantly to a student of Italian customs. Monsignore Cristoforo Cenci, who died about the year 1562, was in holy orders, yet not a priest. One of the clerks of the Apostolic Camera, a Canon of S. Peter's, the titular incumbent of a Roman parish, and an occupant of minor offices about the Papal Court and Curia, he represented an epicene species, neither churchman nor layman, which the circumstances of ecclesiastical sovereignty rendered indispensable. Cristoforo belonged to a good family among that secondary Roman aristocracy which ranked beneath the princely feudatories and the Papal bastards. He accumulated large sums of money by maladministration of his official trusts, inherited the estates of two uncles, and bequeathed a colossal fortune to his son Francesco. This youth was the offspring of an illicit connexion carried on between Monsignore Cenci and Beatrice Amias during the lifetime of that lady's husband. Upon the death of the husband the Monsignore obtained dispensation from his orders, married Beatrice, and legitimated his son, the inheritor of so much

---

[1] *Francesco Cenci e la sua Famiglia.* Per A. Bertolotti, Firenze, 1877.

wealth. Francesco was born in 1549, and had therefore reached the age of thirteen when his father died. His mother Beatrice soon contracted a third matrimonial union; but during her guardianship of the boy she appeared before the courts accused of having stolen clothing from his tutor's wardrobe.

Francesco Cenci disbursed a sum of 88,000 crowns to various public offices, in order to be allowed to enter unmolested into the enjoyment of his father's gains: 8,800 crowns of this sum went to the Chapter of S. Peter's.[1] He showed a certain precocity; for at the age of fourteen he owned an illegitimate child, and was accused of violence to domestics. In 1563 his family married him to Ersilia, a daughter of the noble Santa Croce house, who brought him a fair dowry. Francesco lived for twenty-one years with this lady, by whom he had twelve children. Upon her death he remained a widower for nine years, and in 1593 he married Lucrezia Petroni, widow of a Roman called Velli. Francesco's conduct during his first marriage was not without blame. Twice at least he had to pay fines for acts of brutality to servants; and once he was prosecuted for an attempt to murder a cousin, also named Francesco Cenci. On another occasion we find him outlawed from the States of the Church. Yet these offences were but peccadilloes in a wealthy Roman baron; and Francesco used to boast that, with money in his purse, he had no dread of justice. After the death of his wife Ersilia, his behaviour grew more irregular. Three times between 1591 and 1594 he was sued for violent attacks on servants; and in February of the latter year he remained six months in prison on multiplied charges of unnatural vice. There was nothing even here to single

[1] He was afterwards forced, in 1590, to disgorge a second sum of 25,000 crowns.

Francesco Cenci out from other nobles of his age.[1] Scarcely a week passed in Rome without some affair of the sort, involving outrage, being brought before the judges. Cardinals, prelates, princes, professional men and people of the lowest rank were alike implicated. The only difference between the culprits was that the rich bought themselves off, while the destitute were burned. Eleven poor Spaniards and Portuguese were sent to the stake in 1578 for an offence which Francesco Cenci compounded in 1594 by the payment of 100,000 crowns. After this warning and the loss of so much money, he grew more circumspect, married his second wife Lucrezia, and settled down to rule his family. His sons caused him considerable anxiety. Giacomo, the eldest, married against his father's will, and supported himself by forging obligations and raising money. Francesco's displeasure showed itself in several law-suits, one of which accused Giacomo of having plotted against his life. The second son, Cristoforo, was assassinated by Paolo Bruno, a Corsican, in the prosecution of a love affair with the wife of a Trasteverine fisherman. The third son, Rocco, spent his time in street adventures, and on one occasion laid his hands on all the plate and portable property that he could carry

[1] Prospero Farinaccio, the advocate of Cenci's murderers, was himself tried for this crime (Bertolotti, *op. cit.* p. 104). The curious story of the Spanish soldiers alluded to above will be found in Mutinelli, *Stor. Arc.* vol. i. p. 121. See the same work of Mutinelli, vol. i. p. 48, for a similar prosecution in Rome, 1566; and vol. iv. p. 152 for another involving some hundred people of condition at Milan in 1679. Compare what Sarpi says about the Florentine merchants and Roman *cinedi* in his *Letters*, date 1609, vol. i. p. 288. For the manners of the Neapolitans, *Vita di D. Pietro di Toledo* (*Arch. Stor. It.* vol. ix. p. 23). The most scandalous example of such vice in high quarters was given by Pietro de' Medici, one of Duke Cosimo's sons. Galluzzi, vol. v. p. 174, and Litta's pedigree of the Medici. The *Bandi Lucchesi*, ed. S. Bonghi, Bologna, 1863, pp. 377-381, treats the subject in full; and it has been discussed by Canello, *op. cit.* pp. 20-23. The *Artes Jesuiticæ*, op. cit. Articles 62, 120, illustrate casuistry on the topic.

off from his father's house. This young ruffian, less than twenty years of age, found a devoted friend in Monsignore Querro, a cousin of the family well placed at court, who assisted him in the burglary of the Cenci palace. Rocco was killed by Amilcare Orsini, a bastard of the Count of Pitigliano, in a brawl at night. The young men met, Cenci attended by three armed servants, Orsini by two. A single pass of rapiers, in which Rocco was pierced through the right eye, ended the affair.

In addition to his vindictive persecution of his worthless eldest son, Francesco Cenci behaved with undue strictness to the younger, allowing them less money than befitted their station and treating them with a severity which contrasted comically with his own loose habits. The legend which represents him as an exceptionally wicked man, cruel for cruelty's sake and devoid of natural affection, receives some colour from the facts. Yet these alone are not sufficient to justify its darker hues, while they amply prove that Francesco's children gave him grievous provocation. The discontents of this ill-governed family matured into rebellion; and in 1598 it was decided on removing the old Cenci by murder. His second wife Lucrezia, his eldest son Giacomo, his daughter Beatrice, and a younger son Bernardo, were implicated in the crime. It was successfully carried out at the Rocca di Petrella in the Abruzzi on the night of September 9. Two hired *bravi*, Olimpio Calvetti and Marzio Catalani, entered the old man's bedroom, drove a nail into his head, and flung the corpse out from a gallery, whence it was alleged that he had fallen by accident. Six days after this assassination Giacomo and his brothers took out letters both at Rome and in the realm of Naples for the administration of their father's property; nor does suspicion seem for some time to have fallen upon them. It awoke at Petrella in November, the feudatory of which fief, Marzio Colonna, informed the govern-

ment of Naples that proceedings ought to be taken against
the Cenci and their cut-throats. Accordingly, on December 10,
a ban was published against Olimpio and Marzio. Olimpio
met his death at an inn door in a little village called
Cantalice. Three desperate fellows, at the instigation of
Giacomo de' Cenci and Monsignore Querro, surprised him
there. But Marzio fell into the hands of justice, and his
evidence caused the immediate arrest of the Cenci. It
appears that they were tortured and that none of them
denied the accusation; so that their advocates could only
plead extenuating circumstances. To this fact may possibly
be due the legend of Beatrice. In order to mitigate the guilt
of parricide, Prospero Farinaccio, who conducted her defence,
established a theory of enormous cruelty and unspeakable
outrages committed on her person by her father. With the
same object in view, he tried to make out that Bernardo was
half-witted. There is quite sufficient extant evidence to show
that Bernardo was a young man of average intelligence; and
with regard to Beatrice, nothing now remains to corroborate
Farinaccio's hypothesis of incest. She was not a girl of
sixteen, as the legend runs, but a woman of twenty-two;[1]
and the codicils to her will render it nearly certain that she
had given birth to an illegitimate son, for whose maintenance
she made elaborate and secret provisions. That the picture
ascribed to Guido Reni in the Barberini palace is not a
portrait of Beatrice in prison, appears sufficiently proved.
Guido did not come to Rome until 1608, nine years after
her death; and catalogues of the Barberini gallery, compiled
in 1604 and 1623, contain no mention either of a painting by
Guido or of Beatrice's portrait. The Cenci were lodged
successively in the prisons of Torre di Nona, Savelli, and
S. Angelo. They occupied wholesome apartments and were

[1] De Stendhal's MS. authority says she was sixteen, Shelley's that
she was twenty.

allowed the attendance of their own domestics. That their
food was no scanty dungeon fare appears from the *menus* of
dinners and suppers supplied to them, which include fish,
flesh, fruit, salad, and snow to cool the water. In spite of
powerful influence at court, Clement VIII. at last resolved to
exercise strict justice on the Cenci. He was brought to this
decision by a matricide perpetrated in cold blood at Subiaco,
on September 5, 1599. Paolo di S. Croce, a relative of the
Cenci, murdered his mother Costanza in her bed, with the
view of obtaining property over which she had control. The
sentence issued a few days after this event. Giacomo was condemned to be torn to pieces by red-hot pincers, and finished
with a *coup de grâce* from the hangman's hammer. Lucrezia
and Beatrice received the slighter sentence of decapitation;
while Bernardo, in consideration of his youth, was let off with
the penalty of being present at the execution of his kinsfolk,
after which he was to be imprisoned for a year and then sent
to the galleys for life. Their property was confiscated to the
Camera Apostolica. These punishments were carried out.[1]
But Bernardo, after working at Cività Vecchia until 1606,
obtained release and lived in banishment till his death in
1627. Monsignor Querro, for his connivance in the whole
affair, was banished to the island of Malta, whence he returned
at some date before the year 1633 to Rome, having expiated
his guilt by long and painful exile. In this abstract of the
Cenci tragedy, I have followed the documents published by
Signor Bertolotti. They are at many points in startling con-
tradiction to the legend, which is founded on MS. accounts
compiled at no distant period after the events. One of these
was employed by Shelley; another, differing in some particulars, was translated by De Stendhal. Both agree in
painting that lurid portrait of Francesco Cenci which Shelley

[1] De Stendhal's MS. describes how Giacomo was torn by pincers;
Shelley's says that this part of the sentence was remitted.

has animated with the force of a great dramatist.[1] Unluckily, no copy of the legal instructions upon which the trial was conducted is now extant. In the absence of this all-important source of information, it would be unsafe to adopt Bertolotti's argument, that the legend calumniates Francesco in order to exculpate Beatrice, without some reservation. There is room for the belief that facts adduced in evidence may have partly justified the prevalent opinion of Beatrice's infamous persecution by her father.

The Massimi.

The tragedy of the Cenci, about which so much has been written in consequence of the supposed part taken in it by Beatrice, seems to me commonplace compared with that of the Massimi.[2] Whether this family really descended from the Roman Fabii matters but little. In the sixteenth century they ranked, as they still rank, among the proudest nobles of the Eternal City. Lelio, the head of the house, had six stalwart sons by his first wife, Girolama Savelli. They were conspicuous for their gigantic stature and herculean strength. After their mother's death in 1571, their father became enamoured of a woman inferior at all points, in birth, breeding, and antecedents, to a person of his quality. She was a certain Eufrosina, who had been married to a man called Corberio. The great Marc Antonio Colonna murdered this husband, and brought the wife to Rome as his own mistress. Lelio Massimo committed the grand error of so loving her, after she had served Colonna's purpose, that he married her. This was an insult to the honour of the house, which his sons could not or would not bear. On the night of her

---

[1] The author of De Stendhal's MS. professes to have known the old Cenci, and gives a definite description of his personal appearance.
[2] Litta supplies the facts related above.

wedding, in 1585, they refused to pay her their respects; and on the next morning, five of them entered her apartments and shot her dead. Only one of the six sons, Pompeo Massimo, bore no share in this assassination. Him, the father, Lelio, blessed; but he solemnly cursed the other five. After the lapse of a few weeks, he followed his wife to the grave with a broken heart, leaving this imprecation unrecalled. Pompeo grew up to continue the great line of Massimo. But disaster fell on each of his five brothers, the flower of Roman youth, exulting in their blood, and insolence, and vigour.—The first of them, Ottavio, was killed by a cannon ball at sea in honourable combat with the Turk. Another, Girolamo, who sought refuge in France, was shot down in an ambuscade while pursuing his amours with a gentle lady. A third, Alessandro, died under arms before Paris while serving in the troops of General Farnese. A fourth, Luca, was imprisoned at Rome for his share of the stepmother's murder, but was released on the plea that he had avenged the wounded honour of his race. He died, however, poisoned by his own brother, Marcantonio, in 1599.[1] Marcantonio was arrested on suspicion and imprisoned in Torre di Nona, where he confessed his guilt. He was shortly afterwards beheaded on the little square before the bridge of S. Angelo.

Vittoria Accoramboni.

Next in order, I shall take the story of Vittoria Accoramboni. It has been often told already,[2] yet it combines so

[1] This fratricide, concurring with the matricide of S. Croce, contributed to the rigour with which the Cenci parricide was punished in that year of Roman crimes.

[2] *The White Devil*, a tragedy by John Webster, London, 1612; De Stendhal's *Chroniques et Nouvelles*, Vittoria Accoramboni, Paris, 1855; *Vittoria Accoramboni*, D. Gnoli, Firenze, 1870; *Italian Byways*, by J. A. Symonds, London, 1883. The greater part of what follows above is extracted from my *Italian Byways*.

many points of interest bearing upon the social life of the Italians in my period, that to omit it would be to sacrifice the most important document bearing on the matter of this chapter. As the Signora di Monza and Lucrezia Buonvisi help us to understand the secret history of families and convents, so Vittoria Accoramboni introduces us to that of courts. It will be noticed how the same machinery of lawless nobles and profligate *bravi*, acting in concert with bold women, is brought into play throughout the tragedies which form the substance of our present inquiry.

Vittoria was born in 1557, of a noble but impoverished family, at Gubbio among the hills of Umbria. Her biographers are rapturous in their praises of her beauty, grace, and exceeding charm of manner. Not only was her person most lovely, but her mind shone at first with all the amiable lustre of a modest, innocent, and winning youth. Her father, Claudio Accoramboni, removed to Rome, where his numerous children were brought up under the care of their mother, Tarquinia, an ambitious woman, bent on rehabilitating the decayed honours of her house. Here Vittoria in early girlhood soon became the fashion. She exercised an irresistible influence over all who saw her, and many were the offers of marriage she refused. At length a suitor appeared whose condition and connexion with the Roman ecclesiastical nobility rendered him acceptable in the eyes of the Accoramboni. Francesco Peretti was welcomed as the successful candidate for Vittoria's hand. His mother, Camilla, was sister to Felice, Cardinal of Montalto; and her son, Francesco Mignucci, had changed both of his names to Felice Peretti in compliment to this illustrious relative.[1]

It was the nephew, then, of the future Sixtus V., that

[1] I find a Felice Peretti mentioned in the will of Giacomo Cenci condemned in 1597. But this was after the death of this Peretti, whom I shall continue to call Francesco.

Vittoria Accoramboni married on June 28, 1573. For a short while the young couple lived happily together. According to some accounts of their married life, the bride secured the favour of her powerful uncle-in-law, who indulged her costly fancies to the full. It is, however, more probable that the Cardinal Montalto treated her follies with a grudging parsimony; for we soon find the Peretti household hopelessly involved in debt. Discord, too, arose between Vittoria and her husband on the score of levity in her behaviour; and it was rumoured that even during the brief space of their union she had proved a faithless wife. Yet she contrived to keep Francesco's confidence, and it is certain that her family profited by their connexion with the Peretti. Of her six brothers, Mario, the eldest, was a favourite courtier of the great Cardinal d' Este. Ottavio was in orders, and through Montalto's influence obtained the See of Fossombrone. The same eminent protector placed Scipione in the service of the Cardinal Sforza. Camillo, famous for his beauty and his courage, followed the fortunes of Filibert of Savoy, and died in France. Flaminio was still a boy, dependent, as the sequel of this story shows, upon his sister's destiny. Of Marcello, the second in age and most important in the action of this tragedy, it is needful to speak with more particularity. He was young, and, like the rest of his breed, singularly handsome—so handsome, indeed, that he is said to have gained an infamous ascendency over the great Duke of Bracciano, whose privy chamberlain he had become. Marcello was an outlaw for the murder of Matteo Pallavicino, the brother of the Cardinal of that name. This did not, however, prevent the chief of the Orsini house from making him his favourite and confidential friend. Marcello, who seems to have realised in actual life the worst vices of those Roman courtiers described for us by Aretino, very soon conceived the plan of exalting his own fortunes by trading on his sister's beauty. He worked upon the Duke of Bracciano's mind so cleverly that he brought this haughty prince to the point of an insane passion for Peretti's young wife; and meanwhile he so contrived to inflame the ambition of Vittoria and her mother, Tarquinia, that both were prepared to dare the worst of crimes in expectation of a dukedom. The game was a difficult one to play. Not only had Francesco Peretti first to be murdered, but the inequality of birth and wealth and station between Vittoria and the Duke of Bracciano rendered a marriage almost impossible. It was also an affair of delicacy to stimulate without satisfying the Duke's passion. Yet Marcello did not despair. The stakes were high enough to justify great risks; and all he put in peril was his sister's honour, the fame of the Accoramboni, and the favour of Montalto. Vittoria, for her part, trusted in her power to ensnare and secure the noble prey both had in view.

Paolo Giordano Orsini, born about the year 1537, was reigning Duke of Bracciano. Among Italian princes he ranked almost upon a par with the Dukes of Urbino; and his family, by its alliances, was more illustrious than any of that time in Italy. He was a man of gigantic stature, prodigious corpulence, and marked personal daring; agreeable in manners, but subject to uncontrollable fits of passion, and incapable of self-restraint when crossed in any whim or fancy. Upon the habit of his body it is needful to insist, in order that the part he played in this tragedy of intrigue, crime, and passion may be well defined. He found it difficult to procure a charger equal to his weight, and he was so fat that a special dispensation relieved him from the duty of genuflexion in the Papal presence. Though lord of a large territory, yielding princely revenues, he laboured under heavy debts; for no great noble of the period lived more splendidly, with less regard for his finances. In the politics of that age and country, Paolo Giordano leaned towards France. Yet he was a grandee of Spain, and had played a distinguished part in the battle of Lepanto. Now, the Duke of Bracciano was a widower. He had been married in 1558 to Isabella de' Medici, daughter of the Grand Duke Cosimo, sister of Francesco, Bianca Capello's lover, and of the Cardinal Ferdinando. Suspicion of adultery with Troilo Orsini had fallen on Isabella; and her husband, with the full concurrence of her brothers, removed her in 1576 from this world by his own hand.[1] No one thought the worse of Bracciano for this murder of his wife. In those days of abandoned vice and intricate villany, certain points of honour were maintained with scrupulous fidelity. A wife's adultery was enough to justify the most savage and licentious husband in an act of semi-judicial vengeance; and the shame she brought upon his head was shared by the members of her own house, so that they stood by, consenting to her death. Isabella, it may be said, left one son, Virginio, who became, in due time, Duke of Bracciano.

It appears that in the year 1581, eight years after Vittoria's marriage, the Duke of Bracciano satisfied Marcello of his intention to make her his wife, and of his willingness to countenance Francesco Peretti's murder. Marcello, feeling sure of his game, now introduced the Duke in private to his sister, and induced her to overcome any natural repugnance she may have felt for the unwieldy and gross lover. Having reached this point, it was imperative to push matters quickly on toward matrimony.

But how should the unfortunate Francesco be entrapped? They caught him in a snare of peculiar atrocity, by working on the kindly feelings which his love for Vittoria had caused

---

[1] The balance of probability leans against Isabella in this affair. At the licentious court of the Medici she lived with unpardonable freedom. Troilo Orsini was himself assassinated in Paris by Bracciano's orders a few years afterwards.

him to extend to all the Accoramboni. Marcello, the outlaw,
was her favourite brother, and Marcello at that time lay in
hiding, under the suspicion of more than ordinary crime,
beyond the walls of Rome. Late in the evening of April 16,
while the Peretti family were retiring to bed, a messenger
from Marcello arrived, entreating Francesco to repair at once
to Monte Cavallo. Marcello had affairs of the utmost importance to communicate, and begged his brother-in-law not to
fail him at a grievous pinch. The letter containing this
request was borne by one Dominico d' Aquaviva, *alias* Il
Mancino, a confederate of Vittoria's waiting-maid. This
fellow, like Marcello, was an outlaw; but when he ventured
into Rome he frequented Peretti's house, and he had made
himself familiar with its master as a trusty *bravo*. Neither
in the message, therefore, nor in the messenger was there
much to rouse suspicion. The time, indeed, was oddly
chosen, and Marcello had never made a similar appeal on
any previous occasion. Yet his necessities might surely have
obliged him to demand some more than ordinary favour from
a brother. Francesco immediately made himself ready to
start out, armed only with his sword and attended by a single
servant. It was in vain that his wife and his mother
reminded him of the dangers of the night, the loneliness of
Monte Cavallo, its ruinous palaces and robber-haunted caves.
He was resolved to undertake the adventure, and went forth,
never to return. As he ascended the hill, he fell to earth,
shot with three harquebusses. His body was afterwards
found on Monte Cavallo, stabbed through and through,
without a trace that could identify the murderers. Only, in
the course of subsequent investigations, Il Mancino (February 24, 1582) made the following statements :—That Vittoria's
mother, assisted by the waiting-woman, had planned the
trap; that Marchionne of Gubbio and Paolo Barca of
Bracciano, two of the Duke's men, had despatched the victim.

Marcello, himself, it seems, had come from Bracciano to
conduct the whole affair. Suspicion fell immediately upon
Vittoria and her kindred, together with the Duke of Bracciano;
nor was this diminished when the Accoramboni, fearing the
pursuit of justice, took refuge in a villa of the Duke's at
Magnanapoli a few days after the murder.

A cardinal's nephew, even in those troublous times, was
not killed without some noise being made about the matter.
Accordingly, Pope Gregory XIII. began to take measures for
discovering the authors of the crime. Strange to say, however, the Cardinal Montalto, notwithstanding the great love
he was known to bear his nephew, begged that the investigation might be dropped. The coolness with which he first
received the news of Francesco Peretti's death, the dissimula-
tion with which he met the Pope's expression of sympathy
in a full consistory, his reserve while greeting friends on
ceremonial visits of condolence, and, more than all, the
self-restraint he showed in the presence of the Duke of
Bracciano, impressed the society of Rome with the belief that
he was of a singularly moderate and patient temper. It was
thought that the man who could so tamely submit to his
nephew's murder, and suspend the arm of justice when
already raised for vengeance, must prove a mild and indulgent
ruler. When, therefore, in the fifth year after this event,
Montalto was elected Pope, men ascribed his elevation in no
small measure to his conduct at the present crisis. Some,
indeed, attributed his extraordinary moderation and self-
control to the right cause. '*Veramente costui è un gran
frate!*' was Gregory's remark at the close of the consistory
when Montalto begged him to let the matter of Peretti's
murder rest. '*Of a truth, that fellow is a consummate
hypocrite!*' How accurate this judgment was, appeared
when Sixtus V. assumed the reins of power. The priest who,
as monk and cardinal, had smiled on Bracciano, though he

knew him to be his nephew's assassin, now, as Pontiff and sovereign, bade the chief of the Orsini purge his palace and dominions of the scoundrels he was wont to harbour, adding significantly, that if the Cardinal Felice Peretti forgave what had been done against him in a private station, the same man would exact uttermost vengeance for disobedience to the will of Sixtus. The Duke of Bracciano judged it best, after that warning, to withdraw from Rome.

Francesco Peretti had been murdered on April 16, 1581. Sixtus V. was proclaimed on April 24, 1585. In this interval Vittoria underwent a series of extraordinary perils and adventures. First of all, she had been secretly married to the Duke in his gardens of Magnanapoli at the end of April 1581. That is to say, Marcello and she secured their prize, as well as they were able, the moment after Francesco had been removed by murder. But no sooner had the marriage become known, than the Pope, moved by the scandal it created no less than by the urgent instance of the Orsini and Medici, declared it void. After some while spent in vain resistance, Bracciano submitted, and sent Vittoria back to her father's house. By an order issued under Gregory's own hand, she was next removed to the prison of Corte Savella, thence to the monastery of S. Cecilia in Trastevere, and finally to the Castle of S. Angelo. Here, at the end of December 1581, she was put on her trial for the murder of her first husband. In prison she seems to have borne herself bravely, arraying her beautiful person in delicate attire, entertaining visitors, exacting from her friends the honours due to a duchess, and sustaining the frequent examinations to which she was submitted with a bold, proud front. In the middle of the month of July her constancy was sorely tried by the receipt of a letter in the Duke's own handwriting, formally renouncing his marriage. It was only by a lucky accident that she was prevented on this occasion from committing suicide. The Papal court meanwhile kept urging her either to retire to a monastery or to accept another husband. She firmly refused to embrace the religious life, and declared that she was already lawfully united to a living husband, the Duke of Bracciano. It seemed impossible to deal with her; and at last, on November 8, she was released from prison under the condition of retirement to Gubbio. The Duke had lulled his enemies to rest by the pretence of yielding to their wishes. But Marcello was continually beside him at Bracciano, where we read of a mysterious Greek enchantress whom he hired to brew love-philtres for the furtherance of his ambitious plots. Whether Bracciano was stimulated by the brother's arguments or by the witch's potions need not be too curiously questioned. But it seems in any case certain that absence inflamed his passion instead of cooling it.

Accordingly, in September 1583, under the excuse of a pilgrimage to Loreto, he contrived to meet Vittoria at Trevi, whence he carried her in triumph to Bracciano. Here he openly acknowledged her as his wife, installing her with all the splendour due to a sovereign duchess. On October 10 following, he once more performed the marriage ceremony in the principal church of his fief; and in the January of 1584 he brought her openly to Rome. This act of contumacy to the Pope, both as feudal superior and as Supreme Pontiff, roused all the former opposition to his marriage. Once more it was declared invalid. Once more the Duke pretended to give way. But at this juncture Gregory died; and while the conclave was sitting for the election of the new Pope, he resolved to take the law into his own hands, and to ratify his union with Vittoria by a third and public marriage in Rome. On the morning of April 24, 1585, their nuptials were accordingly once more solemnised in the Orsini palace. Just one hour after the ceremony, as appears from the marriage-register, the news arrived of Cardinal Montalto's election to the Papacy. Vittoria lost no time in paying her respects to Camilla, sister of the new Pope, her former mother-in-law. The Duke visited Sixtus V. in state to compliment him on his elevation. But the reception which both received proved that Rome was no safe place for them to live in. They consequently made up their minds for flight.

A chronic illness from which Bracciano had lately suffered furnished a sufficient pretext. This seems to have been something of the nature of a cancerous ulcer, which had to be treated by the application of raw meat to open sores. Such details are only excusable in the present narrative on the ground that Bracciano's disease considerably affects our moral judgment of the woman who could marry a man thus physically tainted, and with her husband's blood upon his hands. At any rate, the Duke's *lupa* justified his trying what change of air, together with the sulphur waters of Abano, would do for him.

The Duke and Duchess arrived in safety at Venice, where they had engaged the Dandolo palace on the Zueca. There they only stayed a few days, removing to Padua, where they had hired palaces of the Foscari in the Arena and a house called De' Cavalli. At Salò, also, on the Lake of Garda, they provided themselves with fit dwellings for their princely state and their large retinues, intending to divide their time between the pleasures which the capital of luxury afforded and the simpler enjoyments of the most beautiful of the Italian lakes. But *la gioia dei profani è un fumo passaggier*. Paolo Giordano Orsini, Duke of Bracciano, died suddenly at Salò on November 10, 1585, leaving the young and beautiful Vittoria helpless among enemies. What was the cause of his death? It is not possible to give a clear and certain answer. We have seen that he suffered from a horrible and voracious disease, which after his removal from Rome seems to have made progress. Yet, though this malady may well have cut his life short, suspicion of poison was not, in the circumstances, quite unreasonable. The Grand Duke of Tuscany, the Pope, and the Orsini family were all interested in his death. Anyhow, he had time to make a will in Vittoria's favour, leaving her large sums of money, jewels, goods, and houses—enough, in fact, to support her ducal dignity with splendour. His hereditary fiefs and honours passed by right to his only son, Virginio.

Vittoria, accompanied by her brother, Marcello, and the whole court of Bracciano, repaired at once to Padua, where she was soon after joined by Flaminio, and by the Prince Lodovico Orsini. Lodovico Orsini assumed the duty of settling Vittoria's affairs under her dead husband's will. In life he had been the Duke's ally as well as relative. His family pride was deeply wounded by what seemed to him an ignoble, as it was certainly an unequal, marriage. He now showed himself the relentless enemy of the Duchess. Disputes arose between them as to certain details, which seem to have been legally decided in the widow's favour. On the night of December 22, however, forty men, disguised in black and fantastically tricked out to elude detection, surrounded her palace. Through the long galleries and chambers hung with arras, eight of them went bearing torches, in search of Vittoria and her brothers. Marcello escaped, having fled the house under suspicion of the murder of one of his own followers. Flaminio, the innocent and young, was playing on his lute and singing 'Miserere' in the great hall of the palace. The murderers surprised him with a shot from one of their harquebusses. He ran, wounded in the shoulder, to his sister's room. She, it is said, was telling her beads before retiring for the night. When three of the assassins entered, she knelt before the crucifix, and there they stabbed her in the left breast, turning the poignard in the wound, and asking her with savage insults if her heart was pierced. Her last words were, 'Jesus, I pardon you.' Then they turned to Flaminio, and left him pierced with seventy-four stiletto wounds.

The authorities of Padua identified the bodies of Vittoria and Flaminio, and sent at once for further instructions to Venice. Meanwhile it appears that both corpses were laid out in one open coffin for the people to contemplate. The palace and the church of the Eremitani, to which they had been removed, were crowded all through the following day with a vast concourse of the Paduans. Vittoria's dead body, pale yet sweet to look upon, the golden hair flowing around her marble shoulders, the red wound in her breast uncovered, the stately limbs arrayed in satin as she died, maddened the populace with its surpassing loveliness. '*Dentibus fremebant*,' says the chronicler, when they beheld that gracious lady stiff in death. And of a truth, if her corpse was actually exposed in the chapel of the Eremitani, as we have some right to assume, the spectacle must have been impressive. Those grim gaunt frescoes of Mantegna looked down on her as she lay stretched upon her bier, solemn and calm, and, but for pallor, beautiful as though in life. No wonder that the folk forgot her first husband's murder, her less than comely marriage to the second. It was enough for them that this flower of surpassing loveliness had been cropped by villains in its bloom. Gathering in knots around the torches placed beside the corpse, they vowed vengeance against the Orsini; for suspicion, not unnaturally, fell on Prince Lodovico.

The Prince was arrested and interrogated before the court of Padua. He entered their hall attended by forty armed men, responded haughtily to their questions, and demanded free passage for his courier to Virginio Orsini, then at Florence. To this demand the court acceded; but the precaution of waylaying the courier and searching his person was very wisely taken. Besides some formal despatches which announced Vittoria's assassination, they found in this man's boot a compromising letter, declaring Virginio a party to the crime, and asserting that Lodovico had with his own poignard killed their victim. Padua placed itself in a state of defence, and prepared to besiege the palace of Prince Lodovico, who also got himself in readiness for battle. Engines, culverins, and fire-brands were directed against the barricades which he had raised. The militia was called out and the Brenta was strongly guarded. Meanwhile the Senate of S. Mark had despatched the Avogadore, Aloisio Bragadin, with full power, to the scene of action. Lodovico Orsini, it may be mentioned, was in their service; and had not this affair intervened, he would in a few weeks have entered on his duties as Governor for Venice of Corfu.

The bombardment of Orsini's palace began on Christmas Day. Three of the Prince's men were killed in the first assault; and since the artillery brought to bear upon him threatened speedy ruin to the house and its inhabitants, he made up his mind to surrender. 'The Prince Luigi,' writes one chronicler of these events, 'walked attired in brown, his poignard at his side, and his cloak slung elegantly under his arm. The weapon being taken from him he leaned upon a balustrade, and began to trim his nails with a little pair of scissors he happened to find there.' On the 27th he was strangled in prison by order of the Venetian Republic. His body was carried to be buried, according to his own will, in the church of S. Maria dell' Orto at Venice. Two of his followers were hanged next day. Fifteen were executed on the following Monday; two of these were quartered alive; one of them, the Conte Paganello, who confessed to having slain Vittoria, had his left side probed with his own cruel dagger. Eight were condemned to the galleys, six to prison, and eleven were acquitted. Thus ended this terrible affair, which brought, it is said, good credit and renown to the lords of Venice through all nations of the civilised world. It only remains to be added that Marcello Accoramboni was surrendered to the Pope's vengeance and beheaded at Ancona, where also his mysterious accomplice, the Greek sorceress, perished.

The Duchess of Palliano.

It was the custom of Italians in the sixteenth and seventeenth centuries to compose and circulate narratives of tragic or pathetic incidents in real life. They were intended to satisfy curiosity in an age when newspapers and law reports did not exist, and also to suit the taste of ladies and gentlemen versed in Boccaccio and Bandello. Resembling the London letters of our ancestors, they passed from hand to hand, rarely found their way into the printing office, and when they had performed their task were left to moulder in the dust of bookcases. The private archives of noble families abound in volumes of such tales, and some may still be found upon the shelves of public libraries. These MS. collections furnish a mine of inexhaustible riches to the student of manners. When checked by legal documents, they frequently reveal carelessness, inaccuracy, or even wilful distortion of facts. The genius of the *Novella*, so paramount in popular Italian literature of that epoch, presided over their composition, adding *intreccio* to disconnected facts, heightening sympathy by the suggestion of romantic motives, turning the heroes or the heroines of their adventures into saints, and blackening the faces of the villains. Yet these stories, pretending to be veracious and aiming at information no less than entertainment, present us with even a more vivid picture of customs than the *Novelle*. By their truthful touches of landscape and incident painting, by their unconscious revelation of contemporary sentiment in dialogue and ethical analysis of motives, they enable us to give form and substance to the drier details of the law courts. One of these narratives I propose to condense from the transcript made by Henri Beyle, for the sake of the light it throws upon the tragedy of the Caraffa family.[1] It opens with an account of Paul IV.'s ascent to power and a description of his nephews. Don Giovanni, the eldest son of the Count of Montorio, was married to Violante de Cardona, sister of the Count Aliffe. Paul invested him with the Duchy of Palliano, which he wrested from Marc Antonio Colonna. Don Carlo, the second son, who had passed his life as a soldier, entered the Sacred College; and Don Antonio, the third, was created Marquis of Montebello. The Cardinal, as prime minister, assumed the reins of government in Rome. The Duke of Palliano disposed of the Papal soldiery. The Marquis of Montebello, commanding the guard of the palace, excluded or admitted persons at his pleasure. Surrounded by these nephews, Paul saw only with their eyes, heard only what they whispered to him, and unwittingly lent his authority to their lawlessness. They exercised an unlimited tyranny in Rome, laying hands on property and abusing their position to gratify their lusts. No woman who had the misfortune to please them was safe; and the cells of convents were as little respected as the palaces of gentlefolk. To arrive at justice was impossible; for the three brothers commanded all avenues, civil, ecclesiastical, and military, by which the Pope could be approached.

Violante, Duchess of Palliano, was a young woman distinguished for her beauty no less than for her Spanish pride. She had received a thoroughly Italian education; could recite the sonnets of Petrarch and the stanzas of Ariosto by heart, and repeated the tales of Ser Giovanni and other novelists

[1] 'La Duchesse de Palliano,' in *Chroniques et Nouvelles*, De Stendhal (Henri Beyle).

with an originality that lent new charm to their style.[1] Her
court was a splendid one, frequented by noble youths and
gentlewomen of the best blood in Naples. Two of these
require particular notice: Diana Brancaccio, a relative of the
Marchioness of Montebello; and Marcello Capecce, a young
man of exceptional beauty. Diana was a woman of thirty
years, hot-tempered, tawny-haired, devotedly in love with
Domiziano Fornari, a squire of the Marchese di Montebello's
household. Marcello had conceived one of those bizarre
passions for the Duchess, in which an almost religious adoration was mingled with audacity, persistence, and aptitude for
any crime. The character of his mistress gave him but little
hope. Though profoundly wounded by her husband's in-
fidelities, insulted in her pride by the presence of his wanton
favourites under her own roof, and assailed by the importunities of the most brilliant profligates in Rome, she held
a haughty course, above suspicion, free from taint or stain.
Marcello could do nothing but sigh at a distance and watch
his opportunity.

At this point, the narrator seems to sacrifice historical
accuracy for the sake of combining his chief characters in one
intrigue.[2] Though he assumes the tone of a novelist rather
than a chronicler, there has hitherto been nothing but what
corresponds to fact in his description of the Caraffa cabal.
He now explains their downfall; and opens the subject after
this fashion. At the beginning of the year 1559, the Pope's
confessor ventured to bring before his notice the scandalous
behaviour of the Papal nephews. Paul at first refused to
credit this report. But an incident happened which con-

[1] This touch shows what were then considered the accomplishments
of a noble woman.
[2] It was a street-brawl, in which the Cardinal Monte played an
indecent part, that finally aroused the anger of Paul IV. De Stendhal's
MS. shifts the chief blame on to the shoulders of Cardinal Caraffa,
who indeed appears to have been in the habit of keeping bad company.

vinced him of its truth. On the feast of the Circumcision—
a circumstance which aggravated matters in the eyes of a
strictly pious Pontiff—Andrea Lanfranchi, secretary to the
Duke of Palliano, invited the Cardinal Caraffa to a banquet.
One of the loveliest and most notorious courtesans of Rome,
Martuccia, was also present; and it so happened that Marcello Capecce at this epoch believed he had more right to her
favours than any other man in the capital. That night he
sought her in her lodgings, pursued her up and down, and
learned at last that she was supping with Lanfranchi and
the Cardinal. Attended by armed men, he made his way to
Lanfranchi's house, entered the banquet room, and ordered
Martuccia to come away with him at once. The Cardinal, who
was dressed in secular habit, rose, and, drawing his sword,
protested against this high-handed proceeding. Martuccia,
by favour of their host, was his partner that evening. Upon
this, Marcello called his men ; but when they recognised the
Cardinal nephew, they refused to employ violence. In the
course of the quarrel, Martuccia made her escape, followed by
Marcello, Caraffa, and the company. There ensued a street-
brawl between the young man and the Cardinal; but no
blood was spilt, and the incident need have had but slight
importance, if the Duke of Palliano had not thought it
necessary to place Lanfranchi and Marcello under arrest.
They were soon released, because it became evident that the
chief scandal would fall upon the Cardinal, who had clearly
been scuffling and crossing swords in a dispute about a
common prostitute. The three Caraffa brothers resolved on
hushing the affair up. But it was too late. The Pope heard
something, which sufficed to confirm his confessor's warnings;
and on January 27, he pronounced the famous sentence on
his nephews. The Cardinal was banished to Città Lavinia,
the Duke to Soriano, the Marquis to Montebello. The
Duchess took up her abode with her court in the little village

of Gallese. It was here that the episode of her love and tragic end ensued.

Violante found herself almost alone in a simple village among mountains, half-way between Rome and Orvieto, surrounded indeed by lovely forest scenery, but deprived of all the luxuries and entertainments to which she was accustomed. Marcello and Diana were at her side, the one eager to pursue his hitherto hopeless suit, and the other to further it for her own profit. One day Marcello committed the apparent imprudence of avowing his passion. The Duchess rejected him with scorn, but disclosed the fact to Diana, who calculated that if she could contrive to compromise her mistress, she might herself be able to secure the end she had in view of marrying Domiziano. In the solitude of those long days of exile the waiting-woman returned again and again to the subject of Marcello's devotion, his beauty, his noble blood and his manifold good qualities. She arranged meetings in the woods between the Duchess and her lover, and played her cards so well that during the course of the fine summer weeks Violante yielded to Marcello. Diana now judged it wise to press her own suit forward with Domiziano. But this cold-blooded fellow knew that he was no fit match for a relative of the Marchioness of Montebello. He felt, besides, but little sentiment for his fiery *innamorata*. Dreading the poignard of the Caraffas, if he should presume to marry her, he took the prudent course of slipping away in disguise from the port of Nettuno. Diana, maddened by disappointment, flew to the conclusion that the Duchess had planned her lover's removal, and resolved to take a cruel revenge. The Duke of Palliano was residing at Soriano, only a few miles from Gallese. To bring him secret information of his wife's intrigue was a matter of no difficulty. At first he refused to believe her report. Had not Violante resisted the seductions of all Rome, and repelled the advances even of the Duke of Guise? At last she contrived to introduce him into the bedroom of the Duchess at a moment when Marcello was also there. The circumstances were not precisely indicative of guilt. The sun had only just gone down behind the hills; a maid was in attendance; and the Duchess lay in bed, pencilling some memoranda. Yet they were sufficient to rouse the Duke's anger. He disarmed Marcello and removed him to the prisons of Soriano, leaving Violante under strict guard at Gallese.

The Duke of Palliano had no intention of proclaiming his jealousy or of suggesting his dishonour, until he had extracted complete proof. He therefore pretended to have arrested Marcello on the suspicion of an attempt to poison him. Some large toads, bought by the young man at a high price two or three months earlier, lent colour to this accusation. Meanwhile the investigation was conducted as secretly as possible by the Duke in person, his brother-in-law Count Aliffe, and a certain Antonio Torando, with the sanction of the Podestà of Soriano. After examining several witnesses, they became convinced of Violante's guilt. Marcello was put to the torture, and eventually confessed. The Duke stabbed him to death with his own hands, and afterwards cut Diana's throat for her share in the business. Both bodies were thrown into the prison-sewer. Meanwhile Paul IV. had retained the young Cardinal, Alfonso Caraffa, son of the Marquis of Montebello, near his person. This prelate thought it right to inform his grand-uncle of the occurrences at Soriano. The Pope only answered: 'And the Duchess? What have they done with her?' Paul IV. died in August, and the Conclave, which ended in the election of Pius IV., was opened. During the important intrigues of that moment, Cardinal Alfonso found time to write to the Duke, imploring him not to leave so dark a stain upon his honour, but to exercise justice on a guilty wife. On August 28, 1559, the Duke sent the Count Aliffe, and Don Leonardo del Cardine, with a company of soldiers, to Gallese. They told Violante that they had arrived to kill her, and offered her the offices of two Franciscan monks. Before her death, the Duchess repeatedly insisted on her innocence, and received the sacrament from the hands of Friar Antonio of Pavia. The Count, her brother, then proceeded to her execution. 'He covered her eyes with a handkerchief, which she, with perfect *sang froid*, drew somewhat lower in order to shut his sight out. Then he adjusted the cord to her neck; but finding that it would not exactly fit, he removed it and walked away. The Duchess raised the bandage from her face, and said: " Well! what are we about then ? " He answered: " The cord was not quite right, and I am going to get another, in order that you may not suffer." When he returned to the room, he arranged the handkerchief again, fixed the cord, turned the wand in the knot behind her neck, and strangled her. The whole incident, on the part of the Duchess, passed in the tone of ordinary conversation. She died like a good Christian, frequently repeating the words *Credo, Credo*.'

Contrary to the usual custom and opinion of the age, this murder of an erring wife and sister formed part of the accusations brought against the Duke of Palliano and Count Aliffe. It will be remembered that they were executed in Rome, together with the elder Cardinal Caraffa, during the pontificate of Pius IV.

Wife-Murders.

It would be difficult to give any adequate notion of the frequency of wife-murders at this epoch in the higher ranks of society. I will, however, mention a few, noticed by me

FREQUENCY OF WIFE-MURDERS

in the course of study. Donna Pellegrina, daughter of Bianca Capello before her marriage with the Grand Duke of Tuscany, was killed at Bologna in 1598 by four masked assassins, at the order of her husband, Count Ulisse Bentivoglio. She had been suspected or convicted of adultery; and the Court of Florence sent word to the Count, 'che essendo vero quanto scriveva, facesse quello che conveniva a cavaliere di honore.' In the light of open day, together with two of her gentlewomen and her coachman, she was cut to pieces and left on the road.[1] In 1590 at Naples Don Carlo Gesualdo, son of the Prince of Venosta, assassinated his wife and cousin Donna Maria d' Avalos, together with her lover, Fabricio Caraffa, Duke of Andri. This crime was committed in his palace by the husband, attended by a band of cutthroats.[2] In 1577, at Milan, Count Giovanni Borromeo, cousin of the Cardinal Federigo, stabbed his wife, the Countess Giulia Sanseverina, sister of the Contessa di Sala, at table, with three mortal wounds. A mere domestic squabble gave rise to this tragedy.[3] In 1598, in his villa of Zenzalino at Ferrara, the Count Ercole Trotti, with the assistance of a bravo called Jacopo Lazzarini, killed his wife Anna, daughter of the poet Guarini. Her own brother Girolamo connived at the act and helped to facilitate its execution. She was accused—falsely, as it afterwards appeared from Girolamo's confession—of an improper intimacy with the Count Ercole Bevilacqua. I may add that Count Ercole Trotti's father, Alfonso, had murdered his own wife, Michela Granzena, in the same villa.[3]

[1] Mutinelli, *Storia Arcana*, vol. ii. p. 64.
[2] *Ib.* vol. ii. p. 162.   [2] *Ib.* vol. i. p. 843.
[3] *I Guarini Famiglia Nobile Ferrarese* (Bologna, Romagnoli, 1870), pp. 83-87.

The Medici.

The history of the Medicean family during the sixteenth century epitomises the chief features of social morality upon which I have been dwelling in this chapter. It will be remembered that Alessandro de' Medici, the first Duke of Florence, poisoned his cousin Ippolito, and was himself assassinated by his cousin Lorenzino. To the second of these crimes Cosimo, afterwards Grand Duke of Tuscany, owed the throne of Florence, on which, however, he was not secure until he had removed Lorenzino from this world by the poignard of a bravo. Cosimo maintained his authority by a system of espionage, remorseless persecution, and assassination, which gave colour even to the most improbable of legends.[1] But it is not of him so much as of his children that I have to speak. Francesco, who reigned from 1564 till 1587, brought disgrace upon his line by marrying the infamous Bianca Capello, after authorising the murder of her previous husband. Bianca, though incapable of bearing children, flattered her besotted paramour before this marriage by pretending to have borne a son. In reality, she had secured the co-operation of three women on the point of childbirth; and when one of these was delivered of a boy, she presented this infant to Francesco, who christened him Antonio de' Medici. Of the three mothers who served in this nefarious transaction, Bianca contrived to assassinate two, but not before one of the victims to her dread of exposure made full confession at the point of death. The third escaped. Another woman who had superintended the affair was shot between Florence and Bologna in the valleys of the Apennines. Yet after the manifestation of Bianca's imposture, the Duke continued to

---

[1] In addition to the victims of his vengeance who perished by the poignard, he publicly executed in Florence forty-two political offenders.

recognise Antonio as belonging to the Medicean family; and his successor was obliged to compel this young man to assume the Cross of Malta, in order to exclude his posterity from the line of princes.[1] The legend of Francesco's and Bianca's mysterious death is well known. The Duchess had engaged in fresh intrigues for palming off a spurious child upon her husband. These roused the suspicions of his brother Cardinal Ferdinando de' Medici, heir presumptive to the crown. An angry correspondence followed, ending in a reconciliation between the three princes. They met in the autumn of 1587 at the villa of Poggio a Cajano. Then the world was startled by the announcement that the Grand Duke had died of fever, after a few days' illness, and that Bianca had almost immediately afterwards followed him to the grave. Ferdinand, on succeeding to the throne, refused her the interment suited to her rank, defaced her arms on public edifices, and for her name and titles in official documents substituted the words, ' la pessima Bianca.' What passed at Poggio a Cajano is not known. It was commonly believed in Italy that Bianca, meaning to poison the Cardinal at supper, had been frustrated in her designs by a blunder which made her husband the victim of this plot, and that she ended her own life in despair or fell a victim to the Cardinal's vengeance. This story is rejected both by Botta and Galluzzi; but Litta has given it a partial credence.[2] Two of Cosimo's sons died previously, in the year 1562, under circumstances which gave rise to similar malignant rumours. Don Garzia and the Cardinal Giovanni were hunting together in the Pisan marshes, when the latter expired after a short illness, and the former in a few days

---

[1] See Mutinelli, *Storia Arcana*, vol. ii. pp. 54-56, for Antonio's reception into the Order.

[2] I refer, of course, to Galluzzi's *Storia del Gran Ducato*, vol. iv. pp. 241-244. Botta's *Storia d' Italia*, Book xiv., and Litta's *Famiglic Celebri* under the pedigree of Medici.

met with a like fate. Report ran that Don Garzia had stabbed his brother, and that Cosimo, in a fit of rage, ran him through the body with his own sword. In this case, although Litta attaches weight to the legend, the balance of evidence is strongly in favour of both brothers having been carried off by a pernicious fever contracted simultaneously during their hunting expedition.[1] Each instance serves, however, to show in what an atmosphere of guilt the Medicean princes were enveloped. No one believed that they could die except by fraternal or paternal hands. And the authentic crimes of the family certainly justified this popular belief. I have already alluded to the murders of Ippolito, Alessandro, and Lorenzino. I have told how the Court of Florence sanctioned the assassination of Bianca's daughter by her husband at Bologna.[2] I must now proceed to relate the tragic tales of the princesses of the house.

Pietro de' Medici, a fifth of Cosimo's sons, had rendered himself notorious in Spain and Italy by forming a secret society for the most revolting debaucheries.[3] Yet he married the noble lady Eleonora di Toledo, related by blood to Cosimo's first wife. Neglected and outraged by her husband, she proved unfaithful, and Pietro hewed her in pieces with his own hands at Caffaggiolo. Isabella de' Medici, daughter of Cosimo, was married to the Duke of Bracciano. Educated in the empoisoned atmosphere of Florence, she, like Eleonora di Toledo, yielded herself to fashionable profligacy, and was strangled by her husband at Cerretto.[4] Both of these mur-

---

[1] See Galluzzi, *op. cit.* vol. iii. p. 25, and Botta, *op. cit.* Book XII.
[2] See above, p. 295.
[3] Litta may be consulted for details; also Galluzzi, *op. cit.* vol. v. p. 174.
[4] It may be worth mentioning that Virginio Orsini, Bracciano's son and heir, married Donna Flavia, grand-niece of Sixtus V., and consequently related to the man his father murdered in order to possess Vittoria Accoramboni. See Mutinelli, *Storia Arcana*, vol. ii. p. 72.

ders took place in 1576. Isabella's death, as I have elsewhere related, opened the way for the Duke of Bracciano's marriage with Vittoria Accoramboni, which had been prepared by the assassination of her first husband, and which led to her own murder at Padua.[1] Another of Cosimo's daughters, Lucrezia de' Medici, became Duchess of Ferrara, fell under a suspicion of infidelity, and was possibly removed by poison in 1561.[2] The last of his sons whom I have to mention, Don Giovanni, married a dissolute woman of low birth called Livia, and disgraced the name of Medici by the unprincely follies of his life. Eleonora de' Medici, third of his daughters, introduces a comic element into these funereal records. She was affianced to Vincenzo Gonzaga, heir of the Duchy of Mantua. But suspicions, arising out of the circumstances of his divorce from a former wife, obliged him to prove his marital capacity before the completion of the contract. This he did at Venice, before a witness, upon the person of a virgin selected for the experiment.[3] Maria de' Medici, the only child of Duke Francesco, became Queen of France. The history of her amours with Concini forms an episode in French annals.

If now we eliminate the deaths of Don Garzia, Cardinal Giovanni, Duke Francesco, Bianca Capello, and Lucrezia de' Medici, as doubtful, there will still remain the murders of Cardinal Ippolito, Duke Alessandro, Lorenzino de' Medici, Pietro Bonaventuri (Bianca's husband), Pellegrina Bentivoglio (Bianca's daughter), Eleonora di Toledo, Francesco Casi (Eleonora's lover), the Duchess of Bracciano, Troilo Orsini

---

[1] See above, pp. 279-285.
[2] Galluzzi, vol. iii. p. 5, says that she died of a putrid fever. Litta again inclines to the probability of poison. But this must be counted among the doubtful cases.
[3] See Galluzzi, *op. cit.* vol. iv. pp. 195-197, for the account of a transaction which throws curious light upon the customs of the age. It was only stipulated that the trial should not take place upon a Friday. Otherwise, the highest ecclesiastics gave it their full approval.

(lover of this Duchess), Felice Peretti (husband of Vittoria Accoramboni), and Vittoria Accoramboni—eleven murders, all occurring between 1535 and 1585, an exact half-century, in a single princely family and its immediate connexions. The majority of these crimes, that is to say seven, had their origin in lawless passion.[1]

[1] I have told the stories in this chapter as drily as I could. Yet it would be interesting to analyse the fascination they exercised over our Elizabethan playwrights, some of whose Italian tragedies handle the material with penetrative imagination. For the English mode of interpreting southern passion see my *Italian Byways*, pp. 169 *et seq.*, and a brilliant essay in Vernon Lee's *Euphorion*.

CHAPTER VI

SOCIAL AND DOMESTIC MORALS : PART II

Tales illustrative of Bravi and Banditti—Cecco Bibboni—Ambrogio Tremazzi—Lodovico dall' Armi—Brigandage—Piracy—Plagues—The Plagues of Milan, Venice, Piedmont—Persecution of the Untori—Moral State of the Proletariate—Witchcraft—Its Italian Features—History of Giacomo Centini.

THE stories related in the foregoing chapter abundantly demonstrate the close connexion between the aristocracy and their accomplices—bravos and bandits. But it still remains to consider this connexion from the professional murderer's own point of view. And for this purpose, I will now make use of two documents vividly illustrative of the habits, sentiments, and social status of men who undertook to speculate in bloodshed for reward. They are both autobiographical; and both relate tragedies which occupied the attention of all Italy.

Cecco Bibboni.

The first of these documents is the report made by Cecco Bibboni concerning his method adopted for the murder of Lorenzino de' Medici at Venice in 1546. Lorenzino, by the help of a bravo called Scoroncolo, had assassinated his cousin Alessandro, Duke of Florence, in 1537. After accomplishing this deed, which gained for him the name of Brutus, he escaped from the city; and a distant relative of the murdered and the murderer, Cosimo de' Medici, was chosen Duke in Alessandro's stead. One of the first acts of his reign was to publish a ban of outlawry against Lorenzino. His portrait was painted, according to old Tuscan usage, head-downwards, and suspended by one foot, upon the wall of Alessandro's fortress. His house was cut in twain from roof to pavement, and a narrow passage was driven through it, which received the name of Traitor's Alley—*Chiasso del Traditore*. The price put upon his head was enormous—four thousand golden florins, with a pension of one hundred florins to the murderer and his heirs in perpetuity. The man who should kill Lorenzino was, further, to enjoy amnesty from all offences and to exercise full civic rights; he was promised exemption from taxes, the privilege of carrying arms with two attendants in the whole domain of Florence, and the prerogative of restoring ten outlaws at his choice. If he captured Lorenzino and brought him alive to Florence, the reward would be doubled in each item. There was enough here to raise cupidity and stir the speculative spirit. Cecco Bibboni shall tell us how the business was brought to a successful termination.[1]

'When I returned from Germany,' begins Bibboni, 'where I had been in the pay of the Emperor, I found at Vicenza Bebo da Volterra, who was staying in the house of M. Antonio da Roma, a nobleman of that city. This gentleman employed him because of a great feud he had; and he was mighty pleased, moreover, at my coming, and desired that I too should take up my quarters in his palace.'

Bibboni proceeds to say how another gentleman of Vicenza, M. Francesco Manente, had at this time a feud with certain of the Guazzi and the Laschi, which had lasted several years, and cost the lives of many members of both parties and their following. M. Francesco, being a friend of M. Antonio, besought that gentleman to lend him Bibboni and Bebo for a

[1] For the Italian text see *Lorenzino de' Medici*, Daelli, Milano, 1862. The above is borrowed from my *Italian Byways*.

season; and the two bravi went together with their new
master to Celsano, a village in the neighbourhood. ' There
both parties had estates, and all of them kept armed men in
their houses, so that not a day passed without feats of arms,
and always there was some one killed or wounded. One
day, soon afterwards, the leaders of our party resolved to
attack the foe in their house, where we killed two, and the
rest, numbering five men, entrenched themselves in a ground-
floor apartment; whereupon we took possession of their harquebusses and other arms, which forced them to abandon the
villa and retire to Vicenza; and within a short space of time
this great feud was terminated by an ample peace.' After
this Bebo took service with the Rector of the University in
Padua, and was transferred by his new patron to Milan.
Bibboni remained at Vicenza with M. Galeazzo della Seta,
who stood in great fear of his life, notwithstanding the peace
which had been concluded between the two factions. At the
end of ten months he returned to M. Antonio da Roma and
his six brothers, ' all of whom being very much attached to
me, they proposed that I should live my life with them for
good or ill, and be treated as one of the family; upon the
understanding that if war broke out and I wanted to take part
in it, I should always have twenty-five crowns and arms and
horse, with welcome home, so long as I lived; and in case I
did not care to join the troops, the same provision for my
maintenance.'

From these details we comprehend the sort of calling
which a bravo of Bibboni's species followed. Meanwhile
Bebo was at Milan. ' There it happened that M. Francesco
Vinta, of Volterra, was on embassy from the Duke of Florence.
He saw Bebo, and asked him what he was doing in Milan,
and Bebo answered that he was a knight errant.' This phrase
—derived, no doubt, from the romantic epics then in vogue—
was a pretty euphemism for a rogue of Bebo's quality. The

ambassador now began cautiously to sound his man, who seems to have been outlawed from the Tuscan duchy, telling him he knew a way by which he might return with favour to his home, and at last disclosing the affair of Lorenzo. Bebo was puzzled at first, but when he understood the matter, he professed his willingness, took letters from the envoy to the Duke of Florence, and, in a private audience with Cosimo, informed him that he was ready to attempt Lorenzino's assassination. He added that 'he had a comrade fit for such a job, whose fellow for the business could not easily be found.'

Bebo now travelled to Vicenza, and opened the whole matter to Bibboni, who weighed it well, and at last, being convinced that the Duke's commission to his comrade was *bona fide*, determined to take his share in the undertaking. The two agreed to have no accomplices. They went to Venice, and 'I,' says Bibboni, ' being most intimately acquainted with all that city, and provided there with many friends, soon quietly contrived to know where Lorenzino lodged, and took a room in the neighbourhood, and spent some days in seeing how we best might rule our conduct.' Bibboni soon discovered that Lorenzino never left his palace ; and he therefore remained in much perplexity, until, by good luck, Ruberto Strozzi arrived from France in Venice, bringing in his train a Navarrese servant, who had the nickname of Spagnoletto. This fellow was a great friend of the bravo. They met, and Bibboni told him that he should like to go and kiss the hands of Messer Ruberto, whom he had known in Rome. Strozzi inhabited the same palace as Lorenzino. ' When we arrived there, both Messer Ruberto and Lorenzo were leaving the house, and there were around them so many gentlemen and other persons, that I could not present myself, and both straightway stepped into the gondola. Then I, not having seen Lorenzo for a long while past, and because he was very quietly attired, could not recognise the man exactly, but only as it were between certainty and doubt. Wherefore I said to Spagnoletto, "I think I know that gentleman, but don't remember where I saw him." And Messer Ruberto was giving him his right hand. Then Spagnoletto answered, "You know him well enough; he is Messer Lorenzo. But see you tell this to nobody. He goes by the name of Messer Dario, because he lives in great fear for his safety, and people don't know that he is now in Venice." I answered that I marvelled much, and if I could have helped him, would have done so willingly. Then I asked where they were going, and he said, to dine with Messer Giovanni della Casa, who was the Pope's Legate. I did not leave the man till I had drawn from him all I required.'

Thus spoke the Italian Judas. The appearance of La Casa on the scene is interesting. He was the celebrated author of the 'Capitolo del Forno,' the author of many sublime and melancholy sonnets, who was now at Venice prosecuting a charge of heresy against Pier Paolo Vergerio, and paying his addresses to a noble lady of the Quirini family. It seems that on the territory of San Marco he made common cause with the exiles from Florence, for he was himself by birth a Florentine, and he had no objection to take Brutus-Lorenzino by the hand.

After the noblemen had rowed off in their gondola to dine with the Legate, Bibboni and his friend entered their palace, where he found another old acquaintance, the house-steward, or *spenditore* of Lorenzo. From him he gathered much useful information. Pietro Strozzi, it seems, had allowed the tyrannicide one thousand five hundred crowns a year, with the keep of three brave and daring companions (*tre compagni bravi e facinorosi*), and a palace worth fifty crowns on lease. But Lorenzo had just taken another on the Campo di San Polo at three hundred crowns a year, for which swagger (*altura*) Pietro Strozzi had struck a thousand crowns off his allowance. Bibboni also learned that he was keeping house with his uncle, Alessandro Soderini, another Florentine outlaw, and that he was ardently in love with a certain beautiful Barozza. This woman was apparently one of the grand courtesans of Venice. He further ascertained the date when he was going to move into the palace at San Polo, and, 'to put it briefly, knew everything he did, and, as it were, how many times a day he spit.' Such were the intelligences of the servants' hall, and of such value were they to men of Bibboni's calling.

In the Carnival of 1546 Lorenzo meant to go masqued in the habit of a gipsy woman to the square of San Spirito, where there was to be a joust. Great crowds of people would assemble, and Bibboni hoped to do his business there. The assassination, however, failed on this occasion, and Lorenzo took up his abode in the palace he had hired upon the Campo di San Polo. This Campo is one of the largest open places in Venice, shaped irregularly, with a finely curving line upon the western side, where two of the noblest private houses in the city are still standing. Nearly opposite these, in the south-western angle, stands, detached, the little old church of San Polo. One of its side entrances opens upon the square; the other on a lane which leads eventually to the Frari. There is nothing in Bibboni's narrative to make it clear where Lorenzo hired his dwelling. But it would seem from certain things which he says later on, that in order to enter the church his victim had to cross the square. Meanwhile Bibboni took the precaution of making friends with a shoe maker, whose shop commanded the whole Campo, including Lorenzo's palace. In this shop he began to spend much of his time; 'and oftentimes I feigned to be asleep; but God knows whether I was sleeping, for my mind, at any rate, was wide-awake.'

A second convenient occasion for murdering Lorenzo soon seemed to offer. He was bidden to dine with Monsignor della Casa; and Bibboni, putting a bold face on, entered the Legate's palace, having left Bebo below in the loggia, fully resolved to do the business. 'But we found,' he says, 'that they had gone to dine at Murano, so that we remained with our tabors in their bag.' The island of Murano at that period was a favourite resort of the Venetian nobles, especially of the more literary and artistic, who kept country-houses there, where they enjoyed the fresh air of the lagoons and the quiet of their gardens.

The third occasion, after all these weeks of watching, brought success to Bibboni's schemes. He had observed how Lorenzo occasionally so far broke his rules of caution as to go on foot, past the church of San Polo, to visit the beautiful Barozza; and he resolved, if possible, to catch him on one of these journeys. 'It so chanced on February 28, which was the second Sunday of Lent, that having gone, as was my wont, to pry out whether Lorenzo would give orders for going abroad that day, I entered the shoemaker's shop, and stayed awhile, until Lorenzo came to the window with a napkin round his neck—for he was combing his hair—and at the same moment I saw a certain Giovan Battista Martelli, who kept his sword for the defence of Lorenzo's person, enter and come forth again. Concluding that they would probably go abroad, I went home to get ready and procure the necessary weapons, and there I found Bebo asleep in bed, and made him get up at once, and we came to our accustomed post of observation, by the church of San Polo, where our men would have to pass.' Bibboni now retired to his friend the shoemaker's, and Bebo took up his station at one of the side doors of San Polo; 'and, as good luck would have it, Giovan Battista Martelli came forth, and walked a piece in front, and then Lorenzo came, and then Alessandro Soderini, going the one behind the other, like storks, and Lorenzo, on entering the church, and lifting up the curtain of the door, was seen from the opposite door by Bebo, who at the same time noticed how I had left the shop, and so we met upon the street as we had agreed, and he told me that Lorenzo was inside the church.'

To anyone who knows the Campo di San Polo, it will be apparent that Lorenzo had crossed from the western side of the piazza and entered the church by what is technically called its northern door. Bebo, stationed at the southern door, could see him when he pushed the heavy *stoia* or leather curtain aside, and at the same time could observe Bibboni's movements in the cobbler's shop. Meanwhile Lorenzo walked across the church and came to the same door where Bebo had been standing. 'I saw him issue from the church and take the main street; then came Alessandro Soderini, and I walked last of all; and when we reached the point we had determined on, I jumped in front of Alessandro with the poignard in my hand, crying, "Hold hard, Alessandro, and get along with you, in God's name, for we are not here for you!" He then threw himself around my waist, and grasped my arms, and kept on calling out. Seeing how wrong I had been to try to spare his life, I wrenched myself as well as I could from his grip, and with my lifted poignard struck him, as God willed, above the eyebrow, and a little blood trickled from the wound. He, in high fury, gave me such a thrust that I fell backward, and the ground besides was slippery from having rained a little. Then Alessandro drew his sword, which he carried in its scabbard, and thrust at me in front, and struck me on the corslet, which for my good fortune was of double mail. Before I could get ready I received three passes, which, had I worn a doublet instead of that mailed corslet, would certainly have run me through. At the fourth pass I had regained my strength and spirit, and closed with him, and stabbed him four times in the head, and being so close he could not use his sword, but tried to parry with his hand and hilt, and I, as God willed, struck him at the wrist below the sleeve of mail, and cut his hand off clean, and gave him then one last stroke on his head. Thereupon he begged for God's sake spare his life, and I, in trouble about Bebo, left him in the arms of a Venetian nobleman, who held him back from jumping into the canal.'

Who this Venetian nobleman, found unexpectedly upon the scene, was, does not appear. Nor, what is still more curious, do we hear anything of that Martelli, the bravo, ' who kept his sword for the defence of Lorenzo's person.' The one had arrived accidentally, it seems. The other must have been a coward and escaped from the scuffle.

' When I turned,' proceeds Bibboni, ' I found Lorenzo on his knees. He raised himself, and I, in anger, gave him a great cut across the head, which split it in two pieces, and laid him at my feet, and he never rose again.'

Bebo, meanwhile, had made off from the scene of action. And Bibboni, taking to his heels, came up with him in the little square of San Marcello. They now ran for their lives till they reached the Traghetto di San Spirito, where they threw their poignards into the water, remembering that no man might carry these in Venice under penalty of the galleys. Bibboni's white hose were drenched with blood. He therefore agreed to separate from Bebo, having named a rendezvous. Left alone, his ill luck brought him face to face with twenty constables (*sbirri*). ' In a moment I conceived that they knew everything, and were come to capture me, and of a truth I saw that it was over with me. As swiftly as I could I quickened pace and got into a church, near to which was the house of a Compagnia, and the one opened into the other, and knelt down and prayed, commending myself with fervour to God for my deliverance and safety. Yet while I prayed, I kept my eyes well open and saw the whole band pass the church, except one man who entered, and I strained my sight so that I seemed to see behind as well as in front, and then it was I longed for my poignard, for I should not have heeded being in a church.' But the constable, it soon appeared, was not looking for Bibboni. So he gathered up his courage, and ran for the Church of San Spirito, where the Padre Andrea Volterrano was preaching to a great congregation. He hoped to go in by one door and out by the other, but the crowd prevented him, and he had to turn back and face the *sbirri*. One of them followed him, having probably caught sight of the blood upon his hose. Then Bibboni resolved to have done with the fellow, and rushed at him, and flung him down with his head upon the pavement, and ran like mad, and came at last, all out of breath, to San Marco.

It seems clear that before Bibboni separated from Bebo, they had crossed the water, for the Sestiere di San Polo is separated from the Sestiere di San Marco by the Grand Canal. And this they must have done at the Traghetto di San Spirito. Neither the church nor the traghetto are now in existence, and this part of the story is therefore obscure.[1] Having reached San Marco, he took a gondola at the Ponte della Paglia, where tourists are now wont to stand and contemplate the Ducal Palace and the Bridge of Sighs. First, he sought the house of a woman of the town who was his

---

[1] So far as I can discover, the only church of San Spirito in Venice was a building on the island of San Spirito, erected by Sansovino, which belonged to the Sestiere di S. Croce, and which was suppressed in 1656. Its plate and the fine pictures which Titian painted there were transferred at that date to S. M. della Salute. I cannot help inferring that either Bibboni's memory failed him, or that his words were wrongly understood by printer or amanuensis. If for S. Spirito we substitute S. Stefano, the account would be intelligible.

friend; then changed purpose, and rowed to the palace of the Count Salici da Collalto. 'He was a great friend and intimate of ours, because Bebo and I had done him many and great services in times past. There I knocked; and Bebo opened the door, and when he saw me dabbled with blood, he marvelled that I had not come to grief and fallen into the hands of justice, and, indeed, had feared as much because I had remained so long away.' It appears, therefore, that the Palazzo Collalto was their rendezvous. 'The Count was from home; but being known to all his people, I played the master and went into the kitchen to the fire, and with soap and water turned my hose, which had been white, to a grey colour.' This is a very delicate way of saying that he washed out the blood of Alessandro and Lorenzo!

Soon after the Count returned, and 'lavished caresses' upon Bebo and his precious comrade. They did not tell him what they had achieved that morning, but put him off with a story of having settled a *sbirro* in a quarrel about a girl. Then the Count invited them to dinner; and being himself bound to entertain the first physician of Venice, requested them to take it in an upper chamber. He and his secretary served them with their own hands at table. When the physician arrived, the Count went downstairs; and at this moment a messenger came from Lorenzo's mother, begging the doctor to go at once to San Polo, for that her son had been murdered and Soderini wounded to the death. It was now no longer possible to conceal their doings from the Count, who told them to pluck up courage and abide in patience. He had himself to dine and take his siesta, and then to attend a meeting of the Council.

About the hour of vespers, Bibboni determined to seek better refuge. Followed at a discreet distance by Bebo, he first called at their lodgings and ordered supper. Two priests came in and fell into conversation with them. But something in the behaviour of one of these good men roused Bibboni's suspicions. So they left the house, took a gondola, and told the man to row hard to S. Maria Zobenigo. On the way they bade him put them on shore, paid him well, and ordered him to wait for them. They landed near the palace of the Spanish embassy; and here Bibboni meant to seek sanctuary. For it must be remembered that the houses of ambassadors, no less than those of princes of the Church, were inviolable. They offered the most convenient harbouring-places to rascals. Charles V., moreover, was deeply interested in the vengeance taken on Alessandro de' Medici's murderer, for his own natural daughter was Alessandro's widow and Duchess of Florence. In the palace they were received with much courtesy by about forty Spaniards, who showed considerable curiosity, and told them that Lorenzo and Alessandro Soderini had been murdered that morning by two men whose description answered to their appearance. Bibboni put their questions by and asked to see the ambassador. He was not at home. In that case, said Bibboni, take us to the secretary. Attended by some thirty Spaniards, 'with great joy and gladness,' they were shown into the secretary's chamber. He sent the rest of the folk away, 'and locked the door well, and then embraced and kissed us before we had said a word, and afterwards bade us talk freely without any fear.' When Bibboni had told the whole story, he was again embraced and kissed by the secretary, who thereupon left them and went to the private apartment of the ambassador. Shortly after he returned and led them by a winding staircase into the presence of his master. The ambassador greeted them with great honour, told them he would strain all the power of the empire to hand them in safety over to Duke Cosimo, and that he had already sent a courier to the Emperor with the good news.

So they remained in hiding in the Spanish embassy; and

in ten days' time commands were received from Charles himself that everything should be done to convey them safely to Florence. The difficulty was how to smuggle them out of Venice, where the police of the Republic were on watch, and Florentine outlaws were mounting guard on sea and shore to catch them. The ambassador began by spreading reports on the Rialto every morning of their having been seen at Padua, at Verona, in Friuli. He then hired a palace at Malghera, near Mestre, and went out daily with fifty Spaniards, and took carriage or amused himself with horse exercise and shooting. The Florentines, who were on watch, could only discover from his people that he did this for amusement. When he thought that he had put them sufficiently off their guard, the ambassador one day took Bibboni and Bebo out by Canaregio to Malghera, concealed in his own gondola, with the whole train of Spaniards in attendance. And though, on landing, the Florentines challenged them, they durst not interfere with an ambassador or come to battle with his men. So Bebo and Bibboni were hustled into a coach, and afterwards provided with two comrades and four horses. They rode for ninety miles without stopping to sleep, and on the day following this long journey reached Trento, having probably threaded the mountain valleys above Bassano, for Bibboni speaks of a certain village where the people talked half German. The Imperial Ambassador at Trento forwarded them next day to Mantua; from Mantua they came to Piacenza; thence passing through the valley of the Taro, crossing the Apennines at Cisa, descending on Pontremoli, and reaching Pisa at night, the fourteenth day after their escape from Venice.

When they arrived at Pisa, Duke Cosimo was supping. So they went to an inn, and next morning presented themselves to his Grace. Cosimo welcomed them kindly, assured them of his gratitude, confirmed them in the enjoyment of their rewards and privileges, and swore that they might rest

secure of his protection in all parts of his dominion. We
may imagine how the men caroused together after this reception. As Bibboni adds, 'We were now able for the whole
time of life left us to live splendidly, without a thought or
care.' The last words of his narrative are these : 'Bebo from
Pisa, at what date I know not, went home to Volterra, his
native town, and there finished his days; while I abode in
Florence, where I have had no further wish to hear of wars,
but to live my life in holy peace.'

So ends the story of the two bravi. We have reason to
believe, from some contemporary documents which Cantù has
brought to light, that Bibboni exaggerated his own part in
the affair. Luca Martelli, writing to Varchi, says that it was
Bebo who clove Lorenzo's skull with a cutlass. He adds this
curious detail, that the weapons of both men were poisoned,
and that the wound inflicted by Bibboni on Soderini's hand
was a slight one. Yet, the poignard being poisoned, Soderini
died of it. In other respects Martelli's brief account agrees
with that given by Bibboni, who probably did no more, his
comrade being dead, than claim for himself, at some expense
of truth, the lion's share of their heroic action.

Ambrogio Tremazzi.

In illustration of this narrative, and in evidence that it
stands by no means solitary on the records of that century,
I shall extract some passages from the report made by
Ambrogio Tremazzi of Modigliana concerning the assassination of Troilo Orsini.[1] Troilo, it will be remembered, was
the lover of the Medicean Duchess of Bracciano. After the
discovery of their amours, and while the lady was being
strangled by her husband, with the sanction of her brother,

[1] The text is published, from Florentine Archives, in Gnoli's *Vittoria
Accoramboni,* pp. 404-414.

Troilo escaped to France. Ambrogio Tremazzi, knowing that his murder would be acceptable to the Medici, undertook the adventure; moved, as he says, 'solely by the desire of bringing myself into favourable notice with the Grand Duke; for my mind revolted at the thought of money payments, and I had in view the acquisition of honour and praise rather, being willing to risk my life for the credit of my Prince, and not my life only, but also to incur deadly and perpetual feud with a powerful branch of the Orsini family.' On his return from France, having successfully accomplished the mission, Ambrogio Tremazzi found that the friends who had previously encouraged his hopes, especially the Count Ridolfo Isolami, wished to compromise his reward by the settlement of a pension on himself and his associate. Whether he really aimed at a more honourable recognition of his services, or whether he sought to obtain better pecuniary terms, does not appear. But he represents himself as gravely insulted; 'seeing that my tenor of life from boyhood upwards has been always honourable, and thus it ever shall be.' After this exordium in the form of a letter addressed to one Signor Antonio [Serguidi], he proceeds to render account of his proceedings. It seems that Don Piero de' Medici gave him three hundred crowns for his travelling expenses; after which, leaving his son, a boy of twelve years, as hostage in the service of Piero, he set off, and reached Paris on August 12, 1577. There he took lodgings at the sign of the Red Horse, near the Cordeilliers, and began at once to make inquiries for Troilo. He had brought with him from Italy a man called Hieronimo Savorano. Their joint investigations elicited the fact that Troilo had been lately wounded in the service of the King of France, and was expected to arrive in Paris with the Court. It was not until the eve of All Saints' day that the Court returned. Soon afterwards, Ambrogio was talking at the door of a

house with some Italian comedians, when a young man,
covered with a tawny-coloured mantle, passed by upon a
brown horse, bearing a servant behind him on the crupper.
This was Troilo Orsini; and Ambrogio marked him well.
Troilo, after some minutes' conversation with the players,
rode forward to the Louvre. The bravo followed him and
discovered from his servant where he lodged. Accordingly,
he engaged rooms in the Rue S. Honoré, in order to be
nearer to his victim.

Some time, however, elapsed before he was able to ascertain Troilo's daily habits. Chance at last threw them together.
He was playing *primiero* one evening in the house of an
actress called Vittoria, when Troilo entered, with two gentlemen of Florence. He said he had been absent ten days from
Paris. Ambrogio, who had left his harquebuss at home, not
expecting to meet him, 'was consequently on that occasion
unable to do anything.' Days passed without a better opportunity, till, on November 30, 'the feast of S. Andrew, which
is a lucky day for me, I rose and went at once to the palace,
and, immediately on my arrival, saw him at the hour when
the King goes forth to mass.' Ambrogio had to return as he
went; for Troilo was surrounded by too many gentlemen of
the French Court; but he made his mind up then and there
'to see the end of him or me.' He called his comrade Hieronimo, posted him on a bridge across the Seine, and proceeded
to the Court, where Troilo was now playing racquets with
princes of the royal family. Ambrogio hung about the gates
until Troilo issued from the lodgings of Monseigneur de
Montmorenci, still tracked by his unknown enemy, and thence
returned to his own house on horseback, attended by several
servants. After waiting till the night fell, Troilo again left
home on horseback preceded by his servants with torches.
Ambrogio followed at full speed, watched a favourable opportunity, and stopped the horse. 'When I came up with him,

I seized the reins with my left hand, and with the right I set my harquebuss against his side, pushing it with such violence that if it had failed to go off it would at any rate have dislodged him from his seat. The gun took effect, and he fell crying out "Eh! Eh!" In the tumult which ensued, I walked away, and do not know what happened afterwards.' Ambrogio then made his way back to his lodgings, recharged his harquebuss, ate some supper and went to bed. He told Hieronimo that nothing had occurred that night. Next day he rose as usual, and returned to the Court, hoping to hear news of Troilo. In the afternoon, at the Italian theatre, he was informed that an Italian had been murdered, at the instance, it was thought, of the Grand Duke of Florence. Hieronimo touched his arm, and whispered that he must have done the deed; but Ambrogio denied the fact. It seems to have been his object to reserve the credit of the murder for himself, and also to avoid the possibility of Hieronimo's treachery in case suspicion fell upon him. Afterwards he learned that Troilo lay dangerously wounded by a harquebuss. Further details made him aware that he was himself suspected of the murder, and that Troilo could not recover. He therefore conferred upon the matter with Hieronimo in Notre Dame, and both of them resolved to leave Paris secretly. This they did at once, relinquishing clothes, arms, and baggage in their lodgings, and reached Italy in safety.

Lodovico dall' Armi.

The relations of trust which bravi occasionally maintained with foreign Courts, supply some curious illustrations of their position in Italian society. One characteristic instance may be selected from documents in the Venetian Archives referring to Lodovico dall' Armi.[1] This man belonged to a noble

---

[1] See Rawdon Brown's *Calendar of State Papers*, vol. iv.

family of Bologna; and there are reasons for supposing that
his mother was sister to Cardinal Campeggi, famous in the
annals of the English Reformation. Outlawed from his
native city for a homicide, Lodovico adopted the profession of
arms and the management of secret diplomacy. He first
took refuge at the Court of France, where in 1541 he obtained
such credit, especially with the Dauphin, that he was entrusted with a mission for raising revolt in Siena against the
Spaniards.[1] His transactions in that city with Giulio Salvi,
then aspiring to its lordship, and in Rome with the French
ambassador, led to a conspiracy which only awaited the
appearance of French troops upon the Tuscan frontier to
break out into open rebellion. The plot, however, transpired
before it had been matured; and Lodovico took flight through
the Florentine territory. He was arrested at Montevarchi
and confined in the fortress of Florence, where he made such
revelations as rendered the extinction of the Sienese revolt
an easy matter. After this we do not hear of him until he
reappears at Venice in the year 1545. He was now accredited
to the English ambassador with the title of Henry VIII.'s
'Colonel,' and enjoyed the consideration accorded to a powerful monarch's privy agent. His pension amounted to fifty
crowns a month, while he kept eight captains at his orders,
each of whom received half that sum as pay. These subordinates were people of some social standing. We find
among them a Trissino of Vicenza and a Bonifacio of
Verona, the one entitled Marquis and the other Count. What
the object of Lodovico's residence in Italy might be, did not
appear. Though he carried letters of recommendation from
the English Court, he laid no claim to the rank of diplomatic
envoy. But it was tolerably well known that he employed
himself in levying troops. Whether these were meant to be

[1] See Botta, Book IV., for the story of Lodovico's intrigues at
Siena.

used against France or in favour of Savoy, or whether, as the Court of Rome suggested, Henry had given orders for the murder of his cousin, Cardinal Pole, at Trento, remained an open question. Lodovico might have dwelt in peace under the tolerant rule of the Venetians, had he not exposed himself to a collision with their police. In the month of August he assaulted the captain of the night guard in a street brawl; and it was also proved against him that he had despatched two of his men to inflict a wound of infamy upon a gentleman at Treviso. These offences, coinciding with urgent remonstrances from the Papal Curia, gave the Venetian Government fair pretext for expelling him from their dominions. A ban was therefore published against him and fourteen of his followers. The English ambassador declined to interfere in his behalf, and the man left Italy. At the end of August he appeared at Brussels, where he attempted to excuse himself in an interview with the Venetian ambassador. Now began a diplomatic correspondence between the English Court and the Venetian Council, which clearly demonstrates what kind of importance attached to this private agent. The Chancellor Lord Wriothesley, and the Secretary Sir William Paget, used considerable urgency to obtain a suspension of the ban against Dall' Armi. After four months' negotiation, during which the Papal Court endeavoured to neutralise Henry's influence, the Doge signed a safe-conduct for five years in favour of the bravo. Early in 1546 Lodovico reappeared in Lombardy. At Mantua he delivered a letter signed by Henry himself to the Duke Francesco Gonzaga, introducing ' our noble and beloved familiar Lodovico dall' Armi,' and begging the Duke to assist him in such matters as he should transact at Mantua in the King's service.[1] Lodovico presented this letter in April; but the Duchess, who then acted as regent for her son Francesco, refused to receive him. She alleged that the

[1] This letter is dated February 16, 1546.

Duke forbade the levying of troops for foreign service, and declined to complicate his relations with foreign powers. It seems, from a sufficiently extensive correspondence on the affairs of Lodovico, that he was understood by the Italian princess to be charged with some special commission for recruiting soldiers against the French. The peace between England and France, signed at Guines in June, rendered Lodovico's mission nugatory; and the death of Henry VIII. in January 1547 deprived him of his only powerful support. Meanwhile he had contrived to incur the serious displeasure of the Venetian Republic. In the autumn of 1546 they outlawed one of their own nobles, Ser Mafio Bernardo, on the charge of his having revealed State secrets to France. About the middle of November, Bernardo, then living in concealment at Ravenna, was lured into the pine forest by two men furnished with tokens which secured his confidence. He was there murdered, and the assassins turned out to be paid instruments of Lodovico. It now came to light that Lodovico and Ser Mafio Bernardo had for some time past colluded in political intrigue. If, therefore, the murder had a motive, this was found in Lodovico's dread of revelations in the event of Ser Mafio's capture. Submitted to torture in the prisons of the Ten, Ser Mafio might have incriminated his accomplice both with England and Venice. It was obvious why he had been murdered by Lodovico's men. Dall' Armi was consequently arrested and confined in Venice. After examination, followed by a temporary release, he prudently took flight into the Duchy of Milan. Though they held proof of his guilt in the matter of Ser Mafio's murder, the Venetians were apparently unwilling to proceed to extremities against the King of England's man. Early in February, however, Sir William Paget surrendered him in the name of Lord Protector Somerset to the discretion of S. Mark. Furnished with this assurance that Dall' Armi had lost the favour of

England, the Signory wrote to demand his arrest and extradition from the Spanish governor in Milan. He was in fact arrested on February 10. The letter announcing his capture describes him as a man of remarkably handsome figure, accustomed to wear a crimson velvet cloak and a red cap trimmed with gold. It is exactly in this costume that Lodovico has been represented by Bonifazio in a picture of the Massacre of the Innocents. The bravo there stands with his back partly turned, gazing stolidly upon a complex scene of bloodshed. He wears a crimson velvet mantle, scarlet cap and white feather, scarlet stockings, crimson velvet shoes, and rose-coloured silk underjacket. His person is that of a gallant past the age of thirty, high-complexioned, with short brown beard, spare whiskers and moustache. He is good to look at, except that the sharp-set mouth suggests cynical vulgarity and shallow rashness. On being arrested in Milan, Lodovico proclaimed himself a privileged person (*persona pubblica*), bearing credentials from the King of England; and, during the first weeks of his confinement, he wrote to the Emperor for help. This was an idle step. Henry's death had left him without protectors, and Charles V. felt no hesitation in abandoning his suppliant to the Venetians. When the usual formalities regarding extradition had been completed, the Milanese Government delivered Lodovico at the end of April into the hands of the Rector of Brescia, who forwarded him under a guard of two hundred men to Padua. He was handcuffed; and special directions were given regarding his safety, it being even prescribed that if he refused food it should be thrust down his throat. What passed in the prisons of the State, after his arrival at Venice, is not known. But on May 14 he was beheaded between the columns on the Molo.

Venice, at this epoch, incurred the reproaches of her neighbours for harbouring adventurers of Lodovico's stamp. One of the Fregosi of Genoa, a certain Valerio, and Pietro

Strozzi, the notorious French agent, all of whom habitually haunted the lagoons, roused sufficient public anxiety to necessitate diplomatic communications between Courts, and to disquiet fretful Italian princelings. Banished from their own provinces, and plying a petty *condottiere* trade, such men, when they came together on a neutral ground, engaged in cross-intrigues which made them politically dangerous. They served no interest but that of their own egotism, and they were notoriously unscrupulous in the means employed to effect immediate objects. At the same time, the protection which they claimed from foreign potentates withdrew them from the customary justice of the State. Bedmar's conspiracy in 1617–18 revealed to Venice the full extent of the peril which this harbourage of ruffians involved; for though grandees of the distinction of the Duke of Ossuna were involved in it, the main agents, on whose ambition and audacity all depended, sprang from those French, English, Spanish, and Italian mercenaries, who crowded the low quarters of the city, alert for any mischief, and inflamed with the wildest projects of self-aggrandisement by policy and bloodshed. Nothing testifies to the social and political decrepitude of Italy in this period more plainly than the importance which folk like Lodovico dall' Armi acquired, and the revolutionary force which a man like Jaffier commanded.

Brigands, Pirates, Plague.

After collecting these stories, which illustrate the manners of the upper classes in society and prove their dependence upon henchmen paid to subserve lawless passions, it would be interesting to lay bare the life of the common people with equal lucidity. This, however, is a more difficult matter. Statistics of dubious value can indeed be gathered regarding the desolation of villages by brigands, the multitudes destroyed by pestilence and famine, and the inroads of Mediterranean pirates. I propose, therefore, to touch lightly upon these points, and specially to use our records of plague in different Italian districts as tests for contrasting the condition of the people at this epoch with that of the same people in the Middle Ages.

Brigandage, though this was certainly a curse of the first magnitude to Central and Southern Italy, cannot be paralleled, either for the miseries it inflicted, or for the ferocity it stimulated, with the municipal warfare of the twelfth, thirteenth, and fourteenth centuries. In those internecine struggles whole cities disappeared, and fertile districts were periodically abandoned to wolves. The bands of an Alfonso Piccolomini or a Sciarra Colonna plundered villages, exacted black mail, and held prisoners for ransom.[1] But their barbarities were insignificant, when compared with those commonly perpetrated by wandering companies of adventure before the days of Alberigo da Barbiano; nor did brigands cost Italy so much as the mercenary troops, which, after the *condottiere* system had been developed, became a permanent drain upon the resources of the country. The raids of Tunisian and Algerian corsairs were more seriously mischievous; since the whole sea-board from Nice to Reggio lay open to the ravages of such incarnate fiends as Barbarossa and Dragut, while the Adriatic was infested by Uscocchi, and the natives of the Regno not unfrequently turned pirates in emulation of their persecutors.[2] Yet even these injuries may be reckoned light, when we consider what Italy had suffered between 1494 and 1527 from French, Spanish, German, and

[1] See Mutinelli, *Storia Arcana*, vol. ii. p. 167, for the pillage of Lucera by Pacchiarotto.

[2] Sarpi's *History of the Uscocchi* may be consulted for this singular episode in the Iliad of human savagery. See Mutinelli, *op. cit.* vol. ii. p. 182, on the case of the son and heir of the Duke of Termoli joining them; and *ibid.* p. 180 on the existence of pirates at Capri.

Swiss troops in combat on her soil. The pestilences of the
Middle Ages, notably the Black Death of 1348, of which
Boccaccio has left an immortal description, exceeded in viru-
lence those which depopulated Italian cities during the period
of my history. But plagues continued to be frequent; and
some of these are so memorable that they require to be
particularly noticed. At Venice in 1575-77, a total of about
50,000 persons perished; and in 1630-31, 46,490 were
carried off within a space of sixteen months in the city, while
the number of those who died at large in the lagoons
amounted to 94,235.[1] On these two occasions the Venetians
commemorated their deliverance by the erection of the
Redentore and S. Maria della Salute churches, which now
form principal ornaments of the Giudecca and the Grand
Canal. Milan was devastated at the same periods by plagues,
of which we have detailed accounts in the despatches of
resident Venetian envoys.[2] The mortality in the second of
these visitations was terrible. Before September 1629, fourteen thousand had succumbed; between May and August
1630, forty-five thousand victims had been added to the tale.[3]
At Naples, in the year 1656, more than fifty thousand
perished between May and July; the dead were cast naked
into the sea, and the Venetian envoy describes the city as
'*non più città ma spelonca di morti.*'[4] In July his diary is
suddenly interrupted, whether by departure from the stricken
town, or more probably by death, we know not. Savoy was
scourged by a fearful pestilence in the years 1598-1600. Of
this plague we possess a frightfully graphic picture in the

[1] Mutinelli, *Annali Urbani di Venezia*, pp. 470-483, 549-550.
[2] Mutinelli, *Storia Arcana*, vol. i. pp. 310-340, and vol. xiv. pp. 30-65.
[3] It is worth mentioning that Ripamonte calculates the mortality from plague in Milan in 1524 at 140,000.
[4] Mutinelli, *op. cit.* vol. iii. pp. 229-233. Botta has given an account of this plague in the twenty-sixth book of his *History*.

same accurate series of State documents.[1] Simeone Contarini, then resident at Savigliano, relates that more than two-thirds of the population in that province had been swept away before the autumn of 1598, and that the evil was spreading far and wide through Piedmont. In Alpignano, a village of some four hundred inhabitants, only two remained. In Val Moriana, forty thousand expired, out of a total of seventy thousand. The village of San Giovanni counted but twelve survivors from a population of more than four thousand souls. In May 1599, the inhabitants of Turin were reduced by flight and death to four thousand; and of these there died daily numbers gradually rising through the summer from 50 to 180. The streets were encumbered with unburied corpses, the houses infested by robbers and marauders. Some incidents reported of this plague are ghastly in their horror. The infected were treated with inhuman barbarity, and retorted with savage fury, battering their assailants with the pestiferous bodies of unburied victims.

To the miseries of pestilence and its attendant famine were added lawlessness and license, raging fires, and, what was worst of all, the dark suspicion that the sickness had been introduced by malefactors. This belief appears to have taken hold upon the popular mind during the plague of 1598 in Savoy and in Milan.[2] Simeone Contarini reports that two men from Geneva confessed to having come with the express purpose of disseminating infection. He also gives curious particulars of two who were burned, and four who were quartered at Turin in 1600 for this offence.[3] 'These spirits of hell,' as he calls them, indicated a wood in which

[1] Mutinelli, *op. cit.* vol. ii. pp. 287-307.
[2] See Mutinelli, *op. cit.* p. 241 and p. 289. We hear of the same belief at Milan in 1576, *op. cit.* vol. i. pp. 311-315.
[3] *Ibid.* p. 309. See also vol. iii. p. 254 for a similar narration.

they declared that they had buried a pestilential liquid intended to be used for smearing houses. The wood was searched, and some jars were discovered. A surgeon at the same epoch confessed to having meant to spread the plague at Mondovi. Other persons, declaring themselves guilty of a similar intention, described a horn filled with poisonous stuff collected from the sores of plague-stricken corpses, which they had concealed outside the walls of Turin. This too was discovered; and these apparent proofs of guilt so infuriated the people that every day some criminals were sacrificed to judicial vengeance.

The name given to the unfortunate creatures accused of this diabolical conspiracy was *Untori*, or the Smearers. The plague of Milan in 1629-30 obtained the name of 'La Peste degli Untori' (as that of 1576 had been called 'La Peste di S. Carlo'), because of the prominent part played in it by the smearers.[1] They were popularly supposed to go about the city daubing walls, doors, furniture, choir-stalls, flowers, and articles of food with plague stuff. They scattered powders in the air, or spread them in circles on the pavement. To set a foot upon one of these circles involved certain destruction. Hundreds of such *untori* were condemned to the most cruel deaths by justice firmly persuaded of their criminality. Exposed to prolonged tortures, the majority confessed palpable absurdities. One woman at Milan said she had killed four thousand people. But, says Pier Antonio Marioni, the Venetian envoy, although tormented to the utmost, none of them were capable of revealing the prime instigators of the plot. So thoroughly convinced was he, together with the whole world, of their guilt, that he never paused to reflect upon the fallacy contained in this remark. The rack-stretched wretches could not reveal their instigators, because there were none; and the acts of which they accused themselves were the

[1] Mutinelli, *op. cit.* vol. ii. pp. 51-65.

delirious figments of their own torture-fretted brains. We possess documents, relating to the trial of the Milanese *Untori*, which make it clear that crimes of this sort must have been imaginary. As in cases of witchcraft, the first accusation was founded upon gossip and delation. The judicial proceedings were ruled by prejudice and cruelty. Fear and physical pain extorted confessions and complicated accusations of their neighbours from multitudes of innocent people.[1] Indeed the parallel between these unfortunate smearers and no less wretched witches is a close one. I am inclined to think that, as some crazy women fancied they were witches, so some morbid persons of this period in Italy believed in their power of spreading plague, and yielded to the fascination of malignity. Whether such moral mad folk really extended the sphere of the pestilence to any appreciable extent remains a matter for conjecture; and it is quite certain that all but a small percentage of the accused were victims of calumny.

After taking brigandage, piracy, and pestilence into account, the decline of Italy must be attributed to other causes. These I believe to have been the extinction of commercial republics, the decay of free commonwealths iniquitous systems of taxation, the insane display of wealth by unproductive princes, and the diversion of trade into foreign channels. Florence ceased to be the centre of wool manufacture, Venice lost her hold upon the traffic between East and West.[2] Stagnation fell like night upon the land, and the population suffered from a general atrophy.

[1] Cantù's *Ragionamenti sulla Storia Lombarda del Secolo XVII*. (Milano, 1832). The trial may also be read in Mutinelli, *Storia Arcana*, vol. iv. pp. 175-201. Mutinelli inclines to believe in the *Untori*. So do many grave historians, including Nani and Botta. See Cantù, *Storia degli Italiani* (Milano, 1876), vol. ii. p. 215.

[2] Mr. Ruskin has somewhere maintained that the decline of Venice was not due to this cause, but to fornication. He should read the record given by Mutinelli (*Diari Urbani*, p. 157) of Venetian fornication

The Proletariate.

In what concerns social morality it would be almost impossible to define the position of the proletariate, tillers of the soil, and artisans, at this epoch. These classes vary in their goodness and their badness, in their drawbacks and advantages, from age to age, far less than those who mould the character of marked historical periods by culture. They enjoy indeed a greater or a smaller immunity from pressing miseries. They are innocent or criminal in different degrees. But the groundwork of humanity in them remains comparatively unaltered; and their moral qualities, so far as these may be exceptional, reflect the influences of an upper social stratum. It is clear from the histories related in this chapter that members of the lowest classes were continually mixing with the nobles and the gentry in the wild adventures of that troubled century. They, like their betters, were undergoing a tardy metamorphosis from mediæval to modern conditions, retaining vices of ferocity and grossness, virtues of loyalty and self-reliance, which belonged to earlier periods. They, too, were now infected by the sensuous romance of pietism, the superstitious respect for sacraments and ceremonial observances, which had been wrought by the Catholic Revival into ecstatic frenzy. They shared those correlative yearnings after sacrilegious debauchery, felt those allurements of magic arts, indulged that perverted sense of personal honour which constituted psychological disease in the century which we are studying. It can, moreover, be maintained that Italian society at no epoch has been so sharply divided into sections as that of the feudalised races. In this period of one hundred

in 1340, at the time when the Ducal Palace was being covered with its sculpture. The public prostitutes were reckoned then at 11,654. Adulteries, rapes, infanticides were matters of daily occurrence. Yet the Renaissance had not begun, and the expansion of Venice, which roused the envious hostility of Europe, had yet to happen.

MORALS OF THE PEOPLE

years, from 1530 to 1630, when education was a privilege of the few, and when Church and princes combined to retard intellectual progress, the distinction between noble and plebeian, burgher and ploughman, though outwardly defined, was spiritually and morally insignificant. As in the Renaissance, so now, vice trickled downwards from above, infiltrating the masses of the people with its virus. But now, even more decidedly than then, the upper classes displayed obliquities of meanness, baseness, intemperance, cowardice, and brutal violence, which are commonly supposed to characterise villeins.

I had thought to throw some light upon the manners of the Italian proletariate by exploring the archives of trials for witchcraft. But I found that these were less common than in Germany, France, Spain, and England at a corresponding period. In Italy, witchcraft, pure and simple, was confined, for the most part, to mountain regions, the Apennines of the Abruzzi, and the Alps of Bergamo and Tyrol.[1] In other provinces it was confounded with crimes of poisoning, the procuring of abortion, and the fomentation of conspiracies in private families. These facts speak much for the superior civilisation of the Italian people considered as a whole. We discover a common fund of intelligence, vice, superstition, prejudice, enthusiasm, craft, devotion, self-assertion, possessed by the race at large. Only in districts remote from civil life did witchcraft assume those anti-social and repulsive features which are familiar to Northern nations. Elsewhere it penetrated, as a subtle poison, through society, lending its supposed assistance to passions already powerful enough to work their own accomplishment. It existed, not as an endemic disease, a permanent delirium of maddened peasants,

---

[1] Dandolo's *Streghe Tirolesi*, and Cantù's work on the Diocese of Como, show how much subalpine Italy had in common with Northern Europe in this matter.

but as a weapon in the arsenal of malice on a par with poisons and provocatives to lust.

I might illustrate this position by the relation of a fantastic attempt made against the life of Pope Urban VIII.[1] Giacomo Centini, the nephew of Cardinal d'Ascoli, fostered a fixed idea, the motive of his madness being the promotion of his uncle to S. Peter's Chair. In 1633 he applied to a hermit, who professed profound science in the occult arts and close familiarity with demons. The man, in answer to Giacomo's inquiries, said that Urban had still many years to live, that the Cardinal d'Ascoli would certainly succeed him, and that he held it in his power to shorten the Pope's days. He added that a certain Fra Cherubino would be useful, if any matter of grave moment were resolved on ; nor did he reject the assistance of other discreet persons. Giacomo, on his side, produced a Fra Domenico ; and these four accomplices set to work to destroy the reigning Pope by means of sorcery. They caused a knife to be forged, after the model of the Key of Solomon, and had it inscribed with Cabbalistic symbols. A clean virgin was employed to spin hemp into a thread. Then they resorted to a distant room in Giacomo's palace, where a circle was drawn with the mystic thread, a fire was lighted in the centre, and upon it was placed an image of Pope Urban formed of purest wax. The devil was invoked to appear and answer whether Urban had deceased this life after the melting of the image. No infernal visitor responded to the call ; and the hermit accounted for this failure by suggesting that some murder had been committed in the palace. As things went at that period, this excuse was by no means feeble, if only the audience, bent on unholy invocation of the power of evil, would accept it as sufficient. Probably more than one murder had taken place there, of which the owner was dimly conscious. The psychological curiosity to note is that avowed malefactors reckoned

[1] See *Rassegna Settimanale*, September 18, 1881.

purity an essential element in their nefarious practice. They tried once more in a vineyard, under the open heavens at night. But no demon issued from the darkness, and the hermit laid this second mischance to the score of bad weather. Giacomo was incapable of holding his tongue. He talked about his undertaking to the neighbours, and promised to make them all cardinals when he should become the Papal nephew. Meanwhile he pressed the hermit forward on the path of folly; and this man, driven to his wits' ends for a device, said that they must find seven priests together, one of whom should be assassinated to enforce the spell. It was natural, while the countryside was being raked for seven convenient priests by such a tattler as Giacomo, that suspicions should be generated in the people. Information reached Rome, in consequence of which the persons implicated in this idiotic plot were conveyed thither and given over to the mercies of the Holy Office. The upshot of their trial was that Giacomo lost his head, while the hermit and Fra Cherubino were burned alive, and Fra Domenico went to the galleys for life. Several other men involved in the process received punishments of considerable severity. It must be added in conclusion that the whole story rests upon the testimony of Inquisitorial archives, and that the real method of Giacomo Centini's apparent madness yet remains to be investigated. The few facts that we know about him, from his behaviour on the scaffold and a letter he wrote his wife, prejudice me in his favour.

Enough, and more than enough, perhaps, has been collected in this chapter, to throw light upon the manners of Italians during the Counter-Reformation. It would have been easy to repeat the story of the Countess of Cellant and her murdered lovers, or of the Duchess of Amalfi strangled by her brothers for a marriage below her station. The massacres committed by the Raspanti in Ravenna would furnish a whole series of illustrative crimes. From the deeds of Alfonso Piccolomini, Sciarra and Fabrizio Colonna, details sufficient to fill a volume with records of atrocious savagery could be drawn. The single episode of Elena Campireali, who plighted her troth to a bandit, became Abbess of the Convent at Castro, intrigued with a bishop, and killed herself for shame on the return of her first lover, would epitomise in one drama all the principal features of this social discord. The dreadful tale of the Baron of Montebello might be told again, who assaulted the castle of the Marquis of Pratidattolo, and, by the connivance of a sister whom he subsequently married, murdered the Marquis, with his mother, children, and relatives. The hunted life of Alessandro Antelminelli, pursued through all the States of Europe by assassins, could be used to exemplify the miseries of proscribed exiles. But what is the use of multiplying instances, when every pedigree in Litta, every chronicle of the time, every history of the most insignificant township, swarms with evidence to the same purpose? We need not adopt the opinion that society had greatly altered for the worse. We must rather decide that medieval ferocity survived throughout the whole of that period which witnessed the Catholic Revival, and that the piety which distinguished it was not influential in curbing vehement passions.

The conclusions to be drawn from the facts before us seem to be in general these. The link between government and governed in Italy had snapped. The social bond was broken; and the constituents that form a nation were pursuing divers aims. On the one hand stood Popes and princes, founding their claims to absolute authority upon titles that had slight rational or national validity. These potentates were ill combined among themselves, and mutually jealous. On the other side were ranged disruptive forces of the most heterogeneous kinds—remnants from antique party-warfare, fragments of obsolete domestic feuds, new strivings after freer life in mentally down-trodden populations, blending with crime and misery and want and profligacy to compose an opposition which exasperated despotism. These anarchical conditions were due in large measure to the troubles caused by foreign campaigns of invasion. They were also due to the Spanish type of manners imposed upon the ruling classes, which the native genius accepted with fraudulent intelligence, and to which it adapted itself by artifice. We must further reckon the division between cultured and uncultured people, which humanism had effected, and which subsisted after the benefits conferred by humanism had been withdrawn from the race. The retirement of the commercial aristocracy from trade, and their assumption of princely indolence in this period of political stagnation, was another factor of importance. But the truest cause of Italian retrogression towards barbarism must finally be discerned in the sharp check given to intellectual evolution by the repressive forces of the Counter Reformation.

CHAPTER VII

TORQUATO TASSO

Tasso's Relation to his Age—Balbi on that Period—The Life of Bernardo Tasso—Torquato's Boyhood—Sorrento, Naples, Rome, Urbino—His first Glimpse of the Court—Student Life at Padua and Bologna—The 'Rinaldo'—Dialogues on Epic Poetry—Enters the Service of Cardinal d' Este—The Court of Ferrara—Alfonso II. and the Princesses—Problem of Tasso's Love—Goes to France with Cardinal d' Este—Enters the Service of Duke Alfonso—The 'Aminta'—Tasso at Urbino—Return to Ferrara—Revision of the 'Gerusalemme'—Jealousies at Court—Tasso's Sense of His own Importance—Plans a Change from Ferrara to Florence—First Symptoms of Mental Disorder—Persecutions of the Ferrarese Courtiers—Tasso confined as a Semi-madman—Goes with Duke Alfonso to Belriguardo—Flies in Disguise from Ferrara to Sorrento—Returns to Court Life at Ferrara—Problem of his Madness—Flies again—Mantua, Venice, Urbino, Turin—Returns once more to Ferrara—Alfonso's Third Marriage—Tasso's Discontent—Imprisoned for Seven Years in the Madhouse of S. Anna—Character of Tasso—Character of Duke Alfonso—Nature of the Poet's Malady—His Course of Life in Prison—Released at the Intercession of Vincenzo Gonzaga—Goes to Mantua—The 'Torrismondo'—An Odyssey of Nine Years—Death at Sant Onofrio in Rome—Costantini's Sonnet.

IT was under the conditions which have been set forth in the foregoing chapters that the greatest literary genius of his years in Europe, the poet who ranks among the four first of Italy, was educated, rose to eminence, and suffered. The political changes introduced in 1530, the tendencies of the Catholic Revival, the terrorism of the Inquisition, and the educational energy of the Jesuits had, each and all, their manifest effect in moulding Tasso's character. He represents that period when the culture of the Renaissance was being superseded, when the caries of court-service was eating into the bone and marrow of Italian life, when earlier forms of art were tending to decay, or were passing into the new form of music. Tasso was at once the representative poet of his age and the representative martyr of his age. He was the latter, though this may seem paradoxical, in even a stricter sense than Bruno. Bruno, coming into violent collision with the prejudices of the century, expiated his antagonism by a cruel death. Tasso, yielding to those influences, lingered out a life of irresolute misery. His nature was such, that the very conditions which shaped it sufficed to enfeeble, envenom, and finally reduce it to a pitiable ruin.

Some memorable words of Cesare Balbi may serve as introduction to a sketch of Tasso's life. 'If that can be called felicity which gives to the people peace without activity; to nobles rank without power ; to princes undisturbed authority within their States without true independence or full sovereignty ; to literary men and artists numerous occasions for writing, painting, making statues, and erecting edifices with the applause of contemporaries but the ridicule of posterity; to the whole nation ease without dignity and facilities for sinking tranquilly into corruption ; then no period of her history was so felicitous for Italy as the 140 years which followed the peace of Cateau-Cambrésis. Invasions ceased : her foreign lord saved Italy from intermeddling rivals. Internal struggles ceased: her foreign lord removed their causes and curbed national ambitions. Popular revolutions ceased : her foreign lord bitted and bridled the population of her provinces. Of bravi, highwaymen, vulgar acts of vengeance, tragedies among nobles and princes, we find indeed abundance ; but these affected the mass of the people to no serious extent. The Italians enjoyed life, indulged in

the sweets of leisure, the sweets of vice, the sweets of making
love and dangling after women. From the camp and the
council-chamber, where they had formerly been bred, the
nobles passed into petty courts and mouldered in a multitude
of little capitals. Men bearing historic names, insensible of
their own degradation, bowed the neck gladly, grovelled in
beatitude. Deprived of power, they consoled themselves with
privileges, patented favours, impertinences vented on the
common people. The princes amused themselves by debasing
the old aristocracy to the mire, depreciating their honours by
the creation of new titles, multiplying frivolous concessions,
adding class to class of idle and servile dependents on their
personal bounty. In one word, the paradise of mediocrities
came into being.'

Tasso was born before the beginning of this epoch. But
he lived into the last decade of the sixteenth century. In
every fibre of his character he felt the influences of Italian
decadence, even while he reacted against them. His misfortunes resulted in great measure from his not having wholly
discarded the traditions of the Renaissance, though his temperament and acquired habits made him in many points
sympathetic to the Counter-Reformation. At the same time,
he was not a mediocrity, but the last of an illustrious race of
nobly gifted men of genius. Therefore he never patiently
submitted to the humiliating conditions which his own conception of the Court, the Prince, the Church, and the Italian
gentleman logically involved at that period. He could not be
contented with the paradise of mediocrities described by Balbi.
Yet he had not strength to live outside its pale. It was the
pathos of his situation that he persisted in idealising this
paradise, and expected to find in it a paradise of exceptional
natures. This it could not be. No one turns Circe's pigsty
into a Parnassus. If Tasso had possessed force of character
enough to rend the trammels of convention, and to live his

own life in a self-constructed sphere, he might still have been unfortunate. Nature condemned him to suffering. But from the study of his history we should then have risen invigorated by the contemplation of heroism, instead of quitting it, as now we do, with pity, but with pity tempered by a slight contempt.

Bernardo, the father of Torquato Tasso, drew noble blood from both his parents. The Tassi claimed to be a branch of that ancient Guelf house of Della Torre, lords of Milan, who were all but extirpated by the Visconti in the fourteenth century. A remnant established themselves in mountain strongholds between Bergamo and Como, and afterwards took rank among the more distinguished families of the former city. Manso affirms that Bernardo's mother was a daughter of those Venetian Cornari who gave a queen to Cyprus.[1] He was born at Venice in the year 1493; and, since he died in 1569, his life covered the whole period of national glory, humiliation, and attempted reconstruction which began with the invasion of Charles VIII. and ended with the closing of the Council of Trent. Born in the pontificate of Alexander VI., he witnessed the reigns of Julius II., Leo X., Clement VII., Paul IV., Pius IV., and died in that of Pius V.

All the illustrious works of Italian art and letters were produced while he was moving in the society of princes and scholars. He saw the Renaissance in its splendour and decline. He watched the growth, progress, and final triumph of the Catholic Revival. Having stated that the curve of his existence led upward from a Borgia and down to a Ghislieri Vicar of Christ, the merest tiro in Italian history knows what vicissitudes it spanned. Though the Tassi were so noble, Bernardo owned no wealth. He was left an orphan

[1] This is doubtful. Serrassi believed that Bernardo's mother was also a Tasso.

at an early age under the care of his uncle, Bishop of
Recanati. But in 1520 the poniard of an assassin cut short
this guardian's life ; and, at the age of seventeen, he was
thrown upon the world. After studying at Padua, where he
enjoyed the patronage of Bembo, and laid foundations for his
future fame as poet, Bernardo entered the service of the
Modenese Rangoni in the capacity of secretary. Thus began
the long career of servitude to princes, of which he frequently
complained, but which only ended with his death.[1] The
affairs of his first patrons took him to Paris at the time when
a marriage was arranged between Renée of France and Ercole
d' Este. He obtained the post of secretary to this princess,
and having taken leave of the Rangoni, he next established
himself at Ferrara. Only for three years, however; for in
1532 reasons of which we are ignorant, but which may have
been connected with the heretical sympathies of Renée, induced him to resign his post. Shortly after this date, we find
him attached to the person of Ferrante Sanseverino, Prince of
Salerno, one of the chief feudatories and quasi-independent
vassals of the Crown of Naples. In the quality of secretary
he attended this patron through the campaign of Tunis in
1535, and accompanied him on all his diplomatic expeditions.
The Prince of Salerno treated him more as an honoured friend
and confidential adviser than as a paid official. His income
was good, and leisure was allowed him for the prosecution of
his literary studies. In this flourishing state of his affairs,
Bernardo contracted an alliance with Porzia de' Rossi, a lady
of a noble house, which came originally from Pistoja, but had
been established for some generations in Naples. She was
connected by descent or marriage with the houses of Gamba-
corti, Caracciolo, and Caraffa. Their first child, Cornelia, was

[1] He speaks in his letters of the difficulty ' di sottrarre il collo al
difficile noioso arduo giogo della servitù dei Principi.' *Lettere Ined.*
(Bologna: Romagnoli), p. 34.

born about the year 1537. Their second, Torquato, saw the light in March 1544 at Sorrento, where his father had been living some months previously and working at his poem, the 'Amadigi.'

At the time of Torquato's birth Bernardo was away from home, in Lombardy, France, and Flanders, travelling on missions from his prince. However, he returned to Sorrento for a short while in 1545, and then again was forced to leave his family. Married at the mature age of forty-three, Bernardo was affectionately attached to his young wife, and proud of his children. But the exigencies of a courtier's life debarred him from enjoying the domestic happiness for which his sober and gentle nature would have fitted him. In 1547 the events happened which ruined him for life, separated him for ever from Porzia, drove him into indigent exile, and marred the prospects of his children. In that year, the Spanish viceroy, Don Pietro Toledo, attempted to introduce the Inquisition, on its Spanish basis, into Naples. The population resented this exercise of authority with the fury of despair, rightly judging that the last remnants of their liberty would be devoured by the foul monster of the Holy Office. They besought the Prince of Salerno to intercede for them with his master, Charles V., whom he had served loyally up to this time, and who might therefore be inclined to yield to his expostulations. The prince doubted much whether it would be prudent to accept the mission of intercessor. He had two counsellors, Bernardo Tasso and Vincenzo Martelli. The latter, who was an astute Florentine, advised him to undertake nothing so perilous as interposition between the viceroy and the people. Tasso, on the contrary, exhorted him to sacrifice personal interest, honours, and glory, for the duty which he owed his country. The prince chose the course which Tasso recommended. Charles V. disgraced him, and he fled from Naples to France, adopting openly the cause of his imperial sovereign's enemies. He was immediately declared a rebel, with confiscation of his fiefs and property. Bernardo and his infant son were included in the sentence. After twenty-two years of service, Bernardo now found himself obliged to choose between disloyalty to his prince or a disastrous exile. He took the latter course, and followed Ferrante Sanseverino to Paris. But Bernardo Tasso, though proving himself a man of honour in this severe trial, was not of the stuff of Shakespere's Kent; and when the Prince of Salerno suspended payment of his salary he took leave of that master. Some differences arising from the discomforts and irritations of both exiles had early intervened between them. Tasso was miserably poor. 'I have to stay in bed,' he writes, 'to mend my hose; and if it were not for the old arms I brought with me from home, I should not know how to cover my nakedness.'[1] Besides this, he suffered grievously in the separation from his wife, who was detained at Naples by her relatives—'brothers who, instead of being brothers, are deadly foes, cruel wild beasts rather than men; a mother who is no mother, but a fell enemy, a fury from hell rather than a woman.'[2] His wretchedness attained its climax when Porzia died suddenly on February 8, 1556. Bernardo suspected that her family had poisoned her; and this may well have been. His son, Torquato, meanwhile had joined him in Rome; but Porzia's brothers refused to surrender his daughter Cornelia, whom they married to a Sorrentine gentleman, Marzio Sersale, much to Bernardo's disgust, for Sersale was apparently of inferior blood. They also withheld Porzia's dowry and the jointure settled on her by Bernardo—property of considerable value, which neither he nor Torquato were subsequently able to recover. In this desperate condition of affairs, without

---

[1] *Lett. Ined.* p. 100.
[2] *Lettere di Torquato Tasso*, February 15, 1556, vol. ii. p. 157.

friends or credit, but conscious of his noble birth and true to honour, the unhappy poet bethought him of the Church. If he could obtain a benefice, he would take orders. But the King of France and Margaret of Valois, on whose patronage he relied, turned him a deaf ear; and when war broke out between Paul IV. and Spain, he felt it prudent to leave Rome. It was at this epoch that Bernardo entered the service of Guidubaldo della Rovere, Duke of Urbino, with whom he remained until 1563, when he accepted the post of secretary from Guglielmo, Duke of Mantua. He died in 1569 at Ostiglia, so poor that his son could scarcely collect money enough to bury him after selling his effects. Manso says that a couple of door-curtains, embroidered with the arms of Tasso and De' Rossi, passed on this occasion into the wardrobe of the Gonzaghi. Thus it seems that the needy nobleman had preserved a scrap of his heraldic trophies till the last, although he had to patch his one pair of breeches in bed at Rome. It may be added, as characteristic of Bernardo's misfortunes, that even the plain marble sarcophagus, inscribed with the words 'Ossa Bernardi Tassi,' which Duke Guglielmo erected to his memory in S. Egidio at Mantua, was removed in compliance with a papal edict ordering that monuments at a certain height above the ground should be destroyed to save the dignity of neighbouring altars!

Such were the events of Bernardo Tasso's life. I have dwelt upon them in detail, since they foreshadow and illustrate the miseries of his more famous son. In character and physical qualities Torquato inherited no little from his father. Bernardo was handsome, well-grown, conscious of his double dignity as a nobleman and poet. From the rules of honour, as he understood them, he deviated in no important point of conduct. Yet the life of Courts made him an incorrigible dangler after princely favours. The 'Amadigi,' upon which he set such store, was first planned and dedicated to Charles V., then altered to suit Henri II. of France, and finally adapted to the flattery of Philip II., according as its author's interests with the Prince of Salerno and the Duke of Urbino varied. No substantial reward accrued to him, however, from its publication. His compliments wasted their sweetness on the dull ears of the despot of Madrid. In misfortune Bernardo sank to neither crime nor baseness, even when he had no clothes to put upon his back. Yet he took the world to witness of his woes, as though his person ought to have been sacred from calamities of common manhood. A similar dependent spirit was manifested in his action as a man of letters. Before publishing the 'Amadigi' he submitted it to private criticism, with the inevitable result of obtaining feigned praises and malevolent strictures. Irresolution lay at the root of his treatment of Torquato. While groaning under the collar of courtly servitude, he determined that the youth should study law. While reckoning how little his own literary fame had helped him, he resolved that his son should adopt a lucrative profession. Yet no sooner had Torquato composed his 'Rinaldo,' than the fond parent had it printed, and immediately procured a place for him in the train of the Cardinal Luigi d' Este. It is singular that the young man, witnessing the wretchedness of his father's life, should not have shunned a like career of gilded misery and famous indigence. But Torquato was born to reproduce Bernardo's qualities in their feebleness and respectability, to outshine him in genius, and to outstrip him in the celebrity of his misfortunes.

In the absence of his father little Torquato grew up with his mother and sister at Sorrento, under the care of a good man, Giovanni Angeluzzo, who gave him the first rudiments of education. He was a precocious infant, grave in manners, quick at learning, free from the ordinary naughtinesses of childhood. Manso reports that he began to speak at six months, and that from the first he formed syllables with precision. His mother Porzia appears to have been a woman of much grace and sweetness, but timid and incapable of fighting the hard battle of the world. A certain shade of melancholy fell across the boy's path even in these earliest years, for Porzia, as we have seen, met with cruel treatment from her relatives, and her only support, Bernardo, was far away in exile. In 1552 she removed with her children to Naples, where Torquato was sent at once to the school which the Jesuits had opened there in the preceding year. These astute instructors soon perceived that they had no ordinary boy to deal with. They did their best to stimulate his mental faculties and to exalt his religious sentiments; so that he learned Greek and Latin before the age of ten, and was in the habit of communicating at the altar with transports of pious ecstasy in his ninth year.[1] The child recited speeches and poems in public, and received an elementary training in the arts of composition. He was in fact the infant prodigy of those plausible Fathers, the prize specimen of their educational method. As might have been expected, this forcing system overtaxed his nerves. He rose daily before daybreak to attack his books, and when the nights were long he went to morning school attended by a servant carrying torches. Without seeking to press unduly on these circumstances, we may fairly assume that Torquato's character received a permanent impression from the fever of study and the premature pietism excited in him by the Jesuits in Naples. His servile attitude toward speculative thought, that anxious dependence upon ecclesiastical authority, that scrupulous mistrust of his own mental faculties, that pretence of solving problems by accumulated citations instead of going to the root of the matter, whereby his philosophical writings are rendered nugatory, may with probability be traced to the mechanical

---

[1] 'Sentendo in me non so qual nuova insolita contentezza,' 'non so qual segreta divozione.' *Lettere*, vol. ii. p. 90.

and interested system of the Jesuits. He was their pupil for three years, after which he joined his father in Rome. There he seems to have passed at once into a healthier atmosphere. Bernardo, though a sound Catholic, was no bigot; and he had the good sense to choose an able master for his son—'a man of profound learning, possessed of both the ancient languages, whose method of teaching is the finest and most time-saving that has yet been tried; a gentleman withal, with nothing of the pedant in him.'[1] The boy was lucky also in the companion of his studies, a cousin, Cristoforo Tasso, who had come home from Bergamo to profit by the tutor's care.

The young Tasso's home cannot, however, have been a cheerful one. The elderly hidalgo sitting up in bed to darn his single pair of hose, the absent mother pining for her husband and tormented by her savage brothers' avarice, environed the precocious child of ten with sad presentiments. That melancholy temperament which he inherited from Bernardo was nourished by the half-concealed mysteriously haunting troubles of his parents. And when Porzia died suddenly, in 1556, we can hardly doubt that the father broke out before his son into some such expressions of ungovernable grief as he openly expressed in the letter to Amerigo Sanseverino.[2] Is it possible, then, thought Torquato, that the mother from whose tender kisses and streaming tears I was severed but one year ago,[3] had died of poison—poisoned by my uncles? Sinking into the consciousness of a child so sensitive by nature and so early toned to sadness, this terrible suspicion of a secret death by poison incorporated itself with the very essence of his melancholy humour, and lurked within him to flash forth

[1] Bernardo's *Letter to Cav. Giangiacopo Tasso*, December 6, 1554.
[2] Dated February 13, 1556.
[3] See *Opere*, vol. iv. p. 100, for Tasso's description of the farewell to his mother, which he remembered deeply, even in later life.

in madness at a future period of life. That he was well acquainted with the doleful situation of his family is proved by his first extant letter. Addressed to the noble lady Vittoria Colonna on behalf of Bernardo and his sister, this is a remarkable composition for a boy of twelve.[1] His poor father, he says, is on the point of dying of despair, oppressed by the malignity of fortune and the rapacity of impious men. His uncle is bent on marrying Cornelia to some needy gentleman, in order to secure her mother's estate for himself. 'The grief, illustrious lady, of the loss of property is great, but that of blood is crushing. This poor old man has naught but my sister and myself; and now that fortune has deprived him of wealth and of the wife he loved like his own soul, he cannot bear that that man's avarice should rob him of his beloved daughter, with whom he hoped to end in rest these last years of his failing age. In Naples we have no friends; for my father's disaster makes everyone shy of us: our relatives are our enemies. Cornelia is kept in the house of my uncle's kinsman Giangiacopo Coscia, where no one is allowed to speak to her or give her letters.'

In the midst of these afflictions, which already turned the future poet's utterance to a note of plaintive pathos and ingenuous appeal for aid, Torquato's studies were continued on a sounder plan and in a healthier spirit than at Naples. The perennial consolation of his troubled life, that delight in literature which made him able to anticipate the lines of Goethe—

> That naught belongs to me I know
> Save thoughts that never cease to flow
> From founts that cannot perish,
> And every fleeting shape of bliss
> Which kindly fortune lets me kiss
> Or in my bosom cherish—

---

[1] *Lettere*, vol. i. p. 6.

now became the source of an inner brightness which not even
the 'malignity of fortune,' the 'impiety of men,' the tragedy
of his mother's death, the imprisonment of his sister, and the
ever-present sorrow of his father, 'the poor gentleman fallen
into misery and misfortune through no fault of his own,'
could wholly overcloud. The boy had been accustomed in
Naples to the applause of his teachers and friends. In Rome
he began to cherish a presentiment of his own genius. A
'vision splendid' dawned upon his mind; and every step he
made in knowledge and in mastery of language enforced the
delightful conviction that 'I too am a poet.' Nothing in Tasso's
character was more tenacious than the consciousness of his
vocation and the kind of self-support he gained from it. Like
the melancholy humour which degenerated into madness, this
sense of his own intellectual dignity assumed extravagant
proportions, passed over into vanity, and encouraged him to
indulge fantastic dreams of greatness. Yet it must be
reckoned as a mitigation of his suffering; and what was solid
in it at the period of which I now am writing, was the
certainty of his rare gifts for art.

The Roman residence was broken by Bernardo's journey
to Urbino in quest of the appointment he expected from Duke
Guidubaldo. He sent Torquato with his cousin Cristoforo
meanwhile to Bergamo, where the boy enjoyed a few months
of sympathy and freedom. This appears to have been the only
period of his life in which Tasso experienced the wholesome
influences of domesticity. In 1557 his father sent for him to
Pesaro, and Tasso made his first entrance into a Court at the
age of thirteen. This event decided the future of his existence.
Urbino was not what it had been in the time of Duke Federigo,
or when Castiglione composed his 'Mirror of the Courtier' on
its model. Yet it retained the old traditions of gentle living,
splendour tempered by polite culture, aristocratic urbanity
refined by arts and letters. The evil days of Spanish manners

THE COURT OF URBINO 347

and Spanish bigotry, of exhausted revenues and insane taxation, were but dawning; and the young prince, Francesco Maria, who was destined to survive his heir and transfer a ruined duchy to the mortmain of the Church, was now a boy of eight years old. In fact, though the Court of Urbino laboured already under that manifold disease of waste which drained the marrow of Italian principalities, its atrophy was not apparent to the eye. It could still boast of magnificent pageants, trains of noble youths and ladies moving through its stately palaces and shady villa-gardens, academies of learned men discussing the merits of Homer and Ariosto and discoursing on the principles of poetry and drama. Bernardo Tasso read his 'Amadigi' in the evenings to the Duchess. The days were spent in hunting and athletic exercises; the nights in masquerades or dances. Love and ambition wore an external garb of ceremonious beauty; the former draped itself in sonnets, the latter in rhetorical orations. Torquato, who was assigned as the companion in sport and study to the heir-apparent, shared in all these pleasures of the Court. After the melancholy of Rome, his visionary nature expanded under influences which he idealised with fatal facility. Too young to penetrate below that glittering surface, flattered by the attention paid to his personal charm or premature genius, stimulated by the conversation of politely educated pedants, encouraged in studies for which he felt a natural aptitude, gratified by the comradeship of the young prince whose temperament corresponded to his own in gravity, he conceived that radiant and romantic conception of Courts, as the only fit places of abode for men of noble birth and eminent abilities, which no disillusionment in after life was able to obscure. We cannot blame him for this error, though error it indubitably was. It was one which he shared with all men of his station at that period, which the poverty of his estate, the habits of his father, and his own ignorance of home-life almost forced upon his poet's temperament.

At Urbino Tasso read mathematics under a real master, Federigo Comandino, and carried on his literary studies with enthusiasm. It was probably at this time that he acquired the familiar knowledge of Virgil which so powerfully influenced his style, and that he began to form his theory of epic as distinguished from romantic poetry. After a residence of two years he removed to Venice, where his father was engaged in polishing the 'Amadigi' for publication. Here a new scene of interest opened out for him; and here he first enjoyed the sweets of literary fame. Bernardo had been chosen secretary by an Academy, in which men like Veniero, Molino, Gradenigo, Mocenigo, and Manuzio, the most learned and the noblest Venetians, met together for discussion. The slim lad of fifteen was admitted to their sessions, and surprised these elders by his eloquence and erudition. It is noticeable that at this time he carefully studied and annotated Dante's 'Divine Comedy,' a poem almost neglected by Italians in the Cinque Cento. It seemed good to his father now that he should prosecute his studies in earnest, with a view of choosing a more lucrative profession than that of letters or Court-service. Bernardo, while finishing the 'Amadigi,' which he dedicated to Philip II., sent his son in 1560 to Padua. He was to become a lawyer under the guidance of Guido Panciroli. But Tasso, like Ovid, like Petrarch, like a hundred other poets, felt no inclination for juristic learning. He freely and frankly abandoned himself to the metaphysical conclusions which were being then tried between Piccolomini and Pendasio, the one an Aristotelian dualist, the other a materialist for whom the soul was not immortal. Without force of mind enough to penetrate the deepest problems of philosophy, Tasso was quick to apprehend their bearings. The Paduan school of scepticism, the logomachy in vogue there, unsettled his religious opinions. He began by criticising the doubts of others in his light of Jesuit-instilled belief; next he found a satisfaction for self-esteem in doubting too; finally he called the mysteries of the Creed in question, and debated the articles of creation, incarnation, and immortality. Yet he had not the mental vigour either to cut this Gordian knot, or to untie it by sound thinking. His erudition confused him; and he mistook the lumber of miscellaneous reading for philosophy. Then a reaction set in. He remembered those childish ecstasies before the Eucharist; he recalled the pictures of a burning hell his Jesuit teachers had painted; he heard the trumpets of the Day of Judgment, and the sentence 'Go ye wicked!' On the brink of heresy he trembled and recoiled. The spirit of the coming age, the spirit of Bruno, was not in him. To all appearances he had not heard of the Copernican discovery. He wished to remain a true son of the Church, and was in fact of such stuff as the Catholic Revival wanted. Yet the memory of these early doubts clung to him, principally, we may believe, because he had not force to purge them either by severe science or by vivid faith. Later, when his mind was yielding to disorder, they returned in the form of torturing scruples and vain terrors, which his fervent but superficial pietism, his imaginative but sensuous religion, were unable to efface. Meanwhile, with one part of his mind devoted to these problems, the larger and the livelier was occupied with poetry. To law, the *Brod-Studium* indicated by his position in the world, he only paid perfunctory attention. The consequence was that before he had completed two years of residence in Padua, his first long poem, the 'Rinaldo,' saw the light. In another chapter I mean to discuss the development of Tasso's literary theories and achievements. It is enough here to say that the applause which greeted the 'Rinaldo' conquered his father's opposition. Proud of its success, Bernardo had it printed, and Torquato in the beginning of his nineteenth year counted among the notable romantic poets of his country.

At the end of 1563, Tasso received an invitation to transfer himself from Padua to Bologna. This proposal came from Monsignor Cesi, who had recently been appointed by Pope Pius IV. to superintend public studies in that city. The university was being placed on a new footing, and to secure the presence of a young man already famous seemed desirable. An exhibition was therefore offered as an inducement; and this Tasso readily accepted. He spent about two years at Bologna, studying philosophy and literature, planning his Dialogues on the Art of Poetry, and making projects for an epic on the history of Godfred. Yet in spite of public admiration and official favour, things did not go smoothly with Tasso at Bologna. One main defect of his character, which was a want of tact, began to manifest itself. He showed Monsignor Cesi that he had a poor opinion of his literary judgment, came into collision with the pedants who despised Italian, and finally uttered satiric epigrams in writing on various members of the university. Other students indulged their humour in like pasquinades. But those of Tasso were biting, and he had not contrived to render himself generally popular. His rooms were ransacked, his papers searched; and finding himself threatened with a prosecution for libel, he took flight to Modena. No importance can be attached to this insignificant affair, except in so far as it illustrates the unlucky aptitude for making enemies by want of *savoir vivre* which pursued Tasso through life. His real superiority aroused jealousy; his frankness wounded the self-love of rivals whom he treated with a shadow of contempt. As these were unable to compete with him in eloquence, or to beat him in debate, they soothed their injured feelings by conspiracy and calumny against him.

In an age of artifice and circumspection, while paying

theoretical homage to its pedantries, and following the fashion of its compliments, Tasso was nothing if not spontaneous and heedless. This appears in the style of his letters and prose compositions, which have the air of being uttered from the heart. The excellences and defects of his poetry, soaring to the height of song and sinking into frigidity or baldness when the lyric impulse flags, reveal a similar quality. In conduct this spontaneity assumed a form of inconsiderate rashness, which brought him into collision with persons of importance, and rendered universities and Courts, the sphere of his adoption, perilous to the peace of so naturally out-spoken and self-engrossed a man His irritable sensibilities caused him to suffer intensely from the petty vengeance of the people he annoyed; while a kind of amiable egotism blinded his eyes to his own faults, and made him blame fortune for sufferings of which his indiscretion was the cause.

After leaving Bologna, Tasso became for some months house-guest of his father's earliest patrons, the Modenese Rangoni. With them he seems to have composed his Dialogues on the Art of Poetry. For many years the learned men of Italy had been contesting the true nature of the Epic. One party affirmed that the ancients ought to be followed; and that the rules of Aristotle regarding unity of plot, dignity of style, and subordination of episodes, should be observed. The other party upheld the romantic manner of Ariosto, pleading for liberty of fancy, richness of execution, variety of incident, intricacy of design. Torquato from his earliest boyhood had heard these points discussed, and had watched his father's epic, the 'Amadigi,' which was in effect a romantic poem petrified by classical convention, in process of production. Meanwhile he carefully studied the text of Homer and the Latin epics, examined Horace and Aristotle, and perused the numerous romances of the Italian school. Two conclusions were drawn from this preliminary course of reading: first, that Italy as yet possessed no proper epic; Trissino's 'Italia Liberata' was too tiresome, the 'Orlando Furioso' too capricious; secondly, that the *spolia opima* in this field of art would be achieved by him who should combine the classic and romantic manners in a single work, enriching the unity of the antique epic with the graces of modern romance, choosing a noble and serious subject, sustaining style at a sublime altitude, but gratifying the prevalent desire for beauty in variety by the introduction of attractive episodes and the ornaments of picturesque description. Tasso, in fact, declared himself an eclectic; and the deep affinity he felt for Virgil indicated the lines upon which the Latin language in its romantic or Italian stage of evolution might be made to yield a second Aeneid adapted to the requirements of modern taste. He had, indeed, already set before himself the high ambition of supplying this desideratum. The note of prelude had been struck in 'Rinaldo;' the subject of the 'Gerusalemme' had been chosen. But the age in which he lived was nothing if not critical and argumentative. The time had long gone by when Dante's massive cathedral, Boccaccio's pleasure domes, Boiardo's and Ariosto's palaces of enchantment, arose as though unbidden and unreasoned from the maker's brain. It was now impossible to take a step in poetry or art without a theory; and, what was worse, that theory had to be exposed for dissertation and discussion. Therefore Tasso, though by genius the most spontaneous of men, commenced the great work of his life with criticism. Already acclimatised to courts, coteries, academies, formed in the school of disputants and pedants, he propounded his 'Ars Poetica' before establishing it by an example. This was undoubtedly beginning at the wrong end; he committed himself to principles which he was bound to illustrate by practice. In the state of thought at that time prevalent in Italy, burdened as he was with an irresolute and diffident self-consciousness, Tasso could not deviate from the theory he had promulgated. How this hampered him, will appear in the sequel, when we come to notice the discrepancy between his critical and creative faculties. For the moment, however, the Dialogues on Epic Poetry only augmented his fame.

Scipione Gonzaga, one of Tasso's firmest and most illustrious friends, had recently established an Academy at Padua under the name of Gli Eterei. At his invitation the young poet joined this club in the autumn of 1564, assumed the title of Il Pentito in allusion to his desertion of legal studies, and soon became the soul of its society. His dialogues excited deep and wide-spread interest. After so much wrangling between classical and romantic champions, he had transferred the contest to new ground and introduced a fresh principle into the discussion. This principle was, in effect, that of common sense, good taste and instinct. Tasso meant to say: there is no vital discord between classical and romantic art; both have excellences, and it is possible to find defects in both; pedantic adherence to antique precedent must end in frigid failure under the present conditions of intellectual culture; yet it cannot be denied that the cycle of Renaissance poetry was closed by Ariosto; let us therefore attempt creation in a liberal spirit, trained by both these influences. He could not, however, when he put this theory forward in elaborate prose, abstain from propositions, distinctions, deductions, and conclusions, all of which were discutable, and each of which his critics and his honour held him bound to follow. In short, while planning and producing the 'Gerusalemme,' he was involved in controversies on the very essence of his art. These controversies had been started by himself and he could not do otherwise than maintain the position he had chosen. His poet's inspiration, his singer's spontaneity, came thus constantly into collision with his own deliberate utterances. A perplexed self-scrutiny was the inevitable result, which pedagogues who were not inspired and could not sing, but who delighted in minute discussion, took good care to stimulate. The worst, however, was that he had erected in his own mind a critical standard with which his genius was not in harmony. The scholar and the poet disagreed in Tasso; and it must be reckoned one of the drawbacks of his age and education that the former preceded the latter in development. Something of the same discord can be traced in contemporary painting, as will be shown when I come to consider the founders of the Bolognese Academy.

At the end of 1565 Tasso was withdrawn from literary studies and society in Padua. The Cardinal Luigi d' Este offered him a place in his household; and since this opened the way to Ferrara and Court-service, it was readily accepted. It would have been well for Tasso, at this crisis of his fate, if the line of his beloved Aeneid—

> Heu, fuge crudeles terras, fuge littus avarum—

that line which warned young Savonarola away from Ferrara, had sounded in his ears, or met his eyes in some Virgilian 'Sortes.' It would have been well if his father, disillusioned by the 'Amadigi's' ill-success, and groaning under the galling yoke of servitude to princes, had forbidden instead of encouraging this fatal step. He might himself have listened to the words of old Speroni, painting the Court as he had learned to know it, a Siren fair to behold and ravishing of song, but hiding in her secret caves the bones of men devoured, and 'mighty poets in their misery dead.' He might even have turned the pages of Aretino's 'Dialogo delle Corti,' and have observed how the ruffian who best could profit by the vices of a Court, refused to bow his neck to servitude in their corruption. But no man avoids his destiny, because few draw wisdom from the past and none foresee the future. To Ferrara Tasso went with a blithe heart. Inclination, the custom of his country, the necessities of that poet's vocation for which he had abandoned a profession, poverty and ambition, vanity and the delights of life, combined to lure him to his ruin.

He found Ferrara far more magnificent than Urbino. Pageants, hunting parties, theatrical entertainments, assumed fantastic forms of splendour in this capital, which no other city of Italy, except Florence and Venice upon rare occasions, rivalled. For a long while past Ferrara had been the centre of a semi-feudal, semi-humanistic culture, out of which the Masque and Drama, music and painting, scholarship and poetry, emerged with brilliant originality, blending medieval and antique elements in a specific type of modern romance. This culminated in the permanent and monumental work began by Boiardo in the morning, and completed by Ariosto in the meridian of the Renaissance. Within the circuit of the Court the whole life of the Duchy seemed to concentrate itself. From the frontier of Venice to the Apennines a tract of fertile country, yielding all necessaries of life, corn, wine, cattle, game, fish, in abundance, poured its produce into the palaces and castles of the Duke. He, like other princes of his epoch, sucked each province dry in order to maintain a dazzling show of artificial wealth. The people were ground down by taxes, monopolies of corn and salt, and sanguinary game-laws. Brutalised by being forced to serve the pleasures of their masters, they lived the lives of swine. But why repaint the picture of Italian decadence, or dwell again upon the fever of that phthisical consumption? Men like Tasso saw nothing to attract attention in the rotten state of Ferrara. They were only fascinated by the hectic bloom and rouged refinement of its Court. And even the least sympathetic student must confess that the Court at any rate was seductive. A more cunningly combined medley of polite culture, political astuteness, urbane learning, sumptuous display, diplomatic love intrigue, and genial artistic productiveness, never before or since has been exhibited upon a scale so grandiose within limits so precisely circumscribed, or been raised to eminence so high from such inadequate foundations of substantial wealth. Compare Ferrara in the sixteenth with Weimar in the eighteenth century, and reflect how wonderfully the Italians even at their last gasp understood the art of exquisite existence!

Alfonso II., who was always vainly trying to bless Ferrara with an heir, had arranged his second sterile nuptials when Tasso joined the Court in 1565. It was therefore at a moment of more than usual parade of splendour that the poet entered on the scene of his renown and his misfortune. He was twenty-one years of age; and twenty-one years had to elapse before he should quit Ferrara, ruined in physical and mental health—*quantum mutatus ab illo* Torquato! The diffident and handsome stripling, famous as the author of 'Rinaldo,' was welcomed in person with special honours by the Cardinal, his patron. Of such favours as Court-lacqueys prize, Tasso from the first had plenty. He did not sit at the common table of the serving gentlemen, but ate his food apart; and after a short residence, the Princesses, sisters of the Duke, invited him to share their meals. The next five years formed the happiest and most tranquil period of his existence. He continued working at the poem which had then no name, but which we know as the 'Gerusalemme Liberata.' Envies and jealousies had not arisen to mar the serenity in which he basked. Women contended for his smiles and sonnets. He repaid their kindness with somewhat indiscriminate homage and with the verses of occasion which flowed so easily from his pen. It is difficult to trace the history of Tasso's loves through the labyrinth of madrigals, odes, and sonnets which belong to this epoch of his life. These compositions bear, indeed, the mark of a distinguished genius ; no one but Tasso could have written them at that period of Italian literature. Yet they lack individuality of emotion, specific passion, insight into the profundities of human feeling. Such shades of difference as we perceive in them, indicate the rhetorician seeking to set forth his motive, rather than the lover pouring out his soul. Contrary to the commonly received legend, I am bound to record my opinion that love played a secondary part in Tasso's destinies. It is true that we can discern the silhouettes of some Court ladies whom he fancied more than others. The first of these was Laura Peperara, for whom he is supposed to have produced some sixty compositions. The second was the Princess Leonora d' Este. Tasso's attachment to her has been so shrouded in mystery, conjecture, and hairsplitting criticism, that none but a very rash man will pronounce confident judgment as to its real nature. Nearly the same may be said about his relations to her sister, Lucrezia. He has posed in literary history as the Rizzio of the one lady and the Chastelard of the other. Yet he was probably in no position at any moment of his Ferrarese existence to be more than the familiar friend and most devoted slave of either. When he joined the Court, Lucrezia was ten and Leonora nine years his senior. Each of the sisters was highly accomplished, graceful, and of royal carriage. Neither could boast of eminent beauty. Of the two, Lucrezia possessed the more commanding character. It was she who left her husband, Francesco Maria della Rovere, because his society wearied her, and who helped Clement VIII. to ruin her family, when the Papacy resolved upon the conquest of Ferrara. Leonora's health was sickly. For this reason she refused marriage, living retired in studies, acts of charity, religion, and the company of intellectual men. Something in her won respect and touched the heart at the same moment; so that the verses in her honour, from whatever pen they flowed, ring with more than merely ceremonial compliment. The people revered her like a saint; and in times of difficulty she displayed high courage and the gifts of one born to govern. From the first entrance of Tasso into Ferrara, the sisters took him under their protection. He lived with them on terms of more than courtly intimacy; and for Leonora there is no doubt that he cherished something like a romantic attachment. This is proved by the episode of Sofronia and Olinto in the 'Gerusalemme,' which points in carefully constructed innuendoes to his affection. It can even be conceded that Tasso, who was wont to indulge fantastic visions of unattainable greatness, may have raised his hopes so high as sometimes to entertain the possibility of winning her hand. But if he did dally with such dreams, the realities of his position must in sober moments have convinced him of their folly. Had not a Duchess of Amalfi been murdered for contracting marriage with a gentleman of her household? And Leonora was a granddaughter of France; and the cordon of royalty was being drawn tighter and tighter yearly in the Italy of his day. That a sympathy of no commonplace kind subsisted between this delicate and polished princess and her sensitively gifted poet, is apparent, But it may be doubted whether Tasso had in him the stuff of a grand passion. Mobile and impressible, he wandered from object to object without seeking or attaining permanence. He was neither a Dante nor a Petrarch; and nothing in his 'Rime' reveals solidity of emotion. It may finally be said that had Leonora returned real love, or had Tasso felt for her real love, his earnest wish to quit Ferrara when the Court grew irksome, would be inexplicable. Had their *liaison* been scandalous, as some have fancied, his life would not have been worth two hours' purchase either in the palace or the prison of Alfonso.

Whatever may be thought of Tasso's love-relations to these sisters—and the problem is open to all conjectures in the absence of clear testimony—it is certain that he owed a great deal to their kindness. The marked favour they extended to him was worth much at Court; and their maturer age and wider experience enabled them to give him many useful hints of conduct. Thus, when he blundered into seeming rivalry with Pigna (the duke's secretary, the Cecil of that little State), by praising Pigna's mistress, Lucrezia Bendidio, in terms of imprudent warmth, it was Leonora who warned him to appease the great man's anger. This he did by writing a commentary upon three of Pigna's leaden Canzoni, which he had the impudence to rank beside the famous three sisters of Petrarch's Canzoniere. The flattery was swallowed, and the peril was averted. Yet in this first affair with Pigna we already hear the grumbling of that tempest which eventually ruined Tasso. So eminent a poet and so handsome a young man was insupportable among a crowd of literary mediocrities and middle-aged gallants. Furthermore, the brilliant being, who aroused the jealousies of rhymesters and of lovers, had one fatal failing—want of tact. In 1568, for example, he set himself up as a target to all malice by sustaining fifty conclusions in the Science of Love before the Academy of Ferrara. As he afterwards confessed, he ran the greatest risks in this adventure; but who, he said, could take up arms against a lover? Doubtless, there were many lovers present; but none of Tasso's eloquence and skill in argument.

In 1569, Tasso was called to his father's sick-bed at Ostiglia on the Po. He found the old man destitute and dying. There was not money to bury him decently; and when the funeral rites had been performed by the help of money-lenders, nothing remained to pay for a monument above his grave. What the Romans called *pietas* was a strong feature in Torquato's character. At crises of his life he invariably appealed to the memory of his parents for counsel and support. When the Della Cruscans attacked his own poetry, he answered them with a defence of the 'Amadigi;' and he spent much time and pains in editing the 'Floridante,' which naught but filial feeling could possibly have made him value at the worth of publication.

In the spring of the next year, Lucrezia d' Este made her inauspicious match with the Duke of Urbino, Tasso's former playmate. She was a woman of thirty-four, he a young man of twenty-one. They did not love each other, had no children, and soon parted with a sense of mutual relief. In the autumn Tasso accompanied the Cardinal Luigi d' Este into France, leaving his MSS. in the charge of Ercole Rondinelli. The document drawn up for this friend's instructions in case of his death abroad is interesting. It proves that the 'Gerusalemme,' here called 'Gottifredo,' was nearly finished; for Tasso wished the last six cantos and portions of the first two to be published. He also gave directions for the collection and publication of his love-sonnets and madrigals, but requested Rondinelli to bury 'the others, whether of love or other matters, which were written in the service of some friend,' in his grave. This last commission demands comment. That Tasso should have written verses to oblige a friend, was not only natural but consistent with custom. Light wares like sonnets could be easily produced by a practised man of letters, and the friend might find them valuable in bringing a fair foe to terms. But why should anyone desire to have such verses buried in his grave? The hypothesis which has been strongly urged by those who believe in the gravity of Tasso's *liaison* with Leonora, is that he used this phrase to indicate love-poems which might compromise his mistress. We cannot, however, do more than speculate upon the point. There is nothing to confirm or to refute conjecture in the evidence before us.

Tasso met with his usual fortunes at the Court of Charles IX.

That is to say, he was petted and caressed, wrote verses, and paid compliments. It was just two years before the Massacre of S. Bartholomew, and France presented to the eyes of earnest Catholics the spectacle of truly horrifying anarchy. Catherine de' Medici inclined to compromise matters with the Huguenots. The social atmosphere reeked with heresy and cynicism. In that Italianated Court, public affairs and religious questions were treated from a purely diplomatic point of view. Not principle, but practical convenience, ruled conduct and opinion. The large scale on which Machiavellism manifested itself in the discordant realm of France, the apparent breakdown of Catholicism as a national institution, struck Tasso with horror. He openly proclaimed his views, and roundly taxed the Government with dereliction of their duty to the Church. An incurable idealist by temperament, he could not comprehend the stubborn actualities of politics. A pupil of the Jesuits, he would not admit that men like Coligny deserved a hearing. An Italian of the decadence, he found it hard to tolerate the humours of a puissant nation in a state of civil warfare. But his master, Luigi d' Este, well understood the practical difficulties which forced the Valois into compromise, and felt no personal aversion for lucrative transaction with the heretic. Though a prince of the Church he had not taken priest's orders. He kept two objects in view. One was succession to the Duchy of Ferrara, in case Alfonso should die without heirs.[1] The other was election to the Papacy. In the latter event, France, the natural ally of the Estensi, would be of service to him, and the Valois monarchs, his cousins, must therefore be supported in their policy. Tasso had been brought to Paris to look graceful and to write madrigals. It was inconvenient, it was unseemly, that a man

[1] Cardinal Ferdinando de' Medici succeeded in a like position to the Grand Duchy of Tuscany. But Luigi d' Este did not survive his brother.

of letters in the Cardinal's train should utter censures on the Crown, and should profess more Catholic opinions than his patron. Without the scandal of a public dismissal, it was therefore contrived that Tasso should return to Italy; and after this rupture, the suspicious poet regarded Luigi d' Este as his enemy. During his confinement in S. Anna he even threw the chief blame of his detention upon the Cardinal.[1]

After spending a short time at Rome in the company of the Cardinals Ippolito d' Este and Albano, Tasso returned to Ferrara in 1572. Alfonso offered him a place in his own household with an annual stipend worth about 88*l.* of our money. No duties were attached to this post, except the delivery of a weekly lecture in the university. For the rest, Tasso was to prosecute his studies, polish his great poem, and augment the lustre of the Court by his accomplishments.[2] It was of course understood that the 'Gerusalemme,' when completed, should be dedicated to the Duke and shed its splendour on the House of Este. Who was happier than Torquato now? Having recently experienced the discomforts of uncongenial service, he took his place again upon a firmer footing in the city of his dreams. The courtiers welcomed him with smiles. He was once more close to Leonora, basking like Rinaldo in Armida's garden, with golden prospects of the fame his epic would achieve to lift him higher in the coming years. No wonder that the felicity of this moment expanded in a flower of lyric beauty which surpassed all that Tasso had yet published. He produced 'Aminta' in the winter of 1572-3. It was acted with unparalleled applause; for this pastoral drama offered something ravishingly new, something which interpreted and gave a vocal utterance to tastes and

---

[1] See *Lettere*, vol. ii. p. 80: to Giacomo Buoncompagno.

[2] 'Egli mi disse, allor che suo mi fece: Tu canta, or che se' 'n ozio.'

sentiments that ruled the age. While professing to exalt the virtues of rusticity, the 'Aminta' was in truth a panegyric of Court life, and Silvia reflected Leonora in the magic mirror of languidly luxurious verse. Poetry melted into music. Emotion exhaled itself in sensuous harmony. The art of the next two centuries, the supreme art of song, of words subservient to musical expression, had been indicated. This explains the sudden and extraordinary success of the 'Aminta.' It was nothing less than the discovery of a new realm, the revelation of a specific faculty which made its author master of the heart of Italy. The very lack of concentrated passion lent it power. Its suffusion of emotion in a shimmering atmosphere toned with voluptuous melancholy, seemed to invite the lutes and viols, the mellow tenors, and the trained soprano voices of the dawning age of melody. We may here remember that Palestrina, seven years earlier in Rome, had already given his 'Mass of Pope Marcello' to the world.

Lucrezia d' Este, now Duchess of Urbino, who was anxious to share the raptures of 'Aminta,' invited Tasso to Pesaro in the summer of 1573, and took him with her to the mountain villa of Casteldurante. She was an unhappy wife, just on the point of breaking her irksome bonds of matrimony. Tasso, if we may credit the deductions which have been drawn from passages in his letters, had the privilege of consoling the disappointed woman and of distracting her tedious hours. They roamed together through the villa gardens, and spent days of quiet in the recesses of her apartments. He read aloud passages from his unpublished poem, and composed sonnets in her honour, praising the full-blown beauty of the rose as lovelier than its budding charm. The Duke her husband, far from resenting this intimacy, heaped favours and substantial gifts upon his former comrade. He had not, indeed, enough affection for his wife to be jealous of her. Yet it is indubitable that if he had suspected her of infidelity, the Italian code of honour would have compelled him to make short work with Tasso.[1]

Meanwhile it seemed as though Leonora had been forgotten by her servant. We possess one letter written to her from Casteldurante on September 8, 1578, in which he encloses a sonnet, disparaging it by comparison with those which he believes she has been receiving from another poet (Guarini probably), and saying that, though the verses were written, not for himself, but 'at the requisition of a poor lover, who, having been for some while angry with his lady, now is forced to yield and crave for pardon,' yet he hopes that they 'will effect the purpose he desires.'[2] Few of Tasso's letters to Leonora have survived. This, therefore, is a document of much importance; and it is difficult to resist the conclusion that he was indirectly begging Leonora to forgive him for some piece of petulance or irritation. At any rate, his position between the two princesses at this moment was one of delicacy, in which a less vain and more cautious man than Tasso might have found it hard to keep his head cool.

Up to the present time his life had been, in spite of poverty and domestic misfortunes, one almost uninterrupted career of triumph. But his fibre had been relaxed in the irresponsible luxurious atmosphere of Courts, and his self-

---

[1] This is how he wrote in his Diary about Lucrezia. 'Finally the Duke decided upon his marriage with Donna Lucrezia d' Este, which took place, though little to his taste, for she was old enough to have been his mother.' 'The Duchess wished to return to Ferrara, where she subsequently chose to remain, a resolution which gave no annoyance to her husband; for, as she was unlikely to bring him a family, her absence mattered little.' 'February 15, 1598. Heard that Madame Lucrezia d' Este, Duchess of Urbino, my wife, died at Ferrara during the night of the 11th.' (Dennistoun's *Dukes of Urbino*, vol. iii. pp. 127, 146, 156.) Francesco Maria had been attached in Spain to a lady of unsuitable condition, and his marriage with Lucrezia was arranged to keep him out of a *mésalliance*.

[2] *Lettere*, vol. i. p. 47. The sonnet begins, 'Sdegno, debil guerrier.'

esteem had been inflated by the honours paid to him as the first poet of his age in Europe. Moreover, he had been continuously over-worked and over-wrought from childhood onwards. Now, when he returned to Ferrara with the Duchess of Urbino at the age of twenty-nine, it remained to be seen whether he could support himself with stability upon the slippery foundation of princely favour, whether his health would hold out, and whether he would be able to bring the publication of his long-expected poem to a successful issue.

In 1574 he accompanied Duke Alfonso to Venice, and witnessed the magnificent reception of Henri III. on his return from Poland. A fever, contracted during those weeks of pleasure, prevented him from working at the epic for many months. This is the first sign of any serious failure in Tasso's health. At the end of August 1574, however, the 'Gerusalemme' was finished, and in the following February he began sending the MS. to Scipione Gonzaga at Rome. So much depended on its success that doubts immediately rose within its author's mind. Will it fulfil the expectation raised in every Court and literary coterie of Italy? Will it bear investigation in the light of the Dialogues on Epic Poetry? Will the Church be satisfied with its morality; the Holy Office with its doctrine? None of these diffidences assailed Tasso when he flung 'Aminta' negligently forth and found he had produced a masterpiece. It would have been well for him if he had turned a deaf ear to the doubting voice on this occasion also. But he was not of an independent character to start with: and his life had made him sensitively deferent to literary opinion. Therefore, in an evil hour, yielding to Gonzaga's advice, he resolved to submit the 'Gerusalemme' in MS. to four censors—Il Borga, Flaminio de Nobili, vulpine Speroni with his poisoned fang of pedantry, precise Antoniano with his inquisitorial prudery. They were to pass their several criticisms on the plot, characters, diction, and ethics of the 'Gerusalemme;' Tasso was to entertain and weigh their arguments, reserving the right of following or rejecting their advice, but promising to defend his own views. To the number of this committee he shortly after added three more scholars, Francesco Piccolomini, Domenico Veniero, and Celio Magno.[1] Not to have been half maddened by these critics would have proved Tasso more or less than human. They picked holes in the structure of the epic, in its episodes, in its theology, in its incidents, in its language, in its title. One censor required one alteration, and another demanded the contrary. This man seemed animated by an acrid spite; that veiled his malice in the flatteries of candid friendship. Antoniano was for cutting out the love passages: Armida, Sofronia, Erminia, Clorinda, were to vanish or to be adapted to conventual proprieties. It seemed to him more than doubtful whether the enchanted forest did not come within the prohibitions of the Tridentine decrees. As the revision advanced, matters grew more serious. Antoniano threw out some decided hints of ecclesiastical displeasure; Tasso, reading between the lines, scented the style of the Collegium Germanicum. Speroni spoke openly of plagiarism—plagiarism from himself forsooth!—and murmured the terrible words between his teeth, 'Tasso is mad!' He was in fact driven wild, and told his tormentors that he would delay the publication of the epic, perhaps for a year, perhaps for his whole life, so little hope had he of its success.[2] At last he resolved to compose an allegory to explain and moralise the poem. When he wrote the 'Gerusalemme' he had no thought of hidden meanings; but this seemed the only way of preventing it from being

---

[1] Tasso consulted almost every scholar he could press into his service. But the official tribunal of correction was limited to the above-named four acting in concert with Scipione Gonzaga.

[2] *Lettere*, vol. i. p. 114.

dismembered by hypocrites and pedants.[1] The expedient proved partially successful. When Antoniano and his friends were bidden to perceive a symbol in the enchanted wood and other marvels, a symbol in the loves of heroines and heroes, a symbol even in Armida, they relaxed their wrath. The 'Gerusalemme' might possibly pass muster now before the Congregation of the Index. Tasso's correspondence between March 1575 and July 1576 shows what he suffered at the hands of his revisers, and helps to explain the series of events which rendered the autumn of that latter year calamitous for him.[2] There are, indeed, already indications in the letters of those months that his nerves, enfeebled by the quartan fever under which he laboured, and exasperated by carping or envious criticism, were overstrung. Suspicions began to invade his mind. He complained of headache. His spirits alternated between depression and hysterical gaiety. A dread lest the Inquisition should refuse the imprimatur to his poem haunted him. He grew restless, and yearned for change of scene.

The events of 1575, 1576, and 1577 require to be minutely studied; for upon our interpretation of them must depend the theory which we hold of Tasso's subsequent misfortunes. It appears that early in the year 1575 he was becoming discontented with Ferrara. A party in the Court, led by Pigna, did their best to make his life there disagreeable. They were jealous of the poet's fame, which shone with trebled splendour after the production of 'Aminta.' Tasso's own behaviour provoked, if it did not exactly justify, their animosity. He treated men at least his equals in position with haughtiness, which his irritable temper rendered insupportable. We have it from his own pen that ' he could not bear to live in a city where the nobles did not yield him the first place, or at least admit him to absolute equality;' that 'he expected to be

[1] *Lettere*, vol. i. p. 192.   [2] *Ib.* vol. i. pp. 55-215.

adored by friends, served by serving-men, caressed by domestics, honoured by masters, celebrated by poets, and pointed out by all.'[1] He admitted that it was his habit 'to build castles in the air of honours, favours, gifts, and graces, showered on him by emperors and kings and mighty princes;' that 'the slightest coldness from a patron seemed to him a tacit act of dismissal, or rather an open act of violence.'[2] His blood, he argued, placed him on a level with the aristocracy of Italy; but his poetry lifted him far above the vulgar herd of noble men. At the same time, while claiming so much, he constantly declared himself unfit for any work or office but literary study, and expressed his opinion that princes ought to be his tributaries.[3] Though such pretensions may not have been openly expressed at this period of his life, it cannot be doubted that Tasso's temper made him an unpleasant comrade in Court-service. His sensitiveness, as well as the actual slenderness of his fortunes exposed him only too obviously to the malevolent tricks and petty bullyings of rivals. One knows what a boy of that stamp has to suffer at public schools, and a Court is after all not very different from an academy.

Such being the temper of his mind, Tasso at this epoch turned his thoughts to bettering himself, as servants say. His friend Scipione Gonzaga pointed out that both the Cardinal de' Medici and the Grand Duke of Tuscany would be glad to welcome him as an ornament of their households. Tasso nibbled at the bait all through the summer; and in November, under the pretext of profiting by the Jubilee, he travelled to Rome. This journey, as he afterwards declared, was the beginning of his ruin.[4] It was certainly one of the

[1] *Lettere*, vol. iii. p. 41, iv. p. 332.
[2] *Ib.* vol. iii. p. 164, v. p. 6.
[3] *Ib.* vol. iii. pp. 85, 86, 88, 163, iv. pp. 8, 166, v. p. 87.
[4] Letter to Fabio Gonzaga in 1590 (vol. iv. p. 296).

TASSO COURTS THE MEDICI

principal steps which led to the prison of S. Anna. There were many reasons why Alfonso should resent Tasso's entrance into other service at this moment. The House of Este had treated him with uniform kindness. The Cardinal, the Duke, and the princesses had severally marked him out by special tokens of esteem. In return they expected from him the honours of his now immortal epic. That he should desert them and transfer the dedication of the 'Gerusalemme' to the Medici, would have been nothing short of an insult; for it was notorious that the Estensi and the Medici were bitter foes, not only on account of domestic disagreements and political jealousies, but also because of the dispute about precedence in their titles, which had agitated Italian society for some time past. In his impatience to leave Ferrara, Tasso cast prudence to the winds, and entered into negotiations with the Cardinal de' Medici in Rome. When he travelled northwards at the beginning of 1576, he betook himself to Florence. What passed between him and the Grand Duke is not apparent. Yet he seems to have still further complicated his position by making political disclosures which were injurious to the Duke of Ferrara. Nor did he gain anything by the offer of his services and his poem to Francesco de' Medici. In a letter of February 4, 1576, the Grand Duke wrote that the Florentine visit of that fellow, 'whether to call him a mad or an amusing and astute spirit, I hardly know,' had been throughout a ridiculous affair; and that nothing could be less convenient than his putting the 'Gerusalemme' up to auction among princes.[1] One year later, he said bluntly that 'he did not want to have a madman at his Court.'[2] Thus Tasso, like his father, discovered that a noble poem, the product of his best pains, had but small substantial value. It might, indeed, be worth

---

[1] *Lettere*, vol. iii. p. viii.
[2] *Ib.* vol. iii. p. xxx. note 34.

something to the patron who paid a yearly exhibition to its author; but it was not a gem of such high price as to be wrangled for by dukes who had the cares of State upon their shoulders. He compromised himself with the Estensi, and failed to secure a retreat in Florence.

Meanwhile his enemies at Ferrara were not idle. Pigna had died in the preceding November. But Antonio Montecatino, who succeeded him as ducal secretary, proved even a more malicious foe, and poisoned Alfonso's mind against the unfortunate poet. The two princesses still remained his faithful friends, until Tasso's own want of tact alienated the sympathies of Leonora. When he returned in 1576, he found the beautiful Eleonora Sanvitale, Countess of Scandiano, at Court. Whether he really fell in love with her at first sight, or pretended to do so in order to revive Leonora d' Este's affection by jealousy, is uncertain.[1] At any rate he paid the Countess such marked attentions, and wrote for her and a lady of her suite such splendid poetry, that all Ferrara rang with this amour. A sonnet in Tasso's handwriting, addressed to Leonora d' Este and commented by her own pen, which even Guasti, no credulous believer in the legend of the poet's love, accepts as genuine, may be taken as affording proof that the princess was deeply wounded by her servant's conduct.[2]

It is obvious that, though Tasso's letters at this period show no signs of a diseased mind, his conduct began to strike outsiders as insane. Francesco de' Medici used the plain words *matto* and *pazzo*. The courtiers of Ferrara, some in pity, some in derision, muttered 'Madman,' when he passed. And he spared no pains to prove that he was losing

---

[1] Guarini, in a sonnet, hinted at the second supposition. See Rosini's *Saggio sugli Amori*, &c.; vol. xxxiii. of his edition of Tasso, p. 51.

[2] *Lettere*, vol. iii. p. xxxi.

self-control. In the month of January 1577 he was seized with scruples of faith, and conceived the notion that he ought to open his mind to the Holy Office. Accordingly, he appeared before the Inquisitor of Bologna, who, after hearing his confession, bade him be of good cheer, for his self-accusations were the outcome of a melancholy humour. Tasso was, in fact, a Catholic moulded by Jesuit instruction in his earliest childhood; and though, like most young students, he had speculated on the groundwork of theology and metaphysic, there was no taint of heresy or disobedience to the Church in his nature. The terror of the Inquisition was a morbid nightmare, first implanted in his mind by the experience of his father's collision with the Holy Office, enforced by Antoniano's strictures on his poem, and justified to some extent by the sinister activity of the institution which had burned a Carnesecchi and a Paleario. However it grew up, this fancy that he was suspected as a heretic took firm possession of his brain, and subsequently formed a main feature of his mental disease. It combined with the suspiciousness which now became habitual. He thought that secret enemies were in the habit of forwarding delations against him to Rome.

All through these years (1575-1577) his enemies drew tighter cords around him. They were led and directed by Montecatino, the omnipotent persecutor, and hypocritical betrayer. In his heedlessness Tasso left books and papers loose about his rooms. These, he had good reason to suppose, were ransacked in his absence. There follows a melancholy tale of treacherous friends, dishonest servants, false keys, forged correspondence, scraps and fragments of imprudent compositions pieced together and brought forth to incriminate him behind his back. These arts were employed all through the year which followed his return to Ferrara in 1576. But they reached their climax in the spring of 1577. He had lost his prestige, and every servant might insult him, every cur snap at his heels. Even the 'Gerusalemme' became an object of derision. It transpired that the revisers, to whom he had confided it, were picking the poem to pieces; and ignoramuses who could not scan a line, went about parroting their pedantries and strictures. At the beginning of 1576 Tasso had begged Alfonso to give him the post of historiographer left vacant by Pigna. It was his secret hope that this would be refused, and that so he would obtain a good excuse for leaving Ferrara.[1] But the Duke granted his request. In the autumn of that year, one of the band of his tormentors, Maddalò de' Frecci, betrayed some details of his love affairs. What these were, we do not know. Tasso resented the insult, and gave the traitor a box on the ears in the courtyard of the castle. Maddalò and his brothers, after this, attacked Tasso on the piazza, but ran away before they reached him with their swords. They were outlawed for the outrage, and the Duke of Ferrara, still benignant to his poet, sent him a kind message by one of his servants. This incident weighed on Tasso's memory. The terror of the Inquisition blended now with two new terrors. He conceived that his exiled foes were plotting to poison him. He wondered whether Maddalò's revelations had reached the Duke's ears, and, if so, whether Alfonso would not inflict sudden vengeance. There is no sufficient reason, however, to surmise that Tasso's conscience was really burdened with a guilty secret touching Leonora d' Este. On the contrary, everything points to a different conclusion. His mind was simply giving way. Just as he conjured up the ghastly spectacle of the Inquisition, so he fancied that the Duke would murder him. Both the Inquisition and the Duke were formidable; but the Holy Office mildly told him to set his morbid doubts at rest, and the Duke on a subsequent

[1] *Lettere*, vol. i. p. 189.

occasion coldly wrote: 'I know he thinks I want to kill him. But if indeed I did so, it would be easy enough.' The Duke, in fact, had no sufficient reason and no inclination to tread upon this insect.

In June 1577 the crisis came. On the seventeenth evening of the month Tasso was in the apartments of the Duchess of Urbino. He had just been declaiming on the subject of his imaginary difficulties with the Inquisition, when something in the manner of a servant who passed by aroused his suspicion. He drew a knife upon the man—like Hamlet in his mother's bedchamber. He was immediately put under arrest, and confined in a room of the castle. Next day Maffeo Veniero wrote thus to the Grand Duke of Tuscany about the incident. 'Yesterday Tasso was imprisoned for having drawn a knife upon a servant in the apartment of the Duchess of Urbino. The intention has been to stay disorder and to cure him, rather than to inflict punishment. He suffers under peculiar delusions, believing himself guilty of heresy, and dreading poison; which state of mind arises, I incline to think, from melancholic blood forced in upon the heart and vapouring to the brain. A wretched case, in truth, considering his great parts and his goodness!'[1]

Tasso was soon released, and taken by the Duke to his villa of Belriguardo. Probably this excursion was designed to soothe the perturbed spirits of the poet. But it may also have had a different object. Alfonso may have judged it prudent to sift the information laid before him by Tasso's enemies. We do not know what passed between them. Whether moral pressure was applied, resulting in the disclosure of secrets compromising Leonora d' Este, cannot now be ascertained; nor is it worth while to discuss the hypothesis that the Duke, in order to secure his family's honour, imposed on Tasso the

[1] *Lettere*, vol. i. p. 228.

obligation of feigning madness.[1] There is a something not entirely elucidated, a sediment of mystery in Tasso's fate, after this visit to Belriguardo, which criticism will not neglect to notice, but which no testing, no clarifying process of study, has hitherto explained. All we can rely upon for certain is that Alfonso sent him back to Ferrara to be treated physically and spiritually for derangement; and that Tasso thought his life was in danger. He took up his abode in the Convent of S. Francis, submitted to be purged, and began writing eloquent letters to his friends and patrons. Those which he addressed to the Duke of Ferrara at this crisis, weigh naturally heaviest in the scale of criticism.[2] They turn upon his dread of the Inquisition, his fear of poison, and his diplomatic practice with Florence. While admitting 'faults of grave importance' and 'vacillation in the service of his prince,' he maintains that his secret foes have exaggerated these offences, and have succeeded in prejudicing the magnanimous and clement spirit of Alfonso. He is particularly anxious about the charge of heresy. Nothing indicates that any guilt of greater moment weighed upon his conscience.[3] After scrutinising all accessible sources of information, we are thus driven to accept the prosaic hypothesis that Tasso was deranged, and that his Court-rivals had availed themselves of a favourable opportunity for making the Duke sensible of his insanity.

After the middle of July, the Convent of S. Francis

[1] This is Rosini's hypothesis in the Essay cited above. The whole of his elaborate and ingenious theory rests upon the supposition that Alfonso at Belriguardo extorted from Tasso an acknowledgment of his *liaison* with Leonora, and spared his life on the condition of his playing a fool's part before the world. But we have no evidence whatever adequate to support the supposition.

[2] *Lettere*, vol. i. pp. 257-262.

[3] Those who adhere to the belief that all Tasso's troubles came upon him through his *liaison* with Leonora, are here of course justified in arguing that on *this* point he could not write openly to the Duke. Or they may question the integrity of the document.

became intolerable to Tasso. His malady had assumed the form of a multiplex fear, which never afterwards relaxed its hold on his imagination. The Inquisition, the Duke, the multitude of secret enemies plotting murder, haunted him day and night like furies. He escaped, and made his way, disguised in a peasant's costume, avoiding cities, harbouring in mountain hamlets, to Sorrento. Manso, who wrote the history of Tasso's life in the spirit of a novelist, has painted for us a romantic picture of the poet in a shepherd's hut.[1] It recalls Erminia among the pastoral people. Indeed, the interest of that episode in the 'Gerusalemme' is heightened by the fact that its ill-starred author tested the reality of his creation ofttimes in the course of this pathetic pilgrimage. Artists of the Bolognese Academy have placed Erminia on their canvases. But, up to the present time, I know of no great painter who has chosen the more striking incident of Tasso exchanging his Court-dress for sheepskin and a fustian jacket in the smoky cottage at Velletri.

He reached Sorrento safely—'that most enchanting region, which at all times offers a delightful sojourn to men and to the Muses; but at the warm season of the year, when other places are intolerable, affords peculiar solace in the verdure of its foliage, the shadow of its woods, the lightness of the fanning airs, the freshness of the limpid waters flowing from impendent hills, the fertile expanse of tilth, the serene air, the tranquil sea, the fishes and the birds and savoury fruits in marvellous variety; all which delights compose a garden for the intellect and senses, planned by Nature in her rarest mood, and perfected by art with most consummate curiosity.'[2] Into this earthly paradise the wayworn pilgrim entered. It was his birthplace; and here his sister still dwelt with her children. Tasso sought Cornelia's home. After a dramatic

[1] Rosini's edition of Tasso, vol. xxx. p. 144.
[2] Manso, *ib.* p. 46.

scene of suspense, he threw aside his disguise, declared himself to be the poet of Italy and her brother; and for a short while he seemed to forget Courts and schools, pedants and princes, in that genial atmosphere.

Why did he ever leave Sorrento? That is the question which leaps to the lips of a modern free man. The question itself implies imperfect comprehension of Tasso's century and training. Outside the Court, there was no place for him. He had been moulded for Court-life from childhood. It was not merely that he had no money; assiduous labour might have supplied him with means of subsistence. But his friends, his fame, his habits, his engrained sense of service, called him back to Ferrara. He was not simply a man, but that specific sort of man which Italians call *gentiluomo*—a man definitely modified and wound about with intricacies of association. Therefore, he soon began a correspondence with the House of Este. If we may trust Manso, Leonora herself wrote urgently insisting upon his return.[1] Yet in his own letters Tasso says that he addressed apologies to the Duke and both princesses. Alfonso and Lucrezia vouchsafed no answer. Leonora replied coldly that she could not help him.[2]

Anyhow, Ferrara drew him back. It is of some importance here to understand Tasso's own feeling for the Duke, his master. A few months later, after he had once more experienced the miseries of Court-life, he wrote: 'I trusted in him, not as one hopes in men, but as one trusts in God. . . . I was inflamed with the affection for my lord more than ever was man with the love of woman, and became unawares half an idolater. . . . He it was who from the obscurity of my low fortunes raised me to the light and reputation of the Court; who relieved me from discomforts, and placed me in a position of honourable ease; he conferred value on my compositions by listening to them when I read them, and by every mark of

[1] Manso, *ib.* p. 147.   [2] *Lettere*, vol. i. p. 275.

favour; he deigned to honour me with a seat at his table and with his familiar conversation; he never refused a favour which I begged for; lastly, at the commencement of my troubles, he showed me the affection, not of a master, but of a father and a brother.'[1] These words, though meant for publication, have the ring of truth in them. Tasso was actually attached to the House of Este, and cherished a vassal's loyalty for the Duke, in spite of the many efforts which he made to break the fetters of Ferrara. At a distance, in the isolation and the ennui of a village, the irksomeness of those chains was forgotten. The poet only remembered how sweet his happier years at Court had been. The sentiment of fidelity revived. His sanguine and visionary temperament made him hope that all might yet be well.

Without receiving direct encouragement from the Duke, Tasso accordingly decided on returning. His sister is said to have dissuaded him; and he is reported to have replied that he was going to place himself in a voluntary prison.[2] He first went to Rome, and opened negotiations with Alfonso's agents. In reply to their communications, the Duke wrote upon March 22, 1578, as follows: 'We are content to take Tasso back; but first he must recognise the fact that he is full of melancholic humours, and that his old notions of enmities and persecutions are solely caused by the said humours. Among other signs of his disorder, he has conceived the idea that we want to compass his death, whereas we have always received him gladly and shown favour to him. It can easily be understood that if we had entertained such a fancy, the execution of it would have presented no difficulty.

[1] *Lettere*, vol. i. p. 278, ii. p. 26.
[2] Manso, p. 147. Here again the believers in the Leonora *liaison* may argue that by prison he meant love-bondage, hopeless servitude to the lady from whom he could expect nothing now that her brother was acquainted with the truth.

Therefore let him make his mind up well, before he comes, to submit quietly and unconditionally to medical treatment. Otherwise, if he means to scatter hints and words again as he did formerly, we shall not only give ourselves no further trouble about him, but if he should stay here without being willing to undergo a course of cure, we shall at once expel him from our State with the order not to return.'[1] Words could not be plainer than these. Yet, in spite of them, such was the allurement of the cage for this clipped singing-bird, that Tasso went obediently back to Ferrara. Possibly he had not read the letter written by a greater poet on a similar occasion: 'This is not the way of coming home, my father! Yet if you or others find one not beneath the fame of Dante and his honour, that will I pursue with no slack step. But if none such give entrance to Florence, I will never enter Florence. How! Shall I not behold the sun and stars from every spot of earth? Shall I not be free to meditate the sweetest truths in every place beneath the sky unless I make myself ignoble, nay, ignominious to the people and the state of Florence? Nor truly will bread fail.' These words, if Tasso had remembered them, might have made his cheek blush for his own servility and for the servile age in which he lived. But the truth is that the fleshpots of Egyptian bondage enticed him; and, moreover, he knew, as half-insane people always know, that he required treatment for his mental infirmities. In his heart of hearts he acknowledged the justice of the Duke's conditions.

An Epistle or Oration addressed by Tasso to the Duke of Urbino, sets forth what happened after his return to Ferrara in 1578.[2] He was aware that Alfonso thought him both malicious and mad. The first of these opinions, which he knew to be false, he resolved to pass in silence. But he

---

[1] *Lettere*, vol. i. p. 238.   [2] *Ib.* vol. i. pp. 271-290.

openly admitted the latter, 'esteeming it no disgrace to make a third to Solon and Brutus.' Therefore he began to act the madman even in Rome, neglecting his health, exposing himself to hardships, and indulging intemperately in food and wine. By these means, strange as it may seem, he hoped to win back confidence and prove himself a discreet servant of Alfonso. Soon after reaching Ferrara, Tasso thought that he was gaining ground. He hints that the Duke showed signs of raising him to such greatness and showering favours upon him so abundant that the sleeping viper of Court-envy stirred. Montecatino now persuaded his master that prudence and his own dignity indicated a very different line of treatment. If Tasso was to be great and honoured, he must feel that his reputation flowed wholly from the princely favour, not from his studies and illustrious works. Alfonso accordingly affected to despise the poems which Tasso presented, and showed his will that: 'I should aspire to no eminence of intellect, to no glory of literature, but should lead a soft and delicate and idle life immersed in sloth and pleasure, escaping like a runaway from the honour of Parnassus, the Lyceum, and the Academy, into the lodgings of Epicurus, and should harbour in those lodgings in a quarter where neither Virgil nor Catullus nor Horace nor Lucretius himself had ever stayed.' This excited such indignation in the poet's breast that: 'I said oftentimes with open face and free speech that I would rather be a servant of any prince his enemy than submit to this indignity, and in short *odia verbis aspera movi*.' Whereupon, the Duke caused his papers to be seized, in order that the still imperfect epic might be prepared for publication by the hated hypocritical Montecatino. When Tasso complained, he only received indirect answers; and when he tried to gain access to the princesses, he was repulsed by their doorkeepers. At last: 'My infinite patience was exhausted. Leaving my books and writings, after the service of thirteen years, persisted in with luckless constancy, I wandered forth like a new Bias, and betook myself to Mantua, where I met with the same treatment as at Ferrara.'

This account sufficiently betrays the diseased state of Tasso's mind. Being really deranged, yet still possessed of all his literary faculties, he affected that his eccentricity was feigned. The Duke had formed a firm opinion of his madness; and he chose to flatter this whim. Yet when he arrived at Ferrara, he forgot the strict conditions upon which Alfonso sanctioned his return, began to indulge in dreams of greatness, and refused the life of careless ease which formed part of the programme for his restoration to health. In these circumstances he became the laughing-stock of his detractors; and it is not impossible that Alfonso, convinced of his insanity, treated him like a Court-fool. Then he burst out into menaces and mutterings of anger. When he had made himself wholly intolerable, his papers were sequestrated, very likely under the impression that he might destroy them or escape with them into some quarter where they would be used against the interests of his patron. Finally, he so fatigued everybody by his suspicions and recriminations that the Duke forbore to speak with him, and the princesses closed their doors against him.

From this moment Tasso was a ruined man; he had become that worst of social scourges, a courtier with a grievance, a semi-lunatic all the more dangerous and tiresome because his mental powers were not so much impaired as warped. Studying his elaborate apology, we do not know whether to despise the obstinacy of his devotion to the House of Este, or to respect the sentiment of loyalty which survived all real or fancied insults. Against the Duke he utters no word of blame. Alfonso is always magnanimous and clement, excellent in mind and body, good and courteous by nature, deserving the faithful service and warm love of his dependents.

Montecatino is the real villain. 'The princes are not tyrants —they are not, no, no: he is the tyrant.'[1] After quitting Ferrara, Tasso wandered through Mantua, Padua, Venice, coldly received in all these cities; for 'the hearts of men were hardened by their interests against him.' Writing from Venice to the Grand Duke in July, Maffeo Veniero says: 'Tasso is here, disturbed in mind; and though his intellect is certainly not sound, he shows more signs of affliction than of insanity.'[2] The sequestration of his only copy of the 'Gerusalemme,' not unnaturally caused him much distress; and Veniero adds that the chief difficulty under which he laboured, was want of money. Veniero hardly understood the case. Even with a competence, it is incredible that Tasso would have been contented to work quietly at literature in a private position.[3] From Venice he found his way southward to Urbino, writing one of his sublimest odes upon the road from Pesaro.[4] Francesco Maria della Rovere received him with accustomed kindness; but the spirit of unrest drove him forth again, and after two months we find him once more, an indigent and homeless pedestrian, upon the banks of the Sesia. He wanted to reach Vercelli, but the river was in flood, and he owed a night's lodging to the chance courtesy of a young nobleman. Among the many picturesque episodes in Tasso's wanderings none is more idyllically beautiful than the tale of his meeting with this handsome youth. He has told it himself in the exordium to

---

[1] *Lettere*, vol. i. p. 289.   [2] *Ib.* vol. i. p. 233.

[3] Tasso declares his inability to live outside the Court. 'Se fra i mali de l' animo, uno de' più gravi è l' ambizione, egli ammalò di questo male già molti anni sono, nè mai è risanato in modo ch' io abbia potuto sprezzare affatto i favori e gli onori del mondo, e chi può dargli' (*Lettere*, vol. iii. p. 56). 'Io non posso acquetarmi in altra fortuna di quella ne la quale già nacqui' (*Ibid.* p. 243).

[4] It is addressed to the Metaurus, and begins: 'O del grand' Apennino.'

his Dialogue 'Il Padre di Famiglia.' When asked who he was and whither he was going, he answered: 'I was born in the realm of Naples, and my mother was a Neapolitan; but I draw my paternal blood from Bergamo, a Lombard city. My name and surname I pass in silence: they are so obscure that if I uttered them, you would know neither more nor less of my condition. I am flying from the anger of a prince and fortune. My destination is the state of Savoy.' Upon this pilgrimage Tasso chose the sobriquet of *Omero Fuggiguerra*. Arriving at Turin, he was refused entrance by the guardians of the gate. The rags upon his back made them suspect he was a vagabond infected with the plague. A friend who knew him, Angelo Ingegneri, happened to pass by, and guaranteed his respectability. Manso compares the journey of this penniless and haggard fugitive through the cities of Italy to the meteoric passage of a comet.[1] Wherever he appeared, he blazed with momentary splendour. Nor was Turin slow to hail the lustrous apparition. The Marchese Filippo da Este entertained him in his palace. The Archbishop, Girolamo della Rovere, begged the honour of his company. The Duke of Savoy, Carlo Emanuele, offered him the same appointments as he had enjoyed at Ferrara. Nothing, however, would content his morbid spirit. Flattered and caressed through the months of October and November, he began once more in December to hanker after his old home. Inconceivable as it may seem, he opened fresh negotiations with the Duke; and Alfonso, on his side, already showed a will to take him back. Writing to his sister from Pesaro at the end of September, Tasso says that a gentleman had been sent from Ferrara expressly to recall him.[2] The fact seems to be that Tasso was too illustrious to be neglected by the House of Este. Away from their protection, he was capable of bringing on

[1] *Op. cit.* p. 143. [2] *Lettere*, vol. i. p. 268.

their name the slur of bad treatment and ingratitude. Nor would it have looked well to publish the 'Gerusalemme' with its praises of Alfonso, while the poet was lamenting his hard fate in every town of Italy. The upshot of these negotiations was that Tasso resolved on retracing his steps. He reached Ferrara again upon February 21, 1579, two days before Margherita Gonzaga, the Duke's new bride, made her pompous entrance into the city. But his reception was far from being what he had expected. The Duke's heart seemed hardened. Apartments inferior to his quality were assigned him, and to these he was conducted by a courtier with ill-disguised insolence. The princesses refused him access to their lodgings, and his old enemies openly manifested their derision for the kill-joy and the skeleton who had returned to spoil their festival. Tasso, querulous as he was about his own share in the disagreeables of existence, remained wholly unsympathetic to the trials of his fellow-creatures. Self-engrossment closed him in a magic prison-house of discontent. Therefore, when he saw Ferrara full of merry-making guests, and heard the marriage music ringing through the courtyards of the castle, he failed to reflect with what a heavy heart the Duke might now be entering upon his third sterile nuptials. Alfonso was childless, brotherless, with no legitimate heir to defend his duchy from the Church in case of his decease. The irritable poet forgot how distasteful at such a moment of forced gaiety and hollow parade his reappearance, with the old complaining murmurs, the old suspicions, the old restless eyes, might be to the master who had certainly borne much and long with him. He only felt himself neglected, insulted, outraged:

> Questa è la data fede?
> Son questi i miei bramati alti ritorni? [1]

---

[1] From the sonnet, *Sposa regal* (*Opere*, vol. iii. p. 218).

Then he burst out into angry words, which he afterwards acknowledged to have been 'false, mad, and rash.'[1] The Duke's patience had reached its utmost limit. Tasso was arrested, and confined in the hospital for mad folk at S. Anna. This happened in March 1579. He was detained there until July 19, 1586, a period of seven years and four months.

No one who has read the foregoing pages, will wonder why Tasso was imprisoned. The marvel is rather that the fact should have roused so many speculations. Alfonso was an autocratic princeling. His favourite minister, Montecatino, fell in one moment from the height of power to irrecoverable ruin. The famous preacher, Panigarola, for whom he negotiated a Cardinal's hat, lost his esteem by seeking promotion at another Court, and had to fly Ferrara. His friend, Ercole Contrario, was strangled in the castle on suspicion of having concealed a murder. Tasso had been warned repeatedly, repeatedly forgiven; and now when he turned up again with the same complaints and the same menaces, Alfonso determined to have done with the nuisance. He would not kill him, but he would put him out of sight and hearing. If he was guilty, S. Anna would be punishment enough. If he was mad, it might be hoped that S. Anna would cure him. To blame the Duke for this exercise of authority, is difficult. Noble as is the poet's calling, and faithful as are the wounds of a devoted friend and servant, there are limits to princely patience. It is easier to blame Tasso for the incurable idealism which, when he was in comfort at Turin, made him pine 'to kiss the hand of his Highness, and recover some part of his favour on the occasion of his marriage.'[2]

Three long letters, written by Tasso during the early months of his imprisonment, discuss the reasons for his

[1] *Lettere*, vol. ii. p. 67.   [2] *Ibid.* vol. ii. p. 34.

arrest.¹ Two of these are directed to his staunch friend Scipione Gonzaga, the third to Giacomo Buoncompagno, nephew of Pope Gregory XIII. Partly owing to omissions made by the editors before publication, and partly perhaps to the writer's reticence, they throw no very certain light even on his own opinion.² But this much appears tolerably clear. Tasso was half-mad and altogether irritable. He had used language which could not be overlooked. The Duke continued to resent his former practice with the Medici, and disapproved of his perpetual wanderings. The courtiers had done their utmost to prejudice his mind by calumnies and gossip, raking up all that seemed injurious to Tasso's reputation in the past acts of his life and in the looser verses found among his papers. It may also be conceded that they contrived to cast an unfavourable light upon his affectionate correspondence with the two princesses. Tasso himself laid great stress upon his want of absolute loyalty, upon some lascivious compositions, and lastly upon his supposed heresies. It is not probable that the Duke attached importance to such poetry as Tasso may have written in the heat of youth; and it is certain that he regarded the heresies as part of the poet's hallucinations. It is also far more likely that the Leonora episode passed in his mind for another proof of mental infirmity than that he judged it seriously. It was quite enough that Tasso had put himself in the wrong by petulant abuse of his benefactor and by persistent fretfulness. Moreover, he was plainly brain-sick. That alone justified Alfonso in his own eyes.

¹ *Lettere*, pp. 7–62, 80–93.
² We are met here as elsewhere in the perplexing problem of Tasso's misfortunes with the difficulty of having to deal with mutilated documents. Still the mere fact that Tasso was allowed to correspond freely with friends and patrons, shows that Alfonso dreaded no disclosures, and confirms the theory that he only kept Tasso locked up out of harm's way.

And brain-sick Tasso was, without a shadow of doubt.[1] It is hardly needful to recapitulate his terror of the Inquisition, dread of being poisoned, incapacity for self-control in word and act, and other signs of incipient disease. During the residence in S. Anna this malady made progress. He was tormented by spectral voices and apparitions. He believed himself to be under the influence of magic charms. He was haunted by a sprite, who stole his books and flung his MSS. about the room. A good genius, in the form of a handsome youth, appeared and conversed with him. He lost himself for hours together in abstraction, talking aloud, staring into vacancy and expressing surprise that other people could not see the phantoms which surrounded him. He complained that his melancholy passed at moments into delirium (which he called *frenesia*), after which he suffered from loss of memory and prostration. His own mind became a constant cause of self-torture. Suspicious of others, he grew to be suspicious of himself. And when he left S. Anna, these disorders, instead of abating, continued to afflict him, so that his most enthusiastic admirers were forced to admit that 'he was subject to constitutional melancholy with crises of delirium, but not to actual insanity.'[2] At first, his infirmity

---

[1] A letter written by Guarini, the old friend, rival, and constant Court-companion of Tasso at Ferrara, upon the news of his death in 1595, shows how a man of cold intellect judged his case. 'The death by which Tasso has now paid his debt to nature, seems to me like the termination of that death of his in this world which only bore the outer semblance of life.' See Casella's *Pastor Fido*, p. xxxii. Guarini means that when Tasso's mind gave way, he had really died in his own higher self, and that his actual death was a release.

[2] Tasso's own letters after the beginning of 1579, and Manso's Life (*op. cit.* pp. 156-176), are the authorities for the symptoms detailed above. Tasso so often alludes to his infirmities that it is not needful to accumulate citations. I will, however, quote two striking examples. 'Sono infermo come soleva, e stanco della infermità, la quale è *non sol malattia del corpo ma de la mente*' (*Lettere*, vol. iii. p. 160). 'Io sono

did not interfere with intellectual production of a high order, though none of his poetry, after the 'Gerusalemme' was completed in 1574, rose to the level of his earlier work. But in course of time the artist's faculty itself was injured, and the creations of his later life are unworthy of his genius.

The seven years and four months of Tasso's imprisonment may be passed over briefly. With regard to his so-called dungeon, it is certain that, after some months spent in a narrow chamber, he obtained an apartment of several rooms. He was allowed to write and receive as many letters as he chose. Friends paid him visits, and he went abroad under surveillance in the city of Ferrara. To extenuate the suffering which a man of his temper endured in this enforced seclusion would be unjust to Tasso. There is no doubt that he was most unhappy. But to exaggerate his discomforts would be unjust to the Duke. Even Manso describes 'the excellent and most convenient lodgings' assigned him in S. Anna, alludes to the provision for his cure by medicine, and remarks upon the opposition which he offered to medical treatment. According to this biographer, his own endeavours to escape necessitated a strict watch upon his movements.[1] Unless, therefore, we flatly deny the fact of his derangement, which is supported by a mass of testimony, it may be doubted whether Tasso was more miserable in S. Anna than he would have been at large. The subsequent events of his life prove that his release brought no mitigation of his malady.

It was, however, a dreary time. He spent his days in writing letters to all the princes of Italy, to Naples, to Bergamo, to the Roman Curia, declaiming on his wretchedness and begging for emancipation. Occasional poems flowed from his pen. But during this period he devoted

poco sano e tanto maninconico che *sono riputato matto da gli altri e da me stesso*' (*Ib.* p. 262).

[1] *Op. cit.* p. 155.

his serious hours mainly to prose composition. The bulk of his Dialogues issued from S. Anna. On August 7, 1580, Celio Malaspina published a portion of the 'Gerusalemme' at Venice, under the title of 'Il Gottifredo di M. Torquato Tasso.' In February of the following year, his friend Angelo Ingegneri gave the whole epic to the world. Within six months from that date the poem was seven times reissued. This happened without the sanction or the supervision of the luckless author; and from the sale of the book he obtained no profit. Leonora d' Este died upon February 10, 1581. A volume of elegies appeared on this occasion; but Tasso's Muse uttered no sound.[1] He wrote to Panigarola that 'a certain tacit repugnance of his genius' forced him to be mute.[2] His rival Guarini undertook a revised edition of his lyrics in 1582. Tasso had to bear this dubious compliment in silence. All Europe was devouring his poems; scribes and versifiers were building up their reputation on his fame. Yet he could do nothing. Embittered by the piracies of publishers, infuriated by the impertinence of editors, he lay like one forgotten in that hospital. His celebrity grew daily; but he languished, penniless and wretched, in confinement which he loathed. The strangest light is cast upon his state of mind by the efforts which he now made to place two of his sister's children in Court-service. He even tried to introduce one of them as a page into the household of Alfonso. Eventually, Alessandro Sersale was consigned to Odoardo Farnese, and Antonio to the Duke of Mantua. In 1585 new sources of annoyance rose. Two members of the Della Crusca Academy in

---

[1] *Lacrime di diversi poeti volgari*, &c. (Vicenza, 1585).

[2] *Lettere*, vol. ii. p. 103. The significance of this message to Panigarola is doubtful. Did Tasso mean that the contrast between past and present was too bitter? 'Most friendship is feigning, most loving mere folly.'

Florence, Leonardo Salviati and Bastiano de' Rossi, attacked the 'Gerusalemme.' Their malevolence was aroused by the panegyric written on it by Cammillo Pellegrini, a Neapolitan, and they exposed it to pedantically quibbling criticism. Tasso replied in a dignified apology. But he does not seem to have troubled himself overmuch with this literary warfare, which served meanwhile to extend the fame of his immortal poem. At this time new friends gathered round him. Among these the excellent Benedictine, Angelo Grillo, and the faithful Antonio Constantini demand commemoration from all who appreciate disinterested devotion to genius in distress. At length, in July 1586, Vincenzo Gonzaga, heir-apparent to the Duchy of Mantua, obtained Tasso's release. He rode off with this new patron to Mantua, leaving his effects at S. Anna, and only regretting that he had not waited on the Duke of Ferrara to kiss his hand as in duty bound.[1] Thus to the end he remained an incorrigible courtier; or rather shall we say that, after all his tribulations, he preserved a dog-like feeling of attachment for his master?

The rest of Tasso's life was an Odyssey of nine years. He seemed at first contented with Mantua, wrote dialogues, completed the tragedy of 'Torrismondo' and edited his father's 'Floridante.' But when Vincenzo Gonzaga succeeded to the dukedom, the restless poet felt himself neglected. His young friend had not leisure to pay him due attention. He therefore started on a journey to Loreto, which had long been the object of his pious aspiration. Loreto led to Rome, where Scipione Gonzaga resided as Patriarch of Jerusalem and Cardinal. Rome suggested Southern Italy, and Tasso hankered after the recovery of his mother's fortune. Accordingly he set off in March 1588 for Naples, where he stayed, partly with the monks of Monte Oliveto, and partly with the

[1] All the letters written from Mantua abound in references to this neglect of duty.

Marchese Manso. Rome saw him again in November; and
not long afterwards an agent of the Duke of Urbino wrote
this pitiful report of his condition: 'Everyone is ready to
welcome him to hearth and heart; but his humours render
him mistrustful of mankind at large. In the palace of the
Cardinal Gonzaga there are rooms and beds always ready for
his use, and men reserved for his especial service. Yet he
runs away and mistrusts even that friendly lord. In short, it
is a sad misfortune that the present age should be deprived
of the greatest genius which has appeared for centuries.
What wise man ever spoke in prose or verse better than this
madman?'[1] In the following August, Scipione Gonzaga's
servants, unable to endure Tasso's eccentricities, turned him
from their master's house, and he took refuge in a monastery
of the Olivetan monks. Soon afterwards he was carried to
the hospital of the Bergamasques. His misery now was
great, and his health so bad that friends expected a speedy
end.[2] Yet the Cardinal Gonzaga again opened his doors to
him in the spring of 1590. Then the morbid poet turned
suspicious, and began to indulge fresh hopes of fortune in
another place. He would again offer himself to the Medici.
In April he set off for Tuscany, and alighted at the convent
of Monte Oliveto, near Florence. Nobody wanted him; he
wandered about the Pitti like a spectre, and the Florentines
wrote: '*actum est de eo.*'[3] Some parting compliments and
presents from the Grand Duke sweetened his dismissal. He
returned to Rome; but each new journey told upon his broken
health, and another illness made him desire a change of scene.
This time Antonio Costantini offered to attend upon him.
They visited Siena, Bologna, and Mantua. At Mantua, Tasso
made some halt, and took a new long poem, the 'Gerusalemme
Conquistata,' seriously in hand. But the demon of unrest

[1] *Lettere,* vol. iv. p. 147.
[2] *Ibid.* p. 229.   [3] *Ibid.* p. 315.

LAST YEARS AT NAPLES AND ROME

pursued him, and in November 1591 he was off again with the Duke of Mantua to Rome. From Rome he went to Naples at the beginning of the following year, worked at the 'Conquistata,' and began his poem of the 'Sette Giornate.'[1] He was always occupied with the vain hope of recovering a portion of his mother's estate. April saw him once more upon his way to Rome. Clement VIII. had been elected, and Tasso expected patronage from the Papal nephews.[2] He was not disappointed. They received him into their houses, and for awhile he sojourned in the Vatican. The year 1593 seems, through their means, to have been one of comparative peace and prosperity. Early in the summer of 1594 his health obliged him to seek change of air. He went for the last time to Naples. The Cardinal of S. Giorgio, one of the Pope's nephews, recalled him in November to be crowned poet in Rome. His entrance into the Eternal City was honourable, and Clement granted him a special audience; but the ceremony of coronation had to be deferred because of the Cardinal's ill health.

Meanwhile his prospects seemed likely to improve. Clement conferred on him a pension of one hundred ducats, and the Prince of Avellino, who had detained his mother's estate, compounded with him for a life-income of two hundred ducats. This good fortune came in the spring of 1595. But it came too late; for his death-illness was upon him. On the first of April he had himself transported to the convent of S. Onofrio, which overlooks Rome from the Janiculan hill.

[1] Yet he now felt that his genius had expired. 'Non posso più fare un verso: la vena è secca, e l' ingegno è stanco' (*Lettere*, vol. v. p. 90).

[2] During the whole period of his Roman residence, Tasso, like his father in similar circumstances, hankered after ecclesiastical honours. His letters refer frequently to this ambition. He felt the parallel between himself and Bernardo Tasso: 'La mia depressa condizione, e la mia infelicità, quasi ereditaria' (vol. iv. p. 238).

Torrents of rain were falling with a furious wind, when the carriage of Cardinal Cinzio was seen climbing the steep ascent. The badness of the weather made the fathers think there must be some grave cause for this arrival. So the prior and others hurried to the gate, where Tasso descended with considerable difficulty, greeting the monks with these words: "I am come to die among you."'[1] The last of Tasso's letters, written to Antonio Costantini from S. Onofrio, has the quiet dignity of one who struggles for the last time with the frailty of his mortal nature.[2]

'What will my good lord Antonio say when he shall hear of his Tasso's death? The news, as I incline to think, will not be long in coming; for I feel that I have reached the end of life, being unable to discover any remedy for this tedious indisposition which has supervened on the many others I am used to—like a rapid torrent resistlessly sweeping me away. The time is past when I should speak of my stubborn fate, to mention not the world's ingratitude, which, however, has willed to gain the victory of bearing me to the grave a pauper; the while I kept on thinking that the glory which, despite of those that like it not, this age will inherit from my writings, would not have left me wholly without guerdon. I have had myself carried to this monastery of S. Onofrio; not only because the air is commended by physicians above that of any other part of Rome, but also as it were upon this elevated spot and by the conversation of these devout fathers to commence my conversation in heaven. Pray God for me; and rest assured that as I have loved and honoured you always in the present life, so will I perform for you in that other and more real life what appertains not to feigned but to

---

[1] Manso, *op. cit.* p. 215.
[2] This letter proves conclusively that, whatever was the nature of Tasso's malady, and however it had enfeebled his faculties as poet, he was in no vulgar sense a lunatic.

veritable charity. And to the Divine grace I recommend you and myself.'

On April 25, Tasso expired at midnight, with the words *In manus tuas, Domine*, upon his lips. Had Costantini, his sincerest friend, been there, he might have said like Kent:

> O, let him pass! he hates him much
> That would upon the rack of this tough world
> Stretch him out longer.

But Costantini was in Mantua; and this sonnet, which he had written for his master, remains Tasso's truest epitaph, the pithiest summary of a life pathetically tragic in its adverse fate—

> Friends, this is Tasso, not the sire but son;
> For he of human offspring had no heed,
> Begetting for himself immortal seed
> Of art, style, genius and instruction.
>
> In exile long he lived and utmost need;
> In palace, temple, school, he dwelt alone;
> He fled, and wandered through wild woods unknown;
> On earth, on sea, suffered in thought and deed.
>
> He knocked at death's door; yet he vanquished him
> With lofty prose and with undying rhyme;
> But fortune not, who laid him where he lies.
>
> Guerdon for singing loves and arms sublime,
> And showing truth whose light makes vices dim,
> Is one green wreath; yet this the world denies.

The wreath of laurel which the world grudged was placed upon his bier; and a simple stone, engraved with the words *Hic jacet Torquatus Tassus*, marked the spot where he was buried.

The foregoing sketch of Tasso's life and character differs in some points from the prevalent conceptions of the poet. There is a legendary Tasso, the victim of malevolent persecution by pedants, the mysterious lover condemned to misery in prison by a tyrannous duke. There is also a Tasso formed by men of learning upon ingeniously constructed systems; Rosini's Tasso, condemned to feign madness in punishment for courting Leonora d' Este with lascivious verses; Capponi's Tasso, punished for seeking to exchange the service of the House of Este for that of the House of Medici; a Tasso who was wholly mad; a Tasso who remained through life the victim of Jesuitical influences. In short, there are as many Tassos as there are Hamlets. Yet these Tassos of the legend and of erudition do not reproduce his self-revealed lineaments. Tasso's letters furnish documents of sufficient extent to make the real man visible, though something yet remains perhaps not wholly explicable in his tragedy.

www.ingramcontent.com/pod-product-compliance
Lightning Source LLC
Chambersburg PA
CBHW030214170426
43201CB00006B/81